The Court of Philip IV.

SPAIN IN DECADENCE

BY *Andrew Sharp*

MARTIN HUME

SOMETIME EDITOR OF THE CALENDARS OF SPANISH STATE PAPERS
(PUBLIC RECORD OFFICE)
LECTURER IN SPANISH HISTORY AND LITERATURE
PEMBROKE COLLEGE, CAMBRIDGE

Vuestras augustisimas Soberanias vivan, O GRAN
FELIPE, *inclitamente triunfantes, gravadas en los Anales
de la Fama, pues sois sólida columna y mobil Atlante de
la Fe, unica defensa de la iglesia, y bien universal de
vuestras invencibles reinos*

A NEW EDITION

NEW YORK
BRENTANO'S
PUBLISHERS

PRINTED IN GREAT BRITAIN BY
MORRISON AND GIBB LTD., LONDON AND EDINBURGH

5

THE COURT OF PHILIP IV.

Philip IV at the age of 55.

From a portrait by Velazquez in the National Gallery. London.

PREFACE

"I lighted upon great files and heaps of papers and writings of all sorts. . . . In searching and turning over whereof, whilst I laboured till I sweat again, covered all over with dust, to gather fit matter together . . . that noble Lord died, and my industry began to flag and wax cold in the business."

THUS wrote William Camden with reference to his projected life of Lord Burghley, which was never written ; and the words may be applied not inappropriately to the present book and its writer. Some years ago I passed many laborious months in archives and libraries at home and abroad, searching and transcribing contemporary papers for what I hoped to make a complete history of the long reign of Philip IV., during which the final seal of decline was stamped indelibly upon the proud Spanish empire handed down by the great Charles V. to his descendants. I had dreamed of writing a book which should not only be a social review of the period signalised by the triumph of French over Spanish influence in the civilisation of Europe, but also a political history of the wane and final disappearance of the pro-digious national imposture that had enabled Spain, aided by the rivalries between other nations, to dominate the world for a century by moral force unsupported by any proportionate material power.

v

The sources to be studied for such a history were enormous in bulk and widely scattered, and I worked very hard at my self-set task. But at length I, too, began to wax faint-hearted; not, indeed, because my "noble Lord had died"; for no individual lord, noble or ignoble, has ever done, or I suppose ever will do, anything for me or my books; but because I was told by those whose business it is to study his moods, that the only "noble Lord" to whom I look for patronage, namely the sympathetic public in England and the United States that buys and reads my books, had somewhat changed his tastes. He wanted to know and understand, I was told, more about the human beings who personified the events of history, than about the plans of the battles they fought. He wanted to draw aside the impersonal veil which historians had interposed between him and the men and women whose lives made up the world of long ago; to see the great ones in their habits as they lived, to witness their sports, to listen to their words, to read their private letters, and with these advantages to obtain the key to their hearts and to get behind their minds; and so to learn history through the human actors, rather than dimly divine the human actors by means of the events of their times. In fact, he cared no longer, I was told, for the stately three-decker histories which occupied half a lifetime to write, and are now for the most part relegated, in handsome leather bindings, to the least frequented shelves of dusty libraries.

I therefore decided to reduce my plan to more modest proportions, and to present not a universal

history of the period of Spain's decline, but rather
a series of pictures chronologically arranged of the
life and surroundings of the " Planet King " Philip
IV.—that monarch with the long, tragic, uncanny
face, whose impassive mask and the raging soul
within, the greatest portrait painter of all time
limned with merciless fidelity from the King's
callow youth to his sin-seared age. I have adopted
this method of writing a history of the reign,
because the great wars throughout Europe in
which Spain took a leading part, under Philip
and his successor, have already been described
in fullest details by eminent writers in every
civilised language, and because I conceive that
the truest understanding of the broader pheno-
mena of the period may be gained by an intimate
study of the mode of life and ruling sentiments
of the King and his Court, at a time when they
were the human embodiment, and Madrid the
phosphorescent focus, of a great nation's decay.

The ground was practically virgin. John Dunlop,
three-quarters of a century ago, wrote a stolid
history of the reign, mainly concerned with the
Spanish wars in Germany, Flanders, and Italy.
But that was before the archives of Europe were
accessible ; and, creditable as was Dunlop's history
for the time in which it was written, it is obsolete
now. The Spanish reproduction in recent years
of seventeenth-century documents, for the most
part unknown in England, has added much to
recent information ; whilst numerous original manuscripts, and old printed narratives and letters
of the time, in Spanish, English, and French, have
also provided ample material for the embodiment

in the text of first-hand descriptions of events. The book as it stands is far less ambitious than that originally projected ; but it contains much of the contemporary matter which would have provided substance for the wider history ; and though it is limited in its scope, it may nevertheless render the important period it covers human and interesting to ordinary readers who seek intellectual amusement, as well as intelligible to students who read for information alone.

The book—" a poor thing, but mine own "—owes nothing to the labours of previous English historians, except that in describing the Prince of Wales' visit to Madrid I have referred to two documents published by the Camden Society under the editorship of the late Dr. Gardiner. With these exceptions the material has been sought in contemporary unpublished manuscripts and printed records and letters, in most cases now first utilised for the purpose. Whatever its faults may be—and doubtless the critical microscope may discover many—it is the only comprehensive history of Philip IV. and the decadent society over which he reigned that modern research has yet produced. May good fortune follow it ; for, as the Bachiller Carasco sagely said : " *No hay libro tan malo que no tenga algo bueno*," and I hope that in this book, at least, the " good " will be held to outbalance the " bad."

MARTIN HUME.

CONTENTS

CHAPTER I

CHAPTER II

CHAPTER III

CHAPTER VI

CHAPTER VII

CHAPTER VIII

CONTENTS

LIST OF ILLUSTRATIONS

THE
COURT OF PHILIP IV.

CHAPTER I

INTRODUCTORY — PHILIP'S BAPTISM, 1605 — THE
ENGLISH EMBASSY—EXALTED RELIGIOUS FEEL-
ING—DEDICATION OF PHILIP'S LIFE TO THE
VINDICATION OF ORTHODOXY—STATE OF SPAIN
—EFFECTS OF LERMA'S POLICY—POVERTY OF
THE COUNTRY—EXPULSION OF THE MORISCOS
—PHILIP'S CHILDHOOD AND YOUTH—HIS BE-
TROTHAL—FALL OF LERMA—THE PRINCE AND
OLIVARES—DEATH OF PHILIP III

THE mean city of Valladolid reached the summit
of its glory on the 28th of May 1605. Seven
weeks before—on Good Friday, the 8th April—there
had been born in the King's palace an heir to the
world-wide monarchy of the Spains, the first male
child that had been vouchsafed to the tenuous
reigning house for seven-and-twenty years ; and the
new capital, proud of the fleeting importance that
the folly of Lerma had conferred upon it, curtailed
its lenten penance, and gave itself up to sensuous
devotion blent with ostentatious revelry. King
Philip III. and his nobles, in a blaze of splendour,
had knelt in thanksgiving to sacred images of the

A

Holy Mother bedizened with priceless gems ; well-fed monks and friars had chanted praises before a hundred glittering altars ; and famished common folk, in filthy tatters, snarled like ravening beasts over the free food that had been flung to them, and fought fiercely for the silver coins that had been lavishly scattered for their scrambling.[1] From every window had flared waxen torches ; for the hovels of beggars were illumined as well as the palaces of nobles,—nay, the courtly chronicler records that the very bells in the church tower of St. Benedict, seventeen of them, "melted in glittering tears of joy" when, to put it more prosaically, the edifice was gutted by a conflagration accidentally caused by the torches.[2] Cavalry parades, bull fights, and cane-tourneys by knights and nobles had alternated with banquets and balls during the fifty days that had been needed to bring together in the city of the Castilian plain the chivalry of Philip's realms. One after the other grandees and prelates, with long cavalcades of followers as fine as money or credit could make them, had crowded into the narrow streets and straggling plazas of Valladolid ; and as the great day approached for the baptism of the Prince, who had been pledged by his father at his birth to the Virgin of San Llorente as the future champion of Catholic orthodoxy, news came that a greater company than that of any

[1] See a curious contemporary, unpublished, account by Don Geronimo Gascon de Torquemada. Add. MSS. 10,236 British Museum. He says that the Town Council scattered 12,000 silver reals in the plaza on Saturday, 9th April, and that 30,000 wax candles, with as many sheets of white paper to wrap round them for torches, were distributed to the poor ; the whole population of the city at the time being between 50,000 and 60,000.

[2] Narrative of Matias de Novoa, *Documentos Ineditos*, vol. lx.

grandee of them all was slowly riding over the mountains of Leon to honour the festival, and to pledge the most Catholic King to lasting peace and amity with heretic England, that in forty years of bitter strife had challenged the pretension of Spain to dictate doctrine to Christendom ; and had, though few saw it yet, sapped the foundation upon which the imposing edifice of Spanish predominance was reared.

Then grave heads were shaken in doubt that this thing might be of evil omen. Already had the rigid Ribera, Archbishop of Valencia,[1] solemnly warned the King and Lerma of their impiety in making terms with the enemies of the faith ; lamentations, as loud as was consistent with safety, had gone up from churches and guardrooms innumerable at this tacit confession of a falling away from the stern standard of Philip II. But now that Lord Admiral Howard, Earl of Nottingham, who had defeated the great Armada in 1588, and had commanded at the sack of Cadiz in 1596, was to ruffle and feast, with six hundred heretic Englishmen at his heels, in the very capital of orthodox Spain, whilst the baby prince whom God had sent to realise the dream of his house was baptized into the Church, offended pride almost overcame the stately courtesy and hospitality which are inborn in the Spanish character. But not quite: for though priests looked sour, and soldiers swaggered a little more than usual when they met the Englishmen in the

---

[1] The vehement protest of Ribera is reproduced *in extenso* in Gil Gonzalez Davila's *Vida y Hechos de Phelipe III*. Original MS. in possession of the author. Also published, Madrid, 1771. Ribera it was who principally promoted the expulsion of the Moriscos a few years later.

cobbled streets, yet to outward seeming all was kind on both sides ; and even the biting satires of the poets were decently suppressed until the strangers had gone their way.[1]

Howard and his train were lodged on the night of the 25th May in the castle and town of Simancas, on its bold bluff seven miles from the city ; and betimes in the morning the six hundred and more British horsemen, all in their finest garb, set forth over the arid sandy plain on the banks of the Pisuerga, to enter in stately friendship the capital of the realm that they and theirs had harried by land and sea for two score years. For seven months no drop of rain had fallen on the parched earth ; and as the noble figure of the old earl, in white satin and gold, surrounded by equally splendid kinsmen, passed on horseback to the appointed meeting place outside the walls of the city, the dust alone marred the magnificence of the cavalcade. For two hours the Englishmen were kept waiting under the trees,

[1] Gongora's sonnet, for instance, which is thus Englished by Churton—

"Our Queen had borne a Prince. When all were gay,
A Lutheran envoy came across the main,
With some six hundred followers in his train,—
All knaves of Luther's brood. His proud array
Cost us, in one fair fortnight and a day,
A million ducats of the gold of Spain,
In jewels, feasting crowds, and pageant play.
But then he brought us, for our greater gain,
The peace King James on Calvin's Bible swore.
Well ! we baptized our Prince ; Heaven bless the child !
But why make Luther rich, and leave Spain poor ?
What witch our dancing courtiers' wits beguiled ?—
Cervantes, write these doings : they surpass
Your grave Don Quixote, Sancho and his ass."

See also Cervantes' ballad of the Churching of Queen Margaret, in his Exemplary Novel of *The Little Gipsy*, written, however, some years after the event.

where the Grand Constable, the Duke of Frias,[1] and the other grandees were to meet them ; for Spanish pride was never at a loss for a device to inflict a polite snub upon a rival. This time it was a diplomatic illness of the Duke of Alba that delayed the starting of the great crowd of nobles who were to greet the English ambassador, and it was five o'clock in the afternoon before the Spanish horsemen reached their waiting guests. Then, as if by magic, the heavens grew suddenly black as night, and such a deluge as few men had seen [2] descended upon the gaudy throng ; " heaven weeping in sorrow at their reception," said the bigots. In vain the Constable of Castile besought the stiff old Lord Admiral to take shelter in a coach. He would not balk the people of the sight, he said, and the costly finery of both English and Spanish received such a baptism as for ever spoilt its pristine beauty. Wet to the skin, their velvets and satins bedraggled, their plumes drooping, and their great lace ruffs as limp as rags, the thousand noble horsemen passed through dripping, silent, but curious crowds to their quarters.

Howard himself was lodged in seven fine rooms in the palace of Count de Salinas, hard by the yet unfinished palace ; and his six hundred followers were billeted in the houses of nobles and citizens.[3]

[1] Don Juan Fernandez de Velasco, hereditary Great Constable of Castile, Duke of Frias, who in the previous year, 1604, had gone to England to conclude with James I. the Treaty of Peace.

[2] So at least say the eye-witnesses ; though it can hardly have been a more violent downpour than that which overtook the present writer on the same spot, and at a similar date, in a recent year, when, with hardly five minutes' notice, the road was converted into a rushing torrent several inches deep, though previously no rain had fallen for months.

[3] Cabrera (*Documentos Ineditos*) says that care was taken that no

Fifty English gentlemen of rank dined together that evening in Howard's lodging, and their manners, dress, and demeanour furnished food for curious discourse in Spain for many days to come. How tall and handsome they were, though some of them were spoilt by full beards! said the gossips; how careful to show respect for the objects of worship in the churches, although only fourteen of the whole number were avowed Catholics. Many of them spoke Spanish well, as did Howard himself, and their dress was, on the whole, adjudged to be handsome; "though their ornaments were not so fine as ours." But what amused their critics more than anything else was their industrious poking about the city in search of books, and a curious fashion they had of breaking off in their discourse —or in a pause of the conversation—and practising a few steps of a dance, the tune of which they hummed between their teeth.[1] In the innocence of their hearts, too, they imagined that they were

sacred pictures were placed in the rooms, for fear of offence, though they were hung with fine tapestries. Three new beds, he says, were bought for Howard and his sons, etc. As an instance of the great care taken on both sides to avoid offence, Davila mentions that Howard, having learnt that two of his gentlemen had brought English Bibles with them, insisted upon their being returned to the ship; and Gascon de Torquemada asserts that the Englishmen were forbidden to dispute with Spaniards, right or wrong, on pain of death.

[1] "Todos tienen lindos trajes y altos cuerpos; y en habiendo entrado en conversacion con nosotros se apartan luego, y hacen cabriolas, cantando entre dientes; y aunque entre ellos usan esto no lo usava el Almirante." Gascon de Torquemada's MS. B.M., Add. MSS. 10,236. Cabrera de Cordova (*Relacion de las Cosas Sucedidas desde* 1599 *hasta* 1614) also mentions the "cabriolas" or skipping of the English gentlemen in the grand ball given in their honour on the 16th June by the King. The passion for dancing "high and disposedly" was at the time considered peculiarly English, and Englishmen are frequently referred to in Spanish letters of the time as being naturally volatile and mercurial, in marked contrast with their latter-day descendants.

paying a compliment to the Spaniards by saying how little real difference there was between their own creed and that of their hosts ; a view which the latter received in courteous silence in their presence, but rejected with scorn and derision behind their backs.[1] Brave doings there had been, too, the next day, when Howard had his first interview with Philip III. Surrounded by the King's Spanish and Teuton guard, in new uniforms of yellow and red, the Lord Admiral was led by the Duke of Lerma into the presence of the King. Of the genuflections and embraces, of the advances on each side, measured and recorded to an inch by jealous onlookers, of the piled-up sumptuousness of the garments and the gifts, it boots not here to tell in full, but the King's new liveries alone on this occasion are said to have cost 120,000 ducats ; and Howard excused himself for the poverty of his country when he handed to Queen Margaret an Austrian eagle in precious stones worth no more than the same great sum.[2]

All this, however, was a mere foretaste of the overwhelming magnificence of the following day, Whit Sunday, the 28th May, for ever memorable in the annals of Valladolid as the greatest day in its long history ; for then it was that in solemn majesty, and lavish ostentation without example, there was dedicated to the great task in which his ancestors had failed, a babe with a lily-fair skin and wide open light blue eyes, upon whom were

[1] See Geronimo Gascon de Torquemada's MS. B.M., Add. MSS. 10,936.
[2] Full accounts of Howard's reception may be found in Torquemada's MS. already quoted, in Novoa's relation (*Documentos Ineditos*, 60 and 61), in Cabrera de Cordova, in Davila already quoted, and in Yepes' *Felipe III*. Madrid, 1723.

centred the hopes and prayers of a sensitive, devout people, who had seen in a few years their high-strung illusions vanish, their assurance of divine selection grow fainter and fainter, the cause they thought was that of heaven conquered everywhere by the legions of evil, and their own country reduced to chronic penury; burdened with a weight beyond its strength, yet too proud to cast the burden down or to acknowledge its own defeat.

The almost despairing cry that constant disaster had wrung from Philip II: " Surely God will in the end make His own cause triumph," still found an echo in thousands of Spanish hearts; and this child of many prayers was greeted as an instrument sent at last from heaven, on the most solemn day in the Christian year, to put all things right when he should grow to be a man.[1] The presence of the " heretic " peace embassy seemed of no good omen, though some men even affected to interpret it as such when Howard knelt before the King and was raised and embraced by him; but, as if to banish every doubt, and mark for all the world that the vocation of the Prince was irrevocably fixed beforehand, there was brought in solemn pomp, from the remote village of Calguera, the

[1] Cervantes thus writes on the subject—

"This pearl that Thou to us hast given,
Star of Austria's diadem:
What crafty plans, what high designs,
Are shattered by this peerless gem.

What hopes within our breasts are raised,
What soaring schemes have come to nought,
What fears are by his birth aroused,
What havoc with ambition wrought ! "

MacColl's translation of " The Exemplary Novels."

crumbling little font in which, five hundred years before, had been baptized the fierce firebrand St. Dominic, scourge of heresy and founder of the Holy Inquisition, whose work it was to make all Christians one, though blood and fire alone might do it.

Nothing was omitted that could connect the Prince with the Dominican idea. Early in the morning of the day of the baptism, the King, who was to take no public part in the later christening ceremony, walked in state with all his Court [1] in a great procession of six hundred monks of Saint Dominic from their monastery of San Pablo to the cathedral, there again solemnly to dedicate his infant heir to the vindication of the Church ; and at the dazzling ceremony which took place the same afternoon in the Dominican church of San Pablo a similar note was struck. The fair infant, with its vague blue eyes, was borne in triumph by the Duke of Lerma, a half dozen of the proudest dukes in Christendom carried the symbols and implements of the ceremony, cardinals and bishops in pontificals received the baby with royal state at the church porch, the populace pressed in thousands around with tears and blessings to see their future King ; all that lavish extravagance and exuberant

[1] With him, we are told, walked the Princes of Savoy and all the grandees and prelates present in Valladolid, the household of each personage being dressed in new liveries for the occasion, those of the royal servants being white and crimson trimmed with gold. The English ambassador Howard witnessed the procession, as he did later in the day that of the baptism, from a corner balcony in Count Rivadavia's house, his garments glittering with diamonds, and the collar of the Garter on his shoulder. It was noticed that when the King passed beneath the Englishman doffed his bonnet and made a deep reverence. Porreño, *Vida y Hechos de Phelipe III.*

fancy could devise to add refulgence to the solemnity was there ; but, looking back with understanding eyes, we can see that the two significant objects which stand forth clearly in antagonism from all that welter of gew-gaws are the humble rough font of St. Dominic under its jewelled canopy, supported by great silver pillars, and the stately white-haired figure of the " heretic " ambassador with his prominent eyes bowing gravely, yet triumphantly, in his balcony, as the pompous procession swept by.

Other less important things there were which must have told their tale and cast their shadow as plainly to those who witnessed them as to us. The two black-browed Savoyard cousins, who walked in the place of honour, the eldest of them as chief sponsor, must have been but skeletons at the feast, for the birth of the Prince had spoilt their cherished hope of the great inheritance ; and, as we shall see in the course of this history, Victor-Amadeus of Savoy and his kin brought, therefore, abounding sorrow to his god-son and to Spain. When the infant, too, was denuded of his rich adornments for the ceremony, and they were deposited upon the solid silver bed that had been erected in the church for the purpose, some of the great personages, who alone could have had access to the precious objects, stole them all, and the heir of Spain, Prince Philip Dominic, who entered the church with his tiny body covered with gems, left it as unadorned as ascetic St. Dominic himself could have wished.[1]

[1] Cabrera, *Relacion de las Cosas Sucedidas desde* 1599 *hasta* 1614. In addition to the authorities already quoted, there is a curious account of

Thus, in a whirlwind of squandering waste, surrounded by pompous pride, unscrupulous dishonesty, and ecstatic devotion, Philip from his birth was pledged to the hopeless task of extirpating religious dissent from Christendom : the task that had been too great for the Emperor and his steadfast son, that had drained to exhaustion the wealth of the Indies, had turned Castile into a wilderness, and was to drag the Spanish Empire to ruin and dissolution under the sceptre of the babe whose christening we have witnessed. The life-story of the unhappy monarch which we have to tell is one of constant struggle amidst the antagonistic circumstances that surrounded his baptism ; against the impossibility of reconciling the successful performance of the work, to which devotional pride and not national interest had bound him, with the poverty and exhaustion that had forced Philip III. and Lerma to seek peace with Protestants, and had made the victor of the Invincible Armada an honoured guest when the heir of 'Catholic Spain was dedicated to the ideal of Dominic. For, in good truth, it was from no lack of either devotion or pride that Philip III. had been forced to parley with the thing that he had been taught to look upon as accursed of God. Almost the only policy in which he was ever vehemently energetic was the attempt in the first days of his reign to invade Ireland in the interests of the Catholics, and to secure the control of the Crown of England by

the celebrations referred to, sometimes attributed to Cervantes, called *Relacion de lo Subcedido en la Ciudad de Valladolid*, etc. Published at Valladolid in 1605.

means of the anti-Jacobite party.[1] He was, as Llorente truly says, more fit himself for a Dominican friar's frock than a regal mantle; and if rigid obedience to the directions of his spiritual guides had enabled him to root out Protestant dissent from Christendom, as he rooted out the Moriscos from his realms, Philip III. would have succeeded where his greater father and grandfather failed.

But devotion was not enough to secure the triumph of Spain; fervent belief in the divine approval was not enough. Both Philip II. and the Spaniards of his time possessed those qualities to excess, and yet they had failed. What was needed now, even to avert catastrophe, were orderly organisation, industry, celerity in council and in action, economical adaptation of ways and means, ready resource and a flexible conscience; in short, statesmanship,—and these were the very qualities which Philip III. conspicuously lacked. With the accession of Philip III. (1598) the weak point in the system of the Emperor and his son had come out; and their laboriously constructed political machine had broken down. Under Philip II. himself, in his later recluse years, it had grown rusty and sluggish, but whilst the mainspring, the monarch, had laboured ceaselessly, treating his ministers as clerks, and raising them from the gutter that they might be his tools alone, the wheels at least went round; but when the monarch in whom all motion was centred left off working, and did nothing but dance and pray alternately, then came paralysis

---

[1] A detailed account of these attempts will be found in *Treason and Plot*, by the present writer, and in the fourth volume of his *Calendars of Spanish State Papers of the Reign of Elizabeth*.

and consequent disaster. " Ah ! Don Cristobal ;
I fear they will rule him," groaned Philip II. on
his agonised deathbed ; and, though too late, he
had guessed his son's character aright. Thenceforward the favourite, Lerma or another, was
monarch in all but name ; and each problem of
government as it arose, or was submitted to the
King, was considered by Philip III. not in its broad
political aspects, but as a case of private conscience
to be quibbled over by confessors and theologians,
and finally decided with timorous heart-searching
on grounds apart from national interests or expediency.

Philip II. himself had all his life been sternly
conscientious, according to his lights, and his
inflexibility had been one of the main causes of
the partial failure of his policy and the exhaustion
of his country. He was a strong, slow, persistent
man, unwavering in his methods, as he was consistent in his objects ; but he was withal a statesman
of vast ability, with the power of self-persuasion
that all great statesmen must possess, and he
played the game of international politics with
mundane pieces, though he convinced himself
and others that they were divine. His son and
grandson, as will be seen in the course of this
book, had not his power of self-conviction ; they
lived in an age of growing national disillusionment,
and were swayed mainly by sentimental, traditional, and devotional considerations. They were
for ever unlocking with trembling hands the secret
closet of their conscience, to assure themselves
that indeed no stain rested there. Having seen
that all was spotless in their own breasts, they

were content to sit with crossed hands, in almost Oriental fatalism, throwing the whole responsibility for what happened, or failed to happen, upon the divine decrees. *They* had satisfied their confessor and their conscience in the course they had taken, and if things went awry after that it was not *their* fault.[1] This was no doubt all very saintly and good ; but it meant calamity as a system of government when its professors were pitted against rivals unhampered by such scruples and limitations.

It may seem paradoxical to assert that the more purely religious character of the motives that swayed Philip III. and Philip IV., than of those which influenced Philip II., resulted from a weakening of the exalted devotional faith that had dominated Spain during the greater part of the sixteenth century ; and yet, if it be carefully considered, such will prove to be the case. A faith so fervent as that which carried the men-at-arms and explorers of the Emperor and his son triumphant through the world left no room for doubt. What *they* did could not be wrong, because they were chosen to do God's own work ; and for that all means were sanctified. They did not need to be

[1] When the capital of Spain was again transferred to Madrid in 1606, Queen Margarita was much opposed to and distressed at the change. Porreño relates that she went to take leave of her favourite nuns at Valladolid with tears in her eyes, and when asked by the nuns why she did not persuade the King to remain at Valladolid, which agreed so well with his wife and children, she replied that " nothing on earth could move the King now, as the removal of the capital to Madrid had now been presented to him as a case of conscience." " Thus," says Porreño, in admiration, " he was ready to sacrifice the welfare of his wife and children, and all earthly considerations, for his conscience' sake !" Spaniards of the period thought that no higher praise than this could be given to any man

for ever pulling their consciences up by the roots
to satisfy themselves that the fruit was good.   If
Philip II. ordered murder to be committed, or the
Emperor seized private or ecclesiastical property
for his own purposes ; if hundreds of inconvenient
political persons were consigned to a living tomb
in the galleys and dungeons of the Inquisition, we
may be assured that no qualms of conscience were
felt in consequence by the first two sovereigns
of the Spanish house of Austria ; for the spiritual
fervour, which was the secret of the unity and
power of their realms, made all things right which
were done in furtherance of objects which were
considered sacred : and throughout the Reforma-
tion period the Spanish sovereigns quite honestly
and unhesitatingly employed religious forms and
professions to attain purely political ends.[1] But
after the accession of Philip III. disillusion and
faintness of faith set in, and the assurance of
divine selection grew weaker. People in Spain
were, it is true, more outwardly devout than ever,
for the Inquisition increased in strength as it
became more independent and less a political
engine in the hands of the weak monarch ; but the
constant timid misgivings of governors and people,
the universal recourse of gentle and simple to
priests, friars, and nuns for guidance, consolation,
and reassurance, were of themselves a proof that
the old robust self-sufficing faith was declining ;
and in the course of this history we shall see how

[1] For instance, Charles' unblushing manipulation of the Council of
Trent in 1545–46, the juggle with Paul III. about the Italian principalities,
and the clever hoodwinking of Sixtus V. as to the real objects of the
Armada of 1588.

the process continued hand in hand with the national decadence ; the devotional influence upon political action increasing as religious faith grew less positive and conscience more clamorous.

We have seen the wasteful splendour with which young Philip's infancy was surrounded : it will be necessary now for us to examine the state of the country at the time, in order that we may be able to trace in future pages the consequences of Philip's action and character when he came to the throne. Most of the contemporary chroniclers of the reign whose works remain to us, men like Novoa, Davila, Porreño, Cabrera, Malvezzi, and Torquemada, courtiers or placemen all, lose themselves in hyperbolical ecstasy at the colossal riches and greatness of the sovereign who could afford to spend in feasts and shows such vast sums as those squandered on the christening of Prince Philip Dominic and similar celebrations : but they were too much taken up with the pomp and glitter of their patrons, and in recording the interminable lists of high-sounding titles and glittering garments, to give much attention to the reverse side of the picture. For that we must turn to other authorities, especially to the narratives of foreign visitors, and to the remonstrances of the unfortunate members of the Cortes of Castile, who, between the despairing and indignant orders of their constituents, and the ceaseless pressure of the sovereign for fresh supplies of money, were obliged to speak plainly, though fruitlessly, of the ruin that impended unless matters were reformed.[1]

[1] It must be borne in mind that the Cortes of Castile (which comprised Castile, Leon, Andalucia, etc., and consisted of thirty-six deputies for

The first Cortes of the third Philip's reign (1598), when Lerma demanded the previously unheard-of vote of eighteen million ducats, spread over six years, to be raised by a tax on wine, oil, meat, etc., earnestly prayed the King to attend to their long-neglected petitions for a readjustment of expenditure and taxation. When the sum was voted, the King's promise of reform was, as usual, broken, and the Cortes then told the King that his country was already ruined and could pay no more. " Castile is depopulated, as you may see ; the people in the villages being now insufficient for the urgently necessary agricultural work : and an infinite number of places formerly possessing a hundred households are now reduced to ten, and many to none at all." [1] The common people were starving : the formerly prosperous cloth-weaving industry was rapidly being strangled by the terrible " *alcabala* " tax, imposed upon all commodities every time they changed hands by sale. The price of necessary articles was enormously and constantly rising, owing to the tampering of

eighteen cities) had, after the abortive rising of the Comuneros early in the reign of Charles V., in a great measure allowed the control of supply to slip from its hands, and was rapidly becoming effete ; all the members being bribed and influenced by grants and favours of the Court. The three Cortes of the Crown of Aragon, however, still held their own purse-strings, and always made supply a matter of bargain. For this reason practically the whole of the growing national burden rested upon wretched Castile.

[1] Danvila y Collado, *El Poder Civil en Espana*, vol. 6. In this petition the Cortes told the King that, whereas it had cost twelve years previously 60 ducats to maintain a student and his servant at Salamanca for a year, it now cost 120. Wages had risen for a bricklayer from 4 reals to 8, and for a labourer from 2 reals to 4 ; a trimmed felt hat which had previously cost 12 reals now cost 24. Segovia cloth, of which the price was formerly 3 ducats a piece, now fetched nearly double. The ducats quoted are the so-called copper ducat of 2s. 5½d., the real being the silver real worth about 6d.

B

Lerma with the currency, the dwarfing of industry
by the *alcabala*, town tolls, local octrois, and the
greatly increasing demand for commodities by
America. Whilst the sternest decrees were issued
in rapid succession against luxury in dress and
living, the advent of Lerma and the host of greedy
aristocrats to power had caused a perfect frenzy
for magnificence in attire; and the vast amounts
of money spent in costly stuffs and precious embroideries, etc., were almost entirely sent abroad,
inasmuch as the Spanish manufacturers and dealers
in such wares were not only impeded in the production and distribution of them by the economical
causes mentioned, but were practically the only
classes punished for infraction of the sumptuary
decrees. Thus the great sums that arrived in
Seville every year from the Indies to a large extent
never penetrated Spain at all, but were tran-
shipped at once to other countries, either in exchange for foreign commodities which unwise
sumptuary decrees and faulty finance prevented
from being produced in Spain, or else to pay the
Genoese and German loan-mongers,—*asentistas*,
as they were called,—who on usurious terms were
always ready to provide money against future
revenue for the wasteful shows by means of which
the idea of Spain's abounding wealth and power
was kept up. What portion of the American gold
and silver did reach the Spanish people themselves
was mostly hoarded or buried to keep it from
the grasp of tax-farmers, thieves, and extortioners
of all sorts, to whom a man of known wealth was
simply looked upon as fair prey. The copper
money, genuine and forged, with which the country

was flooded [1] was the only sort commonly current, and this had been by decree (1603) raised to double its face value, again increasing the price of articles of prime necessity to the poorer purchaser ; whilst the nobles and other wealthier people who possessed hoarded silver and gold lived comparatively cheaply.

In the very year 1605, when, as we have seen, money was squandered in Valladolid without limit, every source of national revenue had been pledged for years in advance ; and a year or two previously the King's officers had been forced to beg from door to door for so-called voluntary contributions of not less than fifty reals, for the daily expenses of the royal household. The revenue in this year was stated to be nominally 23,859,787 copper ducats of the value of 2s. 5⅓d. each,—more than enough, if it had been received, to meet every necessary expenditure ; but peculation and corruption were so universal, contraband and evasion so general, that according to the Venetian ambassador, every branch of the administration was starved, the national defences in a deplorable condition, and the King unable to raise an army of more than 20,000 or 30,000 men in Spain. [2]   In the meanwhile Lerma and his family and friends and their respective adherents were piling up possessions and riches beyond computation. The first act of Philip III. on his accession had been to give to his favourite the right to receive what presents

---

[1] The quantity of copper coin in circulation increased in five or six years from 6 millions of ducats' worth to 28 millions.

[2] Contarini to the Doge and Senate of Venice (*Relazioni degli Ambasciatori Veneziani*).

were offered to him, and Lerma had exercised
the privilege to the full. What the chief minister
did the subordinates imitated. Rodrigo Calderon,
the favourite of the favourite, and Franquesa,
the clerk of the council of finance, were found in
their subsequent disgrace to have hoarded immense
quantities of gold and silver ; and every one of the
twenty Viceroys, forty-six Governor-Generals, and
their infinite underlings, robbed as much money
as he could grasp, the sooner to come and swagger
in the Court amidst a squalid, starving population,
of which every man was striving within his limits
to imitate his betters, and to share in the easily
won riches of official corruption.[1] The one prosperous trade was the service of the King or the
service of his servants ; and thus, whilst the
sovereign himself was blind and deaf to all but
his innocent frivolities, and the superstitious awe
that constituted his religion, Spain grew yearly
poorer and more miserable as a nation, and the
favoured classes, the nobles and the clergy, practically exempt from taxation, waxed ever fatter,
more insolent, and more lavish.

The policy and aims of Philip II. had kept
his realms at war for a generation. The fatal
possession of the Flemish and Dutch territories

[1] Navarrete says, speaking of the luxury of the Court at this period
—and we shall see that it was exceeded later—" The smallest hidalgo
insisted upon his wife only going out in a carriage, and that her equipage
should be as showy as that of the greatest gentleman at Court. Not even
a carpenter or a saddler, or any other artizan, was seen but he must be
dressed in velvet or satin like a nobleman. He must needs wear his
sword and his dagger, and have a guitar hanging on the wall of his shop."
When it is remembered that the production and distribution in Spain
itself of the precious stuffs mentioned were hampered at every point, it
will be understood how great and constant the drain of wealth was from
a country which now exported little but the products of its soil.

of the House of Burgundy and the traditions of
Catholic unity had cursed poor Castile with a
European policy, and had driven Spain into constant war with Protestant England, her natural
ally ; but Philip II. on his deathbed had done
his best to lighten his son's burden. Flanders
was left to his dear daughter Isabel, and her
destined husband, the Cardinal-Archduke Albert,
with reversion, unfortunately, to Spain, in the
probable case of failure of issue from the Infanta.
To this extent Spain was relieved. There was no
longer any material need for her to spend her blood
and money in fighting the Protestants, either for
the Emperor or for the new Archduchess of
Flanders ; who herself, and especially her husband,
were content to let the Protestant Dutch go
their own way, whilst she enjoyed in peace her
inherited Catholic Belgic sovereignty. The exhaustion of Spain and his own avarice had tended
to make Lerma pacific ; and, as we have seen,
peace was arranged both with France and England :
it must be confessed, on extremely favourable
terms for Spain, as early in the reign of Philip
III. as was practicable. The war with the Dutch
in support of the Infanta still dragged on ; for
the Spaniards would bate not a jot of their pride,
and Maurice of Nassau and his Hollanders were
in no submissive mood after holding their own
for forty years. The Infanta and her husband
ardently longed for peace, and were ready to
acknowledge the independence of Holland ; but
Philip III. was full of scruples of conscience as to
the morality of formally ceding territory to Protestants, even when he could not hold it himself,

and it was 1609 before the punctilious haggling
ended, and the famous truce of twelve years was
signed, practically giving the stout Dutchmen
the independence for which they had fought so
well.

Spain was then at peace for the first time within
most men's memory ; and, with prudence, economy,
and good government, might yet have repaired
the disasters that had befallen her. The promotion of production, the rehabilitation of labour,
a return to the frugal, honest life which prevailed
before the nation was led to its splendid hysteria
by the imperial connection, would have enabled
the great revenues from the Indies to be kept
in Spain, whose shipping was now for a time free
from the depredations of privateers. But we
have seen how demoralised the whole people had
grown. Long wars in foreign lands, usually against
Protestants or infidels, the craze for discovery and
profitable adventure in the Indies, and the dwarfing of industry, except for the very poor, humble,
plodding folk, had made the vast majority of
Spaniards scornful of labour ; and in any case it
would have been hard to set men to work again.
The attempt even was never seriously made.
Peace for Philip III. and his people did not mean
an opportunity for setting their house in order
and reorganising the nation, because they did not
even yet fully recognise the hopelessness of the
national dream of domination through the unity
of Christendom on Spanish Catholic lines.

For the realisation of this dream absolute
unity of faith in Spain itself was the first necessary
condition. The country was peopled by several

unamalgamated racial and political elements, and had been artificially unified by the religious exaltation resulting from the conquest of Granada and the fierce doctrinal pride fostered by the Inquisition, artfully utilised for political ends by Ferdinand the Catholic and his successors. The weak point of the sacred bond that held Spaniards together was the large hard - working Moorish population scattered over the Peninsula, and especially numerous in the south-west. In spite of pledges and promises of toleration, Christian baptism had been forced upon these people. Taxes and disabilities of all sorts had been piled upon them, insulting and oppressive rules had been made to their detriment, alternate cruelty and persuasion had been resorted to in vain : the Moriscos at heart remained true to their own faith, however humbly they conformed to the Christian rites imposed upon them. They were still the most thrifty toilers ; the carrying trade of the Peninsula was almost entirely in their hands, and their means of inter-communication were thus better than those enjoyed even by Christian Spaniards. How to deal with this alien element so as to eliminate the danger that existed from their presence in a Christian state, the realisation of whose great ambition depended upon unbroken religious unification, had puzzled the minds of Spanish statesmen for years. It had been practically decided at one time (1581) by Philip II. to take the whole Morisco population out to sea and sink the ships that carried them ; Gomez Davila of Toledo urged Philip III. in 1598 to massacre the whole of them, whilst others more humane advocated the forcible abduction of all the children, the sterilisation of the males, and other heroic measures. For a time also the milder spirits, such as Father Las Casas, prayed that gentler methods might be tried ; but the attitude of the Moriscos themselves and the bigotry of the churchmen soon silenced the voice of mercy.

For years the Moriscos had been plotting with Spain's enemies ; with Henry IV. of France, with Elizabeth of England, with the Duke of Savoy, with the Sultan, with the King of Fez, or whoever else would promise them aid to break up the Spanish monarchy ; and the very day that the Prince Philip Dominic was born (8th April 1605) was fixed for the great Moslem rising at Valencia which should deliver Eastern Spain to the French King. The plot was discovered in time, and this frustrated treason had added to the religious fervour of the baptism, which has been described at the beginning of this chapter. Thenceforward the black cloud that loomed over the folk of Moorish blood grew ever darker. Not the religious bigots alone, but statesmen too, intent only on the immediate problem before them, urged that if unity of Christendom was the necsssary condition of Spain's greatness, then the faith within her own realms must be made pure and solid beyond all question or doubt, let the sacrifice be what it might.[1] Racial jealousy, economical rivalry, and envy of the superior financial position of the frugal Moriscos over that of their Christian neighbours,

[1] For details of the expulsion see, *inter alia*, Fray Jaime Bleda's *Cronica de los Moros de España* (Valencia, 1618); *The Moriscos of Spain*, by C. H. Lea (London, 1901) ; *Memorable Expulsion*, etc., by Guadalajara (Pamplona, 1614) ; and Porreño's *Felipe III*.

aided the forces of religious bigotry and political expediency : and, just as the baptism of Prince Philip had coincided in point of time with the discovery of the Moorish treason, so did the next ceremony of his infant life coincide with the fatal decision to exterminate root and branch from Spain all those in whose veins was known to flow the blood of the Moslem races. For the attainment of the views of both statesmen and churchmen of the day, purblind as they were to the larger issues, the resolution to expel the Moriscos was necessary, but, as will be seen later, it was disastrous industrially and economically.

In accordance with the condition of political science of the time, the results of the measure were indeed neither considered nor understood in the latter aspects.[1] It was discussed in the King's Council, first as a point of conscience, and secondly as a political necessity, and the breathing time given to Spain by the peace with the Protestants after forty years of strife, instead of being employed in the repair and recuperation of national forces, was seized upon by those who yet pursued the chimera of domination by religious unification, to deplete still further the already exhausted country by the expulsion of the principal productive element of

---

[1] The wise minister of Philip II., Idiaquez, in 1595 almost alone saw the economical evil of the expulsion. In an important letter to a colleague (MS. Loyola No. 1., 31, Royal Academy of History, Madrid) he rebuked the general idea that Spain would be richer for the expulsion of the Moriscos, and pointed out that they almost alone were creating national wealth by their industry, frugality, and skill in agriculture. " But all this," he says, " is of no consideration in exchange for putting away from our throat the knife which threatens it so long as these people remain amongst us in their present condition and we in ours."

its population, amidst the fervent applause of the idle and thriftless majority.

And still the frenzy of waste and magnificence in all classes went on, for no men saw fully yet that ruin was the inevitable result of a state of society in which luxurious idleness, or the pretence of it, was alone regarded as honourable, and where the honey was seized by the drones of the hive before workers had stored it.   On the 13th January 1608 the ceremony of swearing allegiance to the child Philip as heir to the Crown of Spain was celebrated in the church of St. Geronimo in Madrid,[1] with a lavishness that almost rivalled that of his baptism. Once more the King, in white satin and spangles and overloaded with gems, walked in procession with the fair-haired fragile Queen, even more splendidly bedight than he ;[2] once more the lavish Lerma led the baby Prince as sponsor, and the courtiers who followed vied with the favourite in the magnificence of their attire ; once more Cardinal Sandoval de Rojas with a crowd of prelates invested the act with all the solemn state of which the Church was capable, and in the courtly fashion of his house substituted a kiss for the canonical blow in the ceremony of confirmation.[3]   Madrid was

[1] The ancient church in the Prado where this ceremony always took place, and where the young King of Spain and his English bride were married recently.

[2] " His Majesty wore a white doublet and trunks with a grey satin cloak, all embroidered with bugles and gold spangles and lined with ermine.   White shoes and a black velvet cap with strings of pearls and diamonds and a plume of white feathers sprinkled with magnificent diamonds ; a sword beautifully chased and an embroidered belt ; a ruff with crimson silk ribs and the grand collar of the Golden Fleece."   See a curious contemporary MS. account of the ceremony.   British Museum MSS., Egerton, 367.

[3] The Prince was nevertheless so frightened that the silken bands

ablaze with light, and the ball in the palace at night
surpassed anything that the now deposed Valladolid
could show ; but over all the glitter the black
cloud hovered, and even whilst the ceremony of
homage was being celebrated, the Council of State,
despairing now of the conversion of the Moriscos
by softer methods, and alarmed at the prospects of
a great invasion from Morocco, practically decided
to clear the soil of Spain of the descendants of its
former conquerors.

Of the details of the expulsion this is not the
place to speak. We are principally concerned with
it here to show that Philip IV. was bound from his
earliest infancy to an inherited policy, and that
the seeds of social and national decadence were
sown before his time. He was no Hercules to root
them out, but was forced with bitter anguish to
witness the riches and power of his realms choked
and destroyed by the noxious growth which grew
to maturity in his time : whilst he wept and prayed
for the miraculous remedy that never comes, or
sought forgetfulness in vicious indulgence that
added private remorse to his public sorrow.

Young Philip's education and the surroundings
of his childhood were not calculated to increase his
self-reliance or independence of judgment. His
devout, delicate, Austrian mother died in child-
birth when he was but six years old, and his
father's awestricken devotion thereafter grew

necessary in the ceremony meant an intention to bleed him, and he cried
so much in consequence, that he had to be led to a little chair at his
mother's knee before he could be pacified; and there his sister, the
Infanta Ana, weighed down by her stiff gorgeousness, knelt and did
homage, to be followed by the cardinal, the nobles, and the Cortes.
Ibid.

more mystic than ever. Friars surrounded him, dictating the most trifling as well as the most important acts of his life ; supernatural visions and heavenly voices assured him of divine favour in his intervals of terrified despair which reduced him almost to lunacy,[1] and the little boy who was to be the heir of his gilded misery was left to the care of cloistered churchmen, whose ideal of goodness was the suppression of all natural impulse and the extinction of personal initiative as opposed to the dread fatalism which made them supreme.

Beyond dull, ceremonious visits to the royal convent of the Discalced Carmelites, hard by the palace of Madrid, the little Prince saw no relaxation from prayers and lessons, but an occasional stage play or masque performed by himself and his young courtiers of similar age. Even as a small child this was young Philip's sole delight ; and so long as he could declaim verse before his father's Court, or listen to the declamation of others, he was content. On one occasion, in 1614, it is recorded in a gossiping letter of the time, that the Prince, who was then nine years old, represented the character of cupid before the King and his family in the room in the palace devoted to such shows ; and as he had to make his entry upon the stage in a high ornamental chariot, the jolting of the vehicle made the poor child seasick ; and the God of love, when he advanced to the footlights, was reduced to a most unlovely plight in face of the dignified audience,

[1] Gil Gonzalez de Avila, in his MS. *Historia de Phelipe III.*, gives many admiring instances of the King's mystic communications with the heavenly powers, and of his attacks of religious panic. (Original MS. in my possession.)

though we are told that he "performed his part very prettily." There were those who shook grave heads, especially some of the friars, at this early indulgence of the heir of Spain in his passion for a pastime so little in accord with the traditional dignity of the royal house;[1] but little Philip himself very soon learnt his lesson, for he was an apt pupil, and even as a youth assumed a staid gravity on all public and ceremonious occasions entirely at variance with his demeanour in private.

In the meanwhile the country was sunk in the most abject misery. Corruption and plunder of the national resources by Lerma and his favourites and their hangers-on had at last aroused the resentment, or perhaps the jealousy, of rival self-seekers. Spain was at war again, and a league of all liberal Europe under Henry IV. of France was pledged to humble finally the inflated pretensions of the house of Austria ; but just as Lerma's star was waning, and the prompt ruin of Spain seemed imminent, a circumstance happened that gave a new lease of life to the proud dreams of the Philips, and made the subsequent downfall during the reign we have to record the more complete.

In May 1610 the dagger of a crazy fanatic ended the glorious life of " Henry of Navarre "; and the coalition against Spain broke down, and gave way to a struggle between his widow Marie de Medici and James I. of England to secure the friendship of the decadent power which still loomed so large and asserted its high claims so haughtily. The Queen Regent of France, papal and clerical as she

[1] Cabrera de Cordova, *Cosas Sucedidas a la Corte*, etc., *desde* 1599 *á* 1614.

was, succeeded where crafty, servile James Stuart
failed ; and in 1612 the eldest daughter of Spain,
the Infanta Ana, was betrothed in Madrid by
proxy to the boy King of France, Louis XIII., and
young Philip, Prince of Asturias, became the
affianced husband of Isabel of Bourbon, the elder
daughter of Henry IV., the great Béarnais. Of the
lavish splendour that accompanied the betrothals
in Madrid this is not the place to speak,[1] but when
Lerma's fall was at last approaching, engineered by
his own son the Duke of Uceda, in 1615, King
Philip III. and his pompous Court travelled north
in an interminable cavalcade to exchange the brides
on the frontier.

Prince Philip remained at the ancient Castilian
capital of Burgos, whilst the dark-eyed young beauty
who was destined to be his wife rode, surrounded by
Spanish nobles, from the little frontier stream through
San Sebastian and Vittoria to meet her eleven year
old bridegroom. The boy and his father rode a
league or two out of Burgos to greet the girl, who it
was fondly hoped would cement France and Spain
together for the fulfilment of the impossible old
dream of Christian unity dictated from Madrid ;
and eye-witnesses tell that the pale little milksop
Prince, with his lank sandy hair and his red hanging
under-lip, gazed speechless in admiration of the pretty
bright-eyed child, in unbecoming Spanish dress,
who was destined to be the companion of his youth
and prime. The next day Burgos was in a blaze of
splendour to welcome the future Queen, who rode on
her white palfrey and her silver sidesaddle through

---

[1] A full account of the crazy magnificence on the occasion will be
found in *Documentos Ineditos*, lxi.

the narrow frowning streets to the glorious cathedral;
and then, from city to city, through stark Castile,
the little bride, smiling and happy, and her pale boy
bridegroom, followed by the most splendid Court in
Christendom, slowly made their way to the crowning
triumph of the capital.[1]

In the gorgeous crowd of courtiers that accompanied the King on his long journey to and from
the French frontier, intrigue and falsity were rife.
The Duke of Lerma's favourite, Calderon, had
languished in a dungeon already for five years, and
the spoilt favourite himself knew that his fall had
been plotted long since by his son and the powerful clerical clique that swayed the timorous soul of
Philip III. But Lerma was making a brave fight
for his dignity and vast wealth. Philip III. was
kind and tender-hearted, and the habit of subjection
to his favourite was hard to break, so that his enemies
had to tread warily. Their plan was to place
gradually around the King and his heir nobles
whom Lerma had failed to satisfy with sufficient
bribes. One of them was a young man of twenty-
eight, perhaps the most forceful of them all, Gaspar
de Guzman, Count of Olivares, son of that proud
minister of Philip II. who had bullied and hood-
winked Sixtus V. into supporting the Armada in
1588. For years Gaspar de Guzman, and his father
before him, had fruitlessly besought Lerma to
convert their peerage of Castile into a grandeeship of
Spain; and on the journey to France with the King,
the Count, though his branch of the great Guzman

---

[1] An unpublished account of the progress by an eye-witness is in Add.
MSS. 102,36, British Museum. See also *Queens of Old Spain*, by Martin
Hume, and *Documentos Ineditos*, lxi.

house was less rich than noble, had striven to show by the splendour of his train that if he was not a grandee he was magnificent enough to be one.[1]

Philip III. loved lavishness, especially to dazzle the French at this juncture, and was easily persuaded by Lerma's false son to make the Count of Olivares a gentleman of the chamber to the Prince. At first young Philip disliked his masterful attendant, whose imperious manner and stern looks frightened the sensitive boy; but gradually, as the latter grew older and more curious, the address and cleverness of Olivares asserted their influence over the weaker spirit of the Prince. Olivares was supposed by Uceda to be acting entirely in his interest, and had persuaded the latter to give him complete control of the Prince's household, which he took care to pack with friends pledged to himself. When Lerma was finally dismissed with a cardinal's hat and all his riches, young Philip was anxious to know why so great a minister had been disgraced. Olivares was always ready to enlighten the lad, and would spend long periods chatting with him alone as the Prince lay in bed, or as he was riding. In answer to Philip's questions about Lerma, he impressed upon him the insolence of favourites generally, their noxious public influence, their evil effect upon monarchs, and much more to the same purport, pointed at Uceda the new minister quite as much as at his fallen father. The sufferings of the people were described vividly to the sympathising boy, who was told of the vast plunder held by Lerma and his family from the national resources, and the noble task awaiting a monarch who would

[1] Malvezzi, *Historia de Felipe III.*, Yañez.

govern his realm himself and redress the wrongs of his subjects. Young Philip's youthful ambition was aroused, and thenceforward he listened to his mentor eagerly ; whilst he ostentatiously frowned in public upon the Duke of Uceda.[1]

Spain, notwithstanding the change of favourites, went from bad to worse. The vast sums spent by the King upon the building of new convents and in sumptuous shows were still wrung from the humblest classes, who alone did any profitable work, and in vain was the sainted image of the Virgin of Atocha carried in regal state through the streets of the capital, in the hope of averting widespread famine. Lerma at least, in his long ministry, had managed to conceal from the indolent King the utter ruin that threatened ; but the ineptitude of the new favourites made the misery patent even to him. The knowledge overwhelmed his feeble spirit, and his long spells of despair were but rarely relieved now by the frivolities that formerly delighted him. Ill and failing as he was, and his poor spirit broken, he prayed the Council of Castile to tell him the truth as to the condition of his people, and to suggest remedies for their ills. The report, which reached him in February 1619, finally opened his eyes, now that it was too late, to the appalling results of his rule ; and, stricken with panic fear that he would he damned eternally for his life-long neglect of duty, the poor King broke down

---

[1] Matias de Novoa, *Felipe III*. *Documentos Ineditos*, lxi. This writer was a chamberlain of Philip IV. and an agent of Olivares; but receiving from the latter no reward, he wrote a series of bitter attacks upon him.

C

utterly. He knew that his strength was ebbing, and forgiveness for himself was his first thought, and then to pray that his son might do better than he had done.

To distract him, his favourites persuaded him to make a royal progress to Portugal, with all the old lavish splendour, to witness the taking of the oath by the Portuguese Cortes to young Philip as heir to the throne. For months the cities of Portugal were the scene of prodigal pomp and devotion, that once more drove out of the muddled brain of the King all thought of the misery he had left behind him in Castile ; and as he sat, on the 14th July 1619, under his gold and silken canopy in his palace at Lisbon, dressed in white taffeta and gold, and surrounded by the nobles of Portugal and Spain, it seemed as if the lying fable that made him personally the master of boundless wealth must be true, and that his stark and ruined realm was overflowing with happy abundance.[1] By his side sat his hopeful son Philip, a tall slim lad of fourteen, wearing a white satin suit covered with gold and gems, and surmounted by a black velvet shoulder-cape a mass of bullion embroidery ; and as the representatives of the Portuguese nation bent the knee and swore to accept him as King when his father should die, in exchange for his assurance that their ancient rights should be respected, little thought any of the glittering throng that the pale long-faced boy with the loose lower lip would, out of indolent amiability, cause rivers of blood to run between Portugal

[1] The King's and the Prince's splendid dresses and adornments on this occasion are described fully by Porreño in *Dichos y Hechos de Don Felipe III.*

and Spain, and that all the oaths sworn that day on both sides would be broken. Little dreamed they, either, that the dark-visaged man with the big square head, who stood behind the Prince's chair, was to be the mover of this calamity, and of the final disruption of his young master's great inheritance. Olivares, secure in his hold now over the Prince, left Lisbon to go to the home of his house in Seville for a time, knowing well that the jarring rivals around the boy would soon make his return to Court the more welcome. The King was ill and like to die on his way back to Madrid,[1] and Olivares was near the Prince at the critical time, more influential than ever.

Philip was precocious, and Olivares encouraged his precocity. By his influence it was decided that the married life of the fifteen and a half year old Prince and his pretty French bride should commence in November 1620, at the suburban palace of the Pardo ; and thenceforward, whilst the poor King, in alternate fits of agonised remorse and hysterical hope, clung to his mouldering relics of dead saints for comfort, and to the frocks of his attendant friars for reassurance against the wrath of the Most High, his son Philip was yearning impatiently for the coming of the time when he might as King carry into effect the lessons his mentor Olivares had whispered to him ; banish the whole brood of Sandoval y Rojas, and revive, as

[1] His recovery from this grave illness after the doctors had given up hope was ascribed to the miraculous effect produced by the dead body of the newly beatified Saint Isidore of Madrid, which was brought to his bedside at Covarrubias. The King kissed and embraced the corpse, and improved from that hour.

by magic, the potency of his country and the
happiness of his people.

Through the month of March 1621, King Philip
III. lay dying in his palace at Madrid, overlooking
the bare Castilian plain.[1] He was not much over
forty years of age, but though his malady was
slight his vitality had fled, and all desire to prolong
his disillusioned life. His remorse and horror of
heaven's vengeance were terrible to behold, though
during all his reign his habits had been those of a
frivolous friar rather than of a bad man, which he
certainly was not.[2] On the 30th March young
Philip took a last farewell of his father. " I have
sent for you," said the King, " that you may see
how it all ends " ; and he gave the weeping lad
similar advice to that given by his own greater
father, Philip II., to him on his deathbed, counsel
to be treated in a similar way. He was to marry
his sister Maria to the German Emperor, and to set
his face sternly against all temptations to make a
less Catholic alliance for her ; for James of England

[1] The ridiculous story, related by entirely untrustworthy French
travellers, of the cause of Philip's fatal illness being the Court etiquette,
which forbade any attendant but a high noble who happened to be absent
to remove a brazier from too close proximity to the King, may be dismissed as a fable. Anything which exaggerated the strangeness, the
romance, and the inflation of Spanish manners found ready belief in
seventeenth-century France, and has done so ever since. The absurd
ideas relative to Spain even at the present time are mainly due to this
insistence on the part of French writers in seeing everything Spanish
through the coloured medium of the romantic school. Madame D'Aulnoy's
overdone " local colour " and evidently invented stories are largely
responsible for this, aided by Bassompiere, Saint Simon, Mme. Villars,
and the later romantic school of French novelists.

[2] Terrible accounts of Philip's awful deathbed are given by Gil Gonzales
de Avila, his chronicler and friend, in his *Historia de Felipe III.*, original
MS. in my possession, in Yañez's additions to Malvezzi, and in Novoa,
Documentos Ineditos, lxi.; all contemporaries.

had been striving hard, seconded by Gondomar, to win her for Charles, Prince of Wales, and to secure the Palatinate of the Rhine for his son-in-law Frederick. The dying Philip urged his son to strive for the happiness of his people, cherish his sisters and brothers, to avoid new counsellors, and to stand steadfast to the faith of Spain ; but when the young Prince left the room Uceda and his crew knew that it was to go straight and take counsel of Olivares and his supporters for making a clean sweep of all those who had not bent the knee to the cadet of the house of Guzman, the dark man with the bent shoulders, the big square head, flashing fierce black eyes, and brusque imperious manner, who was already assuming the airs of a master.

For many months the palace had been a swarming hive of intriguers, where hate, jealousy, and uncharitableness reigned supreme ; but one by one the friends of the Sandovals had been pushed into the background, and no one but Olivares and his creatures were now allowed to approach the lad who was soon to be King of Spain. It was clear to Uceda that he was not strong enough to resist the coming storm alone ; perhaps the father he had ousted, the Cardinal Duke of Lerma, who had acted on the death of Philip II. as Olivares was acting now, might with his experience and prestige yet win the day. The dying King had already raised the exile of all the other courtiers who had been banished from Court ; though on their return they had been excluded by Olivares from access to the Prince ; and now, in the last days of the King's life, Uceda obtained

from him a decree recalling the Duke of
Lerma.

Like a thunderbolt the news fell in the camp of
the Guzmans. Olivares summoned his kin, headed
by the wisest of them, old Baltasar de Zuñiga.
From this meeting Olivares went to the Prince and
told him that as his father was dying it was necessary
to look ahead and take measures for securing prompt
obedience when the crucial moment came. Young
Philip acquiesced, for he was as wax in the hands
of his imperious mentor ; and Olivares, thus rein-
forced, proceeded to the King's apartments, where
by cajolery and threats he obtained from the two
great nobles on duty, the aged Duke of Infantado
and the Marquis of Malpica, not only a knowledge
of the provisions of the King's will, but also a
promise that prompt information of everything
that passed in the death chamber should be sent
direct to the Prince's adviser. The Cardinal Duke
was hurrying across Castile towards Madrid, full
of hope for a revival of his greatness ; for young
Philip, whom he had dandled as a babe, always
liked him, and had wept for his " Gossip," as he
called him, when he had been banished from
Court. If once the Duke reached Madrid, Guzman
was in danger, and no time was to be lost. So the
Prince, at the bidding of Olivares, took the bold
and dangerous course of assuming sovereign power
to countermand his father's orders whilst yet the
King lived.

Young Philip was alone in the dusk of the
evening in his panelled chamber in the old palace
of Madrid, when the president of the Council of
Castile, the highest functionary in Spain and

Archbishop of Burgos, stood bowing before him in obedience to his call. The Prince, who lounged against a carved oak sideboard, was dressed in black, and his long sallow face had assumed the haughty immobility that for the rest of his life was his official mask of majesty. " I have sent for you, he mumbled to the Archbishop in slow, measured tones, to direct you to despatch a member of the Council to forbid the Duke of Lerma from entering Castile, and to command him to return immediately to Valladolid to await my orders." [1] The Archbishop knelt and promised obedience, though he knew, we are told, that if the King recovered he would have to suffer for his weak compliance with an illegal command. [2]

There was little to fear in the world now, however, from Philip III., who in the intervals of his bodily anguish was occupied solely in his panic-stricken intercessions for pardon. His room was encumbered with ghastly remains of saintly humanity, and the sacred offices succeeded each other day and night : but around the bed worldly ambitions were raging bitterly. In the morning of the 30th March a consultation of physicians pronounced the end to be near ; and the Duke of Uceda, as principal minister and first chamberlain, announced his intention of conveying the news to the Prince. Then the Duke of Infantado, secure in the favour of Olivares, to whom only two days before he had betrayed the secrets of the

---

[1] Novoa, *Documentos Ineditos*, lxi.
[2] Novoa says that when the Archbishop signed the order he broke into tears and cast away the pen he had used.

death chamber, broke out tempestuously: " No, indeed ; that is my place, for the Prince has specially ordered me to go." Uceda knew his day was past, and meekly bent his head : and thus, in the midst of greedy bickering, his nerveless hand grasping to the last the rough crucifix that had comforted the glazing eyes of his grandfather the Emperor, and his father Philip II., the third Philip passed the dread divide, revered and beloved by the people whom his ineptitude had ruined, because he had still upheld throughout Europe the claim of his house to impose Christian orthodoxy upon the world, and had purged the sacred soil of Spain of the taint of Moorish blood, to his country's permanent undoing.

Olivares had played his cards cleverly. For weeks he had feigned a desire to seek retirement in his home at Andalusia, knowing well that young Philip, in the welter of difficulties and intrigues that surrounded him, looked to him alone for guidance ; and the adviser had only to hint at a wish to retire for the Prince to assent to whatever he demanded. As the King lay dying Uceda had met Olivares in the corridor. " How goes it," he asked, " in the Prince's chamber ? " " All is mine," replied the Count. " All ! " exclaimed the Duke of Uceda ruefully ; " Yes, without exception," retorted Olivares ; " for his Highness overrates me in all things but my goodwill." [1] Before many hours had passed Uceda and his kin knew to their cost that Olivares had not boasted in vain. All was

---

[1] *Fragmentos Historicos de la Vida de D. Gaspar de Guzman*, etc. Unpublished contemporary MS. biography of Olivares in my possession ; the work of his partisan Vera y Figueroa, Count de la Roca.

indeed his, and the strong hand fell ruthlessly
upon those who had ruled and plundered Spain
since the greatest of the Philips had passed his
heavy crown to his weak son twenty-two years
before.

CHAPTER II

ACCESSION OF PHILIP IV.—OLIVARES THE VICE-KING
— CONDITION OF THE COUNTRY — MEASURES
ADOPTED BY THE NEW KING—RETRENCHMENT
—MODE OF LIFE OF PHILIP AND HIS MINISTER—
PHILIP'S IDLENESS—HIS APOLOGIA—DISSOLUTE-
NESS OF THE CAPITAL—VILLA MEDIANA—THE
AMUSEMENTS OF THE KING AND COURT — A
SUMPTUOUS SHOW — ARRIVAL OF THE PRINCE
OF WALES IN MADRID — HIS PROCEEDINGS —
OLIVARES AND BUCKINGHAM

PRINCE PHILIP lay in his great square tentlike
bedstead in the palace of Madrid, at nine o'clock
on the morning of the 31st March 1621, when an
usher announced his Dominican confessor, Sotomayor. The friar entered, and, kneeling by the
bedside with a grave face, saluted his new sovereign
as King Philip IV. For a moment the boy was
overwhelmed at the long-looked-for news, and bade
the attendants draw the curtains close that he
might indulge his grief unseen. But soon the
eager worshippers of the risen sun flocked into the
room to pay their court to the new monarch when
he should deign to show his face. Anon there was
stir in the antechamber, and the crowd divided,
bowing low as the stern, masterful man who
was now lord over all stalked through the room,
accompanied by his aged uncle the white-haired

Don Baltasar de Zuñiga, destined by him to be nominally the King's chief minister, behind whom Olivares might rule unchecked. Advancing to the King's bed, Olivares threw back the curtains and peremptorily told Philip that he must get up, for there was much to be done. Uceda was still officially first minister and great chamberlain, with right of free access to the Sovereign; but when, a few moments later, he and his secretary entered the antechamber, amidst the scarcely concealed sneers of the courtiers, and the whisper reached Philip that they were coming, the King leapt from his bed and cried out that no one else was to be admitted until he was dressed.

Dressing on this occasion was a long process, for the young King broke down with grief and excitement several times whilst his attendants were preparing him for public audience; and Uceda, in the antechamber, fumed and fretted at the insult put upon him by the King, who thus disregarded his father's dying injunctions in the first moments of his bereavement. Whilst Uceda awaited the King's pleasure, Olivares, leaving the bed-chamber, met his falling rival face to face, and a violent altercation took place as to the premature action of Philip in ordering the Duke of Lerma, a Prince of the Church now, and immune from lay commands, to stay his journey to Madrid. Pointing to the State papers, seals, and keys in the hands of the secretary who accompanied him, Uceda asked who but the Duke of Lerma was worthy of taking charge of them. " My uncle, Don Baltasar de Zuñiga is here," replied Olivares, " to do so, and to give to the State the advantage of his long experience, and wisdom second to none." Uceda was then notified that the King, being dressed, would receive him; and entering the room, he knelt and proffered to Philip the seals and papers of his office. Pouting and frowning, the King waved his hand towards the sideboard, and said, "Put them there," and Uceda went out unthanked, to weep his now certain ruin and disgrace.[1]

Whilst the King was busy condoling with his young wife and sister and his two brothers Carlos and Fernando, and receiving the homage of his nobles, the preparations were hastily made in the great hall of the Alcazar for the lying in state of the body of Philip III. in his habit as a friar of St. Francis. And as the muffled death bells boomed from the steeples of the capital, one man at least there was whose heart fainted at the sound. "The King is dead, and so am I," cried Don Rodrigo de Calderon from the prison where he had suffered and languished for years, the scapegoat for others, borne down by accusations innumerable, from theft to witchcraft and regicide. In his pride and power he had piled up wealth beyond compute, as his master Lerma had done, but it is clear now that the other charges against him were mainly false. His long trial had resulted in no mortal crime being proved, and had Philip III. lived he would doubtless have been pardoned; but he had belonged to the old greedy gang, and Olivares had no mercy upon them. Before Philip's nine days mourning reclusion in the

---

[1] Novoa, who was present at the scene described, *Documentos Ineditos*, lxi.

monastery of St. Geronimo was ended a clean
sweep was made of the men who had surrounded
the dead King. Calderon's head fell on the scaffold
in the Plaza Mayor of Madrid; the great Duke of
Osuna, who had ruled Naples with so high a hand
as to be accused of the wish to make himself a King,
was incarcerated and persecuted till his proud
heart broke; Uceda met with a similar fate; the
powerful confessor Aliaga was disgraced and
banished; and even Lerma was not spared, though
he fought stoutly for his plunder; and all the clan
of Sandoval and Rojas were trampled under the
heels of the Guzmans and their allies.

The state of things which the new Sovereign
had to face was positively appalling. The details
of the abject penury and misery universal throughout Spain, except amongst those who managed
the public revenues and their numerous hangers-on,
sound almost incredible. Idleness and pretence
were everywhere. Insolent gentlemen in velvet
doublets and no shirts, workmen who strutted
and clattered in ruffs and rapiers, seeking prey
as sham soldiers instead of earning wages by
honest handicrafts, led poets, and paid satirists,
gamesters, swindlers, bravos and cutpurses, pretended students who lived like the rest of the idle
crew on alms and effrontery, crowds of friars and
priests whose only attraction to their cloth was the
sloth which it excused; ladies, rouged and over-
dressed, who deliberately and purposely aped the
look and manners of prostitutes,—these were the
prevailing types of the capital, as described by eye-
witnesses innumerable, as well as by the romancers
who revelled in the colour, movement, and squalid

picturesqueness of such a society.[1]　And to maintain
the real and false splendour in Madrid the starving
agriculturists, who had not abandoned their hold-
ings in sheer despair, were ground down to their
last real by the crushing alcabala tax, by local
tolls and octrois, and by the heartless extortions
of the tax farmers.

There is no doubt that, so far as their light
extended, both the King and Olivares sincerely
wished to reform abuses of which the results were
patent to all. Young Philip himself was good
hearted and kindly, as his father had been, but far
more sensual and less devout in his habits. Though
in public he assumed the marble gravity traditional
thenceforward in Spanish kings, he was gay and
witty in private discourse with those whose society
he enjoyed, especially writers and players. His
love of books, music, and pictures, as well as of
poetry and the drama, made him, as time went
on, the greatest patron of authors and artists in
Spain's golden age of social and political decadence.
But idleness marred all his qualities, and the
lust for pleasure which he was powerless to resist
made him the slave of favourites and his passions
all his life. A man such as this, endowed with a
gentle heart and a tender conscience, was doomed
to a life of misery and remorse in the intervals
of his thoughtless pleasures ; and in the course
of this book we shall see that sorrow ever followed
close on joy's footsteps in the life of the " Planet
King," until final ruin overtook the nation, cursed
with the gayest and wickedest Court since that of

[1] Especially Gil Blas, Guzman de Alfarache, Marcos de Obregon,
Estevanillo Gonzales, and El Diablo Cojuelo.

Heliogabalus, and all was quenched in a great wave of tears.

The man to whom Philip handed his conscience, as has been described, on the first day of his reign, was nearly twenty years his senior. An indefatigable worker, with an ambition as voracious as his industry, Olivares was the exact reverse of the idle, courtly, conciliatory Lerma. His greed was not personal, as that of Lerma had been, though his love of power led him to absorb as many offices as he. He was vehement and voluble, arrogant and impatient even with the King, and impressed upon Philip incessantly the need for exertion on his own part.[1] Able as he unquestionably was, he appraised his ability too highly, and contemned all opinions but his own; whilst his attitude towards the foreign Powers was insolent in the extreme, and quite unwarranted by Spain's position at the time. From an economic point of view, Olivares, though he began his rule by cutting down expenses in drastic fashion, was no wiser than his predecessors; though his ruling idea that the political unity of Spain was the thing primarily needful was sage and statesmanlike. But in this he was before his time, and his disregard for provincial traditions and rights in his determination to force unity of sacrifice upon the country, led to his own ruin and the disintegration of Spain. The portraits of him by Velazquez enable us to see the man as he lived,—stern, dark, and masterful,

---

[1] This was constantly denied by his many enemies, but original documents, to which I shall refer later, will prove that in this as in so many other things they did him an injustice, whatever his real aim might have been.

with bulging forehead and sunken eyes and mouth, his massive shoulders bowed by the weight of his ponderous head, we know instinctively that such a man would either dominate or die. He was the finest horseman in Spain, and he treated men as he treated his big-boned chargers, breaking them to obedience by force of will and persistence.

Such was the man who led Spain during the crucial period which was to decide, not only whether France or Spain should prevail politically, but whether the culture and civilisation of Europe should in future receive its impulse and colour from Spanish or French influences. In that great contest Spain was beaten, not so much because Olivares was inferior to Richelieu, as because of the old tradition that hampered Spain at home and abroad and pitted a decentralised country, where productive industry had been stifled and the sources of wealth choked, against a homogeneous nation where active work was fostered, and whose resources were at the command of the central authority.[1]

This much it was necessary to say in order to make clear the manner of men that in future ruled the Court of which we have to write : a King to whom pleasure was a business; and a minister to whom business alone was pleasure, who loved the reality of rule whilst his master loved the ceremonial of it. Not many days passed before the ambition of the Guzmans for the grandeeship was satisfied. The King was still passing his first days of mourning in the monastery of St. Geronimo when the sermon of the day, either by chance or

[1] *Cambridge Modern History*, vol. iv. "Spain," by Martin Hume.

design, inculcated the need for properly rewarding services done to us. The sermon over, Philip went to dinner, the room being crowded with nobles, amongst whom was Uceda, not yet finally banished. When the King had finished his meal and the cloth was drawn, Olivares entered very unobtrusively, and sidled against the wall behind the other nobles in attendance, well knowing, probably, what was coming. The King, catching his eye, said : " Let us obey the good friar who preached to-day ; Count of Olivares, be covered ! " This was the form used in the raising of a peer to the grandeeship, and Olivares, putting on his widebrimmed hat, threw himself at the King's feet with his uncle and those of his kin who were in the room, overjoyed at the honour done to their house ; and their joy was increased when, a few hours later, Uceda was told that he must surrender to Olivares at once one of his two great offices in the household.

Offices and honours thenceforward crowded upon the favourite, who was soon made Duke of San Lucar and principal chamberlain. Almost ostentatiously he professed a desire to leave politics entirely to his uncle, and to confine himself to the duties of his household offices near the King. Nobody was deceived by his apparent modesty, for even before Zuñiga's death, which happened in a year, it was known that his nephew's long personal conversations with the King, facilitated by his courtly palace duties, were mainly concerned with questions of Government and State. The Count-Duke, as he came to be called universally, would allow nothing to be done for the King but by himself. Before Philip was out of bed the minister

D

was the first to enter the room, draw the curtains
and open the window. Then on his knees by the
bedside he rehearsed the business of the coming
day. Every garment that the King put on passed
first through the hands of Olivares, who stood by
whilst Philip dressed. After the midday meal, at
which Olivares was often present, the minister was
wont to amuse the King by entertaining chat,
detailing the gossip of the capital, and late in the
evening he attended to give him an account of the
despatches received, and consult him as to the
answers, after which he saw the monarch to bed.[1]
This constant attendance upon the King made it
impossible for any person not an absolute creature
of Olivares to approach Philip's ear with doubt as
to the policy of the favourite in political matters.

When Philip's first parliament met, a few
months after his accession, it was stated in the
assembly that so terrible was the distress that
" people had abandoned their lands and were
now wandering on the roads, living on herbs and
roots, or else travelling to provinces where they had
not to pay the awful food excises and alcabalas " ;
whilst every source of revenue was anticipated for
years to come on usurious terms.[2] Philip himself,
in an important original paper hitherto unpublished
(British Museum, Egerton MSS. 338), gives the
following account of the state of affairs he had to face
on his accession, whilst complaining of the little
help he had received from his officers : " I found

---

[1] *Fragmentos Historicos MSS.*, by Vera y Figueroa, also Novoa, and Yañez,
and *Relazioni degli Ambassciatori Veneti*, British Museum MSS., Add. 8701.

[2] *Discursos y Apuntamientos*, by Lison y Biedma, a member of this
Parliament. (Secretly printed book of the period in my possession, which
gives a sad picture of affairs.)

finance so exhausted (apart from the dreadful state it had been left in at the death of Philip II., who had pledged it deeply) that all resources were anticipated for several years, and my patrimony had been so reduced that in my father's time alone 96,000,000 crowns had been granted in gifts, etc.; besides what had been spent in the other realms (*i.e.* Aragon, Catalonia, etc.), from which no returns have been received. The currency had been raised to three times its face value, an unheard-of thing in any realm. . . . Ecclesiastical affairs were in such disorder, that it was asserted from Rome that innumerable dispensations for simony had been obtained for archbishoprics, bishoprics, prebends, etc. . . . As for justice, on the very first day of my reign I was obliged to put my foot down, as will be recollected, . . . for the ministers who received bribes were more numerous than those who did not . . . My State, too, was so discredited that in the truce that the Dutch had made with my father they were treated as independent sovereigns, although every minister, from the King my father and the Archduke downward, refused to acknowledge such a claim. . . . I had only seven ships of war in the fleet. . . . India and the Indies were well-nigh lost. . . . The truce with Flanders was just expiring. . . . German affairs were more pressing than ever. . . . The marriage of the Prince of Wales with my sister was so far advanced that it seemed impossible to avoid it without a great war, which, indeed, followed, as we could not give way on the religious point.[1] Portugal was discontented

[1] There are two letters in *Cabala*—the first from Philip to Olivares, and the second the minister's reply to the King—which show that there

with the Viceroy, . . . whilst all the other parts of the monarchy was neglected or misgoverned. . . . We were at war with Venice; the Kingdom of Naples was almost in revolt, and the money there was utterly corrupted. All this was from no fault of my father, nor of his predecessors, as all the world knows, but simply because God so ordained it."

This document, written by Philip himself a few years afterwards for his own justification, proves how pressing was the need for an abatement of untenable claims on the part of Spain to interfere with the affairs of other nations, and the absolute necessity for a policy of retrenchment. And yet at the bidding of Olivares, against the opinion even of wise old Zuñiga, the first minister, the interminable war with the Dutch for the assertion of Spain's sovereignty over Holland was resumed as soon as the truce ended, only a few months after the young King's accession.

In his address to his first Cortes, Philip struck the unwise note of Dominican intolerance and pride

was never any intention on their part of carrying the English match through. The long letter from Olivares to the King is an adaptation of a Spanish original which is well known, and to which I shall refer later, proposing the marriage of Charles with the Emperor's daughter; but the King's letter which produced Olivares' reply is not, to my knowledge, printed elsewhere.

" The King my father declared at his death that his intention never was to marry my sister the Infanta Doña Maria with the Prince of Wales, which your uncle Don Baltasar well understood; for he so treated this match with an intention to delay it, notwithstanding it is so far advanced that, considering with all the averseness unto it of the Infanta, it is high time to seek some means to divert the treaty which I would have you discover, and I will make it good whatsoever it may be; but in all other things procure the satisfaction of the King of Great Britain, who hath deserved very much, and it shall content me, so that it be not the match." This must have been written before Charles' arrival in Madrid.

which had pervaded his baptism, setting forth in the midst of the miserable state of things just described that his first duty as a Spanish sovereign was, " with holy zeal befitting so Catholic a Prince, to undertake the defence and exaltation of our holy Catholic faith ; . . . to aid the Emperor in Bohemia ; to fight the rebel Hollanders again, and to defend everywhere our sacred faith and the authority of the Holy See." So, whilst Olivares made efforts to stop the peculation of high officers of State, to compel restitution of past plunder, to prevent further alienation of national property, and to reduce to a minimum the cost of the royal establishment, and whilst he passed ferocious sumptuary laws enjoining modesty and economy in dress, the real root of the evil was not touched ; for taxation continued to strangle production and fell mainly upon the poor, and the wasteful drain of unnecessary wars for an exploded idea continued as if Spain was still wallowing in wealth. Good, therefore, as the intentions of Olivares may have been, it is clear that he was a disastrous adviser for an inexperienced, idle young sovereign of sixteen.

And if his political influence was unfortunate, his social and moral influence was no less evil. There exists, for instance, in manuscript in various collections, and notably in the British Museum (Egerton MSS. 329), a pregnant correspondence between the Archbishop of Granada, Philip's tutor, and Olivares, written shortly after the accession, in which the Archbishop indignantly reproaches the favourite, who was certainly old enough to know better, for taking the young King out into the streets of the capital at night, and introducing him into evil company. "People," says the prelate, "are gossiping about it all over Madrid, and things are being said about it which add little to the Sovereign's credit or dignity." Madrid is, even now, fond of scandal, but early in the seventeenth century, isolated as it was from the world, Philip's capital found its most piquant pursuit from morn till night in slander and tittle-tattle, both in the form of malicious satirical verses that passed from hand to hand, and in whispered immoralities touching high and low. The long raised walk by the side wall of the Church of St. Philip at the entrance of the Calle Mayor (High Street), from the Puerta del Sol, opposite the still standing Oñate Palace, was the recognised centre of such confidences, and came to be called by the appropriate name of the *Mentidero* (Liars' Walk). The Archbishop in his letter proceeds to say that not only have these people begun to whisper things about the King's proceedings which were better unsaid; but the example shown of a young monarch and his principal minister scouring the streets at night in search of adventure is a bad one for the people at large; and he reminds Olivares of the great grief and anxiety of the late King on this very account, and of his dread that his youthful heir was already before his death being inducted into dissipation. The answer to the bold prelate's remonstrance is just such as might have been expected from the arrogant favourite. He tells him, in effect, that he is an impertinent meddler, and ought to be ashamed, at his age and in his high position, to trouble him with the vulgar gossip of the streets. " The King is sixteen," he says, " and he (Olivares) is thirty-four,

and it is not to be expected that they are to be kept
in ignorance of what is going on in the world.   It is
good that the King should see all phases of life, bad
as well as good.   Besides, he never trusts the
King with anyone else " ; and the favourite's letter
ends with a barely concealed threat that if the
Archbishop does not mind his own business in
future, ill might befall him.

Early, however, as was Philip's introduction into
the profligacy that was the curse of his life, and the
endless subject of his remorse in later years, he was a
gallant young husband to his pretty French wife,
though with the fall of her mother, Marie de Medici,
and her Italianate crew the political object of the
marriage had already failed, and France and Spain,
once more at issue, were rapidly drifting into war.
Scandalous and notorious as Philip's infidelity to
his wife very soon became, he appears to have been
devotedly attached to her, and was violently jealous
of any appearance of special love or homage to her
beauty.   She, on her part, true daughter of the
gallant *Béarnais* as she was, was gay and debonair
in her bearing, and followed, though decorously, the
fashion in Spain of her time, which allowed women
an amount of licence of speech with gallants impossible in other countries or at other periods.[1]   As

---

[1] Nearly all foreigners who visited Madrid during the reign of Philip IV.
remarked the extraordinary liberty which existed in the demeanour of
the women, even ladies of high birth and position, no doubt a reaction
from the conventual strictness with which they had been kept during
the two previous reigns.   There is no need to multiply authorities ; but
the following passage, from the report of the Venetian ambassador in
Spain at the time of Olivares' fall, will give an idea of the prevailing
laxity—even in the royal entourage.   " In the royal palace the gentlemen
are permitted to carry on with the ladies of the Queen the relations they
call ' gallanting,' in which lavishness, ostentation and expenditure are

with all other ladies of the Court, there was unkind tittle - tattle about the gay young Queen ; but apparently without the slightest foundation, though a supposed passion for her on the part of one of the most brilliant nobles of the Court led to tragic results for the gallant.

At a royal bull-fight—one of the earliest shows to celebrate the King's accession in the summer of 1621—the Count of Villa Mediana, Don Juan de Tassis, rode into the arena at the head of his troop of cavaliers, bearing as his device a mass of silver coins called " reals " (or royals), and above them the audacious motto of " My loves are ——," which was taken to mean, in conjunction with his daring glances and marked salutes, that his love was set upon the Queen. The Count was over forty years of age, and no beauty ; and his malicious satirical verses had been aimed at everybody in Court, from the King downward. He was therefore well provided with enemies, who were ready to place the worst construction on his acts. It is now proved— as far as any such thing can be proved [1]—that the real object of the Count's regards was a lady named Doña Francisca de Tavara, with whom the King was carrying on an intrigue at the time. But in either case the young King's jealousy was aroused, and his annoyance was increased by an innocent

carried to such an extraordinary excess as to be beyond belief, although here it is considered the most ordinary thing in the world, for rivalry and competition do away with all moderation. Those who go the greatest lengths are held in the highest esteem, not only by the courtiers in general, but also by the royal personages, who make quite a recreation of hearing the accounts of the presents given and attentions paid to them, that the ladies narrate daily to their Majesties. British Museum MS., Add. 8701.

[1] Address by J. E. Hartzenbusch, *Transactions of the Royal Spanish Academy*, 1861.

ISABEL DE BOURBON, FIRST WIFE OF PHILIP IV.

From a portrait by Velazquez in the possession of
Edward Huth, Esq.

COUNT DE VILLA MEDIANA   57

remark of his wife that " Villa Mediana aimed well."
" Ah!" replied Philip crossly, "but he aims too high";
and soon the ill-natured story with due embellishments was being whispered all over Madrid.[1]

But in the following spring of 1622 there
was a great series of festivals at Aranjuez, where
the Court was then in residence, to celebrate Philip's
seventeenth birthday. Already the glamour of
the stage had seized upon Philip and his wife,
and one of the attractions of the rejoicings was
the representation in a temporary theatre of
canvas erected amidst the trees on the " island
garden," and beautifully adorned, of a comedy
in verse by Count de Villa Mediana dedicated to the
Queen. The comedy was called *La Gloria de
Niquea*, and Isabel herself was to personate the
goddess of beauty. It was night, and the flimsy
structure of silk and canvas was brilliantly lit
with wax lights when all the Court had assembled
to see the show ; the young King and his two
brothers and sister being seated in front of the
stage, and the Queen in the retiring-room behind
the scenes. The prologue had been finished successfully, and the audience were awaiting the
withdrawing of the curtain that screened the
stage, when a piercing shriek went up from the
back, and a moment afterwards a long tongue of
flame licked up half the drapery before the stage,
and immediately the whole place was ablaze.
Panic seized upon the splendid mob, and there
was a rush to escape. The King succeeded in
fighting his way out with difficulty, and made his

[1] It is fair to say that this story depends upon the very untrustworthy
evidence of Mme. D'Aulnoy.

way to the back of the stage in search of his wife. In the densely wooded gardens that surrounded the blazing structure he sought for a time in vain, but at last found that Villa Mediana had been before him, and that the half-fainting figure of the Queen was lying in the Count's arms. Whatever may have been the truth of the matter, this, at all events, made a delightful *bonne bouche* for the scandal-mongers, who hated Villa Mediana for his atrabilious gibes, and it soon became noised abroad that the Count had planned the whole affair, and had purposely set fire to the theatre that he might gain the credit of having saved the Queen, and enjoy the satisfaction of having clasped her in his arms, if but for a moment.

Four months afterwards, in August 1622, Villa Mediana was returning home in his coach soon after dark, when, from an archway in the Calle Mayor, opposite the alley leading to the Church of St. Gines, there darted the cloaked figure of a man, who discharged at him a bolt from a cross-bow which pierced his chest. The Count had just time to leap from the coach and draw his sword, shouting "It is done," when he fell dead upon the road. Villa Mediana had been noted in a splendid Court as the most splendid and extravagant courtier. Amongst men to whom gallantry was an obsession, he was looked upon as the most gallant; in a society of literary and artistic dilettanti, he was held to be the most critical and refined ; and his murder, almost at his own door in the midst of the capital, caused a profound sensation. Murders in the open streets, it is true, had become scandalously frequent, mostly, it was said, prompted

by private vengeance, and rarely punished; but
the killing of Villa Mediana in the circumstances
related set tongues wagging in a way that had
not been equalled since that luckless secretary of
Don Juan of Austria, Escovedo, had been assassinated nearly fifty years before by the secret
orders of Philip II. As if by common consent, all
fingers pointed at young King Philip as the in-
stigator of the crime.[1] It was asserted that the
man who struck the blow was one Alonso Mateo,
a crossbowman of the King; but though hundreds
affirmed it, neither he nor any other was ever
prosecuted for the crime, and the immortal Lope
de Vega, who firmly believed that the young
Sovereign connived at the murder of the Duke of
Lemos, the former minister of his father, in November
1622, only interpreted the general belief in the
capital, if it was indeed he who wrote that whoever
struck the fatal blow at Villa Mediana, "*the impulse that guided it was sovereign.*"

Whilst murders such as this were of frequent
occurrence in the capital, whilst war was looming
daily closer, whilst industry lay ruined and the
fields unproductive, whilst poverty and famine
stalked unchecked through the land, the nobles
and officials dependent upon the Court grew richer
in plunder and more insolent in ostentation, not-

[1] The tradition that this was the case existed from the first, and has
never been lost; although most of the stories of the relations of Villa
Mediana with the Queen are quite unsupported by serious contemporary
evidence. Lord Holland, in his *Lope de Vega*, says that only a few days
after Philip's accession, the Prime Minister Zuñiga, Olivares' uncle,
warned Villa Mediana that his life was in danger. The tradition that
Philip was involved in the murder from motives of jealousy is too firm
and long-standing to be ignored, though whether his jealousy concerned
his wife is very doubtful.

withstanding the sumptuary decrees and the frantic efforts of Philip and Olivares to impose strict economy in one direction, as a counterbalance to lavish squandering in others. Almost any pretext was good enough for Philip to seize for a wasteful show. In after - times people blamed Olivares for purposely leading the lad into these frivolous extravagances, with the set object of diverting him from his duty; but I am inclined to believe that this view is an unjust one as regards the beginning of the reign. Olivares, of course, wished to please and flatter his master; but whilst he worked like a giant himself, and behind a perfect multitude of boards and juntas con- trived to keep in his own hands supreme control of national affairs, he unquestionably urged Philip again and again to apply himself diligently to work and to spend less time in pleasure.[1]

Philip's own inclinations led him to idle and profitless pleasures, especially those which lent themselves to theatrical display or ostentatious decorations. The bull - fights, combats between wild beasts, equestrian parades, cane tourneys, masques, balls, comedies and banquets, alternated with religious processions and church ceremonies. In these rejoicings Philip and his wife took equal pleasure. It was the Augustan age of Spanish literature, and the drama of intrigue which Spaniards had invented to delight Europe in future was then in its full flood of malicious fertility. From October 1622 every Sunday and Thursday, except during the height of summer, dramas

---

[1] Transcripts (contemporary) of these letters, etc., to which reference will be made later, are in British Museum, Egerton MSS. 338.

were performed by regular actors and actresses in the private theatre of the palace, the Queen being nominally the principal patron of the pastime. Some of the comedies then first represented may be mentioned as indicating the taste of the time. " The Scorned Sweetheart," " Jealousy of a Horse," and " The Loss of Spain " were three plays by Pedro Valdés, for which the Queen paid 300 reals, or £6 each. " The Fortunate Farmer," " The Woman's Avenger," " The Husband of his Sister," and " The Power of Opportunity " were other plays paid for by the Queen ; and the total number of new dramas represented in the Queen's apartments in the palace during the winter of 1622–23 was forty-three, the fees for which reached 13,500 reals, equal to £270.[1]

The favourite convent of the Discalced Carmelites, by the Church of St. Martin, was the scene of constant royal visits and semi-religious dissipations, and one of the most pompous of the ceremonious festivities that beguiled the dazzled crowd at the beginning of the reign was the series of shows that celebrated the canonisation of three of the most popular of Spanish saints in 1622, when all Madrid, in alternating devotional ecstasy and frivolous jollity, followed the King and his wife in honouring St. Isidore, the husbandman, now the patron of Madrid, St. Teresa of Avila, and St. Ignatius Loyola, founder of the Jesuits. Accompanied by the bull - fights and ceremonial trials of accused heretics, called *autos-de-fe*, which specially delighted the crowd, this canonisation fete also

---

[1] *Historia del Arte Dramatica en España,* from the German of A. F. Schack.

revived an ancient Spanish diversion, which thenceforward became under Philip's patronage one of the most highly appreciated of the pleasures of his literary Court, namely, the Literary Academies, as they were called, and Floral Games, or poetical competitions, in which the poetasters tried their mettle one against the other, in hope of gaining the ear of powerful patrons for their verses. It was a struggle of keen wits ; for in no time or court was poetry, especially satirical and dramatic poetry, ever so fashionable ; and that it degenerated later into preciosity, extravagance, and affectation was the natural result of the universal struggle to gain a hearing in a chorus of verse.

There are abundant and for the most part tedious contemporary descriptions of these various courtly festivities, descriptions usually as pompous and dry as is to our taste the affected frivolity of the festivities themselves.[1] But though these turgid productions cannot be quoted to any great length in a book like the present, which is intended to suggest a general picture of the Court and times rather than a series of minute sectional photographs, an idea may be gained of the scale upon which the festivities were arranged, by giving a rigidly condensed translation of the account of a great masque and equestrian display given by Philip and his brother Carlos on the 26th February 1623.[2]

[1] Especially in the MS. of the Royal Academy of History, Madrid by Soto y Aguilar, one of the courtiers and writers of the time, and in the MS. at the National Library at Madrid (M. 299) called Noticias de Madrid. These are contemporary news letters from 1621 to 1627.

[2] From the Soto y Aguilar MS. already mentioned.

"All the Court was anxious for the day when his Majesty and the Infante Don Carlos should honour and delight it with the promised feast. It took place on Palm Sunday, with a magnificent mask notable not only for its beauty, its ingenuity, and costly garments, and the high nobles and gentlemen who took part, but also because his Majesty and his Highness appeared in it.

"Four enclosed courses had been made; the principal one before the palace, and the others before the Convent of Discalced Carmelites, in the Plaza Mayor, and at the Gate of Guadalajara,[1] many (side) streets being barricaded and occupied by mounted alguacils (constables), and no coaches being allowed in the streets. The best horses Andalucia could breed or the world could see were brought out that day, with glittering trappings and harness, liveries, devices and accoutrements, richer than had ever been beheld. The King had ordered all the maskers to be ready mounted at the Convent of the Incarnation[2] at one o'clock, a stage and canopy having been erected there from which his Majesty was to mount. At about two o'clock the Spanish and German Guards arrived,[3] very smart and handsome, under Don Fernando Verdugo and the Marquis de Rentin; and soon afterwards the

[1] This was a narrow street forming part of the line of the Calle Mayor, in which it is now incorporated. It is quite close to the other three courses.

[2] A tremendous and costly monastic house (of which the church still stands in the Calle Mayor) upon which Philip III. and his wife had squandered incredible sums.

[3] This is very Spanish. The whole of the company had been ordered to be ready mounted at one o'clock, and yet the royal guard which was to keep the space and maintain order did not appear until an hour later, the maskers of course coming later still.

royal horses came, having gone in procession through the streets where the maskers were to pass. This was the order in which they came. First twelve drummers, thirty trumpeters, and eight minstrels, all on horseback, and dressed in white and black velvet; after them came the pioneers on foot, and then the royal grooms, and thirty-six splendidly caparisoned horses covered with housings of crimson velvet fringed with gold, bearing upon each a crown of cloth of gold and a cipher of " Philip IV." They were led by thirty-six lackeys, some in black and some in crimson, their garments being trimmed with frizzed velvet, like embroidery. The farriers came next, distinguished from the lackeys by wearing caps instead of hats. Thirty-six postillions followed, dressed like slaves in silvered plush on a black ground, with hats to match. . . .

"The first noble to put in an appearance (*i.e.* at the Incarnation) was Don Pedro de Toledo, Marquis of Villafranca, general of the Spanish cavalry. He was dressed in black, with cape and bonnet, and bore the insignia and baton of a general. With him came twelve lackeys in liveries of black velvet trimmed with gold, and twelve pages dressed similarly, but with white plumes in their caps. In like guise came the Marquis of Flores D'Avila, chief equerry of the King, whose noble presence and snowy hair, even if he had been alone, would have sufficed to dignify the feast. When the greater part of the nobles, the flower of Spain, had collected, the sun, to speak in poetical terms, envious of so much splendour and majesty, summoned up dark clouds which for a long time ceased not to pour water upon the festival. The feelings on the matter of the rain were divided. First it was a pity if the show were spoilt, the preparations being more beautiful and costly than had ever been made for a masquerade at Court, there being forty-eight pairs of horsemen, each with different liveries, besides his Majesty and his brother. The livery of the King and the Count of Olivares was steel grey with white plumes, whilst those of the Infante and the Marquis de Carpio were black and white with plumes to match. The second emotion aroused by the rain was rejoicing at the good it would do to the poor people who needed it so much for their crops, even though the maskers and merry-makers had to take shelter under the eaves. But soon the sky cleared, and the rain ceased ; so that all were satisfied. The clarions by and by rang out and announced that the King and the Infante had mounted, and the maskers did the same. Then Don Fernando Verdugo and the Guards clearing the way, Don Pedro de Toledo led the cavalcade to the palace, where the course ended in front of the balcony in which our lady the Queen with the Infanta Maria, and the Cardinal Archbishop of Toledo, the Infante Fernando, were seated, the ladies in waiting occupying the rest of the balconies of the royal apartment. If I described the precious stones, the gold, the rich dresses and the wealth displayed, this work would be a long one. The first to run was Don Pedro de Toledo, with his accustomed gravity and dignity ; and, having reached the end of the course, he bowed low to the Queen and their royal Highnesses, and then made a signal for the rest of the maskers to follow one

E

another along the course. (Here follow the resounding names of the ninety-six Spanish nobles,
dukes, marquises, and counts who formed the
company.) The last pair to run were his Majesty
the King and the Count of Olivares, with the
dexterity and gallantry to be expected of them.
The effect was strange and brilliant in the extreme,
for each pair of horsemen wore different colours
and devices. The splendid squadron was closed by
the Spanish and German Guards and other troops,
led by Verdugo. All the horsemen rode with great
rapidity, but the Infante Carlos and the Marquis of
Carpio went by like a flash of lightning, to the
astonishment of everyone. This pair had hardly
covered half the course when the Queen and the
Infanta and the Cardinal Infante stood up in
their balcony, because they saw that the King and
the Count of Olivares were starting out, they being
the last to run. They swept by, not on steeds, as it
seemed, but on the wind itself, wafted onward by
the blessings of those who saw them. Again they
covered the course thus, and then the whole
cavalcade rode to the plaza before the Convent of
the Discalced Carmelites."

At various parts of the capital the same sumptuous show was repeated; the most popular and
crowded exhibition being in the great square (the
Plaza Mayor) then recently built, and but little
altered since that time. The King, we are told,
rode a beautiful bay stallion presented to him by
the Marquis of Carpio; and when the running
was over and night fell the horsemen still paraded
the streets, which were illuminated by thousands

of torches, the cost of the feast having amounted
to more than 200,000 ducats.

But ten days after the wasteful ostentation
just described an event happened which not only
stirred Spain and all Europe, but was an occasion
for the display of lavishness by Philip that threw
into the shade all the festivities that had gone
before it. Between five and six in the evening
of the 7th March 1623, as the twilight began to
fall, two young Englishmen, travel-stained and
unaccompanied, rode into the noisome, unpaved
streets of Madrid. Inquiring the way to the
house of the English ambassador, the Earl of
Bristol, they were directed to the " house of the
seven chimneys," lying in a retired street off the
Calle de Alcalá. When they arrived there, the
elder of the two travellers was told, in answer to
his summons at the wicket, that his Excellency
the ambassador was busy, and could not be disturbed. The visitor persisted, and sent word that
he brought an important letter from Sir Francis
Cottington, who was on his way from England,
and had broken down on the road a day's journey
away. At length, upon being admitted, the
cloaked and dishevelled stranger, shouldering a
small valise that formed their only luggage, left
his younger companion in the shadow of the wall
across the way to guard the horses during his
parley with the ambassador.

Lord Bristol (Sir John Digby) was full of care,
for matters were not going very smoothly with
the difficult negotiation upon the successful issue
of which his whole future depended, as well as
great international issues. For twelve years he

had been backwards and forwards to Spain as King James' ambassador to bring about a marriage of the Prince of Wales with the Infanta Maria. James Stuart was a cunning fool, who was easily beaten in diplomacy, because he flattered himself that he could beat everybody else in duplicity. Most of his life, from long before he inherited the English crown, he had been playing the same game : trying to make other men his tools by pretending to agree with them. He had professed himself both Catholic and Protestant so often that now no one believed or trusted him, least of all the Catholics, whom he had deceived again and again.

When it had been necessary for Philip III. and Lerma to divert England from a threatened coalition with France, they had feigned to listen to the British King's advances, which they had previously repelled with scorn. Though insincere, they always had in view the prospect of gaining great immediate advantages for the Catholics of England, and subsequently they hoped the re-entry of Great Britain into the fold of the Church. The King of Spain and his minister had also been somewhat led astray by the sanguine hopes in this direction, given by their own ambassador in London, Count de Gondomar, whose diplomatic position was as much at stake as that of the Earl of Bristol. Gondomar, confident, as well he might be, of his power to bend King James ultimately to his will, had, there is no doubt, systematically minimised for years the obstacles to the match on both sides, and had led both his own Government and King James to believe that the other side would ultimately make concessions, which

we now see clearly would have been impossible
for either. James or his son dared not become
openly Catholic, nor could they force the English
Parliament to reverse the whole religious policy
of the last half century at the bidding of a foreign
Power ; whilst, with their traditions behind them,
it was equally impossible for Philip and Lerma to
mate their Princess with a " heretic." In order
to keep James from breaking away from Spain,
the intrigue had for some years past been transferred to Rome, where a dispensation from the Pope
for the marriage was being interminably discussed.

This was the position when Philip IV. ascended
the throne, and it is quite certain that, whatever
may have been the real intentions of the ministers
of Philip III. at an earlier period, neither Philip IV.
nor Olivares, with their revived arrogant claims
for Spain as the dictatress of Europe, meant to
marry the Infanta to the English Prince against
the dying injunction of Philip III., unless, indeed,
and even that is doubtful, upon terms quite impossible for the English to accept.[1] Bristol had

[1] In a document quoted on page 51, it will have been noticed
that Philip refers to the match as being one that it was necessary to
avoid, even at the cost of a war with England. In a notable document
in Spanish in the British Museum (MSS. Add. 14,043), reproduced by the
Camden Society under the editorship of Dr. Gardiner (*El Hecho de los
Tratados de Matrimonio*, etc.), there is a long memorandum written by
Olivares for Philip's information in 1622, proposing as a way out of the
difficulty the marriage of the Infanta to the son of the Emperor, the
marriage of the Prince of Wales with the Emperor's elder daughter, and
the betrothal of the Palatine's eldest son Maurice to the second daughter
on condition that the Prince was sent to Vienna to be brought up as a
Catholic, the Palatinate being restored to him after his marriage. This
solution, however, it is quite evident, would have been unacceptable to
James for many reasons. In any case it is quite clear that when Charles
appeared in Madrid, Olivares had no intention of allowing the Infanta
to marry him, unless indeed England became Catholic.

been sent once more to Madrid as ambassador in
June 1622. He had found Olivares and Philip
full of soft words about the match, though he
promptly guessed that their real aim was still to
delay matters, whilst securing Catholic concessions
from England, and he urged King James to insist
upon a settlement of the points at issue.[1]

Whilst he was labouring at his impossible task,
and almost despairing of success, an underhand
intrigue was carried on behind his back by those
who thought that his diplomatic caution stood
in the way of a settlement of the affair. James
badly wanted ready money in form of a dowry
for his son's bride, and a guarantee that the Palatinate should be restored by the Emperor to his
son-in-law, Frederick. Olivares wanted to lead
England on to the slope of Catholicism, and to
ensure Spain's hegemony over Europe. Gondomar,
who had returned to Spain, and Buckingham,
whom he had bought, wanted to gain the honour
and profit of having effected so important a match.
So, at Gondomar's instance, Buckingham sent his
half-Spanish secretary, Endymion Porter, a late
page of Olivares, to Madrid with secret orders to
promise religious concessions, which, had they
been known in England, would have caused serious
trouble, and to hint that the Prince himself might
come to Spain to fetch his bride. Porter, who
was no diplomatist, saw Olivares early in November
1622, and bluntly asked for assurance that in
return for the concessions promised, Spain would
at once consent to the marriage and force the
Emperor to restore the Palatinate to the Elector,

[1] The Earl of Bristol's defence. *Camden Society Miscellany,* vol. vi.

at which Olivares haughtily scoffed, and said that,
as for the match, he did not know what Porter
meant.[1] Bristol soon heard of this, and quite lost
heart, but he did not know that Endymion took
back to London a private message from Gondomar
to Buckingham, telling him that the only way
to make the match was for the Prince to come
suddenly to Madrid incognito and force the hands
of the slow-moving diplomatists, who would be
unable to draw back when the honour of England
was so far pledged.

Poetic and romantic Prince Charles was soon won
over to so compromising and dangerous a course ;
but King James wept and slobbered like a frightened
infant when " Baby " and " Steenie " wrung from
him unwilling permission to undertake so hare-
brained an adventure.[2] Only Cottington and Porter
were to go with them to Spain, and the former at
least, who knew Spain well, was dead against the
voyage ; but Buckingham's violence gained the day.
Distancing all posts, and riding for a fortnight an
average of sixty miles a day, through France and
over the rough mule tracks in the north of Spain,

[1] A very interesting and, as I believe, unpublished contemporary
manuscript account of the proceedings of Charles and Buckingham in
Madrid, and of the events that followed their return to London, so far
as regards the Spanish match, has been brought to my notice whilst this
chapter is being written. The manuscript, evidently an original, appears
to have been the work of someone who accompanied the Prince in his
journey. Many expressions in it are the same as those which I have
quoted from other sources, especially from certain letters of Endymion
Porter in the Record Office, and from those of Buckingham to the King,
most of which were written by Porter. I am therefore led to the conclusion that this interesting new document, which is the property of
Dr. Rosedale of the Royal Society of Literature, is the work of Endymion
Porter. I am informed that it will shortly be published by the Society.

[2] Clarendon, *Great Rebellion*.

the little party pushed onwards. Cottington and Porter were distanced and left behind a day's journey from Madrid ; and when the man with the valise, who gave his name as Thomas Smith, entered Lord Bristol's study, and, throwing aside his cloak and hat, disclosed the handsome face of "Steenie," the Marquis of Buckingham, the King's favourite, the ambassador was in dismay, increased almost to terror when he learnt that the Prince of Wales, the only son of King James, masquerading under the name of John Smith, was holding the horses on the other side of the dark street.[1]

What was to be done ? The presence of the heir of England could not be hidden for many hours from gossiping Madrid, for the couriers from Paris, where he had been recognised, were following close upon his heels. A voyage to Spain in those days was a far greater adventure than an expedition to Thibet would be now, and the temerity, nay the foolhardiness, of putting such a pledge as the Prince of Wales unconditionally in the hands of the Spaniards, who if they chose to detain him could exact what terms they liked as the price of his safe return, struck the harassed ambassador with alarm. " My Lord Bristol in a kind of astonishment brought him (*i.e.* Prince Charles) up to his chamber, where he presently called for pen and ink, and despatched a post that night to England to acquaint his Majesty how in less than sixteen days he was come safely to the Court of Spain." [2]

After grave discussion in Bristol's room, it was

[1] Howel's *Familiar Letters*.   Howel was in Madrid at the time.
[2] Howel's *Familiar Letters*.

decided to send at once for Gondomar, to whom, as Buckingham well knew, the arrival of the Prince would cause no surprise. It was past nine o'clock at night when Gondomar entered the " house with the seven chimneys," full of glee at the success of his bold diplomacy ; and not long afterwards he was at the door of Olivares' rooms in the palace, anxious to give to the favourite the first news of the great event. The Count-Duke was seated at supper as Gondomar entered the apartment. The famous Spanish ambassador in England owed much of his success to the assumed bluff jocosity with which he was wont to cover his cunning ; but when he bounced into the Count-Duke's supper chamber on this occasion, he was so exuberant in his joy that grave Olivares looked up in surprise, and said : " Ah, Count ! what brings you here at such an hour as this ? You look as jolly as if you had the King of England himself in Madrid." " If we have not the King," chuckled Gondomar, " we have the next best thing to him,—the Prince of Wales." [1]

Olivares was far from sharing Gondomar's delight. To him the news meant infinite anxiety, danger, and expenditure ; for not only must the Prince be entertained lavishly, but somehow he must be got rid of without marrying the Infanta, and if possible without a national war with England for the slight put upon the Prince. The Count-Duke hurried to the King's apartments with the great news, and Philip was as much taken aback as his minister, for young as he was he fully understood the gravity of the situation. One thing, however,

[1] *Fragmentos Historicos de la Vida de Gaspar de Guzman*, etc. MS. by Count de la Roca in my possession.

he was quite determined upon. Already the
adulation of which he had been made the object,
and the high hopes aroused by the new measures
and men that had been introduced upon his
accession, had convinced the lad he was the heaven-
sent instrument destined to restore to Spain its
proud supremacy over a united Christendom, and
religious exaltation had claimed him henceforth
for its own, however ungodly his daily life might be.
When Olivares had laid before him the difficulties
that arose from the unexpected descent of Charles
Stuart upon them, Philip rose, and walking to where
a figure of Christ crucified hung at the head of his
bed, he kissed the feet of the figure, and burst out
into the following impassioned oath : " O Lord !
I swear to Thee by the human and divine alliance
crucified that in Thee I adore, and upon whose feet
I seal this pledge with my lips, that not only shall
the coming of this Prince be powerless to make me
concede one point in the matter of the Catholic
religion, not in accordance with what Thy Vicar the
Pontiff of Rome may resolve, but even if I were to
lose all the realms I enjoy, by Thy grace I will not
give way a single iota." Then turning to Olivares
(who says that this was one of the only two oaths
he ever knew the King to take), Philip told him
they must nevertheless fulfil the duties of hospitality
that the Prince had thrown upon them.[1]

For the greater part of that night the minister
worked hard laying out all the plans for the entertainment of the Prince, and for avoiding without
giving mortal offence the marriage he sought. At

---

[1] *Fragmentos Historicos*, etc. MS. by Count de la Roca, the great
friend and confidant of Olivares.

eight o'clock next morning a meeting of high councillors, with Gondomar and the King's confessor,
met in the Count-Duke's room in the palace, the
result of their deliberations being highly characteristic : namely, " first, to offer public prayers
to God in thanks for the event, and in supplication
for His guidance"; and secondly, to instruct
Gondomar to sound Buckingham and Cottington
(who was expected to arrive that day) as to how far
the King of England might be squeezed, " in order
to bring this visit to be a great and very signal
service to the Church." [1]

A dozen knotty points of etiquette had to be
settled, and Gondomar was busy all day speeding
backward and forward between the palace and the
" house with the seven chimneys " ; [2] but at last
it was arranged that the pride of Olivares should
be saved from making the first visit, by the device
of an apparently chance meeting with Buckingham.
Already Madrid was agog with the news that some
great personage, the King of England some said,
had arrived in disguise ; and when, late on Saturday afternoon, the great swaying gilded coach of
Olivares, with its leather curtains, its six gaudily
decked mules, and its crowd of liveried servants
and pages around it, was seen threading the green

[1] *Hecho de los Tratados*, etc.,   British Museum MS., Add. 14,043, and
Camden Society.

[2] Gondomar had been raised to the Council of State during the early
morning sitting, and on his first visit that day (Saturday) to the English
embassy he came rushing to the Prince in his usual boisterously jocose
fashion, saying that he had a strange piece of news to convey.   "An
Englishman had been sworn a Privy Councillor of Spain," meaning, as
Howel (who tells the story) says, himself, who, he professed, was an
Englishman at heart.   This was the kind of joke by which he had managed
to dominate King James.

alleys of the gardens below the palace on the banks
of the Manzanares, all the idlers on "Liars Walk"
knew that the Count-Duke was going to meet, "by
chance," the Admiral of England, the favourite
of his King. When the carriages met, Olivares
alighted and greeted Buckingham half - way between their coaches, where, with carefully arranged
politeness and high-flown compliments, as false
as they were pompous, the great Guzman first
measured his strength with brilliant, rash, unscrupulous George Villiers.

After many professions of delight on both sides,
the Count-Duke entered the English coach with
Buckingham, Bristol, and Cottington, and for an
hour they drove in close confabulation. On their
return they entered the palace gateway, and Olivares
secretly led Buckingham into the King's presence,
where again the compliments were repeated. There
is no doubt that the Spaniards, from the King
downward, were flattered with the embarrassing
visit, which was a patent proof, it was proudly
claimed, of the reality of Spain's regained power
and superiority under the new régime, when the
heir of England came wooing her at so great a risk.
So Philip was all smiles to Buckingham ; and when
the latter returned to the " house with the seven
chimneys," Olivares insisted upon accompanying
him to greet the Prince personally in the King's
name. The Spanish narratives say that the Count-
Duke performed his part with all the dignity and
splendour characteristic of him ; but Howel, who
was in Madrid at the time, and knew Porter well,
writes that the Count-Duke " knelt, and kissed his
(*i.e.* the Prince's) hands and hugged his thighs,

and delivered how immeasurably glad his Catholic Majesty was at his coming, and other high compliments, which Mr. Porter did interpret." [1]

During the interview Charles expressed his ardent desire to see his lady love, the Infanta—"to discover the wooer," as Buckingham called it; and it was agreed that on the next day, Sunday, 9th March, the coaches of the royal family should parade the Prado, where the Infanta should be distinguished by a blue ribbon tied round her arm; and the Prince in Bristol's coach might meet the royal party as if by chance, and incognito. Little enough of incognito there was about the affair, when, at four o'clock in the afternoon the ambassador's coach with the Prince, Buckingham, Aston, Gondomar, and Bristol in it, stood in the narrow street of the Puerta de Guadalajara in the Calle Mayor to await the coming of the King's party. Every foot of the streets was crowded with sightseers, and the pride and joy of the show-loving Madrileños knew no bounds. By and by the long line of coaches accompanying the King rumbled by, and at last young Philip with his pretty dark-eyed girl wife, his two young brothers, Carlos and Fernando, almost exact replicas of himself, with their lank sandy hair, their long white faces, thick red lips, under-hung jaws and great pale eyes. In the door-seat of the carriage sat the Infanta Maria. She was much like her brothers : " a very comely lady, rather of Flemish complexion than Spanish, fair haired, and carrying a most pure mixture of red and white in her face. She is full and big lipped,

---

[1] *Familiar Letters.* The sequence of events, meetings, etc., as given in *Life and Times of James I.*, is untrustworthy.

which is held a beauty rather than a blemish." [1]
As the King's carriage passed that of the Prince,
Philip, who was not supposed to see Charles, bowed
low, as did his brothers, to Lord Bristol; but it
was noticed that the Infanta first flushed and then
turned deadly pale as her lover's eyes fell upon
her.

The poor girl, indeed, was getting seriously
alarmed. She was, of course, devout and ignorant.
To her heretics were an abomination, and the
prospect of living amongst such was worse than
death. Her monkish confessor painted in lurid
colours the horror of the fate that threatened her ;
worse than hell it was, he said, to lie by a heretic's
side, and bear heretic children. Only that morning
she had sent her confidential lady, Margaret
Tavara, to Olivares, passionately protesting against
the marriage being seriously negotiated. She
would, she said, take refuge in the Convent of the
Discalced Carmelites, and assume the nun's veil
the moment she heard that the capitulations were
signed. Charles on his part appears to have been
really smitten with the pink and white charms of
the little lady, and played the eager wooer well.
The Prince and Buckingham, writing to their " Dear
Dad and Gossip " (the King), calls this first
meeting " a private obligation hidden from
nobody ; for there was the Pope's Nuncio, the
Emperor's ambassador, the French, and all the
streets filled with guards and other people. Before
the King's coach went the best of the nobility,
after followed by the ladies of the Court. We sat
in an invisible coach, because nobody was suffered

[1] Howel.

to take notice of it, though seen by all the world."[1] The cavalcades then wended their ways by different roads to the Prado, where, parading up and down, the Prince had several opportunities of looking upon his blushing sweetheart. Soon Olivares came and entered the Prince's coach ; and again fulsome compliments passed as they drove back to the English embassy.[2]

Buckingham, indeed, was fairly dazzled and deceived, for both he and Charles believed now that the match was as good as completed. Alas! they did not know Olivares or Spanish methods so well as Bristol did.

"If we can judge by outward shows," wrote Charles and Steenie to the King, "or general speeches, we have reason to condemn your ambassadors for rather writing too sparingly than too much. To conclude, we find the Conde de Olivares so overvaluing our journey, he is so full of real courtesy, that we can do no less than beseech your Majesty to write the kindest letter of thanks and acknowledgment you can unto him. He said, no later to us than this morning, that if the Pope would not give a dispensation for a wife they would give the Infanta to thy Baby as his wench,[3]

[1] Hardwicke, *State Papers.* Charles and Buckingham to the King.

[2] We are told that on this occasion Olivares, notwithstanding the Prince's remonstrance, insisted upon taking the humble seat at the carriage doorstep ; and that throughout the whole visit he treated Charles with the same honours as he did the King, kneeling when he spoke to him, kissing his hand, etc. Charles, on the other hand, appears to have been equally polite to Olivares ; but Buckingham soon got tired of an attitude so unusual to him, and behaved himself with extraordinary rudeness and ill-breeding, as will be told later. *Hecho de los Tratados*, etc.

[3] Lord Bristol, in his defence (*Camden Miscellany*, vi.) gives an account of a conversation in the coach when the Prince, Bristol, Gondomar,

and hath this day written to Cardinal Ludovico, the Pope's nephew, that the King of England hath put such an obligation upon this King in sending his son hither, that he entreats him to make haste of the dispensation, for he can deny nothing that is in his kingdom. . . . The Pope's Nuncio works as maliciously and as actively as he can against us, but receives such rude answers that we hope he will soon weary on't. We make this collection that the Pope will be very loth to grant a dispensation, which, if he will not do, then we would gladly have your directions how far we may engage you in the acknowledgment of the Pope's special power, for we almost find, if you will be contented to acknowledge the Pope as chief head under Christ, that the match will be made without him." [1]

It is difficult to know what to condemn most in this astounding letter,—whether the simplicity that made Buckingham so easy a dupe of Olivares' soft speeches, or the proposal at the end, which, as the reply shows, was too much even for King James, that the latter should abandon the main condition upon which he held the Protestant crown of England. It is clear that the intention of

Olivares, Buckingham, and Aston were waiting for the royal party to pass on the Sunday referred to in the text. This shows how entirely Olvares had convinced them all of his sincerity. Gondomar in boastful mood had asked Olivares if he was not justified now in all he had written from England about the real desire of King James for the marriage ; and whether Bristol and himself had not proved themselves honest men. "Yes," replied Olivares, "you may both say your *Nunc Dimitis* now, and trouble no more about it, except to claim the reward of success." No blame, he said, could attach to them in any case.

[1] Hardwicke, *State Papers.*

Olivares was to cast upon the Pope the whole of the blame for the failure of the match, and this, at least from the Spanish point of view, was a statesmanlike policy, although the full falsity of it is evident to us now that we have before us the communications that passed between Madrid and Rome on the subject.[1]

Leaving Charles at the embassy after the drive, Olivares and Buckingham, with Porter as their interpreter, re-entered a coach and drove off in the gathering darkness to the gardens behind the palace, to arrange the details of the coming private interview to be held that night between Philip and the English Prince. Whilst the coach, with Olivares and Buckingham, was in the green alleys of the garden, a man, unaccompanied, with his cloak masking his face, and sword and buckler by his side, was seen walking towards them. "This is the King," said Olivares, to Steenie's intense astonishment. "Is it possible," exclaimed Buckingham, "that you have a King who can walk like that ? What a marvel ! " and, leaping from the carriage, he knelt and kissed the young King's hand. Entering the coach again, the party, accompanied now by the King, were driven through the quiet streets of the unlit capital, for it was ten o'clock at night, to the Prado, where the Prince, with Gondomar, Bristol, Aston, and Cottington, in another coach, awaited their coming. Descending and embracing warmly, the King and Prince then re-entered the carriage with Bristol alone, and for more than half an hour discoursed amiable banalities in the darkness under the overhanging trees of the promenade.

[1] *Hecho de los Tratados,* etc. B.M. MSS. Add. 14,043.

Thenceforward Buckingham and Olivares by
agreement changed offices, the former constituting
himself chief equerry in waiting to Philip, whilst
Olivares attended Prince Charles. In pursuance
of this idea, the suite of apartments in the palace
occupied by Olivares as master of the horse were
hastily prepared with great magnificence for the
occupation of the English Prince ; and whilst their
redecoration and furnishing were being accomplished,
Charles was invited to transfer his lodging to the
rooms in the monastery of St. Geronimo in the
Prado, to which the Kings of Spain usually retired in
times of mourning, and previous to state entries to
the capital, an invitation which he did not accept.

In the week that followed the first meeting of
Charles and his host, until Sunday the 16th March,[1]
which was the day fixed for his public entry into
the city, Madrid was astir with excitement. The
pragmatic decrees recently promulgated forbidding
starched and fluted ruffs, embroidered dresses,
and the use of gold in tissues, and generally sup-
pressing extravagance of living, were all suspended
by proclamation during the visit of the Prince ;
the streets were ordered to be swept and garnished,
and the houses on the line of route richly adorned ;
and Madrid, by the morning of the day fixed for
the public entry, had covered its squalor and dirt
by an overcoating of finery. All the gaols, too,
were emptied of prisoners, by way of welcoming
the English guest.[2]

In the week of waiting Charles sought per-

---

[1] The dates given throughout are old style, according to the English
calendar of the time.   The Spanish dates are ten days later.
[2] MSS. Soto y Aguilar.

mission to visit Philip privately in return for the
interview in the Prado on Sunday night, and he
and Buckingham gave the following account of
the meeting to their " Dear Dad and Gossip."

" The next day your Baby desired to kiss the
King's hand privately in the palace, which was
granted, and thus performed. First, the King
would not suffer him to come to his chamber,
but met him at the stair-foot, then entered into
the coach and walked in his park. The greatest
matter that passed between them was compliments, . . . and then by force he would needs
convey him (*i.e.* Charles) half way home, in which
doing they were both almost overthrown in brick
pits. Two days after we met his Majesty again
in his park with his two brothers ; they spent
their time in seeing his men kill partridges flying
and conies running with a gun." [1]

In the meanwhile the people with pride and
delight had quite satisfied themselves that the
coming of the Prince meant the intended conversion
of himself to Catholicism and the return of England
to the fold of the Church,[2] and Olivares pressed this

[1] Hardwicke, *State Papers.*

[2] Most of the poets and poetasters of the Court were convinced of
this, and the romantic love-making of the Prince, who for the sweet eyes
of the Infanta was to make England Catholic, inspired many verses.
Howel sends to a friend in England one stanza of such a poem written
at this time, he says by Lope de Vega—

Carlos Estuardo, soy,	Charles Stuart, here am I,
Que siendo amor mi guia,	Guided by love afar
Al cielo de España voy,	Into the Spanish sky,
Par ver mi estrella Maria.	To see Maria my star.

Gongora's fine sonnet, translated by Churton, is worth quoting entire—
Fair from his cradle springs the star of day,
Rock'd on bright waves fair sinks his parting light :

point so persistently and publicly upon Charles,
that Buckingham himself began to take fright.
He noticed that whenever the Count-Duke found
himself near Charles, which indeed was continually,
he turned the conversation towards the Catholic
religion. Charles was young, the son of a Catholic
mother, and was certainly for the time smitten by
the Catholic Infanta : his father had professed himself Catholic again and again ; and at this moment
was writing thus to his " Sweet boys " : " I send you,
my Baby, two of your fittest chaplains for this
purpose, Mawe and Wren, together with all stuff
and ornaments fit for the service of God. I have
fully instructed them, so as all their behaviour and
service shall, I hope, prove decent and agreeable to
the service of the primitive Church ; *and yet as
near the Roman form as can lawfully be done ; for
it hath ever been my way to go with the Church
of Rome usque ad aras.*" But whatever may
have been the tendencies of Charles himself,
Buckingham in his saner moments, and certainly
Bristol, must have seen the pitfall laid for the
Prince, and thus early, in the midst of all the
complimentary billing and cooing before the state
entry, the young adventurers began to realise the

> Such be thy course, in sunlike beauty bright,
> Daughter of kings and born to be as they,
> The world's majestic wonder. Lo ! thy ray
> Hath called a royal bird, in venturous flight,
> From realms where keen Arcturus fires by night
> The polar skies : from regions far away
> He wheels on swiftest wing : within thy sphere
> Secure his bold eye drinks the soft clear fires,
> Now Heaven and Love be kind ; and both ordain
> What time his suit shall win thy beauty's ear.
> The Northern Eagle won with chaste desires,
> By Truth's pure light may live to God again.

difficulty of the task, which looked so easy from a distance.

On the day following the state entry, Charles and Buckingham wrote to the King—

" For our chief business, we find them by outward shows as desirous of it as ourselves, yet they are hankering upon a conversion ; for they say that there can be no firm friendship without union in religion, but they put no question in bestowing their sister, and we put the other quite out of the question, because neither our conscience nor the time serves for it." [1]

Delay, as they said, was the worst denial; for King James was in a hurry,—in a hurry to get his heir married, in a hurry for the Infanta's dowry, and in a hurry to get the Palatinate back for his son-in-law ; and as yet the priests were still squabbling over the dispensation in Rome, and Olivares, equally with his master, was determined to delay until either England became practically Catholic, or the English themselves broke off the negotiations by refusing the terms upon which Rome, prompted by the Spanish agents, alone would consent to the match. This, indeed, as Olivares saw, was the only slender chance of preventing war with England, and to avoid throwing James into the arms of France.

[1] Hardwicke, *State Papers.*

CHAPTER III

ALL being ready for the public entry of Charles on
Sunday, 16th, the Prince, though he declined the
invitation to sleep the previous night at the
monastery of St. Geronimo, as was customary
with Spanish sovereigns who entered the capital in
state, went thither early in the morning, and was
entertained at a sumptuous banquet by the Count
Gondomar, as near as he could manage it in
English fashion. Then, as was also the usage with
Spanish sovereigns, all the members of the numerous
Councils and *juntas* rode in full state, accompanied
by their officers and escorts, to pay their respects to
the Prince. Charles received this glittering crowd,
numbering some hundreds, standing by a velvet-

covered table beneath a canopy of silver tissue in the royal apartment of the monastery, the empty throne being behind him, and the walls of the chambers covered with rich hangings and pictures, amongst which were portraits of King James and his councillors. As each pompously named official knelt and begged permission to kiss the Prince's hand, Charles gracefully threw his arms upon their shoulders instead, and raised them from the ground.[1] The impression generally produced by the Prince now and during his stay was excellent, and it was noticed throughout that he never took advantage, as Buckingham and the crowd of noisy English courtiers who soon arrived in Spain did, of the Spanish politeness which places everything at the disposal of a guest. The behaviour of these courtiers, indeed, and especially Buckingham's insolence, very soon produced disgust amongst the grave, courteous Spaniards.

At midday, when the councils had retired and taken their places on the line of route, a flourish of drums and pipes heralded the coming of the Spanish Guard in orange and scarlet to the monastery, followed by the German Guard, in crimson satin and gold with white sleeves and plumed caps ;

[1] Soto y Aguilar. Another unpublished contemporary account in Spanish of the state entry in the British Museum, MSS. Add. 10,236, says that Charles advanced to the centre of the room and took off his hat as the councillors entered. It is mentioned that Charles retained his English dress and had " a gallant figure" (bizarro en el talle). He was noticed to doff his hat whenever Philip did on passing a church or sacred image, and this greatly impressed the crowd in his favour. When the royal personages arrived at the palace at half-past six, having taken three hours to cover the distance of about a mile from St. Geronimo to the palace, the Prince was led to salute the Queen, Lord Bristol kneeling before them to interpret their conversation. This account is very enthusiastic as to Charles' graciousness and dignity.

then came the municipality of Madrid, with a great following of town officers dressed in orange satin with silver spangles. Nobles and princes followed in pairs, led by Prince Edward of Portugal and the Count of Villamor, each pair of high gentlemen resplendent in satin, velvet and gold, jingling and flashing on their showy Andalusian horses. Following these and a hundred other ostentatious groups, the mention of which would fill pages, King Philip left his palace as the great clock in the courtyard—one of the marvels of Madrid—struck the hour of one, and reached a side door of the monastery in his coach by a circuitous route. Until three o'clock Charles and Philip chatted in friendly converse, and then the signal was given for the cortege to start, the King and Prince mounting their horses at the same moment.

The drums, pipes, clarionets, and trumpets led off, followed by judges, officials, courtiers, and nobles, heralds, guards, pages, lacqueys, and grooms by the hundred, upon whose grand dresses Soto y Aguilar dwells with tedious minuteness. Then came the King and the Prince, under a canopy of white damask and gold, mounted upon silver poles borne by six officers of the corporation, the Prince riding on the right hand of his host. They must have looked a gallant pair, for they were mere youths, and both fine horsemen. Olivares and Buckingham side by side followed them, and then came a great troop of Spanish grandees with the English ambassadors and officers. Through the streets, decked lavishly, and crowded with cheering people, flattered at the coming conversion of England by means of Spain, the cavalcade rode by the Puerta del Sol and Calle Mayor to the ancient Alcazar upon the cliff, which looks across the arid plain to the snow-capped Guadarramas. On the line of route national dances and the eternal comedies were played until the Prince approached, when special dances were performed in his honour, at which, we are told, he was much delighted. Upon entering the palace the King himself conveyed the Prince to his apartments, and surpassed himself in courtly welcome to his guest; and that same night the Queen sent to the Prince a great present of white linen for table use and personal wear, with a rich dressing gown and toilet paraphernalia in a scented casket with gold keys.[1] It was all as Howel wrote, " a very glorious sight to behold, for the custom of the Spaniard is, tho' he go plain in his ordinary habit, yet upon some great festival or cause of triumph there's none goes beyond him in gaudiness." [2]

The next day the municipality of Madrid celebrated a royal bull-fight on a scale of magnificence rarely approached. The great Plaza Mayor of Madrid, 340 feet square, was surrounded by stagings, and every one of the hundreds of balconies of the high houses overlooking the plaza was hung with crimson silk and gold, and filled with noblemen and ladies whose names were as splendid as the clothes, of which Solo y Aguilar [3] spares us no detail. The royal balcony was erected on the first floor of the municipal bakery (still standing),

[1] MS. Soto y Aguilar.
[2] *Familiar Letters.*
[3] MS. Royal Academy of History, Madrid. Transcript in my possession. The writer, in this official capacity, was present at all these feasts.

and must have been a mass of crimson and cloth
of gold, with its hangings, its canopies, its curtains,
and its balustrades.   Every council and board, and
under Olivares they were infinite, had its special
tribune.   Nobles, officials, officers, and foreign representatives, all of whose fine garb the literary
quarter-master details for us until his description
produces but a vague impression of sumptuous
stuffs without end, smothered in bullion, arrived
in procession to occupy their places as spectators
or actors in the glittering show.   The English
visitors were accommodated in a special stand
occupying the opening of the Street of Bitterness
(Calle de Amargura), which gave rise to much
satirical comment.   When all was ready, and
around the vast plaza a packed mass of bedizened
humanity had assembled, the royal coaches entered
and drove around the arena to the central entrance
of the Queen's balcony before the bakehouse.
Here Isabel alighted, dressed, we are told, like
the Infanta, who accompanied her, in brown silk
embroidered with gold, and covered with gems,
the plumes of their jaunty toques being white
and brown, sprinkled with diamonds.   With them
came the two Infantes, Carlos, in black velvet
and gold, with diamond chains and buttons, and
the boy Cardinal Infante Fernando, in the purple
of his ecclesiastical rank.   Behind them came
scores of ladies, and then officers of the Guards,
and finally a " great company of Spanish and
English gentlemen, courtiers, grandees, and attendants."

The Prince of Wales was very beautifully dressed
in black with white plumes, and was mounted on

a bright bay horse, whilst the King, also in sober brown, for it was Lent, rode a silver grey charger, " both horses showing by their majestic port that they were conscious of the preciousness of their burdens." After them rode the Admiral of England (*i.e.* Buckingham) and the Count of Olivares, with the English ambassador, councillors of state, gentle-men-in-waiting, and archers of the guard. . . . The Queen and Infanta sat in the right-hand balcony, and separated only by a rail from them in the next balcony were Don Carlos, the King, the Prince of Wales, and the Cardinal Infante Don Fernando ; the Marquis of Buckingham, the Count of Olivares, and the other English and Spanish gentlemen being in the balcony on the left. The trumpets sounded, and when a hundred lacqueys, in brown jerkins and floating silver ribbons, had cleared the arena, the Duke of Cea pranced in on a grey horse, preceded by fifty lacqueys in doublets of cloth of silver and fawn-coloured breeches, wear-ing silver thread caps, and followed by a group of famous bull-fighters. The Duke bowed low before the royal balcony, whereupon Prince Charles uncovered. Then came the Duke of Maqueda, with his gallant party, who performed the same courtly ceremony as the Duke of Cea, " looking like a Cæsar," as Soto y Aguilar says. And so noble after noble, each with his glittering train of mounted gentlemen and host of servants, passed before the King and his English guest, until, in the written description of the scene, gorgeous fabrics, fine colours, and precious metals seem to lose their separate significance, so lavish is the re-petition of them.

Then came the many bulls, each despatched by a grandee's spear (*rejon*); many hairbreadth escapes being recorded, but no noble killed. When the feast was ended the rain was falling heavily, and we are told by the courtly chronicler " that amidst the falling torrents there fell a torrent of pages with torches who inundated with light the realms of darkness." It would be tedious to give particulars of the many such shows provided for Prince Charles, but at one subsequent bull-fight, more splendid still, described by Soto, no less than twenty bulls were done to death by noble bull-fighters on horseback, and prodigality itself ran riot to show the English Prince how rich Spain was.

For three days more the rejoicings of the State entry of Charles went on day and night : comedies, music, cane tourneys, and illumination and fireworks continuing without cessation. Even Buckingham was dazzled, extravagant as he was, and he says in his letter to the King—

They " made their entry with as great a triumph as could be, where he (Philip) forced your Baby (Charles) to ride on his right hand. . . . This entry was made just as when the Kings of Castile came first to the crown, all prisoners set at liberty, and no office nor matter of grace falls but is put into your Baby's hands to dispose of. . . . We had almost forgotten to tell you that the first thing they did at their arrival in the palace was to visit the Queen, where grew a quarrel between your Baby and lady for want of a salutation ; but your dog's (*i.e.* Buckingham's) opinion is that it is an artificial forced quarrel to beget hereafter greater kindness."

But in this letter, written the day after the state entry, when the municipality were offering as a present to Buckingham the costly canopy that had served in the ceremony,[1] the flustered visitors forgot to tell the King how his " Baby " liked the Infanta, whom he had now seen at close quarters for the first time, and a hurried little note was scribbled and enclosed with the letter just quoted, saying—

" Baby Charles himself is so touched at the heart that he confesses that all he ever saw is nothing to her [2] (*i.e.* the Infanta), and swears that if he want her there shall be blows. I (Buckingham) shall lose no time in hastening their conjunction, in which I shall please him, her, you, and myself most of all, in thereby getting liberty to make the speedier haste to lay myself at your feet ; for never none longed more to be in the arms of his mistress. So, craving your blessing, I end, your humble slave and dog, Steenie." [3]

But withal the negotiations got no nearer. The dispensation still tarried in Rome, and Olivares staved off all definite discussion, on the lying

---

[1] MS. Soto y Aguilar.

[2] Charles really seems to have fallen in love with her. Howel writes in July. There are comedians once a week come to the palace, where, under a great canopy the Queen and the Infanta sit in the middle and our Prince and Don Carlos on the Queen's right hand, and the little Cardinal on the Infanta's left hand. I have seen the Prince have his eyes immovably fixed upon the Infanta half an hour together in a thoughtful speculative posture, which sure would needs be tedious unless affection did sweeten it. It was no handsome comparison of Olivares that he watched her as a cat doth a mouse." Endymion Porter, writing to his wife soon after the Prince's arrival in Spain, says : " The Prince hath taken such a liking to his mistress that now he loves her as much for her beauty as he can for being sister to so great a King. She deserves it, for never was there a fairer creature." *State Papers, Domestic,* March 1623.

[3] Hardwicke, *State Papers.*

pretext that he did not know upon what the Pope would insist. To keep things going and beguile the English, the Count-Duke persuaded Charles to listen to a disputation in the monastery of St. Geronimo as to the truth of the Catholic religion, and set all the most persuasive clerics of the Court upon the task of converting the English Prince. An English priest named Wallsfort (?) was specially charged to tackle Buckingham, in conjunction with Friar Francisco de Jesus, the King's preacher; but, as may be supposed, with little success, though they asserted that Buckingham, though a heretic for political reasons, was really a Catholic at heart. But when the great attempt was made to bring to bear all the priestly artillery in Madrid upon the Prince's Protestantism, and Charles showed some signs of acquiescence in the Catholic arguments,[1] Buckingham put his foot down firmly, and rudely told Olivares he should not allow the Prince to continue the discussion, to which Olivares retorted by warning him that any attempt to introduce the Protestant chaplains from England into the Prince's apartment in the palace would be resisted by force,[2] for all their pretence that the

---

[1] From a somewhat ungenerous letter from Charles to Bristol (who was made the scapegoat), written on the 21st January 1625, he says: " you will remember how at our first coming into Spain, when taking upon you to be so wise as to foresee our intention to change our religion, you were so far from dissuading us that you offered your services and secrecy to concur in it ; and in many other open conferences pressing to show how convenient it was for us to be Roman Catholic, it being impossible in your opinion to do any great action otherwise." The letter is full of reproaches and condemnation of Bristol's conduct, but it is quite clear that Bristol saw the only condition under which the match was possible from the first, which Charles and Buckingham, deceived by Olivares, did not. Cabala (ed. 1691), p. 188.

[2] *Hecho de los Tratados.* Camden Society.

rites they used were similar to those of Rome. Charles, indeed, flattered himself with the idea that he had half converted the Infanta's confessor, Rahosa,[1] though certainly no signs appear of it in the subsequent actions of the priest. In every diocese in Spain, too, orders were given that religious processions, rogations, and penitential exercises should be celebrated in all churches and convents, in supplication to God for the fortunate issue of the negotiations for the marriage, which, of course, meant the conversion of the Prince and his country, whilst ecclesiastics were bombarding the King and Olivares with solemn addresses, denouncing the idea of the marriage of the Infanta to any Prince not a devout Catholic.

It is fair to say that Olivares, whilst professing platonically an ardent desire for the match, never attempted to disguise that it would only be conceded on terms quite impossible for England. The self-deception was indeed entirely on the part of Buckingham and the Englishmen of Catholic leanings whose hopes prompted the belief. From the first no pretence was made on the Spanish side of trusting to the word, or even the oath, of King James; the Spaniards knew him too well. Deeds must precede words, repeated Olivares again and again. The Catholics of England must have full toleration, and Parliament must repeal the Penal Acts of Elizabeth against them before the Infanta left Spain. James was ready to promise much, and did promise much at various times, though not so much as Buckingham; but it was clear that he could not coerce the English

[1] Carey, Earl of Monmouth, *Guerre d' Italia.*

Parliament into a course of action that would have made his crown not worth a week's purchase ; and, charm as he and Buckingham might, the Spaniards never budged an inch on the main point, amiable and flattering as they were to Charles, in the hope, probably, that some solid concession to the English Catholics might be wrung from his father, in any case, as a preliminary to the more than problematical marriage.

It is impossible in this book to follow the daily changing phases of the negotiations through the many months that the Prince stayed in Madrid, but some accounts, contained in the correspondence and other contemporary manuscripts, of the manner in which he and his followers passed their time at Court, will convey the best idea of the dexterity with which Olivares beguiled and befooled the Prince and his advisers into the position which threw upon them the onus of a rupture, whilst the Spaniards appeared to be only too anxious for the marriage and for the friendship of England.

Charles usually spent his afternoons with Philip or Olivares, witnessing fencing bouts or other sports from a window in the palace, or walking in the garden, or in hunting the boar or hawking ; and though he did not accompany the King and Court in their frequent visits to the Discalced Carmelite convent, or to the other religious houses where celebrations were held, he often saw the processions from closed jalousies, or through the drawn leather curtains of a coach. The mornings were passed in studying Spanish or writing, and in the evening he frequently visited the royal family, where, on a few occasions, the Infanta was present.

One such visit, on Easter Day 1623, is thus described in Bristol's diary [1]—

· "In the morning the Prince sent to desire leave to repay the visit and the *buenas pascuas* he had received the day before, and was accordingly appointed about four o'clock in the afternoon to be brought up by a private way to the King, with whom, when he had been a short space and performed that compliment, he intimated a desire to do the like to the Queen, and was presently conducted by the King, who accompanied him publicly, attended by all the grandees and great ministers of the Court, from his own side of the square, which is on the opposite side of the palace (to the Queen's), and there found the Queen and the Infanta together, attended by all the ladies of the Court. This being the first time that his Highness had personally visited the Infanta, there were four chairs set : in the middlemost sat the Queen and the Infanta, on the right hand of the Queen sat the Prince, and on the left of them all sat the King. When the Prince had given the Queen the *buenas pascuas* (*i.e.* compliments of the season), and passed some other compliments of gratitude for the favours he had received from her since his coming to this Court, in which it pleased his Highness to call me (*i.e.* Bristol) to do him service as interpreter, he rose out of his chair and went towards the Infanta, who likewise rose to entertain (*i.e.* to receive) him ; and, after fitting courtesies on both sides performed, the Prince

[1] Lord Bristol's diary, MS. in the Advocates' Library, Edinburgh, gives a minute account of the Prince's movements from day to day.

told her that the great friendship which was
between his Catholic Majesty and the King his
father, had brought him to this Court to make
a personal acknowledgment thereof, and to assure,
for his part, the desire he had to continue and
increase the same, and that he was glad on this
occasion to kiss her Highness's hands and offer
her his services. To which the Infanta answered,
that she did highly esteem what the Prince had
said unto her. His Highness then told her that
he had been troubled to understand that of late
she had not been in perfect health, and asked her
how she had passed the Lent, and how she did
now, whereunto the Infanta answered : " *Que
quedava buena á servicio de su Alteza* (that she was
now well, and at his Highness's service). The
Prince then retired himself to his chair and sat
down again by the Queen, with whom he passed
some short compliments, and so they all rose,
and with much courtesy took their leaves.

"And I do assure you (*i.e.* Mr. Secretary Conway,
to whom the diary was sent) that in all things
the Prince's comportment was so natural and
suitable to his quality and greatness, that he hath
given instant cause to the Spaniards to admire
him, as I find they generally do. From hence he
was conducted by the King in the same equipage
that he had come thither unto the King's side,
where, when the King had entertained his Highness
awhile with beholding from a window certain
masters and gentlemen exercising fencing before
them, the King had him to another window which
looketh upon a large place before the court-gate,
and, telling the Prince that he would only go and

see the Queen, took his brother, Don Carlos, with him, and left the Infante Cardinal with the Prince, expecting his return.

"But before much time had passed there appeared about three score of the principal nobility of the kingdom in the gallery (*i.e.* course) before the window, who were very richly apparelled with embroideries, and being on horseback came two and two together their several careers. They all had their faces uncovered save only the King, Don Carlos, the Count of Olivares, and the Marquis of Carpio, who wore vizards." [1]

The extremely slow courtship here described seems to have struck Charles as unsatisfactory, and a few weeks afterwards, probably encouraged by the general laxity and freedom he saw about him in the intercourse of the sexes, the Prince seriously violated the royal etiquette by an attempt to make love to the Infanta in less formal fashion. Howel tells the story in a letter to Tom Porter :

"Not long since the Prince, understanding that the Infanta was used to go some mornings to the *Casa de Campo*, a summer-house the King hath on t'other side of the river, to gather May-dew, he rose

---

[1] Soto y Aguilar gives a glowing and pompous account of this festivity, which, according to him, was a cane tournament and competition of horsemanship got up in honour of Charles by the Admiral of Castile. Charles is described as being dressed in black satin, with the blue ribbon and jewel of the Garter on his breast, the simplicity of his garb being praised as being very distinguished in appearance, as it may well have been amidst so gorgeous a crowd as that described by Soto. It should be noted, however, that Philip himself rarely dressed in bright colours, though his red doublet in the Dulwich College picture is splendid enough, his favourite colour being brown with steel or silver trimmings. On this occasion he is described as being dressed in this way, with a chain consisting of four linked jewelled crowns on his breast.

betimes and went thither, taking your brother (*i.e.* Endymion Porter) with him. They were let into the house, and so into the garden; but the Infanta was in the orchard, there being a high partition-wall between, and the door, doubly bolted, the Prince got on the top of the wall and sprung down a great height, and so made towards her. But she, spying him first of all the rest, gave a shriek and ran back. The old marquis that was then her guardian came towards the Prince and fell on his knees, conjuring his Highness to retire, in regard that he hazarded his head if he admitted any to her company. So the door was opened, and he came out under that wall over which he had got in. I have seen him watch a long hour together in a close coach in the open street to see her as she went abroad. I cannot say that the Prince did ever talk with her privately, yet publicly often, my Lord of Bristol being interpreter; but the King sat hard by to overhear all. Our cousin Archy (*i.e.* Archy Armstrong, King James's jester, who had joined Charles in Madrid with a large number of English courtiers) hath more privileges than any, for he often goes with his fool's coat where the Infanta is with her *meninas* (maids) and ladies of honour, and keeps a'blowing and blustering among them, and slurts out what he lists." [1]

Festivities kept Charles well occupied; and now that his father's courtiers had joined him

---

[1] *Familiar Letters.* Several references are made in Spanish documents of Archy's insolence whilst in Madrid, though that was no new thing in Philip's Court, where the buffoons were numerous.

with full baggage, he could play the Prince more effectively than on his first arrival. King James, indeed, seems to have imagined that by gifts and ostentation he could carry the point he had at heart,[1] though in one of his letters to his "sweet boys" he says that "for the honour of England he had curtailed the train of courtiers that went by sea of a number of rascals." Those who went, however, behaved very badly, and did little to

[1] Writing on the 17th March, he says : "I send you also your robes of the order, which you must not forget to wear upon St. George's day, and dine together in them if they come in time, which I pray God they may, for it will be a goodly sight for the Spaniards to see my two boys dine in them. I send you also the jewels I promised ; some of mine, and such of yours, I mean both of you, as are worthy of sending. For my Baby's presenting to his mistress, I send him an old double cross of Lorraine, not so rich as ancient, and yet not contemptible for the value, a good looking-glass with my picture in it to be hung at her girdle, which ye must tell her ye have caused it so to be enchanted by art magic as whensoever she shall be pleased to look in it she shall see the fairest lady that either her brother's or your father's dominions can afford. Ye shall present her with two long fair diamonds set like an anchor, and a fair pendant diamond hanging to them ; ye shall give her a goodly rope of pearls, ye shall give her a carcanet or collar, thirteen great ball rubies and thirteen knots or conques of pearls, and ye shall give her a head dressing of two-and-twenty great pear pearls ; and ye shall give her three goodly peak pendants, diamonds whereof the biggest to be worn at a needle on the forehead and one in each ear. For my Baby's own wearing ye have two good jewels of your own, your round brooch of diamonds and your triangle diamond with the great round pearl, and I send ye for your wearing three bretheren that ye know full well, but newly set ; the mirror of France, the fellow of the Portugal diamond, which I would wish you to wear alone in your hat with a little black feather. You have also good diamond buttons of your own to be set to a doublet or jerkin. As for your ' J,' it may serve as a present for a Don. As for thee, my sweet Gossip, I send thee a fair table diamond, which I would once have given thee before if thou would'st have taken it for wearing in thy hat or where thou pleases ; and if my Baby will spare thee two long diamonds in form of an anchor it were fit for an Admiral to wear." After minute instructions as to how Charles is to give his presents to the Infanta, the King continues : "I have also sent four other crosses of meaner value, with a great pointed diamond in a ring, which will save charges in presents to Dons, according to quality ; but I will send with the fleet divers other jewels for presents." Hardwicke, *State Papers*.

raise Spanish opinion of English nobles generally.
Buckingham was accused of having introduced
bad company even into the palace, and to have
behaved outrageously to the women who acted on
the stage during a comedy. " For outward usage "
(writes Howel in July), " there is all industry used
to give the Prince and his servants all possible
contentment, and some of the King's own servants
wait upon them at table in the palace, where I
am sorry to hear some of them jeer at the Spanish
fare, and use other slighting speeches and demeanour." [1] Worst of all, many of these fine
gallants went out of their way to offend Spanish
religious susceptibilities; and Howel mentions
one such case which nearly led to grave trouble.
One of the Prince's pages, Mr. Washington, had
died of fever, and before his death an English
priest named Ballard visited him, in the hope of
converting him. Sir Edmund Verney met the
priest on the stairs, and attacked him, first with
words and then with blows.

" The business was like to gather very ill blood
and to come to a great height, had not Count
Gondomar quashed it ; which I believe he could
not have done unless the times had been favourable, for such is the reverence they bear to the
Church here, and so holy a conceit have they of
all ecclesiastics, that the greatest Don in Spain
will tremble to offer the meanest of them any
outrage or affront. Count Gondomar hath also
helped to free some English that were in the Inquisition in Toledo and Seville, and I could allege

[1] *Familiar Letters.*

many instances how ready and cheerful he is to assist any Englishman whatsoever, notwithstanding the base affronts he hath often received from the London boys.[1] I heard a merry saying of his to the Queen, who, discoursing with him of the greatness of London, and whether it was as populous as Madrid : " Yes, madam," he said, " and more populous when I came away, though I believe there's scarce a man left now, but all women and children, for all the men both in court and city were ready booted and spurred to go away."

Madrid was not quite so full of English courtiers as that, though their presence was conspicuous and assertive enough at Court. At the weekly representation of the comedies in the palace, only the royal party were provided with chairs ; the ladies, in the usual Spanish Court fashion, being seated on cushions on the floor, and the gentlemen standing behind the royal family. This did not suit either Buckingham or the most ostentatious nobleman of his time, the upstart Hay, Earl of Carlisle, and they both fumed and fretted at what they considered a slight upon them. Buckingham, of course, was obliged to stay, but Hay and many others of the insolent crew left Madrid in dudgeon before the great heats came on. Hay, indeed, found it extremely difficult to obtain audience of the Infanta, whom the English already called Princess of Wales ; and when, after much importunity, he was admitted, " he was brought into a room where the Infanta was placed on a throne

---

[1] Gondomar was specially obnoxious to the London prentices, who attacked him in his carriage on more than one occasion.

aloft, gloriously set forth with her ladies about her : my lord, with his compliments, motions, and approaches, could not draw from her so much as the least nod, she remaining all the while as immovable as the image of the Virgin Mary. . . . At his coming away the Infanta gave him leave to kneel to her above an hour, whereupon our great ladies begin to consult how they shall demean herself when she comes." [1]

During the whole of the spring, matters in Madrid remained thus, the arrival of the dispensation being constantly delayed, whilst England was being every day more deeply pledged to an impossible policy by the folly of Buckingham and Charles and the eagerness of King James. James had made the fatal mistake—after saying, through Bristol, that the Pope's dispensation meant nothing whatever to him—of sending agents, Father Gage particularly, to Rome to negotiate for the dispensation to be modified and expedited, and he showed himself more squeezable on the religious point at every turn of the negotiation. "As for myself," he wrote to his son and Buckingham late in March, " I would with all my heart give my consent that the Bishop of Rome should have the first seat. I, being a western King, would go with the Patriarch of the West. And as for his temporal seigniory of Rome, I do not quarrel with that either. Let him, in God's name, be *primus episcopus inter omnes episcopos, et princeps episcoporum*, so it be no otherwise but as St. Peter was *princeps episcoporum*." So confident were they all that no serious hitch would stand in the way of the wedding

[1] News-letter from London.

at last, that the fleet which was intended to carry back the Infanta and her husband to England was ready to sail for Spain in April, and the silly doting King was busy settling the smallest details of the voyage for the comfort of his " sweet boys."

At length, late in April, news came to Madrid that the dispensation was on its way to Spain, but "clogged" with new guarantees and conditions in favour of English Catholics, which Buckingham still thought he could avoid granting, and asked that the English fleet should be sent to Corunna at once to convey them back triumphant with the Infanta. They soon found that matters were not so easily settled, for, as we know now, Olivares was determined that no marriage should take place, and a device for delay was easily found in the assembly of a commission of divines at St. Geronimo to discuss how far the conditions of the dispensation might be modified. Buckingham conceived the extraordinary plan of asking James to give a blank commission to his son, and Charles accordingly wrote to his father to send him the following pledge signed by his own hand: " *We do hereby promise by the word of a King that whatsoever you, our son, shall promise in our name we shall punctually perform.*" " Sir, I confess," wrote the Prince, " that this is an ample trust ; and if it were not mere necessity I should not be so bold " ; and Buckingham accompanied the Prince's letter by a note that he knew would touch the King. " This letter of your son's is written out of an extraordinary desire to be soon with you again. He thinks if you sign thus much, though they would be glad (which he doth not yet discover)

to make any further delay, this will disappoint
them. The discretion of your Baby you need not
doubt." [1] Needless to say, the weak King sent
the power as requested, in order, as he wrote,
" that ye may speedily and happily return and
light in the arms of your dear Dad."

Provided with this unlimited pledge, the Prince
and Buckingham, assisted by Bristol, Aston, and
Cottington, met a commission appointed by Philip.
For weeks the discussions continued. In vain the
English pointed out the impossibility of acceding
to the demands that religious toleration in England
should be decreed forthwith, and that the consent
of the English Parliament should be obtained
within a year or so for the abrogation of all the
penal laws against English Catholics, with the
many other points which were now insisted upon
by the Pope for the first time. The Pope had
even written a letter direct to Charles, urging his
immediate conversion ; and Charles had further
compromised himself by answering it in a way
which, although vague, would have caused, if it
had been known, intense indignation in England.
As the English negotiators advanced, Olivares
retired, whilst Buckingham became daily more
impatient and angry, throwing the blame now
entirely upon the Count-Duke. [2]

At length, at the end of May, Buckingham
came to an open quarrel with Olivares, and threatened to leave with the Prince at once and abandon
the negotiation. This angry departure did not

---

[1] Hardwicke, *State Papers*.
[2] Full details of the discussion from day to day are in *El Hecho de los
Tratados*, etc.   Camden Society.

suit the Spaniards ; and, after much protest and entreaty on the part of Philip and Olivares, it was agreed that the Prince should stay in Madrid at least until King James was made acquainted with the point insisted upon, and sent his instructions ; although, after having consented to remain, Charles, seeing the persistent attempts to put pressure upon him to marry at once on the Pope's conditions, endeavoured to withdraw his promise altogether and retire. Eventually, however, the cajolery of Olivares prevailed, and Cottington went off post haste to England, carrying with him the details of the Spanish papal demands. In the letter written by Charles and Buckingham to James, and taken by Cottington, they still express a hope that he may accede to the terms, though they dared not do so themselves without his consent.

" Dear Dad and Gossip," this letter runs, " the Pope having written a courteous letter to me, your Baby, I have been bold to write to him an answer. . . . We make no doubt but to have the opinions of the busy divines reversed (for already the Count of Olivares hath put out ten of the worst), so that your Majesty will be pleased to begin to put in execution the favour towards your Roman Catholic subjects, and ye will be bound by your oath as soon as the Infanta comes over, which we hope you will do for the hastening of us home, with this protestation to reverse all, if there be any delay in the marriage. We send you here the articles as they are to go, the oaths, public and private, that you and your Baby are to take, with the councils, wherein if you scare at the least clause of your private oath (where you promise that the Parliament shall revoke all penal laws against the Papists within three years), we thought good to tell your Majesty our opinion, which is that if you think you may do it in that time (which we think you may if you do your best), although it take not effect, you have not broken your word, for this promise is only security that you will do your best. The Spanish ambassador for respect of the Pope will present to you the articles as they came from Rome, as likewise to require that the delivery of the Infanta may be deferred till the spring. . . . We both humbly beg of your Majesty that you will confirm these articles soon, and press earnestly for our speedy return." [1]

King James was in despair when he received this letter and Cottington's intelligence. Olivares had cleverly turned the whole negotiation on the acceptance by the English of the religious demands, and had remained quite unpledged as to the restoration of the Palatinate, which was the thing nearest to James' heart. The reply of the King is too characteristic for compression, and is here reproduced entire.

" My sweet Boys, your letter by Cottington hath strucken me dead! I fear it shall very much shorten my days, and I am more perplexed that I know not how to satisfy the people's expectation here ; neither know I what to say to our Council, for the fleet that staid upon a wind

[1] Hardwicke, *State Papers.*

this fortnight. Rutland and all abroad must now be staid, and I know not what reason I shall pretend for doing it. But as for my advice and directions that ye crave in case they will not alter their decree, it is, in a word, to come speedily away, if ye can get leave, and give over all treaty. And this I speak without respect of any security they may offer, except ye never look to see your old Dad again, whom I fear ye shall never see if ye see him not before winter. Alas! I now repent me sore that ever I suffered you to go away. I care for match, nor nothing, so I may once have you in my arms again. God grant it! God grant it! God grant it! Amen, amen, amen! I protest ye shall be as heartily welcome as if ye had done all things ye went for, so that I may once more have you in my arms again, and God bless you both, my sweet son and my only best sweet servant, and let me hear from you quickly with all speed as ye love my life ; and so God send you a happy, joyful meeting in the arms of your dear Dad.—

JAMES R.

GREENWICH, 14 *June* 1623."

The poor King was nearer to his difficulties than was Buckingham, for Archbishop Abbott and the English Puritan divines were becoming clamorous at all this coquetting with the Scarlet Lady, and to have conceded openly a half of the papal demands as payment for the Spanish match would have meant a revolution in England. In the meanwhile Charles and Buckingham continued their struggle to get the conditions modified; whilst Olivares, supported by his theologians, still insisted that the marriage might be celebrated conditionally in Madrid, to be confirmed at some future time when the measures in favour of the English Catholics had been put into operation.

The events of the next few weeks are related by the Spanish authority,[1] very differently from the version given by the Prince and Buckingham to King James. The Spaniards aver that Charles' counter-proposals and amendments were considered exhaustively by the various commissions, and unhesitatingly rejected, the Prince, in his final interview with Olivares on the subject, when the answer was given to him, signifying his intention to return to England at once, and requesting an audience to take leave of the King. The Prince is represented by the Spaniards to have asked Bristol to draw up for him a valedictory address which he might read to Philip, but when Lord Bristol submitted his draft the Prince expressed dissatisfaction with it, and said that he would trust to the inspiration of the moment and take leave of the King in his own words. The leave-taking was fixed for the 17th July, in the evening, and when Charles, with Buckingham and the whole of his train, were in the presence of Philip, to the intense astonishment and dismay of Bristol, the Prince expressed his intention of accepting the conditions laid down by the Spaniards with regard to religion, and said that he would, in his father's name, give due security for their fulfilment. Couriers were sent post haste to Rome to obtain the Pope's final consent to the slightly modified conditions accepted by Charles ; and for a time

[1] *Hecho de los Tratados.* Camden Society.

the Spanish Court ostensibly regarded the marriage as irrevocably fixed.

This is the story as told by the Spaniards, and it is probably not far from the truth ; but in the letters to King James [1] the Prince and Buckingham naturally represent the conditions they accepted as being an important modification of the previous Spanish demands, which, so far as can be seen, they were not. On the very day when the reconsidered conditions were first handed to Charles, and, according to the Spanish story, rejected, he and Buckingham wrote to King James. (26th June–6th July.)

" DEAR DAD AND GOSSIP,—Though late, yet at last we have gotten the articles drawn up in the forms we sent you by Lord Rochford, without any new addition or alteration. The foolery of the Conde de Olivares hath been the cause of this long delay, who would willingly against thee have pulled it out of the junta's and Council's hands and put it into a wrangling lawyer's, a favourite of his, who, like himself, had not only put it into odious form, but had slipped in a multitude of new unreasonable, undemanded, and ungranted conditions, which the Council yielded unto merely out of fear ; for when we met the junta they did not make one answer to our many objections, but confessed with blushing faces that we had more than reason on our side ; and concluded with us that the same oath should serve which passed between Queen Mary and King Philip (II.) being put to the end of every article which is to be sworn

[1] Hardwicke, *State Papers.*

to. By this you may guess the little favour with
which they proceed with us, first delaying us as
long as they possibly can, then, when things are
concluded, they throw in new particulars in hope
that they will pass, out of our desire to make haste.
But when our business is done we shall joy in it
the more that we have overcome so many difficulties, and in the meantime we expect pity at
your hands. But for the love of God and our
business let nothing fall from you to discover
anything of this, and comfort yourself that all
will end well to your contentment and honour.
Our return now will depend upon your quick
despatch of these, for we thank God we find the
heats such here that we may well travel both
evenings and mornings. The divines have not
yet recalled their sentence, but the Conde tells us
that he hath converted very many of them, yet
keeps his old form in giving us no hope of anything
till the business speaks it itself. But we dare say
they dare not break it upon this, nor, we think,
upon any other, except the affairs of Christendom
should smile strangely upon them."

How completely Olivares had outwitted them
is plain by this letter. He still insisted verbally
upon the whole of the pretensions originally formul-
ated, but had by subtle hints led them into the
self-deceiving condition displayed by their fatuous
words in the letter just quoted.

A few hours only after the above letter was
written, the courier Crofts arrived in Madrid
with King James' peremptory order for his son to
return, printed on page 109. With this order in

their hands, Charles and Buckingham thought to bring matters to a crisis, and, as they say, told Olivares with a sad face that the King of England had ordered them to return immediately. How, they asked him, could they obey the command without sacrificing the marriage ?

" His answer was that there were two good ways to do the business and one ill one. The two good ones were either with your Baby's conversion, or to do it with trust, putting all things freely with the Infanta into our hands. The ill one was to bargain and stick upon conditions as long as they could. As for the first (*i.e.* conversion) we had utterly rejected it ; and, for the second, he confessed that if he were King he would do it ; and, as he is, it lay in his power to do it : but he cast many doubts, lest he should hereafter suffer for it if it should not succeed. The last he confessed impossible, since your command was so peremptory. To conclude, he left us with a promise to consider it ; and when I, your dog (*i.e.* Buckingham) conveyed him to the door, he bade me cheer up my heart, and your Baby's, both. Our opinion is the longest time we can stay here is a month, and not that neither without bringing the Infanta with us. If we find ourselves sure of that, look for us sooner. Whichever of these resolutions be taken, you shall hear from us shortly, that you may in that time give order for the fleet. We must once more entreat your Majesty to make all the haste you can to return those papers confirmed, and in the meantime give order for the execution of all these things (*i.e.* the abrogation of

H

all penal enactments against Catholics, and the granting of religious toleration, etc.), and let us here know so much." [1]

The next night Charles sent for Olivares, and asked him what advice he had to give him. The matter was still under discussion, replied the minister ; and two or three days more would have to be given before King Philip could send his final decision. Charles and Buckingham demurred at further delay, and again talked of immediate departure ; but, as usual, Olivares hinted and implied much, whilst he pledged himself to nothing, and when he returned he left " Baby " and " Steenie " once more in a fool's paradise of confident hope. From day to day they were thus kept ; Olivares hinting that as soon as news came that King James had given liberty to English Catholics, all obstacles would be removed, and the Infanta might accompany her bridegroom to England. Charles and his adviser begged James urgently and often to fulfil their promises in this respect without delay ; for, said they, they were convinced that Olivares would stand out no longer when the news came.

" We know you will think a little more time will be well spent to bring her with us, when by that means we may upon equaller terms treat with them of other things. Do your best there (*i.e.* in England), and we will not fail of ours here. . . . Of all this we must entreat you to speak nothing ; for if you do our labour here will be the harder, and when it shall be hoped there and not take

[1] Hardwicke, *State Papers.*

effect they will be the more discontented.[1] I, your Baby, have, since this conclusion, been with my mistress, and she sits publicly with me at the plays, and within these two or three days shall take place of the Queen as Princess of England."

James in London was sorely perplexed, for the Marquis of Hinojosa and Carlos Coloma, the Spanish ambassadors, were pressing him still more to make the concessions to the English Catholics thorough and irrevocable; whilst the Council, even Buckingham's sycophantic creatures, Conway and Calvert, the Secretaries of State, were ill at ease. But the step had to be taken, and James, with many prickings of conscience, or more worldly fears, summoned his Council at Whitehall on Sunday the 20th July, and, after feasting the two Spanish ambassadors, the King of England took an oath before them and a Catholic priest, with Cottington and the two Secretaries of State only in attendance, to comply with all the conditions of the marriage which had been accepted in Madrid, the English Catholics being given immediate and complete toleration.[2] This ceremony in the palace of Whitehall having come to an end, King James was entering his coach to go to the Spanish embassy, and take a secret oath there to obtain within a

---

[1] The meaning of this somewhat obscure passage appears to be that if King James made public the conditions to which he was to pledge himself the opposition in England might prevent the measures promised from being carried out, in which case the disappointment in Spain would be redoubled.

[2] Secretary Conway to Buckingham. Hardwicke, *State Papers*. Conway says concerning this : "The acts of favour are gone for the King's signature, which, known, will create cold sweat and fear until the return of his Highness."

given time the abrogation by Parliament of all the penal laws, when, as he says, Lord Andover, travel-stained with his long rapid journey from Madrid, " came stepping in the door like a ghost," and delivered the letter from Charles and Buckingham, saying that the Spaniards were insisting upon deferring the departure of the Infanta until the spring, to give time for the reception of the Pope's consent to the modified conditions, and for the full execution of the decrees, relieving the English Catholics from their disabilities.

Poor James must have seen now clearly that he had been outwitted. He was pledged, pledged up to the hilt. He had just solemnly sworn to accept all the Spanish conditions. His son was still in the hands of Spain ; no promise whatever binding Spain had been given for the return of the Palatinate to Frederick ; and now the gage that he and his shallow favourite had thought would guarantee their demands upon Spain was not to be delivered until next spring, which might mean never !

" This course is both a dishonour to me and double charges, if I must send two fleets. But if they will not send her till March, then let them, in God's name, send her by their own fleet, . . . but if no better may be, do ye hasten your business : the fleet shall be at you as soon as wind and weather can serve, and this bearer (*i.e.* Cottington) will bring you the power to treat for the Palatinate, and in the matter of Holland. And, sweet Baby, go on with the contract, and the best assurance ye can get of sending her next year. But, upon my blessing, lie not with her in Spain, except ye be sure to bring her with you ; and forget not to make them keep their former conditions anent the portion (*i.e.* dowry), otherwise both my Baby and I are bankrupt for ever."

Cottington lost no time ; and by the 5th (15th N.S.) August was back again in Madrid with the news of the King of England's compliance on oath with the Spanish conditions. Again the divines, at Olivares' bidding, began wrangling over the form and substance of James' oath ; for Hinojosa, the Spanish ambassador in England, had reported unfavourably upon the real intentions of James towards the Catholics, and three weeks more passed before the whole marriage treaty was embodied in a formal document, which Charles, on the 28th August (7th September), swore solemnly on the Gospels in the hands of the Patriarch of the Indies to fulfil, whilst Philip simply promised that the marriage should take place *when the Pope's consent arrived*, in which case the Infanta should be sent to England in the following spring. It was indeed a triumph for the diplomacy of Olivares, and Charles endeavoured to save appearances by asking, now that it was too late, for some assurance that the Pope's consent would be given by Christmas and the marriage solemnised. Philip was all smiles. Nothing would delight him better ; but, as it was a case of conscience, the theologians must decide. When they met to do so they raked up many stories, old and new, to show that Englishmen could not be trusted further than you could see them in matters of religion, and decided that all of

King James's promises to the Catholics must come into actual effect before any further step could be taken by Philip. Cottington, it appears, had fallen ill with the fatigue of his rapid journey; and, in the belief that he was dying, sent for a priest and confessed himself a Catholic, yet as soon as the fit passed off and he recovered he withdrew his professions, and this was cited as a proof of the falsity of Englishmen. The story, already quoted from Howel, of Varney's coming to fisticuffs with the English priest Ballard was made the most of. Besides, said they, a gentleman of King Philip's chamber only the other day had seen on a sideboard in Prince Charles's apartment, in the palace of the Catholic King himself, "a Protestant catechism in which all the heresies and errors are taught, translated into Spanish and richly and curiously bound." This was really too shocking, and the divines decided that Charles was not to be trusted an inch beyond the conventions already made.

In vain a grander bull-fight than ever was given to celebrate the so-called betrothal, in which Charles cut a gallant figure in white satin, and in which, amidst a mad prodigality of splendour, three-and-twenty bulls were done to death by nobles;[1] in vain feasts[2] and banquets hailed

[1] Soto y Aguilar MS.

[2] One of these, a cane tourney, is fully described in a Spanish account translated in Somers' Tracts. Philip was always a lover of this showy diversion, in which bodies of gaily clad horsemen manœuvred in opposing squadrons, throwing small cane javelins at each other, the skilful horsemanship being the criterion of excellence. After the usual parade through the gaily decked streets, in which Philip and Charles rode side by side, the King went to the palace of the Countess de Miranda to change his dress and prepare for the evolutions. The palace was splendidly fitted

Charles as the husband of a Spanish Princess, and the future restorer of England to the Catholic faith ; both Charles and Buckingham now saw that they had been fooled, and were only anxious to get away with a good face and such dignity as they might. Olivares personally still pretended to be eager for the match, and feigned a desire to send the Infanta with the Prince, " to turn them all out of Spain together, as he said jocosely " ; but Buckingham now profoundly distrusted him— and, indeed, told him at this juncture that he would always be his enemy—and was determined that the Prince should not be further pledged to the marriage, unless the Infanta accompanied them to England. " Send us peremptory commands to come away, with all possible speed," they wrote to King James ; " we desire this, not that we fear we shall need it, but in case we have, that your son, who hath expressed much affection to the Infanta, may press his coming away under colour of your command without appearing an ill lover."

The love romance, in good truth, was at an end, and the foolish adventure had resulted in one side being pledged to a course that threatened the stability of England, whilst the other was bound to nothing whatever, since the Pope's consent would be given or withheld as Spain desired. Worst blow of all to King James was the contemptuous treatment of his demands about the Palatinate.

up with white damask for his reception ; the halls being artificially cooled and perfumed. His hostess received him in state at the door, and served him with a refection, " consisting of all manner of conserves, dried suckets and rosewater confections of eight different sorts." Philip, by the way, was a great lover of sweetmeats.

"As for the business of the Palatinate," wrote Charles to his father, " now that we have pressed them we have discovered these two impediments : first, they say they have no hope to accommodate it without the marriage of your grandchild with the Emperor's daughter, . . . to be brought up in the Emperor's Court ; and the second is, that though they will restore his lands (to the Palatine) they will not restore his honour." It was, indeed, time that Charles was gone, for the sorry part he and Buckingham had played in Madrid, and their long absence, had provoked serious discontent in England ; and even Archy Armstrong in Madrid, with his fool's privilege, goaded Buckingham with taunts and sneers, until the enraged favourite threatened that he would have him hanged. " No one ever heard of a fool being hanged for talking," retorted Archy, " but many Dukes in England have been hanged for insolence." [1]

On the 29th August (8th September, N.S.), Charles was conducted in state by Philip to take his leave of the Queen and the Infanta, to whom he made all manner of professions and promises. Buckingham on this occasion did not accompany the Prince, being desirous, as the Spaniards said, of having a separate honour for himself ; but even whilst this ostentatious ceremony was being used towards him, a secret paper was being drafted by skilful hands and brains in Madrid that was destined to precede him and the Prince to London, and to set before King James the long tale of Buckingham's transgressions and omissions whilst in Spain, his violence, his rudeness, his lack of

[1] *Hecho de los Tratados.*

diplomacy, his inexpertness in affairs, his pride and insolence. The Spaniards, indeed, had determined to make Buckingham the scapegoat as an additional security for themselves, and they, or rather Olivares, thus laid the foundation of the spoilt favourite's ruin.

Splendid presents were given on both sides: Philip sending to his guest four-and-twenty Spanish and Arab horses and six mares, twenty hackneys in velvet housings, fringed and embroidered with gold, two pairs of fine Spanish asses for the stud, a dagger, a sword, and a pistol, all richly encrusted with diamonds, eighty muskets and eighty crossbows and a hundred of the best swords in Spain ; whilst Charles, in return for this, apart from his gifts to the King, gave to the bearer of his presents a great diamond jewel. Buckingham also received from the King a fine stud of horses and mares, with arms and jewels of immense value.[1] The Queen's present to Charles consisted of an enormous quantity of linen under-garments of great fineness, worked by the discalced nuns, fifty dressed and perfumed skins, and two hundred and fifty scented glove skins of great rarity and value ; whilst Olivares, knowing Charles' artistic tastes and the interest he had taken in the fine pictures in the palace, presented him with many beautiful paintings, some chamber hangings, and three Sedan chairs, fit, as Soto says, for the greatest king on earth ; one entirely of tortoiseshell and gold, these chairs being for the use in London of King James, the Prince of Wales, and Buckingham respectively. All the principal courtiers came

[1] They are all described, *ad nauseam*, in the Soto y Aguilar MS.

with similar gifts ; but when, with many false tears
on both sides, Charles went to the Convent of the
Discalced Carmelites to take a last private farewell
of his betrothed, she gave him, amongst many
rich and beautiful toys, perfumes, and the like, a
letter from which she said she hoped great things
would come. It was addressed to a saintly nun
at Carrion, which lay in his road towards the sea,
and the Infanta prayed that he would visit and
confer with the holy woman for the good of his
soul.[1] She made Charles promise her, moreover,
that he would have a care for the Catholics of
England, for any one of whom, she said, she would
lay down her life.

Charles was as lavish in his gifts as were his
hosts, jewels of inestimable value being given to
the King and Queen, and, indeed, to everybody,
apparently, with whom the Prince had been brought
into contact at the Spanish Court. The Infanta
received from her lover a string of two hundred and
fifty great perfect pearls, with similar pearls for
the ears and breast, and a diamond ornament so
precious " that no one dared to estimate its value." [2]
Amongst the shower of jewels that fell upon the
Spanish courtiers, that which came to Olivares
seems to have been one of the most precious. It
was the great " Portuguese " diamond of purest
water, that once had been the pride of the crown
jewels of Portugal, and had been brought to
England by the pretender Don Antonio, who,

[1] The Nuncio sent the same night a special messenger to the nun,
directing her how she was to endeavour to do the great service to the
Catholic Church.

[2] These jewels were afterwards returned when the match was
abandoned.

whilst his jewels lasted, had found so warm a welcome in the Court of Elizabeth.

At dawn on Saturday, 30th August, King Philip and his brother Carlos, with their English guest, and followed by hundreds of gallant gentlemen, rode across the bridge of Segovia out of the Castilian capital, over the arid plain towards the vast monastery palace of the Escorial in the Guadarramas, the enduring gloomy monument of the first of the Spanish Philips. The next day was spent in seeing the wonders of the building, and on Monday hunting in the woods and moors around occupied the day. On Tuesday morning, 3rd September, the party set forth, and a few miles on the road the King, after an alfresco luncheon and a long private conversation with his guest, took final leave of Charles, with much ceremonial salutation and professions of eternal regard. That night the English Prince, in whose coach travelled Buckingham, Bristol, and Gondomar, arrived at the village of Guadarrama, and the next night was spent at the ancient city of Segovia.

Charles had left in Bristol's hands a power to conclude the marriage on the arrival in Madrid of the consent of the Pope to the modified conditions; but at Segovia he signed two letters, one to King Philip reiterating his intention and desire to carry the match through, and the other revoking the full powers he had given to Bristol to conclude the espousals when the Pope's consent arrived, on the ground that there was nothing in the conventions to prevent the Infanta from embracing a conventual life after the marriage.[1] With Charles's slow progress through Spain to Santander, and so to England, this book has naught to do, nor with the extraordinary set of intrigues by which, to Bristol's indignation and subsequent ruin, Buckingham on his return drew the pliant James into alliance with France against Spain.

Bristol, during his short further stay in Madrid, laboured hard, aided by Gondomar, to keep the negotiations afoot, the Spanish party in the English Court endeavoured with the same object to arouse the fears of James against Buckingham, and nearly succeeded in doing it. Bristol's colleague and successor at Madrid, Sir Walter Aston, hoping to smooth matters, incurred Buckingham's violent resentment by provisionally agreeing to a day for the espousals, when at last the Pope's conditional consent came. James, and now apparently Charles, had quite made up their minds that no marriage should take place without the Palatinate being surrendered by the Emperor ; and Philip, as Olivares had said again and again, would never coerce his Catholic kinsman to do that for the sake of a heretic. Thenceforward, though the bickering both in Madrid and London still continued for months, the marriage of Charles and the Infanta was impracticable, and the unwise attempt to force the hands of cunning statesmen by a romantic *coup de théâtre* came to the undignified and unsuccessful end that it deserved.

---

[1] Lord Bristol's remonstrance to the Prince on this disingenuous proceeding is in Cabala, p. 101.

[2] Buckingham, in his haughty letter of rebuke to Aston (Cabala, p. 120), says that Charles wrote to Aston from Santander to the effect that he would never marry the Infanta unless good conditions were agreed to with regard to the Palatinate. Aston's letters from Madrid are in Cabala.

The Spaniards pretended that the match would have been carried through but for Buckingham's bad faith and his personal quarrel with Olivares, and they found it convenient to defend their own character for sincerity by using the favourite for a scapegoat. But it is quite certain now, with the abundant authoritative documents before us, that, except upon quite impossible conditions, there never was any intention on the part of Philip and Olivares to give the Infanta to Charles. Olivares played the game with consummate skill, obtaining concessions to the English Catholics, which, if they had been sincerely carried out, would have endangered James's crown; and presenting to Europe the spectacle of the English King and Prince soliciting an alliance with Spain in a way which allowed such a rebuff to be administered to England as might have made the great Elizabeth turn in her grave.

That Buckingham was keenly alive to his defeat, and was determined to avenge it upon Spain, is seen in his letter to James as soon as he left Madrid,[1] and by the strenuous and successful efforts which he made on his return to London to defeat the Spanish party, to which he had, thanks to Gondomar's bribery, formerly belonged. The subsequent ignominious war with Spain into which England was dragged by Buckingham and the French alliance, was a fitting sequel, in its inept mismanagement, to the utter foolishness of the policy which had precipitated it. The comparison between

[1] I'll bring all things with me you have desired except the Infanta, which hath almost broken my heart, because your, your son's, and the nation's honour is touched by the miss of it. Hardwicke, *State Papers.*

the incompetence of Sir Edward Cecil with his disorganised and futile fleet before Cadiz in 1625, and the English attack upon the same city in 1596 under Howard, Raleigh, and Essex, is as complete and humiliating as the contrast between shallow Buckingham and sagacious Burghley, or between the doting poltroon whose letters to his "sweet Boys" we have seen, and the proudly patriotic termagant whom he succeeded on the throne of England.

CHAPTER IV

FOREIGN WAR RENDERED INEVITABLE BY OLIVARES'
POLICY — ITS EFFECT IN SPAIN — CONDITION
OF THE COURT—WASTE, IDLENESS, AND OSTEN-
TATION OF ALL CLASSES — EXTRAVAGANCE IN
DRESS—PHILIP'S EFFORTS TO REFORM MANNERS
—RETRENCHMENT IN HIS HOUSEHOLD — THE
SUMPTUARY ENACTMENTS—THE *GOLILLA*—THE
INDUSTRY OF OLIVARES—HIS CHARACTER AND
APPEARANCE — HIS MAIN OBJECT TO SECURE
POLITICAL AND FISCAL UNITY IN SPAIN — THE
DIFFICULTIES IN THE WAY OF THIS — THE
COMEDIES — THEATRES IN MADRID — PHILIP'S
LOVE FOR THE STAGE—AN AUTO-DE-FE—LORD
WIMBLEDON'S ATTACK ON CADIZ—RICHELIEU'S
LEAGUE AGAINST SPAIN—SPANISH SUCCESSES—
" PHILIP THE GREAT "—VISIT OF THE KING TO
ARAGON AND CATALONIA IN 1626—DISCONTENT
AND DISSENSION—PHILIP'S LIFE TRAGEDY

THE policy of Olivares, which had estranged
England and revived the haughty old claims of
Spain to dictate to Europe, had already begun to
produce widespread effects. France, no longer
under the papal Italian rule of the Queen-mother,
but in the firm hands of Richelieu, could not be
expected to submit to such claims now ; and during
1624 Europe once more divided itself into two
camps, one to assert and the other to dispute the

supremacy of the house of Austria under the hegemony of Spain. Richelieu did not believe in beginning the game until he held all the cards in his hands, and delayed an open declaration of war until he could join with him in a league against Spain, the United Provinces, and Savoy, and had bought at least the neutrality if not the active aid of England.

In the meanwhile we will glance at the effects which had been produced in Spain, and particularly in the Court, by the joint action of the young King and his mentor, the Count-Duke. The ruin and disappearance of the greedy crew that had followed Lerma and his family, and the accession of a promising youth like Philip IV. to the throne, had filled the lieges with the belief that, as if by a fairy wand, all Spain's troubles would cease and national power and general prosperity would flood the long-suffering land with joy. The happy dream was of short duration, for the ills were too deep seated to be quickly cured, if even wise measures had been adopted. But the reforms of Olivares had been merely of a palliative character, leaving the system and incidence of taxation radically bad. Whilst rigid investigation of past peculations was effected, whilst the squandering of the royal resources in grants was limited, and economy severely enjoined in the expenditure of private citizens, the most lavish waste was perpetrated in other directions ; and this, with the cost incurred by a forward foreign policy, had, in the three years that succeeded the accession of Philip, again brought affairs to a crisis, in which the national penury was the conspicuous fact.

As soon as the echoes had died away of the festivals that had been organised to dazzle the English Prince, the discontent of the people began to find voice amongst those whose mordant speech and fluent pen were so eager always to seize upon a pretext for the exercise of their powers. Quevedo, the greatest wit of his time, who had once more been recalled from the exile into which his biting satire so often cast him,[1] and was the idol both of the quidnuncs of Liars' Walk and of the dilettante nobles of the Court, launched his darts against the grumblers, and told Spaniards boldly that the continued misery was the fault of the degenerate race of his countrymen, "the well perfumed but ill conducted hosts" who impatiently resisted or evaded the decrees of those who endeavoured to mend matters.

The decrees, it is true, were from their intricacy and their thoroughness not easy to follow, for they sought to revolutionise the customs and ways of life rendered familiar by almost immemorial usage. The evils to be cured had been patent to all, but the remedies were too sudden and too drastic to be effectual. When Philip had first come to the throne, and the new broom was to be wielded, the reforming member of the Cortes, Lison y Biedma, had told the King[2]—

"Your subjects spend and waste great sums in the abuse of costly garb, with so many varieties of trimmings that the making costs more than the

---

[1] He wrote a series of interesting descriptions of the ceremonies and feasts in honour of Charles's visit to Madrid. *Terpsichore.*

[2] *Apuntamientos.* Secretly printed in Madrid, 1623.

I

stuff; and as soon as the clothes are made there is a change of fashion and the money has to be spent over again. When they marry the wealth they squander on dress alone ruins them, and they remain in debt for the rest of their lives; . . . such is the excess that the wife of an artisan nowadays needs as much finery as a lady, even though she have to get money for it by dishonest means and to the offence of God. . . . As for collars and ruffs, the disorder in their use is very scandalous. A single ruff of linen with its making and ravelling will cost over 200 reals, and six reals every time it is dressed, which at the end of the year doubles its cost, and much money is thus wasted. Besides, many strong, able young men are employed in dressing and goffering these extravagant things, who might be better employed in work necessary for the commonwealth or in tilling the ground. The servants, too, have to be paid higher wages in consequence of the money they spend in wearing these collars, which indeed consumes most of what they earn; and a great quantity of wheat is wasted in starch which is sorely wanted for food. The fine linens to make these collars have, moreover, to be brought from abroad, and money has to be sent out of the country to pay for them. With respect to coaches, great evil is caused and offence given to God, seeing the disquiet they bring to women who own them; for they never stay at home, but leave their children and servants to run riot, with the evil example of the mistress being always gadding abroad. The art of horsemanship is dying out, and those who ought to be mounted crowd, six or eight of them together, in a coach, talking to wenches rather than learning how to ride. Very different gentlemen, indeed, will they grow up who have all their youth been lolling about in coaches instead of riding."

And so on, almost every item of the daily life of Madrid is shown by the writers of the day to be vicious, wasteful, and corrupt. Idlers crowd in the monasteries, and hosts of other idlers, sham students, poetasters, bullies, and beggars, depend for their daily sustenance upon the garlic soup and crusts which are doled out at the gates from the superfluity of the friars; and servants, with or without wages, but living slothfully upon their patron's food in tawdry finery and squalid plenty, pester the noble houses from stable court to roof.[1] Philip and Olivares in the early days did not lack courage, and they came out with a decree so drastic to restrict the wearing of rich clothes, the abuse of ornament, and the possession of rich furniture, the use of trimmings, bullion, silks, velvets, embroideries, and fringes, and to limit the employment of silver and gold plate for household use,[2] as to be quite inoperative; besides which, almost as soon as the decree was promulgated the visit of Charles Stuart caused its suspension.

The number of servants to be kept was rigidly restricted, the use of coaches was only to be allowed to people of a certain rank, women were forbidden to drive up and down unattended by father or

---

[1] When the Duke of Osuna was arrested early in Philip's reign he had 300 servants resident in his house.

[2] There are copies of many of these decrees in British Museum MSS. Add. 9933 and 9934.

husband, and, what caused more gibes than anything else, the houses of ill fame, of which, in the alleys leading out of the Calle Mayor, there was an enormous number, were ordered to be closed. Above all, the most severe orders were given against the wearing of ruffs and the using of starch for any purpose. Pillory, confiscation, and exile were to be the fate of any person who wore any pleated or goffered linen in any shape, and the broad, flat Walloon collar, which fell upon the shoulders, alone was to be allowed. Alguacils were provided with shears, and at a given signal raided the fashionable promenades, cutting the fine lace ruffs which the fops still insisted upon wearing, seizing and burning the stocks of them in the shops, lopping hat-brims to the requisite narrowness, confiscating jewels, and even snipping off the lovelocks before the ears which were the mark of the exquisite.

The ladies, too, were no better treated, and many a brazen-faced madam was hauled out of her trundling coach and put to shame, or had portions of her forbidden finery profaned by the coarse hands of catchpoles. The Calle Mayor and the Prado were up in arms at such sacrilege, and bewailed the time when, the stern pragmatics notwithstanding, each hidalgo and his dame who could get money or credit dressed as splendidly as they liked. The worst of it was, that except the time when all the Court was ablaze with the welcome to its English visitor, the King, for the first time, followed his own pragmatics. Philip, like his grandfather, disliked gorgeous attire for himself ; though, when the dignity of his position demanded it, he could be refulgent. He was, moreover,

sincerely desirous of remedying the terrible penury
that existed everywhere. He had been told by
his advisers that one of the ways to do this was to
limit personal expenditure, in order that there
might be more money for the State to spend, and
he endeavoured in his own person to set the example
of economy.

Philip has left a document in his own hand,[1]
setting forth the reforms he introduced in the
service of his own palace (February 1624). It is
addressed to the master of the household, the
Duke of Infantado, and although far too long to
reproduce entire here, some few passages of it may
be quoted, as showing that, severe as the cutting
down might be, the royal household was still much
larger than would now be considered necessary
for a monarch.[2] The distressed condition of the
public revenues, says the King, the many calls
upon it, the end of the truce with the Dutch, and
Spain's many foes on sea and land, make it im-
perative to cut down every unnecessary expense.
A beginning is to be made in the salary of the
master of the household himself, all *future* holders
of the office to receive a million maravedis less
salary (*i.e.* £330 less), but to retain all the perquisites of the office. Only the four senior stewards
are in future to be paid, the rest to serve without
payment, but to retain their rations, with some
small reductions, namely, the dish of chicken
custard or rice is to be suppressed, and the allow-

---

[1] Contemporary transcript by Father Torquemada. MSS. Add. 10,236
British Museum.   The original is in the Biblioteca Nacional, Madrid.

[2] It may be noted that Olivares, who of course cut down his own
household, still had 122 servants after that process. *Revista de Archivos*,
iv. p. 20.

ance of twenty pounds of ice hitherto given to each steward daily to be stopped. The number of "gentlemen of the mouth" is in future to be restricted to fifty, the gentlemen of the chambers to forty, who are not to have more than two lacqueys each. The pages in future are to be only twenty-four. The numbers of officials of the bakery, fruitery, cellar, spicery, chandlery, and butchery are all reduced to what still seems an extravagant personnel according to modern ideas, and the old scandal of the enormous "rations" drawn (and in many cases sold) by all the palace officials is once more attacked. For instance, the perquisite of sixty wax torches taken by the chief gentlemen of the bed-chamber is abolished; and only eight sets of rations are to be served to the gentlemen of the bed-chamber, whilst the chief groom of the bed-chamber is in future to go without his fifty reals a month in lieu of salads, and his jam on fast days. The controller of the household will no longer be entitled to fresh meat, pastry, bacon, chicken custard, salad and jams, and will have to content himself in future whilst on a journey with two dishes of roast meat and one dish of boiled, and two dishes for supper,—"and he must not take anything out of the store."

Through every branch of the household this process of reduction was decreed by Philip, and even the pay of the guards was rigidly cut down. The members of the Spanish guard had recently had their pay doubled to 200 ducats a month, and now found themselves reduced to their former pay of 100. The King, by these reforms, decreed that a saving of 67,300 ducats a year was to be effected. In another manuscript of the King's,[1] in which a year or two afterwards he recapitulates his personal efforts to remedy the evils of his country, he refers particularly to the sacrifices he made in his household for the commonweal at this time.

"I have twice reformed my household," he says, "and although my servants may be more numerous than before, I have had no other money to pay them with than honours, and they have received no pecuniary pay. As for my personal expenses, the moderation of my dress and my rare feasts prove how modest it is, and I spend no money voluntarily on myself, for I try to give my vassals an example to avoid vain ostentation. So I have reconciled myself to ask for nothing for my own person, but only the indispensable funds for the defence of my realm and the Catholic faith. I want no more, not a maravedi, from my vassals, and I charge you (the Council of Castile) on your conscience to let me know if anything is being spent beyond this."

Philip spoke truly and from his heart when he expressed his desire to avoid as much as possible the oppression of his subjects, but the science of political economy had not yet been born, and neither he nor his advisers could see that a system of taxation that largely consisted of a crushing fine upon every sale of commodities and food stopped production and trade, and tapped the stream of revenue before it had time to fructify the land. The money from the Indies, or what was left of it after the peculations of officers, all

[1] British Museum, Egerton MSS. 338, f. 136.

drifted abroad immediately, mostly before landing, to pay for the loans raised on usurious interest, and in return for the articles of extravagance and luxury which were forbidden to be made in Spain, or of which the vicious taxation had killed the production. And so Philip, with the best of intentions, still, be it remembered, a mere boy of nineteen, was enclosed in the vicious circle which the impossible policy of saddling Spain with the defence and assertion of the Catholic faith throughout the world had imposed upon his doomed house.

He might, and did, as I have just shown, do his best to economise for the supposed benefit of his people ; but it was his people themselves who needed reforming. Whilst they complained that matters got no better, they shouted as loudly as ever that Spain must teach heretics their error at the point of the pike, and they themselves resisted and evaded by every means in their power the sumptuary and other measures intended for the general relief. That these sumptuary measures were to a great extent absurd, and the methods of enforcing them undignified and often ridiculous, is, of course, clear to us now ; but the resistance to them was not founded on that ground, but because they went against the prevailing sentiment of the people, at least the people of the capital. The general pretentiousness, idleness, and love of luxury unearned by labour were, indeed, symptomatic of the natural decadence of society, produced by the unfounded inflation and unreal exaltation of the nation for the greater part of a century previously. The decay had gone too far now for any but a great governing genius to remedy it ;

and Philip, though good hearted, well meaning, and not without ability, certainly was not that. The poison had to work itself out of the national system by slow and painful process, until the patient, exhausted but sound, could build up its strength again. Philip, throughout his life a brilliant idler with good heart and a tender conscience, was condemned to witness the progress of the disease without being able to understand or remedy it ; and to watch at the same time with failing heart the parallel decline and threatened extinction of his own historic house.

Whilst the male, and especially the female, swaggerers of the Calle Mayor gave grudging and evasive obedience to the royal pragmatics against extravagance in most respects, there was one enactment of Philip's which, though at first resisted more sulkily than any of them, gave rise at length to a new fashion, which was seized upon by the whole of Spain with avidity, and became for the rest of the century—seventy-five years—the most entirely characteristic acticle of Spanish male dress. The ruffs under Philip III. had become enormous, and the costly lace edging and elaborate devices for keeping the frills stiff had made them, perhaps, the most extravagant articles of dress ever generally and diurnally worn in any country. Many attempts had been made to suppress them before Philip and Olivares tried their hands, but all had failed. The alternative collar decreed by Philip's pragmatics was either a plain linen band or the flat Walloon collar falling on the shoulders. The former of these was rejected utterly by people who aspired to be well dressed, as being mean and lacking in distinction after the spreading splendour of the " lettuce frill " ruff. The Walloon collar, unstarched, soon got wrinkled, creased, and soiled ; and moreover, it had become to a great extent identified with the " heretic " Hollanders and unpopular Flemings, so that Madrid never looked upon it with favour, though the King wore it after his first pragmatic. The problem was to find a new collar which should be dignified and stiff without the forbidden starch, " or other alchemy," as the pragmatics said; should present the light contrast becoming to swarthy faces, without employing the fine foreign lawn and lace which the royal decree made illegal, and should render unnecessary the puritanical wrinkled Walloon.

An ingenious tailor in the Calle Mayor, early in 1623, submitted to the King and to his brother Carlos a new device, consisting of a high spreading collar of cardboard, covered with white or grey silk on its inner surface, and on the outside with dark cloth to match the doublet. By means of heated iron rollers and shellac the cardboard shape was permanently moulded into a graceful curve which bent outwards at the height of the chin, presenting in juxtaposition with the face the surface of light coloured silk.[1] Philip was pleased with the novelty, which was distinctly more " dressy " than the Walloon, and had none of the objections of the ruff, and ordered some to be made for his brother Carlos and himself. The tailor, in

---

[1] The first idea of this collar, which was promptly dubbed *Golilla* (little gorget), was merely as a support for the linen Walloon, which would thus be made to stand out like a ruff, but the silk-lined golilla alone was soon generally adopted.

high glee, went home to his shop to make them.
But, alas! the pragmatics had forbidden " any
sort of alchemy " to make collars stiff, and, moreover, the Inquisition was soon told by its spies
that some secret incantations, needing the use of
mysterious smoking pots and heated machines turned
by handles, were being performed by the tailor in the
Calle Mayor.

This was suspicious, and smelt of the Evil One ;
and soon the poor tailor and his uncanny instruments were haled before the dread tribunal on
suspicion of witchcraft and sorcery. It could not
make much of the tools, but as, in any case, the
collars were lined with silk, and that was against
the pragmatic, the poor tailor's stock and instruments
were ordered to be publicly burnt before his door.
The tailor, in trouble, went to Olivares, who was
furious at the King's collars being burnt, and he
and the Duke of Infantado sent for the president
of the Inquisition Council, and rated him soundly.
The president declared that he knew not that the
strange things were for his Majesty ; but pointed
out how dangerously new they were in shape,
how mysteriously stiffened, and how they sinned
against the pragmatic. But he was soon silenced
by the Count-Duke, who told him they were the
best and most economical neck-gear ever invented,
as they needed no washing or starching, and would
last for a year without further expense. Philip [1]
and Carlos, with many of the courtiers, wore the
new *Golilla* for the first time during the visit of

---

[1] Philip during his life was rarely seen in any other collar, though
in his fine portrait as a young man at Dulwich he wears a large lace
Walloon.

the Prince of Wales, and the fashion caught the
popular taste. Thenceforward all Spain, Spanish
Italy, and South America wore golillas, the curve,
size, and shape changing somewhat as other fashions
changed, but the principle remained the same,
until Spain was born again and a French King
banned the golilla as barbarous, and imposed upon
his new subjects the falling lace cravat and jabot
of the eighteenth century.

Though the satirists and poetasters might gibe
anonymously at the small remedial effect that
followed the well-meant measures of the King
and his " bogey," as they called Olivares, and
might whisper spitefully, as they did, that the latter
purposely kept Philip absorbed in frivolous pursuits,
the better to be able to rule unchecked himself,
the favourite went on his way sternly and force-
fully, pushing aside roughly those who stood in
his path, and behaving none too generously to
those who aided him. He gave up none of the
duties of personal attendance upon the King,
although now the whole of the details of every
department of State passed through his hands.
The jealous courtiers, whose perquisites he had
curtailed, sneered beneath their breath at him for
coming into the King's room hung all round with
packets of papers, with similar packets stuck
in sheafs under the band of his hat, and bulging
from his pockets, the very way, they said, to
disgust with affairs a youth already disinclined for
business and constitutionally idle.

It is quite evident, however, that someone had
to do the business of the State ; and the numerous
and very able State papers and memoranda of

advice from Olivares to Philip, still in existence,[1]
show that every subject of importance was exhaustively explained to the King, naturally from
Olivares' point of view, and that, if Philip left
the executive power in the hands of the minister,
it was not because he was kept in ignorance of
the issues involved. Even thus early the main
tendency of Olivares' policy was avowed to the
King, a policy which was in its essence wise and
statesmanlike, but impossible of expeditious consummation. The difficulty which faced Olivares
had faced Ferdinand and Isabel and all subsequent Spanish sovereigns, namely, the want of
political unity of the country. The " Catholic
Kings" had attained a factitious homogeneity by
promoting a common spiritual pride, which had
given to Spain the temporary force, already well-
nigh dead when Olivares took the reins. How
could Spain face half Europe in arms, and force
orthodoxy on unwilling princes and populations
with the resources of ruined Castile alone?
Aragonese and Catalans were rich, but held their
purse-strings tight. Portugal, with its fine harbours
and its rich Oriental trade, held stiffly to the constitution, to respect which Spanish kings had
solemnly sworn, and not a ducat of taxes could,
be imposed upon it by the King of Spain without
Portuguese consent, or for other than Portuguese
purposes.

The expiry of the truce with the Hollanders,
and the evident approach of war after the departure
of Charles Stuart from Spain, made necessary the

[1] There is a most important collection of these, originals and transcripts, in the Egerton MSS., British Museum.

raising of large funds somehow. It has been
shown how terribly exhausted the national resources
of the Castilian realms were ; and the poverty of
the country had wrung a cry from the Cortes of
Castile, which met late in 1623 to vote new supplies
for three years. They could not vote, nor could
Castile pay, more than the usual amount, which for
the needs of a new war, in addition to the resumed
struggle with Holland, was quite insufficient. It
would be necessary, therefore, for Philip soon to go
and face the independent Parliaments of Aragon,
Catalonia, and Valencia; and, whilst renewing
and taking the usual oaths, beg for generosity
from his eastern subjects. There is extant a
paper,[1] bearing date of 1625, in which Olivares
unfolds to Philip his ideas of the relations that
ought to exist between the various dominions of
which Spain consisted : the object in view, as he
says, being to arrange that " in case any of the
States was at war, the rest should be obliged to
come to its aid and defence." He cites many
examples, ancient and modern, of the need for
national unity in the matter of finance and reciprocal obligation, and points out for the benefit
of the outer realms of Spain that they can only
expect to form a great Power by making such
sacrifices for their King as other subjects are
obliged to make. His idea, evidently, was to
use the obligation of mutual defence as the first
step to a complete political fusion of the crowns,
and he tried to gild the pill by saying that each
of the outer realms may now be considered feudatories of Castile, whereas if they were all united

[1] British Museum, Egerton MSS. 338.

each would be the head. There was, and is, no
sentiment or tradition so strong in these regions,
especially in Catalonia, as that of political independence of Castile, and any such argument as
that of Olivares was bound to meet with stout
resistance if he attempted to enforce it. The very
rumour was sufficient, and even before the journey
of Philip to the eastern realms was begun, in
January 1626, ominous murmurs came that Castile
might fight her own battles. The crowns of Aragon
would provide money and men to defend themselves, and pay their stipulated tribute to their
King on the ancient conditions ; but that if an
attempt was made to coerce any further payment
trouble would ensue. How this threat was carried
out to the bitter end the later pages of this book
will tell ; but before we accompany Philip and
his mentor on their first regal visit to the stubborn
realms of the east, the further progress of events
in the capital must be told.

Philip's routine of life had already become fixed,
and for many years to come changed but little.
Olivares, as before, was always the first to enter
his room in the morning, and assisted him to rise,
afterwards reciting to him the business of the day,
to which, except in the short but frequent fits of
penitence and remorse that throughout his life
plagued him, it is to be feared the King paid but
little attention. He rose early, and ate and drank
very soberly, dining at about eleven in the morning
after an early cup of chocolate, and performing
his religious duties. Like all his house, he was a
devoted lover of the chase, and the large preserves
in the neighbourhood of all his palaces provided

him with ample sport ; besides which, as will be described in a later chapter, he enjoyed frequent wild boar drives, in which his fine horsemanship was displayed with advantage. His dress was usually a close-fitting doublet of brown duffel with trunks to match, or on occasions of greater ceremony black silk or velvet with the thin chain and tiny badge of the Golden Fleece at the neck, but no other ornament. The golilla was almost invariably worn, his doublet being, for outdoor wear, surmounted by a serviceable long shoulder cape of similar dark colour. The galligaskins were full, and tied at the knee with ribbons, and confined at the waist by a leather belt, square-toed shoes with buckles, and stockings of lighter colour than the galligaskins, but not usually pure white, completed the leg coverings, except for hunting wear, when gaiters or boots to the knee were used. A broad-trimmed felt hat with a band, and sometimes a side feather, was his head-dress ; and in the spring or autumn, when the cloak would have been too heavy, his outdoor garment over the close-fitting doublet was a *ropilla* or outer jacket with false sleeves cut open and hanging from the shoulder.

Both Philip and his wife Isabel [1] were indefatigable in their pursuit of pleasure, in which their tastes agreed. The two main amusements were the theatre and the devotional celebrations in churches and monasteries ; and the inmense number of these in Madrid and the principal cities provided an endless choice of such festivities. The splendour and glitter which the sumptuary

[1] A biography of the Queen is given in the author's *Queens of Old Spain*.

PHILIP IV. AS A YOUNG MAN

From a contemporary portrait in the possession of His Grace the Duke of Wellington, at Strathfieldsaye

decrees prohibited so sternly in secular life ran riot in the temples, and a generation forbidden to be extravagant in their own persons flocked to the garish festivities of the Church to find the sensuous enjoyment which the mere sight of richness gave them. No opportunity, indeed, was lost of getting up a religious show. Philip's second child [1] was born in November 1623,—the condition of the Queen at the time of Charles Stuart's departure having been the reason why Philip did not accompany his guest farther on his road to the coast. The infant Princess, Margarita Maria, only lived a month; but the ceremonial to celebrate her baptism reads like the relation of a fairy-tale.[2]

In July of the next year, 1624, a splendid

---

[1] The first had been a girl, prematurely born in August 1621, who died in a few hours.

[2] There is a very long and detailed account of the ceremony in MS. (Biblioteca Nacional, Madrid, p. v. c. 27), transcribed by the writer. The new-born babe was borne down the great staircase of the Alcazar in the arms of a lady of the house of Spinola, the Count-Duke of Olivares walking backwards with golden candlesticks escorting the new Princess to the rooms of her governess, the Countess Duchess of Olivares, in the ground floor apartment that had only a few months before housed the Prince of Wales. The King with all his Court attended the Royal Chapel for the *Te Deum*, pontifically celebrated by the Patriarch and Cardinal Zapata. For three nights in succession every balcony in Madrid was illuminated by a wax torch, and at night a great masked equestrian display of 120 nobles of the Court with new costumes and liveries was performed, the Count of Olivares and Don Pedro de Toledo being the most brilliant and skilful riders. The great cavalcade paraded the principal streets of the capital, and ran two courses, one in the Calle Mayor and the other before the Convent of Discalced Carmelites. The next day the King rode in state with all the Court to give thanks to the Virgin of Atocha, returning in coaches and admiring the illuminations. The baptism took place in the little parish church of St. Gil, hung for the occasion with cloth of gold. There the Nuncio with cardinals and bishops galore made a Christian of the babe. The tremendous ceremony, with silver cradle, its rich offerings and its pompous names, must be taken for granted here, but the pride of the narrator in the grandeur of it all is significant of the time. There is extant a news-letter from Don Antonio de Mendoza

K

opportunity for devotional display was provided
by the action of a madman. The most crowded
church in Madrid was that of the Augustinian
Monastery of St. Philip, at the entrance to the
Calle Mayor, upon whose steps and raised side-
walk the idlers and gossips of the Court met to
whisper scandal and bandy satiric verse. Every
morning from matins until the angelus bell tolled
the hour of noon, when the soup and bread at the
gates were doled to hungry authors, stranded
poets, and idlers out of luck, Liars' Walk was
full. But rarely had such a sensation of horror
pervaded it as on the day just mentioned, when
the congregation rushed in panic from the church,
with cries of horror that a heretic had knelt before
the high altar and had deliberately insulted the
Holy Mystery there displayed.[1]   Horror upon
horrors ! and in the Court of the Catholic King !
For eight days the King and Queen, with all their
Court in the deepest mourning, peregrinated the
capital, visiting shrines and making propitiatory
offerings. Every church in Madrid was draped
in black, and processions, rogations, and public
flagellations of devotees went on ceaselessly for a
week, during the whole of which time " no stage
plays were allowed, and public women were forbidden

to the Duke of Bejar of the date (quoted by Hartzenbusch in his *Calderon*)
giving an account of the great festivity held by Marquis of Alcañices in
his palace in Madrid to celebrate the birth of this Infanta. " Two comedies
by different authors were represented, with excellent dancers and a dance
of maskers in which elegance and skill vied with each other ; the great
saloon in which it was held inciting envy in the heavenly spheres, such
was the beauty and the brilliancy it contained."

[1] He was a French pedlar named Reynard de Peralta, and was of
course garotted and burnt by the Inquisition for his crime, which amounted
to a denial of the Immaculate Conception.

to ply their trade." In the corridors of the palace
itself separate altars were raised for every royal
personage, and all the jewels that the crown of Spain
could provide were piled upon them to appease the
outraged divinity.

The deprivation, even for a week, of the pleasures of the theatre must have been to the citizens
of the Court a greater penance for the offence of the
madman than any other; for Spain had literally
gone crazy for the stage, and Philip and his wife
led or followed the fashion eagerly. Actors, or
histrions, as they were called, were popular heroes,
and upon the Liars' Walk they swaggered and exchanged quips with the fecund poets who supplied
them with lines of facile verse by the fathom.[1]
There walked Quevedo, with his great tortoiseshell goggles and his sober black garb; there, ob-
served of all observers, was the " phoenix of wits,"
the great Lope; there, Moreto and Calderon; and
there also the rival comedians of the two theatres,
the Corral de la Pacheca and the Teatro de la
Cruz, twisted moustachios of defiance at one
another, and talked of the King's compliments at
their last appearance in the palace.

The two theatres of the capital consisted of
large courtyards enclosed by houses, which were
usually held by the owners of the theatres.[2] A
raised stage at the farther end, with tiled eaves

---

[1] The actors had also another Mentidero or Liars' Walk of their own,
where they were wont to congregate on an open space at the corner of
the Calle de Leon, opposite to what is now the great literary club of Madrid,
the Ateneo.

[2] The original pretext for the establishment of the public theatres
was to provide funds for the charitable fraternities who partly owned
them, and always received a considerable share of the takings.

and a curtain, was faced by a number of benches protected from sun and rain by an awning. In these seats men alone were allowed to sit, whilst in the open uncovered space behind them other men, who had paid a smaller sum, witnessed the show standing. On the left hand on the ground level was a sort of enclosed gallery called the *cazuela*, the stew-pan, where the women were accommodated ; and, as upon the English stage at the time, some of the more privileged of the gallants were allowed to be seated on stools upon the stage itself. In the closely grated windows of the houses surrounding the courtyard the aristocracy saw the play and the audience without being seen ; and as these windows corresponded with rooms (*aposentos*) in different houses with separate entrances, but yet in most cases of easy access to the stage, infinite opportunities for intrigue were provided. So scandalous did this state of affairs become at a somewhat later period, that murderous affrays even between the highest nobles of Spain on the subject of the actresses were of frequent occurrence.[1] Philip, by the Court etiquette, was not supposed to go to public theatres, and had

[1] Frequent attempts were made by the authorities to suppress the scandals and abuses in the theatres, which, although the performances always took place by daylight, were inevitable in such a state of society as that we are now describing. It was forbidden, for instance, for men in the courtyard or pit to converse with women in the cazuela or on the stage ; the actresses were not allowed to dress in masculine garb, and an alguacil was always to be on duty in the auditorium during the performance. See Schack's *Historia del arte dramatica en España* ; Pellicer's *Tratado Historico sobre el origen . . . de la Comedia en España* (1804) ; *El Corral de la Pacheca,*" by Juan Comba ; *Origen Epocas y Progresos del Teatro Español,* by Hugalde (1802), and the valuable MS. *Memorias Cronologicas sobre el origen . . . de Comedias en España,* by Antonio de Armona, in the Royal Academy of History, Madrid.

a regular stage erected in the Alcazar and other palaces, where comedies were performed twice a week ; but, in fact, he was a constant visitor to both the public theatres, going, of course, incognito, and often masked, as was the fashion of the time. There he would sit in one of the private rooms, unseen behind a heavily grated window, but vigilant for any new beauty who appeared on the stage or in the cazuela.[1]

Sometimes, too, the Queen would go with similar precautions, and it is to be feared, from the stories of eye-witnesses, that her tastes were, at all events in these joyful early years of her life, not too refined. Not only was she an ardent lover of the bull-fight, but she would in the palace or public theatres countenance amusements which would now be considered coarse. Quarrels and fights between country wenches would be incited for her to witness unsuspected ; nocturnal tumults would be provoked for her amusement in the gardens of Aranjuez or other palaces ; and it is related that, when she was in one of the grated *aposentos* of a public theatre, snakes or noxious reptiles would be secretly let loose upon the floor or in the *cazuela*, to the confusion and alarm of the spectators, whilst the gay red-cheeked young

---

[1] Philip's passion for the theatre was so well understood, that a comedy formed part of the entertainment at every place he visited. In the spring of 1624 he made a short but very splendid progress in Andalucia, and every great noble and city that received him gave him a new play. On the 18th March the Duke of Medina Sidonia, the great Andalucian magnate and kinsman of Olivares, entertained the King in his country house near St. Lucar, and presented a new comedy before him every day of his stay. On the 7th April we learn that during his visit to Granada the King witnessed a comedy in the Alhambra ! The King himself wrote some plays, now lost.

Queen would almost laugh herself into fits to see the stampede.

Nor were bull-fights, comedies, equestrian shows and church spectacles the only amusements of a Court which actually lived for idle pleasures. There was another in which poignancy of excitement and devotion of the peculiar Spanish sort were equally blended ; and, though not so frequent as the other diversions, was still more popular. These were the *autos-de-fe*. Heretics of the Protestant kind there were now practically none to burn ; but sorcery, impiety, and above all Judaism, or the suspicion of it, provided enough victims to furnish forth an occasional public holiday. The description of one such ceremonial at this period will suffice.[1]   It was not long after the mad French pedlar had outraged the religious proprieties in the Church of St. Philip, when the branch of the Inquisition at Madrid received advice from one of its ubiquitous familiars that certain persons, believed to be of Jewish origin, were in the habit of meeting at the house of a certain Licentiate in the Calle de las Infantas, where, amongst other impious rites, they flogged and maltreated a wooden crucifix. Before many hours had passed, the whole of the accused and their friends were in the dungeons of the Inquisition ; and, as a warning to other backsliders, it was determined to hold a solemn public ceremonial judgment of the offenders in the Plaza Mayor of Madrid on Sunday, 4th July 1624.

The municipality provided the stands and

[1] Leon Pinelo's *Anales Manuscritos de Madrid* and other contemporary writings describe many such.

decorations of the great square, with a splendidly
adorned balcony for the King and Queen, six
other balconies being reserved for the ladies in
attendance, with nine balconies for gentlemen of
the palace party ; a vast concourse of citizens
filling the public space, and the hundreds of balconies looking down upon the square. An immense
staging was erected facing the royal balcony,
upon which, in their state robes, were to be seated
the Town Council of Madrid, the Inquisition of
Toledo, the Supreme Tribunal, all the Royal
Councils and other official bodies. The ceremonies
began on the evening before the great day. At
five o'clock on Saturday afternoon, a solemn procession left the Convent of Doña Maria de Aragon,[1]
near the palace, carrying the gigantic green cross
which upon these occasions held the place of
honour. The standard was borne by the first
official noble in the land, the Constable of Castile,
whilst the Admiral of Castile carried the tassels
of the sacred banner. Then, amidst a crowd of
priests with flaring waxen tapers, came the white
cross in the hands of the representative of Toledo,
followed by the green cross itself, in the hands of
the prior of St. Thomas. Torch-bearers and faggot-
bearers came after, many scores of them, and the
procession closed by long lines of friars bearing
tapers from every monastery in Madrid.

At seven o'clock the next morning the King
and Queen left the palace in their coach, followed
by the whole Court ; and when the royal party
had seated themselves in their gay bedizened
balconies, the long procession of the Inquisition,

---

[1] Now the Senate.

with swaying censers, flaming tapers, and propitiatory dirges, wound into the plaza under the
archway from the Calle Mayor. First came the
alguaciles of the municipality and the town officials,
then the alguaciles of the Court and the officers
of the Royal Council; seventy hooded familiars of
the dread tribunal with their big crosses upon their
sombre garb, followed with the crowd of con-
sultants, notaries, and prosecutors of the Holy
Office. After them walked the municipality of
Madrid, then the Chief Constable of the Inquisition alone, followed by the fiscal of the Inquisition
of Toledo bearing the banner of the Holy Office,
whose tassels were held by fiscals of Castile. The
Inquisition of Toledo came next, and then the
Supreme Council of the Inquisition itself, the last
and most important member being Cardinal Zapata,
the Inquisitor-General.

When all had taken their places, the Cardinal,
as usual, ascended to the royal balcony and administered to the King the oath to keep inviolate
the purity of the Church at any cost, an oath
afterwards repeated by the members of the tribunal
itself and the Councils. Upon a lower staging
before the official platform were grouped the forty
wretched creatures in their flaming tabards of
shame, whose offence this pompous show was to
punish. An interminable sermon was preached
by the King's confessor, Sotomayor, exhorting the
accused to repent and the faithful to increased
zeal in the extermination of the enemies of the
holy faith; and then the dread sentences were
read out by the relator. Seven of the accused
were condemned to be burned alive that night

outside the gate of the city, and four more were to be executed in effigy, whilst their bodies rotted for life in the secret dungeons of the Holy Office ; the rest being sent back to their prison, probably never again to see the light of day, and to suffer unrecorded tortures until death should release them. The house where the offence was said to have been committed was doomed to be swept utterly from the face of the earth, and a church and monastery dedicated to Christ crucified erected in its place.[1] By the time the condemned were led away it was three o'clock in the afternoon ; and whilst the wretched prisoners in their *sambenitos*, amidst the curses and insults of the crowd, went to their doom, the smart company of courtiers, together with King Philip and his wife, returned to their respective homes and their much-needed repast, doubtless in an exceedingly self-approving and pharisaical mood.[2]

Whilst the King and his people were thus absorbed in the pursuit of demoralising pleasures, and loudly proclaiming to Europe that Spain had abandoned none of its past pretensions, the European league against her had been fully organised. It had been clear to Richelieu from the beginning of Philip's reign, that unless France struck boldly and promptly she would be in danger of finding herself once more shut in by the House of Austria, more solid than ever now that Olivares was determined to aid the Emperor to keep the

[1] The site is now converted into a pretty public garden, called the Plaza de Bilbao.
[2] The *auto* is described by Leon Pinelo (*Anales Manuscritos*), by Montero de los Rios (*Historia de Madrid*), and others.

Palatinate, and the blood and treasure of Castile were again to be squandered in fighting heresy abroad. Spinola, victorious in Germany with Spanish troops, was seriously threatening the United Provinces, and Spain, in defiance of treaties, still held by force the Valtelline, which connected Lombardy with Tyrol. The Duke of Savoy, ambitious and discontented with his Spanish kinsman, tired of the rôle of catspaw to which he was condemned, and greedy to seize Lombardy and Genoa, readily listened to Richelieu's approaches ; and England, still smarting under the humiliation she had suffered from Olivares, did the same, whilst the United Provinces, already at war with Spain, willingly joined the enemies of her enemy. Europe found itself for a short time again thus divided in its old way : France, Savoy, and the Protestant Powers being on one side ; whilst the House of Austria in Germany and Spain, with the Italian principalities, were on the other. The first object of Richelieu was to break the territorial circle by ousting the Spaniards from the Valtelline, which he invaded with French and Swiss troops in 1625. Then followed the ignominious attack upon Cadiz by the English fleet under Sir Edward Cecil (Lord Wimbledon) in October of the same year,[1] and Spain thus found herself at war with half Europe.

Poor and exhausted as we have seen that the country was, the labours of Olivares had not been quite without result, and with great effort funds were raised to present a front to the enemies of

[1] A full account of this little known inglorious episode is given from the Elliot papers in the Camden Society, 1883.

the faith worthy of Spanish traditions. The Queen offered her personal jewels to fight her own country-men, the French ; the nobles contributed a million ducats in cash from their ill-gotten hoards ; the pulpits and altars of Spain and the Indies rang with priestly exhortations to sacrifice for the faith ; and the clergy itself undertook to maintain twenty thousand troops during the war. The property of all French subjects in Spain was confiscated, and for once the energy of Olivares was felt in all branches of the Spanish service. It was as if the old times of Philip II. had returned. Feria and Spinola, the one on land, the other at sea, forced the French to abandon their conquests in the Valtelline and Genoa. Spain, in a fever of pride and jubilation, hailed the young King, who personally had done nothing and had never left Madrid, as " Philip the Great," and Olivares caused the title to be officially accorded to his young master. But after a time the diplomacy of the Spanish Queen of France and Olivares did more to end the war than the skill of the generals. Richelieu was a cardinal of the Church, and could not entirely ignore the remonstrances of the Pope, prompted by Olivares, against his making common cause with heretics to fight the orthodox Catholic Power ; and a treaty between France and Spain was patched up in January 1626 with regard to the Valtelline, where the Catholics were to enjoy full liberty of conscience on payment of a tribute to the Protestant Grisons.

But in Germany the war, now mainly a religious one, went on, the arms of the Emperor being to a great extent successful, thanks to

the genius of Tilly and the ample aid in men
and money poured into mid-Europe by Spain.
Spanish resources, too, were plentifully sent to the
Infanta Archduchess to carry on the eternal war
with the Dutch, who were, as of yore, upheld by
their brother Protestants in England and France.
Once more the Dutch privateers harried Spanish
commerce, and again all traffic between Holland
and Spain was prohibited, to Spain's detriment.
But the new-born spurt of energy favoured Spanish
arms even here ; for Don Fadrique de Toledo
destroyed the Dutch fleet off Gibraltar, and Spinola
at last, after a siege of ten months, captured
Breda. To complete the picture of Spain's un-
wonted success, the Dutch were expelled from
Guayaquil in South America and from Puerto
Rico in the West Indies, and the Moorish pirates
who had harried the Mediterranean, and even the
Spanish coasts, for years, were crushed by Philip's
galleys.

The pride and jubilation in Spain passed all
bounds, and Philip himself, in a recapitulation of
the situation made to the Council of Castile,[1] sets
forth in words of proud satisfaction the rise in the
national prestige that had followed his accession.
It is significant, however, that the occasion that
gave rise to this document, congratulatory and
exculpatory at the same time, was the absolute
destitution of the country, as a consequence of the
expense caused by the renewal of the war of which
they were all so proud.

  " Our prestige," says the King, " has been

[1] British Museum, Egerton MSS. 338, 136.

immensely improved. We have had all Europe against us, but we have not been defeated, nor have our allies lost, whilst our enemies (*i.e.* the French) have sued me for peace. Last year, 1625, we had nearly 300,000 infantry and cavalry in our pay, and over 500,000 men of the militia under arms, whilst the fortresses of Spain are being put into a thorough state of defence. The fleet, which consisted of only seven vessels on my accession, rose at one time in 1625 to 108 ships of war at sea, without counting the vessels at Flanders, and the crews are the most skilful mariners this realm ever possessed. Thank God, our enemies have never captured one of my ships, except a solitary hulk. So it may truly be said that we have recovered our prestige at sea; and fortunately so, for, lacking our sea power, we should lose not only all the realms we possess, but religion even in Madrid itself would be ruined, and this is the principal point to be considered. This very year of 1626 we have had two royal armies in Flanders and one in the Palatinate, and yet all the power of France, England, Sweden, Venice, Savoy, Denmark, Holland, Brandenberg, Saxony, and Weimer could not save Breda from our victorious arms."

In a similar gratulatory spirit the young King reviews the wars in which Spain has held her own in the Grisons, Venetian territory, France, and Genoa.

" We have," he continues, " held our own against England, both with regard to the marriage and at Cadiz; and yet, with all this universal conspiracy against us, I have not depleted my patrimony by 50,000 ducats. It would be impossible to believe this if I did not see it with my own eyes, and that my own realms are all quiet and religious. I have written this paper to you to show you (*i.e.* the Council of Castile, the supreme administrative, judicial, and financial authority in Spain) that I have done my part, and have put my own shoulder to the wheel without sparing sacrifice. I have spent nothing unnecessary upon myself, and I have made Spain and myself respected by my enemies."

The political blindness that afflicted Philip in common with other Spaniards of the day, is strikingly exhibited in this paper. The liberty or supremacy of the Valtelline Catholics mattered not one jot to Spain. The religious fate of Bohemia and the Palatinate was equally foreign to purely Spanish interests, whilst it must have been patent to all the world that a recognition of the inevitable independence of Protestant Holland, which it was clear now Spain could never prevent, would have resulted in a perfectly honourable peace in that direction, and would have freed Spain from the drain which was exhausting her. And yet there is in the document just quoted, and in scores of others of the period emanating from Philip or his ministers, not one word to indicate any idea that it was unwise or unstatesmanlike to lead suffering Spain to utter ruin for the sake of championing the Catholic faith, and all the causes masquerading under its name, in any part of Europe.

But though Philip and his Castilian subjects were blinded to political expediency by what they

proudly considered their religious privilege and
duty, the subjects of his eastern realms, hard-
headed men of other racial origins and political
traditions, had no notion of allowing themselves
to be ruined for a sentimental idea, however
grandiose. When the King had asked the Aragonese
Cortes for the usual grant in 1624, he was told that
he must first present himself before the Aragonese
Parliaments (Aragon, Catalonia, and Valencia) to
take the usual oath to respect their constitutions,
before they could make a grant ; and as they
stiffly held to the principle, which the Castilian
Parliament had lost, of " redress before supply,"
they could vote nothing until their legislative
demands were satisfied. The anger of Olivares at
such a reply may be guessed by the tenour of the
document of his quoted on page 142, but there
was no help for it, and Philip with as good a grace
as he might promised to visit his eastern subjects,
perfectly well aware that his progress was not
likely to be a mere voyage of pleasure, as his trip
to Andalucia had been a year previously.

The disappointed courtier Novoa [1] gives an
amusing account of the meeting of the Council of
State which decided upon the King's voyage. He
says that Olivares, " careful as usual of the un-
essential point and careless of what was most
important," was determined to show off his oratory,
and begged the King and his brothers to sit behind
the grating in the council chamber, where unseen

---

[1] *Memorias de Matias de Novoa ; Ayuda de Camara de Felipe IV.*
These invaluable memoirs, written by a bitter enemy of Olivares, were
formerly supposed to have been written by another favourite courtier
of Philip, called Vivanco. Though vivid, they are unfair to Olivares.

they could watch the proceedings, in order to hear his speech. The wisest and oldest councillors in their speeches dwelt upon the gravity of the situation, and expressed hope that the alliance of their enemies would soon fall to pieces, and Lord Wimbledon's fleet be wrecked on its way home.

" Then came the Count's turn to speak. Settling himself firmly on his legs, and thrusting his crutch stick between his bald patch and his false hair, he made a longer pause than the occasion demanded, and said that there was no reason for alarm, nor to make so much of the power of many other potentates, for his Majesty was greater than all of them put together. Even if France, England, Venice, Holland, Savoy, Piedmont, Sweden and Denmark were to join together, none of them, and hardly the whole of them united, were so great as the realms under the dominion of King Philip. The realm of Castile, they all knew the greatness of, and so they did of Portugal, Aragon, Valencia, Catalonia, Sicily, Navarre, Naples, Milan, Flanders, the East Indies and the West and other islands, and great territories elsewhere. Well, then! if his Majesty alone had in various parts of the world greater possessions than many of the others together, why should we be so frightened of the power of many united ? [1] Let his Majesty leave Castile, and as

[1] It is rather a curious fact that the Count-Duke's father, the second Count of Olivares, had been the first councillor in 1603 to speak plainly in the Council of Philip III. on the projects of Spain to dominate England. He pointed out very strongly that extension of territory did not mean increase of power, but the contrary, as it meant the distribution instead of the concentration of national strength. See the writer's *Calendar of Spanish State Papers of Elizabeth*, vol. iv.

Photo]   [Hanfstaengl

GASPAR DE GUZMAN, COUNT-DUKE OF OLIVARES

From a portrait by Velazquez in the possession of Edward Huth, Esq.

Portugal is only one realm, Naples and Sicily, so far away and across the sea, let him go to Aragon, Valencia, and Catalonia. Let him call their Cortes together, and ask them for supplies. Let him show them how many years Castile has borne the burden alone, and demand that these three realms shall do their part in providing men and money for his Majesty; and those who cannot go to the war themselves, let them provide capable and experienced men to replace them. By this means we shall be able to outweigh with our own forces the powers against us, without having to go and beg for help from foreign princes. Who doubts, he continued, that by this means we shall raise great armies and fleets to defend the country. We can then easily send the aid necessary to Italy, Flanders, and elsewhere, and to our own coasts, so that our enemies will all be in fear of us, and perhaps will desist from their evil intentions. This is what appears to me, in the present case, as being necessary to carry out the plans I have formed, which I cannot explain at this juncture, but by which I hope to render signal service to his Majesty."

Novoa says that Olivares delivered an empty, pompous harangue for two hours, but that the above was the substance of his speech, and, after making due allowance for the narrator's bias against Olivares, it is evident that the speech as given represents fairly the policy by which Olivares stood and fell. It is difficult to understand how a clever man could be so blind as he appears to have been to facts that now seem so patent, namely, that the extent and scattered position of Spain's

L

vast territories were a source of weakness, rather than of the strength of which Olivares boasted so vainly ; that Philip in resources was not more powerful than all the enemies together ; and that France or England alone could raise from their own resources, homogeneous and commercially prosperous as they were, larger and steadier contributions than could disunited Spain, and especially ruined Castile ; whilst the brave talk of demanding heavy grants of men and money from the eastern realms of Spain for foreign wars was very soon proved to be hollow. Olivares thought to bounce and bully Aragon, Catalonia, Valencia, and later, Portugal, into stultifying their Parliaments and abandoning their constitutions as Castile had done, but he did not realise the fact that in adopting this policy *à outrance* he was pitting himself against the most powerful sentiment in Spain, namely, local individuality ; and it is not too much to say that all of Spain's internal troubles from the days of Olivares to the present have sprung from the attempts to override this sentiment.

The Aragonese nobles were numerous and powerful, and the merchants and shipmen of Catalonia were immensely more wealthy than any others in Spain ; and even before the King left Madrid it was evident that Olivares would have to face strenuous opposition. Power so absolute and so arrogant as his, so regardless of the feelings and the dignity of others, had already in the six years of his power raised up against him the bitter, if discreetly veiled, enmity of many of the older nobles, especially those of the outer realms, and the speech we have just quoted, shadowing

forth his policy in Aragon publicly—in addition to
the document addressed to the King and quoted
on page 142, gave the signal for the gradual drawing
together of the elements against him.

The King and his brother Carlos left Madrid
on the 7th September 1625, attended by Olivares,
his son-in-law, the Marquis of Heliche, the Admiral
of Castile (the Duke of Medina de Rio Seco), the
Marquis of Castel Rodrigo, and other nobles, but
with much less state than usual and a smaller
attendance, the plan being to travel rapidly, and
" rush " the three Cortes into voting what was
needed. But the Aragonese and the others were
already full of suspicion. The three Cortes had
been convened,—that of Aragon at Barbastro, that
of Catalonia at Lerida, and that of Valencia at
Monzon, a town outside the realm of Valencia.
The Valencians had flared up at once, and had
sent a deputation to Madrid to remonstrate with
the King for thus disregarding their privileges.
After several interviews with Olivares, who had
treated them very off-handedly, the deputation
waited upon him for a final interview the day
before the King left Madrid. " Why should you
put this slight upon us ? " asked the Valencians.
" You do not act thus with the Aragonese and
Catalans." " Oh ! " replied the Count-Duke, " we
think you Valencians are softer." " If you mean,"
said the offended deputation, " that we are softer
in giving way to the wishes of our King and his
ministers, regardless of our rights, that seems to
be a reason why you should grant our request
instead of rejecting it." " Well," continued Olivares drily, " all I can say is, that the King is,

going to Monzon; if the Valencian Cortes are
assembled there when he arrives, well and good.
If not, we shall have to take the course we think
best." "Shall I write that to my principals?"
said the spokesman. "You may do as you like,"
retorted the Count-Duke, as he called his page to
show the deputation out.[1]

Philip entered Zaragoza, the capital city of
Aragon, on the 13th January 1626, and the official
rejoicing of the citizens, though respectful, was
marred by their discontent at the lack of the Court
splendour they looked for; for the Aragonese,
though dour, are loyal and love show. In the
great cathedral on the banks of the Ebro, Philip
swore upon the Gospels, held in the hand of the
Chief Justice of the realm, never to impair the
liberties of Aragon, and to the Cortes the King made
a pitiable statement of the needs of his realm, and
asked for 3330 armed soldiers for the war, and the
right of freely enlisting 10,000 more to be drilled
and kept ready in case of need. The Deputies said
that such a vote was impossible, but offered instead
to provide a million ducats, payable in ten annual
instalments. Philip, with Olivares at his elbow, was
angry and threatening; and at last in dudgeon
he adjourned the Parliament to Calatayud, and
hurried off to Barcelona.

But in the meanwhile a much more serious
conflict had taken place between the King and
the offended Cortes of Valencia at Monzon. There
for weeks the King was kept waiting. The clergy
and popular estates were bribed and frightened

---

[1] Dormer, *Anales de Aragon*, MS., Royal Academy of History, Madrid.
The published portion of the book only covers the sixteenth century.

into promising to vote the amount demanded ;
but, deaf to the King's anger and the violent
threats of Olivares, the landed gentlemen's estate
obstinately stood out.   The expulsion of the
Moriscos, their best tenants, they said, had ruined
them, and they could not pay.   Philip, in a formal
document, almost raved at their obstinacy, and on
one occasion said that there could not have been
loyal gentlemen amongst them, or they would have
stabbed a particularly bold speaker who advocated
resistance.   It was necessary that the three estates
should vote together, and that the decision should
be unanimous ; and at length, in the face of open
threats, the vote was cast as the King demanded,
with the exception that one member, Don Francisco
Millan, obstinately held out.   He ought to be
garroted, said one of Philip's secretaries, and at the
alarmed persuasion of his colleagues he gave way.
But then other difficulties were raised.   The estates
could not agree amongst themselves as to their
shares of the vote, but after much wrangling promised to contribute in material, but not in money,
one half as much as the Aragonese paid.   This
did not suit Philip, and fresh trouble, more acute
than ever, arose.   The Cortes asked the King to
stay in Monzon twelve days more, whilst the Cortes
remained in legislative session ; to which request
the King replied by a haughty intimation that he
should leave next day, and that the matter of the
vote of supply must be settled within half an hour,
which, taking out his watch, he told the deputation had already begun.   This message fell like a
thunderbolt upon the Cortes, which had not yet
even discussed any legislation.   Some were for

defiance, and an immediate dissolution of the assembly without voting or discussion on any subject. All night long they sat, considering this grave crisis in their national history, and at six in the morning a messenger from the King entered the chamber, and told the members that his Majesty had decided to punish them by abolishing their famous right of *nemine discrepante*, by which no vote of supply could be enforced unless it was unanimous. In future, he said, a bare majority would suffice, and he was leaving for Barcelona at once.

This was illegal and unconstitutional, and the Valencians never forgave it, but, rather than enter then upon the new path of open rebellion—up to that time an unheard-of thing in Spain since the loss of Castilian legislative power at Villalar a hundred years before—the Cortes of Valencia gave way, and at the stern order of the King voted the supply unconditionally and unanimously; after which the members were expelled the chamber, and sooner or later an armed struggle between the regal Castilian power and the Parliament of Valencia was rendered inevitable. This was the first result of Olivares' attempt to override sentiment and ancient constitutional rights.

Far more serious in the long run was the conflict in the stubborn Cortes of Catalonia. Even before the King made his splendid state entry into Barcelona, the dissensions amongst the nobles in immediate attendance upon him had come at last to an open quarrel. The proud nobles of ancient title looked down upon the new grandeeship of Olivares, and his insolence had deeply wounded them. The matter came to a head upon a trivial point. The King's coach had been occupied by Philip and his brother Carlos, Olivares, as first minister and lord chamberlain, the Admiral of Castile as the senior official grandee by hereditary right, with the Marquis of Heliche, Olivares' young son-in-law, and the Marquis of Carpio, another relative of the Count-Duke and acting master of the horse. The party was to pass the night before entering Barcelona at the house of the Duke of Cardona, the proudest of Catalan nobles; and when they were setting out in the morning the King called for his host Cardona to accompany him in his coach. The Admiral of Castile, determined not to be ousted, pushing forward, took his place in the coach and refused to move or make way for Cardona; whereupon the King, in a rage, rebuked the admiral roughly. To make matters worse, the admiral and his friends at once threw the blame upon Olivares, and the latter, feigning an attack of gout, sulked and ostentatiously absented himself from the solemnities of Holy Week in Barcelona. The King thereupon appointed young Heliche to replace his father-in-law at court, and consequently to take precedence of the admiral. This was too much, and the proud noble gave the King a bit of his mind about his favourite, and ended by flinging his key, the insignia of office as chamberlain, upon the table, resigned his Court appointment, and went off to Madrid in a towering rage, there to be placed under arrest and to suffer all sorts of investigations and humiliations.[1]

[1] Novoa and British Museum, Egerton MSS. 338.

After the splendours and plausibilities of Barcelona,[1] the change to the hard-fisted Cortes at Lerida was a shock to the King and his minister. There was no hesitation in the demand of the Catalan Cortes that they must be heard before they would vote anything at all, and they were more inclined to ask the King to repay them what they had advanced to him than to grant him more money. The tone of Philip towards them at first was supplicatory, for they were rich, strong, and united. Mildness, however, was wasted upon the Catalans, and the private meetings of the members and other signs of resistance were considered to be dangerous. Olivares began to threaten, and gave them three days to pass the vote, but the Catalans were still unmoved. Then the Count-Duke, in a panic of fear, suddenly and without notice hurried Philip back to Madrid (May 1626). The Catalans, when he was gone, frightened in their turn, voted what was asked for, but all grace in the act was gone, and a deep chasm thenceforward existed between the eastern realms and the King's favourite in a hurry, who had tried to undermine their ancient liberties.

Philip from Madrid tried to appease the Aragonese by voluntarily reducing the contribution they had at length voted ; but the result of his journey left not only resentment in the hearts of his non-Castilian subjects, but led to outrageous raids of angry Castilian soldiery into Aragon, and aroused in the King himself a bitter feeling towards the

---

[1] There is a most interesting and full unpublished account of Philip's entry and stay in Barcelona in British Museum, Add. MSS. 10,236, called *Entrada que el Rey Nuestro Señor hizo en la ciudad de Barcelona y fiestas que se hicieron,* 1626.

peoples who had been the first to challenge the despotic supremacy which Olivares had taught him was his divine birthright. Philip, indeed, like his immediate predecessors on the throne, was saturated with the idea of his divinely delegated authority. To oppose his will was not disloyalty alone, but impiety, and it was naturally difficult for him to understand that this view, which was generally held by his Castilian subjects, whose kingly traditions were sacerdotal, could not be shared by peoples whose institutions were based upon a purely elective military monarchy, and feudalism modified by a representative democracy. How the anger rankled in his breast is seen in the long exculpatory document which I have several times quoted, which on his return to Madrid he addressed to the Council of Castile.[1] In the course of the document, whilst showing how he, personally, has striven to improve matters, he rates them, and indeed almost everybody, for so imperfectly seconding his efforts. But the hardness of his eastern subjects was evidently that which touched him most.

"Anything is better," he says, "than to burden more heavily these poor unhappy vassals of Castile, who, by their love, their efforts, and their sufferings have made us masters of the rest of what we possess, and still preserve it for us, as the head and part principal of our commonwealth. I would far rather take burdens from these poor people than impose further sacrifices upon them, and when I think of what they have to pay, and also the

[1] Egerton MSS. 338.

trouble and annoyance they have to submit to in the collection of it, in good truth I would rather beg for charity from door to door, if I could, to provide for the funds necessary for the national defence, than deal so harshly with such vassals as these. . . . I grieve in my very soul to see such good subjects suffer so much from the faults of my ministers. If my own life-blood would remedy it I would cheerfully give it. And yet, though you (the Council of Castile) know how this cuts me to the heart, and though I reproach you, you propose no remedy. . . . I tried the Cortes of Aragon, running, as you well know, serious risk, and incurring great trouble and inconvenience, solely for the purpose of alleviating the pressure upon these Castilian subjects, and I am directing my efforts in the same way with my other realms, so that some day I hope we may be able to lighten the taxes in Castile. God knows, I yearn for the coming of that day more than to conquer Constantinople."

We shall see as time goes on that this attitude is the one natural to Philip through all the troubles which gathered blacker and blacker, as the evil seed sown by him and Olivares grew and ripened. He himself, acting conscientiously and under divine inspiration, was never wrong in the measures he adopted. If suffering and adversity came, they always came either from the wiles of the evil one, or for some wise inscrutable purpose of God. They were never at this time a consequence of any want of wisdom or prescience of his. His heart bled, as we see by his own passionate words quoted above, for the misery of his subjects, but it never seemed through his life to occur to him that the way to remedy it was to abandon an untenable position in his foreign relations, and devote his energies to the concentration of national resources for the promotion of productive industry and interior economy.

This was Philip's tragedy, the tragedy of a lifetime which this book will try to follow to its sad disillusioned end. The haunting, sorrow-stricken, compassionate face shows through its proud mask of impassivity and its leaden eyes deep traces of the terrible struggle within ; of the throes of a man who dared not show his pain, and who in later years bared his soul but to one woman in the world. Weak of will, tender of conscience, sensitive of soul. A rake without conviction, a voluptuary who sought sensuous pleasures from vicious habit long after they had ceased to be pleasures to him, and yet expiated them with agonies of remorse which made his soul a raging hell.

This is the man. Philip the Great ! "The Planet King," as the flattering poets called him ; this pale, long-faced, sallow young man of twenty-one, who came back to his capital in the spring of 1626 already embittered and disillusioned, confronted by wars and threats of wars on all sides, overwhelmed with poverty yet inflated with pride : seeking escape from his troubles in the company of poets, painters, actors, and courtesans, and in the buffoonery of distorted dwarfs and half-idiotic monstrosities, whilst the dark heavy man with the big square head and arrogant mien led the nation down the slope that ended in inevitable disruption and ruin.

CHAPTER V

RISE OF THE PARTY OPPOSED TO OLIVARES—THE
QUEEN AND THE INFANTES CARLOS AND FER-
NANDO—OLIVARES REMONSTRATES WITH PHILIP
FOR HIS NEGLECT OF BUSINESS—PHILIP'S REPLY
—ILLNESS OF THE KING—FEARS OF OLIVARES—
PHILIP'S CONSCIENCE—ASPECT OF MADRID AT
THE TIME—HABITS OF THE PEOPLE—A GREAT
ARTISTIC CENTRE—MANY FOREIGN VISITORS—
VELAZQUEZ—PHILIP'S LOVE OF ART, LITERATURE,
AND THE DRAMA—CONTEMPORARY DESCRIPTION
OF A PLAYHOUSE—PHILIP AND THE CALDERONA,
MOTHER OF DON JUAN OF AUSTRIA—BIRTH
AND BAPTISM OF BALTASAR CARLOS—PHILIP'S
FIELD SPORTS—GENERAL SOCIAL DECADENCE

ON the King's return to Madrid in the spring of
1626 the almost simultaneous baptism of another
short-lived infant Princess and the betrothal of
the Infanta Maria, the erstwhile " Princess of
Wales," to the King of Hungary, heir to the empire,
gave another pretext for one of those interminable
rounds of pompous shows in which Philip delighted. The marriage of yet another Princess of
the Spanish branch of Hapsburg to a future emperor
was a provocation flung in the face of Europe,
and so Richelieu understood it ; and again patiently
knitted his plans for taking up the challenge in
due time, and defeating finally the threatened

hegemony of the house of Austria to the detriment of that of Bourbon.

During the absence of the Court at Aragon, the party against Olivares had taken courage in Madrid ; for already it was seen that the young Queen, full of spirit as she was, chafed under the complete subjection in which the King was held, and the almost equal tutelage which the Countess of Olivares endeavoured to exercise over her. Isabel loved diversion as much as her husband did, though her amusements were less intellectual than his ; but she could not help seeing, even if there had not been those who were eager to tell her, that the high hopes that the domination of Olivares had first aroused were very far from being fulfilled, and that the distress in the country was greater than ever with the increased drain of the never-ending war. Olivares, moreover, took no pains to conciliate the Queen, and his attitude towards ladies in general was frankly insolent and contemptuous. He was determined, in any case, to brook no possible interference with his supremacy, and deliberately endeavoured to lessen the Queen's influence by encouraging the formation of other ties by Philip. Not that Philip, indeed, needed much encouragement ; but a regular network of agents in the principal cities kept the favourite informed of the appearance of any new and charming actress on the provincial stage, in order that she might be brought to the theatres of the capital and placed before the eyes of the King.

Nor was the Queen the only person of the family whose influence Olivares was determined to check. The two young Infantes, the King's brothers, were now growing into manhood, the elder, Charles, born in 1607, being twenty years of age, and the Cardinal Infante Fernando two years younger. A curious memorandum from Olivares to the King on the subject of his brothers is extant,[1] and shows plainly the method by which Olivares kept his hold upon the King by arousing suspicion of all others, even of the members of the royal family. It appears that at the instance of the minister Philip had appointed a commission, headed, of course, by Olivares, to consider and report upon what should be done for the future of the King's brothers ; and the series of memoranda referred to set forth the result of their deliberations. The points to be settled, says the document, are full of difficulty, and though there has been a period of nineteen years to consider it (*i.e.* since the Infante Carlos was born), it is as full of perplexity as ever. The great danger and risk is to make a choice of servants for the Princes. " We must approach this by taking into account the characters and dispositions of their Highnesses. We consider Don Carlos to be of easy and yielding disposition, and that he will tend the way that those who are near him may desire. But in Don Fernando may be seen a greater natural vivacity, which, with a little help, might be inflamed to a point that would cause serious harm, which we must try to prevent." It is far better, says Olivares and his colleagues, to face the matter now

[1] British Museum, Egerton MSS. 2081, p. 261. Some of the papers in question were also published many years ago by Valladares in the *Semanario Erudito.*

than to let it drift until it becomes unmanageable.
" The best thing will be for Fernando to continue
in the ecclesiastic state ; but not to take higher
steps in it than at present, in view of the succession.[1]
Let him have sufficient money, but let us be careful
not to arouse his spirit and ambition by giving him
the power that too much money bestows, and do
not let us in our generosity to him defraud the
poor flocks and the other bishops. Or else give him
the bishopric of Oran and arouse his zeal in Africa,
like Cardinal Ximenez." [2] This project was not
approved of by the commission, as the desire for
arms and conquest might set him against his pro-
fession. " Or we might make him Inquisitor-General,
in order to introduce him into government affairs,
as was done with Prince Henry the navigator.
But the worst of that is that he is yet very young,
and the Inquisition is a very serious matter. Or
we might send him to Flanders, or even put him
into the Council of State here ; but if we did that
we must put Carlos in too, and we can see many
reasons against doing so. Carlos, of course,
must be married or set to some active exercise, to
keep him employed and out of mischief until God
shall point out to us what had better be done with
him. At present there is no available princess for
him." Several princesses are then suggested, such
as one of the Savoy cousins, a younger daughter
of the Emperor, and a sister of the Duke of Lorraine ; but all are rejected, and after an inter-

[1] Fernando was as yet only a deacon, not a full priest, and the King
when this was written had only one child, an epileptic girl infant, who
died soon afterwards.

[2] *i.e.* the great minister of Isabel and Ferdinand.

minable prologue the final recommendation of
Olivares is reached, namely, to get Fernando,
evidently the one he dreaded most, out of the way
by sending him to Flanders. But even this is full
of suspicion and difficulty. The people there want
a Prince of their own. The old Infanta might leave
him the throne when she died, and the Flemings
might use the Infante to conquer and hold independence of you with your (i.e. Philip's) own arms,
and that, of course, must be avoided. If the
States of Flanders could be left without a master
when the Infanta dies, that would be best, but
as it cannot be your Majesty must keep them.[1]
Or if your Majesty thought well, you might make
him Grand Admiral and Prince of the Sea. In that
capacity, as the authority would be so much divided,
it would not be easy for him to do anything to
your Majesty's detriment, especially as he will
be surrounded by persons of unquestionable
fidelity. But it is difficult to know how we can
do this. If he were appointed to supreme command, both in the Atlantic and the Mediterranean,
with both ships and galleys under him, he would
have to depute much of his authority, and we
think this would be good. But still, it would be
putting vast power into the lad's hands. Besides,

[1] This was the worst possible advice, and its ultimate adoption con-
summated the ruin of Spain. Philip II. had left the sovereignty of Flanders
to his daughter the Infanta Isabel and her husband the Archduke Albert,
in the hope that they might remain Catholic and friendly, but separate
thenceforward from the Spanish crown. The Infanta had no children,
and when she died the resumption by Spain of the sovereignty of Flanders,
on the advice of Olivares, was disastrous. Fernando, in effect, became
Governor of Flanders for his brother a few years afterwards on the death
of the Infanta, and turned out a Prince of great promise, and a military
commander of real distinction, but he died young, and of course unmarried,
in Flanders, after years of ceaseless war.

perhaps he would not be contented with the place unless a viceroyalty like that of Sicily was attached to it.

And so every possibility is discussed at length, and every suggestion either rejected altogether or approved of with many qualifications and drawbacks, pointing out the danger of giving power to princes. But though the commission could come to no decided conclusion, Olivares, in a private letter to Philip, recommended that Carlos should eventually be made Viceroy of Sicily, and Fernando sent to Flanders with a wise old household, although, for the present, it was decided that nothing should be done, except to keep the Princes quiet and as much apart from affairs as possible.

I have given to these curious documents perhaps more space than their intrinsic importance deserved, because they seem to me to illustrate exactly the almost diabolical distrust that Olivares sought to instil into the young King, even of his own brothers. Philip's, however, was an affectionate nature, and he was never soured against his brothers, as Philip II. by similar Machiavellian counsels from Perez was fatally estranged from his. Distrust was the note struck everywhere by Olivares : distrust of relatives, of nobles, even of councillors, except those who were creatures of his own ; and it is evident that on the return of the Court to Madrid, after the absence of five months in Aragon, the favourite found the atmosphere less grateful to him than before. The Queen, as Regent in Philip's absence, had enjoyed an increase of power and consideration, and the nobles, priests, and ladies around her had been able to speak more

M

boldly whilst they were relieved of the alarming presence of the Count-Duke.

Olivares soon struck a blow to regain any power or prestige that he had lost and to fill his enemies with confusion. The King, as we have seen, was indolent and pleasure-loving, leaving all the hard work of the Government to Olivares, upon whom he depended absolutely. The minister knew full well that without his guidance his master would be utterly at sea, and the threat of his retirement always brought Philip to heel. No step, therefore, could have been more effectual in stopping the mouths of the carpers opposed to the favourite, than for the latter himself to protest against the King's neglect of his duties. The State paper in which Olivares remonstrated with the King in the autumn of 1626 for his lack of attention to work, and the King's reply, have been printed several times in Spanish ; but they deserve to be quoted here as specimens of the consummate skill of the minister in facing the situation in which he found himself and his clever management of the young King.[1]

The document is headed, " Paper from the Count-Duke to his Majesty, in which he urges him to consider and despatch current and private affairs himself, without obtaining the opinions of the junta, and, above all, the opinion of the Count-Duke, so that the King himself may, by a step later, take entire control of affairs of State and Government." " Your Majesty is good witness of the many times during the long period I have

---

[1] Contemporary transcripts are in British Museum, Egerton MSS. 338, fol. 571.

served you, that I have told you how important it was for your best interests that people should not only see the result of your own actions, but that they should also recognise them as such, and give you the full credit for them, thus also endowing with force those actions upon which you must needs take counsel. For it is certain, sire, that in the present state of this republic no other course will remedy our ills. Let people recognise in your Majesty attention, resolution, a determination to be obeyed, and if this be not sufficient, let it be recognised in the orders you give, and even in your own person in insignificant acts, nay in the most private actions in your own chamber, where most of the fears which the people entertain have their origin. I have also on many occasions begged your Majesty to give me leave to retire, and to recognise how impossible it is for me to succeed in any of my efforts to serve your Majesty, without your own attention, resolution, and application to the papers. Feeling, as I do, the weight of the duty and love I owe to your Majesty, I have tried to impress this need upon you in the preamble of my various requests ; and to show you how indispensable it is for your Majesty's conscience, for your reputation, and for the redress of the evils of the Government, that you should work, or everything will sink to the bottom, no matter how desperate my efforts may be to keep things going. I have decided, therefore, to make a last appeal to you, because during the last few months affairs have become so urgent that there really is no other course but that your Majesty should put your shoulder to the wheel, or commit a mortal sin.

I must protest, with due respect to your Majesty,
as your humble slave and faithful minister, that
if your Majesty will not at once adopt this resolution, I shall be looked upon as a traitor if I continue in this place, knowing as I do that, however
I may strive, it is quite impossible, without the
personal aid and support of your Majesty, for me
to do what is necessary for the State, and this is
being proved now to me by daily experience. It
may be that the reason why your Majesty will not
consent to work and do as I beg you, arises from
the entire confidence you place in me, and that if
I were not here you might apply yourself more
to work, because you might not trust others as
you trust me. This thought, together with the
zeal and desire, as God knows, I have to serve your
Majesty, have brought me to the point of saying
resolutely, that if your Majesty will not do as I
ask you, I will go away at once without asking
your leave or even letting you know I am going,
even though your Majesty may punish my disobedience by sending me to a fortress, because,
God forbid that I, who owe what I do to your
Majesty, should with my eyes open fail to act as
I believe for the best, even at the risk of ruin to
myself and all my kin, a loss which would be well
repaid if it resulted in inducing your Majesty to do
what is necessary to remedy the evils which demand
the personal attention of your Majesty. I have
said all that a subject may say, clearly and boldly ;
I would rather risk your anger than fail in my
duty. The evil is great. Reputation has been
lost, the treasury has been totally exhausted,
ministers have grown venial and slack, taught to

neglect the execution of the laws or to administer them with laxity, and this is one of the great causes of the evils that afflict the country and justice. Take, I pray you, sire, the work into your own hands. Let the very name " favourite " (*privado*) disappear. I will continue to urge your Majesty to shoulder this burden that God Himself has cast upon you, to labour with it, if you will, without overworking yourself, but not without work at all. 4th September 1626."

The appeal sounds genuine, and no doubt to some extent it was so, for it did not suit Olivares to be the person to be held solely responsible for the grave state of things that was already arousing even long-suffering Castile to passionate protest; and the privation and misery of the greater part of the population were, it must have been evident to the Count-Duke, powerful instruments against him in the hands of his enemies, now growing daily bolder. Philip always wanted to do well, that was the tragedy of his life, and if good resolutions had sufficed, no better ruler could have been desired. Any appeal, moreover, to his conscience always found an immediate echo, though a fleeting one ; and in his reply to the minister the weakness as well as the rectitude of his character are touch-ingly displayed. In his own great sprawling hand Philip wrote on Olivares' letter—

" Count,—I have resolved to do as you ask me, for the sake of God, of myself, and of you. Nothing is boldness from you to me, knowing, as I do, your zeal and love. I will do it, Count, and I return you this paper with this reply, so that

you may make it an heirloom of your house, that
your descendants may learn how to speak to kings
in matters that touch their fame, and that they may
know what an ancestor they had. I should like
to leave it in my archives to teach my children, if
God grant me any, and other kings, how they should
submit to what is just and expedient.—I, THE KING."

Whatever may have been Philip's intention,
and it is impossible to doubt his sincerity, his
good resolutions, as Olivares probably foresaw,
did not last long ; but the cavillers for a time
were silenced, and Olivares at any future crisis
could and did always point to his letter, and shift
a full share of his responsibility upon the King.
The responsibility, in good truth, was a heavy one.
The constant drain of men and money to Germany,
Italy, and Flanders fell mainly upon the realms
of Castile, where the poverty was greatest. The
expulsion of the Moriscos (1610), the most ingenious and industrious craftsmen in the land, had
already produced its dire effects, and skilled
industry, which formerly paid most of the taxes,
had well-nigh disappeared. Without doing anything to revive manufactures in Spain itself, the
Government of Olivares now began the fatal policy
of prohibiting commerce of all sorts with the
countries at war with Spain, which soon meant all
maritime Europe; and the consequence was a complete
dearth of commercial movements, a terrible rise
in prices, universal contraband and untold suffering,
which the purblind minister sought to remedy by
the puerile device of suddenly reducing by one
half the value of copper money (May 1627), and

fixing a maximum price at which farmers might
sell food stuffs !

Anxiety and dissipation acted upon a physique
never strong, and Philip, in the summer of 1627,
fell seriously ill in Madrid. The last baby girl had
died, and though the Queen was pregnant, the
next heir, failing issue to the King, was his brother
Carlos, a gentle, easy-going young man, in appearance and character wonderfully like his elder
brother. But for all his gentleness Carlos was no
friend of Olivares, who had taken from his side
all the friends he depended upon, most of them,
be it said, kinsmen of Lerma, whose sister had been
the Prince's governess.

Young Fernando, the cardinal, as we have seen,
was much more able and ardent than his brother ;
and when courtiers began to shake grave heads
and doctors doubted of the King's recovery, it was
Fernando rather than Carlos who took the lead in
resenting the attempts of Olivares to isolate the
King.[1] By means of his wife, also, Olivares endeavoured to set the Queen against her brothers-
in-law, and to extract a pledge from her that if
the King died she would retain the minister in his
place in the interests of her unborn child. As
Philip grew worse, and himself despaired of recovery, the Infantes, strengthened now by a large
party of nobles, made no secret of their anger with
Olivares, and the latter lost heart and fell ill (or,
as spiteful Novoa says, feigned illness), giving
himself up for lost, and groaning that everyone

---

[1] Novoa says that Olivares turned Fernando out of his bedroom,
which adjoined that of the King, in order that he (Olivares) might occupy
it during the King's danger.

hated him so much that they even wished the King dead in order to get rid of him. The palace of Madrid became a buzzing nest of intrigues, in which, however, the principal song was that of gleeful anticipated vengeance on Olivares and all his kin; though, unknown to his foes, arrangements had been made by him and his party to seize the Government and propitiate the Queen and Don Carlos the moment the King died, as he was expected to from one hour to the other.[1]

Whilst Olivares still kept his bed from illness and fear, an attendant entered and said that the King had recovered consciousness and showed signs of improvement. " Who says so ? " cried Olivares, springing up in his bed. " Dr. Polanco." " Then send Dr. Polanco to me immediately." Dr. Polanco bore no love to the arrogant favourite, and he came tardily to the call, and gave a dry and reticent statement of the King's condition. His Majesty, though better for the moment, he said, could hardly survive another crisis. But there were other royal physicians more courtly than Dr. Polanco, and one soon entered the Count-Duke's room with the welcome news that the King was really better, and had asked for Olivares. The Count-Duke's malady left him as if by magic at the news, and in a few minutes he was at Philip's bedside. On the opposite side of it stood the young Cardinal Infante, who exchanged with him

---

[1] The principal conspirator with Olivares is represented by Novoa to have been the Marquis of Hinojosa, who had until recently been the ambassador in London, and had specially signalised himself by his bitter enmity against Buckingham, whom he had tried to ruin by means of statements damaging to him, and impugning his loyalty to King James. See the correspondence in Cabala.

a glance of undisguised enmity, whilst Carlos at
his side was all mildness, only unselfishly delighted
that the King was better. After a few words of
greeting only from the King, who said he was very
ill and in want of rest, Olivares retired, disturbed
and uneasy at the open hatred of him shown by
the Cardinal Infante. In the present state of uncer-
tainty he dared not quarrel with the King's brother,
the cleverest member of the family, and by submissive diplomacy and professions of devotion
soon managed to patch up a reconciliation with
him,[1] whilst resolving in his own mind to lose no
opportunity that offered of getting away from
Madrid so inconvenient a Prince.

Again the King's life was despaired of, when,
after many mouldering relics had been piled up
fruitlessly, until the King's bedroom looked like
a rag and bone warehouse, the prayed-for miracle
was worked by a shoeless Austin friar, " who
brought that admirable and miraculous relic of
the little loaves of St. Nicholas, which the King
took from the hands of the friar with fervent
prayers and supplication for divine help and
mercy, and the King recovered." [2] Olivares did
not spare those who had thrown him into such a
panic whilst the King lay ill, and the plans for the
future made by the minister's enemies were represented to Philip as treason against himself. " Ah,
sire," he said on his first long conversation after
the King's recovery, " we have had an anxious
time. In future must keep our eyes open." " Yes,
no doubt," assented the King languidly. " As
for me," continued the minister, " I considered

[1] Novoa.   [2] *Ibid.*

myself as already being almost thrown out of the window. The Infante Fernando, sire, is in very bad hands!" "And how about Carlos," asked the King, "is he in any better hands?" But though Philip listened to the whispers of treason against all but those who were the creatures of Olivares, he was too amiable and kind to allow any harsh measures against his brothers, and Olivares had to postpone for the present the greater part of his vengeance.[1]

Philip's tender conscience had, as usual, plagued him during his illness and convalescence. In later years, as calamity after calamity fell upon him and his, it became his settled conviction that the wrath of heaven poured upon his country and upon those whom he loved best in the world was the awful retribution exacted for his personal transgressions ; but even in this, his first severe illness, apparently the same idea assailed him, and as soon as he recovered he addressed a curious and characteristic document to each of his many councils, treating the administrative actions of his reign as a case of conscience for himself. The document is dated 14th August 1627, and the preamble states that it is drawn up for the discharge of the King's conscience after his serious illness.[2]

"1. If I have caused any damage or loss of

---

[1] An important series of letters from Olivares to the King soon after his illness, mainly about the Infantes, their characters, their friends, and their proceedings, is in Egerton MSS., British Museum, 2081, from which I have already quoted some papers on the same subject of an earlier date. The whole object of the letters is evidently to arouse the suspicion of the King against his brothers.

[2] Contemporary draft, British Museum MSS., Add. 10,236 f. 382.

property to anybody by any act or order of mine or otherwise, I desire that redress shall be given to the sufferers.

"2. If by any means or way property belonging to any person be unjustly taken or withheld by any act of ours, I command that the wrong be righted at once.

"3. Consider the means that can be devised to pay all my debts, so that in this respect my conscience may be clear, and in future as far as possible let all necessary expenses be justly met and paid.

"4. Consider whether any of the contributions payable by my vassals can be abolished, and what reform is possible, both as to the amounts levied and the mode of collection.

"5. If any minister of your Council does any unjust act, if he fails to administer justice righteously, or if any grievance is inflicted by him on my subjects, severe punishment must be meted out to him. Great vigilance must be exercised by you in this respect.

"6. If, in order to favour or benefit me, any injustice has been done, it must be redressed at once, regardless of every other consideration.

"Consider all this maturely, and report to me.— I, THE KING."

However well intentioned such decrees as this might be, in the existing state of the country they were absurd. If a foreign policy was persisted in which brought Spain into conflict with every progressive and prosperous country in Europe, which shut the ports of Spain to foreign commerce, and excluded Spanish ships from foreign harbours; if a system of finance were persisted in which ruined taxpayers and paralysed production; if industry was a disgrace and idleness respectable; if corruption existed from the base to the summit of the administration at home and abroad, and ostentation, vanity, greed, and self-indulgence permeated every class of society in the capital, the heart from which flowed the tainted life-blood of the nation, it was futile to order redress to be given for individual wrongs, and for the surface administration to be cleansed, whilst the mass was corrupt; and it is needless to say that the King's conscience was rapidly lulled to rest again, leaving matters much as they were before, and as they remained for years to come, whilst Madrid was the artistic and literary centre of the world, and the rest of Spain was sunk in utter misery and debasement.

A glance at the material and moral aspect of society in Philip's Court during this period, the flower of his reign and life, will be necessary in order to understand what followed. After the restoration to Madrid of its rank as the capital in 1606, the increase in the size and population of the town had been extraordinary; and it was at this period that Madrid assumed the extent and appearance that it retained with little change until the middle of the nineteenth century. As now, the great palace on its bold spur looking over the Manzanares and the plains of Castile to the snow-capped Guadarramas, formed the conspicuous boundary of the capital on the west, and the precipitous slope on that side to the bridge of Segovia, then recently built, checked expansion in that direction. But to the north and east the new streets stretched forth in a way which was at the time looked upon as prodigious. The Puerta del Sol, the present centre of the capital, had even in Philip's time begun to acquire importance as leading to the broad new street of Alcalá, which afforded a less congested approach to the promenade of the Prado than the ancient and narrow Carrera de San Geronimo. The Calle Mayor, leading from the palace to the Puerta del Sol, was not, as now, one broad street in its entire length, the wide portion being, indeed, only the newer stretch near the Puerta del Sol, but in the greater part of its length consisted of a continuous line of narrow and somewhat tortuous streets called by different names. This, however, being the road to and from the palace, was the fashionable promenade, especially for the great swaying coaches then the rage in Madrid. In hot summer nights the dry bed of the Manzanares attracted fashionable promenaders to enjoy such coolness as could be found there ; whilst the Prado itself, from the street of Alcala to the Atocha, on certain occasions, especially on saints days, church festivals, and in the evenings of spring, was the crowded resort of the idlers. The Plaza Mayor, or great square, standing much as it does to-day, had been built in the previous reign, the houses that enclosed it being capable of accommodating in their lines of balconies as many as fifty thousand spectators to the bull-fights, *autos-de-fe*, or equestrian shows, which were held there on great occasions.[1]

The construction of the houses, for the most

---

[1] All one side of the great square was destroyed by fire a few years after the time of which we are writing (in 1631).

part rapidly run up to meet the sudden increase of
the population—the Court, as has been explained,
attracting everybody in Spain with brains, ambition,
or money—was extremely mean and shabby, the
heavy ostentatious palaces of the nobles, many of
which still stand, being surrounded by wretched
little shanties with mud walls and filthy exteriors.[1]
The windows towards the street were heavily
grated, and mostly small, which gave a gloomy
dungeon-like appearance to the buildings, whilst the
total absence of drainage made the roadways a
mere middenheap, through which the heavy coaches
ploughed, and bespattered the pedestrians. To
the enormous number of strangers and foreigners
whom curiosity, politics, or business brought to
Madrid at this period, the filthy condition of the
streets became a byword. The gutters of the
houses projecting far out from the eaves threw
great jets of water when it rained into the middle
of the narrow roadways, and with the mere warning of "*Agua va*" all the house garbage, débris, and
excrement were cast forth into the open street,
there to fester until the salutary sun had deodorised
it and reduced it to dust.

In these streets, and especially in the portion
of the Calle Mayor near the Church of St. Philip
and the Puerta del Sol, the idlers of the capital,

---

[1] The fact of so many of the wretched houses of the capital having
only one storey is explained by the oppressive arrangement which placed
at the disposal of the Court one entire floor of every house of more than
one storey, a right grossly abused by Court hangers-on to quarter their
relatives and friends rent free upon the citizens. In Philip IV.'s time
this oppressive right had been partially commuted to a payment of
250,000 ducats annually by the municipality, which was estimated to be
one-sixth of the rental value of such houses. Mesonero Romanos, *El
Antiguo Madrid*.

which meant the greater part of the population, loved to promenade for hours every day, preferably in coaches, bandying coarse jests with the people on foot. This objectless promenading and gossiping was so characteristic that a special verb was coined to describe it, namely, to *ruar*. Everybody pretended to be wealthier, more highly placed, and better dressed than he really was ; and though sumptuary pragmatics and decrees, announced by heralds in the Calle Mayor, constantly threatened transgressors with all sorts of pains and penalties, the people, especially the women, continued to defy the law in their dress and behaviour. The insolent dames would wear outrageous garments; flattened farthingales (*guardainfantes*) so immensely wide as to be indecent, starched ruffs, pattens so high with jingling heels as to be like musical stilts, and would still insist upon covering their faces, all but one eye, the more to pique curiosity and indulge with impunity in their not too delicate badinage.

The large spaces occupied by the frowning religious houses, whilst adding to the gloom of the city, must have increased its salubrity, in consequence of the large shady gardens that they usually enjoyed. At twelve o'clock, when the angelus sounded, the monastery gates opened, and there came forth a lay brother with an immense cauldron of soup and a basket of bread, which formed the principal meal of many hundreds of poor people and idlers all the year round. The students, real or pretended, who in token of their dependence on these eleemosynary meals wore a wooden spoon tucked into the brim of their hats, formed a considerable portion of those who attacked the garlic

broth with avidity. Broken soldiers and led
captains, gamblers out of luck and varlets out of
place, fought too for the food with the maimed and
diseased beggars who crowded the most frequented
streets at fashionable hours.[1]   In addition to these
charity meals given by the religious houses, there
were numerous lay brotherhoods established to
relieve the sick and impotent ; and one particular
brotherhood, which went its rounds at night,
especially in the outer districts of the capital,
was called by the people the " bread and egg
watch," because the brethren carried with them
baskets of bread and eggs to distribute to the
needy whom they found exhausted and homeless
by the way.

It may be asked if Madrid was so forbidding in
appearance, as it was certainly difficult of access
and lacking in comfort and convenience, what was
the attraction that drew to it at the time not only
the enriched Spaniards from the Indies, and the
ambitious and idle of the Peninsula itself, but the
immense number of foreign visitors who now
frequented it.   So far as the Spaniards were concerned, it has already been explained that by the
time of which we are writing the Court had, in fact,
drawn to itself all that was left of available wealth
in the country.   There alone could the Spanish
love of ostentation be indulged ; there alone could
bravery of dress and demeanour find the attention
and emulation it always seeks ; there alone could
advancement in any unlaborious career be found,
for where all the patronage, wealth, and taste were,

---

[1] A vivid picture of Madrid of the time is given in *El Diablo Cojuelo*,
by Velez de Guevara, a judge, and favourite of Philip IV.

there also must be those who sought patronage or provided things that taste and wealth alone could buy, and so the Court—"*la Corte*" as Madrid was always called—shone brightly, like the last phosphorescent spot in a decaying body, and attracted by its brilliancy when all the rest of Spain was dark.

The fame of the splendid shows of Philip's Court, the traditional wealth of the monarch, and the reputation for gallantry and gaiety which the place obtained, brought to it pleasure-seekers from all Europe. The close connection with Austria naturally attracted Germans to Spain in numbers ; Flemish Catholics were, of course, almost as much at home in Madrid as in Brussels ; whilst the marriage of Philip's sister Anna of Austria in France had made the romantic view of Spain fashionable there. The war with France somewhat restricted the French incursion, but Burgundian and Franche-Comtois craftsmen were numerous, and the enemies of Richelieu always found a welcome in the Spanish Court. Italians, especially Neapolitan and Milanese subjects of Philip, who served in his armies and provided his finest weapons, were frequent visitors to his capital. It was, moreover, a dilettante age, when all over Europe, and particularly in Madrid, where for a century the monarchs had been generous patrons of art, a perfect craze had seized wealthy people to collect and display rare and beautiful artistic objects of all sorts, and the ostentatious nobles who surrounded Philip IV., many of whom had lived in Italy, had shared the King's love of such objects, and had made their palaces perfect museums of art treasures of every description.

N

Olivares himself exacted from viceroys and Spanish officers abroad presents of tapestries and articles of virtu.[1] The Count of Monterey and the Marquis of Leganes, both kinsmen of the Count-Duke, had crammed their palaces with rarities,—clocks, mirrors, enamels, medals, marqueterie, and paintings ; and Monterey, who had been viceroy of Naples, had brought back with him to Madrid a whole cargo of silver repoussé work, tapestries, ivory carvings, gems, and such treasures as the red chalk drawing of the cartoon of Michael Angelo's famous " Bathers."[2] V. Carducho, who lived in Madrid at the time, describes in his *Diálogos* the regular meetings there of connoisseurs and patrons of art, to inspect, exchange, or criticise paintings, models and other rare and beautiful things ; where, he says, " originals by Raphael, Correggio, Titian, Tintoretto, Palma, Bassano, and living painters were admired, and where much taste and knowledge were displayed." Besides paintings, he continues, there were to be seen at these meetings " coats of armour and weapons of famous armourers, damascened swords and daggers, rock crystal work and pyramids and globes of jasper and glass." On one particular occasion Carducho mentions that the host of the meeting-place was engaged in arranging some

[1] In this he only followed the recognised rule of Spanish ministers. Quevedo, writing from Madrid to his patron the Duke of Osuna, Viceroy of Sicily, shortly before Philip's accession, says : " Men here are like strumpets, every one of them has to be bought. . . . The Marquis of Siete Iglesias (*i.e.* Calderon) would like a present for his cabinet, and it would be worth while to send some trifle for his cell to the King's confessor." The " trifle" he did accept was a diamond reliquary worth 20,000 reals and a splendid altar jewel.

[2] Carl Justi.

articles for an exchange he was negotiating with the Admiral of Castile, a great art patron, whom he was expecting. They comprised an original by Titian, six heads by Antonio Mor, two bronze statues and a small culverin, whilst the admiral had left with the host a good copy of a painting by Caracci ; and Carducho mentions that Monterey had there at the same time an original Madonna by Raphael from the convent of Discalced Carmelites at Valladolid.[1]

The agglomeration of such works of art at Madrid during a long period naturally led to the dispersion of the great collections on the death or fall of the noble owners, and this was effected by the usual Spanish form of sale still common, called an *almoneda*, such articles as are for sale usually remain *in situ*, but on public view, with the prices marked ; and the German ambassador, Count Harrach, mentions no less than twenty of such *almonedas* of artistic collections belonging to Madrid nobles within the space of five years, at a somewhat later period of Philip's reign than that of which we are now writing.[2]   Of one such noble collector in Madrid (Juan de Espina) Quevedo says : "For years his house was an epitome of the marvels of Europe, visited by strangers, to the great honour of our nation, for they had often nothing to tell of Spain except their recollections of him."

I have mentioned that one of the presents given by Olivares to the Prince of Wales on his departure was a set of paintings, but these were by no means the only pictures that Charles took back

[1] Carl Justi.   [2] *Ibid.*

with him to enrich the royal galleries of England.
The unfortunate murdered Count Villa Mediana's
great collection was still being dispersed by *almoneda* at the time, and here Charles bought several
specimens. Lope de Vega says that the Prince
" collected with remarkable zeal all the paintings
that could be had, paying for them excessive
prices." He was unable to persuade Quevedo's
friend Espina to sell him the gem of his collection,
two volumes of original drawings by Leonardo da
Vinci, which, however, eventually came to England
as the property of Philip Howard, Earl of Arundel.[1]
Many other paintings and precious objects were
secured by Charles during his stay by purchase
and gift ; and it may be fairly assumed that so
great an art lover as he must have found his
principal solace for his long absence from home
in the inspection and acquisition of objects he
prized so highly. In the Calle Mayor, against the
wall of the Oñate Palace, opposite Liars' Walk,
on the raised path along the side of St. Philip's
Church, the Spanish painters of the day, on the
lookout for patrons, were wont to exhibit their canvasses for sale,[2] and some of the modern Spanish
pictures that Charles took home with him were
doubtless seen and bought in the course of his

[1] When Sir Francis Cottington went to Spain to negotiate peace in
1629, Endymion Porter asked him to try and buy these drawings by
Leonardo da Vinci from D. Juan de Espina, whom everybody knows, for
Lord Arundel. The half-Spanish Porter gave a good many other commissions to Cottington on his departure : some paintings by Titian, some
orange-flower water, some orange confection, a dozen baskets of oranges,
six barrels of large Seville olives, caraways, figs, chestnuts, marmalade,
wine, gloves, perfumes, matting, wine, dried peaches, fine crocks, etc., in
considerable quantities. (Record Office SP. Spain MS. 34, November 1629.)

[2] At a somewhat later period Murillo sprang into fame and fortune
through Philip seeing a picture of his exposed for sale here.

daily promenade through the fashionable street of
the capital.

There was one young painter of the day, a
stripling of twenty-four, though already married
and with two children when he arrived in Madrid
at the same time as the Prince of Wales, who at
least had no need to seek purchasers for his canvasses upon the rough side walk, though he did
exhibit them there for the admiring criticism of
the connoisseurs opposite. To have come from
Seville, as he did, was, to begin with, a good creden-
tial in the time of Olivares, whose own noble house
was of Andalucia, and who himself was Sevillano to
the marrow. But this young man, Diego Velazquez,
had married the daughter of his master, Pacheco,
the best known painter in Seville, and the bosom
friend of Francisco de Rojas, the literary henchman
and devoted adherent of Olivares. Three years
before this, Diego had come to Court full of high
hopes and ambitions; for the painting of convent
altar-pieces in Seville was a narrow field for genius,
and Diego yearned for the wide recognition that
the "Court" alone could give. But though he
had the help of the Sevillians who abounded in
Olivares' household, and notably that of Dr.
Fonseca, the Court chaplain and King's "curtain-
drawer" in the royal chapel, business was so
pressing, both for King and minister, in the early
days of the reign, that there was no time to be
spared for portrait painters, and Velazquez returned home disappointed.

But in the spring of 1623, whilst Charles Stuart
was in Madrid, Fonseca, at Olivares' bidding,
wrote to the artist telling him that he might now

with good hope return to Madrid, and sending him
fifty ducats for his travelling expenses. He needed
no further urging, nor did his famous father-in-law,
who, if he was not a genius himself, at least realised
genius when he saw it, and together they set forth,
with the assurance that young Diego was going to
conquer Madrid. There was no heart-breaking
struggle for him, though his triumph was not so
immediate as he would have wished. The effort
to get to the palace, the fountain of all patronage,
was universal ; and the rivalry of competitors
was keen. Poets, dramatists, actors, placemen, and
artists were all struggling eagerly to catch the
eye of royalty, or the ministers of royalty, and for
a time even Fonseca could not secure for his
protégé an admission to the King's presence. In
the meanwhile Velazquez painted a portrait of the
priestly patron Fonseca, in whose house he lived.
As soon as it was finished the chamberlain of the
Cardinal Infante Fernando, the Count de Peñaranda, visited the house by chance, saw the picture,
and insisted upon carrying it off with him to the
palace. Everybody at Court knew the reverend
" royal curtain-drawer " in chapel, and within an
hour the portrait had been seen by all the *palaciegos*,
from the King downward, and praised to the skies.

Promises were sent to the young painter that
he should be commissioned to portray the King and
his brother ; but the King's work and play, more
momentarily pressing, still delayed the anticipated
honour until the end of August, when Philip, on his
prancing charger—for the King was a splendid
and intrepid horseman—carracoled in the garden
of the palace before the grave, lean young painter

with the jet black hair and flashing Andaluz eyes, who for the first time fixed there upon canvas the face and form which his genius was to immortalise. Philip was a good judge of art, and when he saw the picture, though no muscle of his impassive face moved, he expressed his satisfaction with courteous condescension. Olivares, vehement as usual, and proud that a Sevillian should have succeeded, swore that no one else had ever painted the King as he was, and that in future Diego Velazquez alone should paint his Majesty. When the last touch was given to it, the great life-sized equestrian portrait of Philip was exhibited upon the pavement opposite Liars' Walk, not for sale, but for the astonishment and delight of loyal Madrileños.[1]

Diego Velazquez's fortune was made. Within a few weeks he was appointed Court painter, with a salary of twenty ducats a month, with extra payment for each picture and a studio in the palace ; and thenceforward pensions and favours of all sorts testified to Olivares' pride in his fellow-countryman and the King's recognition of a genius. From the time of the great Emperor and his son the tradition had existed that intimate familiarity was permissible between the King of Spain and those household servants whom he cared thus to honour. Both the Emperor and Philip II. had allowed the greatest liberty to their jesters, dwarfs, and body servants, and had extended their friendship to the artist carftsmen who had served them. Philip IV. bettered the instruction, for he at heart was a poet and an artist himself ; and whilst he

[1] Pacheco, *Arte de la Pintura.*

delighted in the company of clever people generally, he distinguished with life-long regard and considerate kindness the young artist, only a few years older than himself, who did so much to ennoble and illustrate his Court. In Velazquez's studio in the palace a leather armchair was always kept sacred for the King, who was wont to come in unannounced when the fancy seized him, and watch the painter at work. Indeed, during his stay in Madrid he hardly missed a day in his visits, and would often come accompanied by his wife to the studio. There he witnessed, gradually growing under the magic brush, the counterfeit presentments of those who made up his life, his wives, brothers, and children, the latter in their chubby babyhood, stiff with irksome splendour; the distorted and deformed beings who ministered to the merriment of those whose surroundings were otherwise far from merry ; the poets who solaced his life, the women he loved, the famous captains of his armies ; Spinola, Pimentel, Pulido-Pareja, and the rest of them ; the great Olivares himself, and all the rout of glittering satellites who revolved around the Planet King.

Philip enjoyed almost as much the society of Quevedo as that of Velazquez, but the satiric wit was less careful than the painter, and his medium was more risky ; so that, though his biting verse and malicious prose had in the King an appreciative listener, the poet was almost as often in exile as in favour.[1] The literary contests and discussions which amused Philip as he grew older

[1] He offended Olivares somehow in 1627, and remained in exile until the minister fell.

always, when Quevedo was not in disgrace, bene-
fited by his ready wit. Philip himself took part
in these literary orgies in the palace, frequently
proposing a subject for an impromptu play in the
facile blank verse which comes so trippingly upon
Spanish lips. The subject would sometimes be a
sacred one, in which case the treatment was such
as would shock modern ears, though for abject
lip devotion the persons who spoke so slightingly
of sacred things were never surpassed. It is related that on one such occasion Philip set the
Creation of the World as the subject for an impromptu play, assigning to himself the character of
the Maker. The poet, whom he had cast for Adam,
made his part unduly long, and Philip elaborately
expressed his grief, as the Eternal Father, that ever
he should have afflicted the world with such a
long-winded Adam. But though these literary
diversions had already become attractive to him
at the period at which we are now writing (1626–
1630), the gloomy old Alcazar was not a congenial
setting for frivolity ; and it was not until later,
when the new suburban palace of the Buen Retiro
was specially devised by Olivares for the purpose,
that the poetic and dramatic exercises of the
Court reached their zenith, as will be related in a
future chapter.

But from the first Philip's devotion to the
theatre never wavered, and in this his people, high
and low, agreed with him. The two public theatres
of the capital, the Corral de la Pacheca (on the
site of the present Teatro Espanol) and the Corral
de la Cruz, in the street of the same name, were
crowded every day, and sometimes twice a day ;

the performance before noon being attended mainly by women, and that of the afternoon by men, and women of a better class. The appurtenances of the stage were extremely rough, and the scenery widely adaptable where it existed at all, as the constant changes of comedy made special scenery impossible. The plays presented, hundreds of which are still extant, are marvellous in the inventive fertility of their plots ; the intrigues that spring from mistaken personality, marital wiles, and lovers' stratagems furnishing the foundations of most of them. The speeches, according to modern ideas, appear intolerably pompous and long, but the mere sound of the flowing rhythm pleased the ears of Spaniards, as similar speeches do to-day, and the Madrileños never grew weary of their shows.

The following lively description of one of the theatres in the reign of Philip IV. will give an idea of the scene they presented on a holiday.[1]

" You must dine hurriedly at noon, and not stay long at table if you are going in the afternoon and wish to find a seat. The first thing you do when you arrive at the door of the theatre is to try to get in without paying. Many work and as few pay as possible. That is the actor's first misfortune. It would not be so bad for twenty people to get in for four farthings, if many more did not try to imitate them. As it is, if one person gets in without payment others expect to do the same. Everybody wishes to enjoy the privilege of free admission, in order that people may see that they are worthy of it. For this reason they

[1] Zabaleta, *El dia de fiesta*, Coimbra, 1666.

strive so hard to enjoy it that it gives rise to endless
disputes and altercations ; with all the more reason
that by these means they usually succeed in their
aim.   When once a person gets entrance without
payment he adopts it as a general rule, and never
wants to pay.   A fine way this to remunerate
those who merit some return for their work in
trying to amuse them.   And perhaps you will think
that he who pays not is more easy to please.   On
the contrary, when the actor is not properly dressed,
those who have not paid insult and hiss him most.
At last our man gets into the theatre, and asks
those who are seated on the benches to make
room for him.[1]   They tell him that there is no
seat for him, but that perhaps one of those who
have paid for a seat will not come, so he had better
wait until the guitar players appear and he may
then occupy the vacant seat.   This being agreed
upon, our friend goes to the dressing-room to
amuse himself in the meanwhile.   There he finds
the actresses taking off their usual clothes and
assuming those necessary for their characters ;
they being sometimes as naked as if they were
going to bed.   He stops and stares before one of
them, who, having come through the streets on
foot, is changing her boots by the aid of her servant.
This cannot be done without some sacrifice of
decorum, and the poor actress is much put out,

---

[1] The mere admission to the theatre was, and still is in Spanish
theatres, paid for separately from the seat.   And from the extract quoted
it would appear that the bench seats at the time were sometimes booked
beforehand, as they may be to-day.   The *entrada* in Spanish theatres
gives the right to the run of the house, but nothing more.   The noble
army of deadheads appears to have been as numerous and unblushing
three hundred years ago in Spain, as they are in England at the present
time.

but she dares not protest, because, as her main object is to gain applause, she is afraid of offending. A hiss, however unjustified, discredits an actor, because people in general incline more to the censure of others than to their own judgment. The actress consequently does not suspend the changing of her boots, and suffers the importunity of the visitor patiently. In the meanwhile the blockhead never takes his eyes off her.

"After that he looks from the stage to see what is happening with the doubtful seat he covets. It is still vacant, and in the hope that the legitimate owner of it will not come he runs to occupy it. The moment he does so the owner appears and defends his claim. The other does the same, and both grow heated and come to blows. The last comer, as he has come to the theatre for amusement, and finding no amusement in shouting and fighting, thinks it better to stand for three hours than to continue clawing, and retires from the fray, another seat being provided for him by those who have intervened and pacified the dispute. When this hurly-burly has ended, our intruder settles down quietly and casts an eye upon the cazuela,[1] and passes in review the women who fill it. He takes a sudden fancy to one of them, and begins to manifest his feelings by making signs to her. But, my good friend! you have surely gone to the theatre to see the play, not the cazuela.

"It is four o'clock in the afternoon by this time, and the performance has not begun yet. Our friend, looking vaguely about him, first on one side and then on another, suddenly feels that

[1] The side gallery where the women were seated.

someone is pulling at his cloak. He turns his head and sees an orange-seller, who, bending towards him between the two spectators behind, whispers in his ear that the lady who is tapping her knee with her fan has watched with sincere pleasure the spirit he showed in the quarrel about the seat, and that it would be a gracious thing if he bought her a dozen oranges in recognition of her sympathy. Our friend scans the cazuela again, and sees that the lady in question is the one that caught his fancy before ; so he pays for the oranges, and tells the orangeman to let the lady know that he will willingly pay for anything else she would like. When the orangeman disappears with this message, our friend thinks of nothing else than how he shall approach the lady when they leave the theatre, cursing the comedy in the meanwhile, which appears to him interminable, such is his impatience. He signifies his disapproval aloud, and groans without cause, exciting the musqueteers [1] below to imitate him and to break forth in offensive cries. This is not only rude and uncultivated, but monstrously ungrateful, for, of all men, actors are those who strive hardest to gain applause. What a bad time they pass, and how laborious whilst they rehearse a piece. And when the first representation comes, any of them would give a year's wage to be applauded for his part. What anxiety assails them, what inexpressible yearning they feel on the stage to please the public. When they have to cast themselves down from some

---

[1] The men who had only paid for the entrance and stood at the back of the patio (or pit) were so called, but they soon became a recognised paid claque.

precipice, they throw themselves off the painted canvas rock with desperation ; when they have to represent a dying man and to writhe in agony, how they soil their clothes, which have often cost much money, and tear their hands with the nails and splinters of the boards ! ''

The rest of the chapter is more concerned with the evils of the actor's life than with the audience, which is the point most interesting to us ; but it is clear from what has been quoted that the comedies, witty and facile as they were, nevertheless did not form the only attraction that drew crowds daily to the theatres of the Court. In the first place, they were a pretext for the prevailing idleness, and the sure sign of decadence which manifests itself in the inactive many gazing upon and criticising the hired exertions of the active few. But the ''corrales'' of Madrid are also shown in the above extract, and in hundreds of allusions in the comedies themselves, to have been places of assignation and incentives to promiscuous gallantry.[1] The King himself, behind the impenetrable window grating of a first-floor private room (*aposento*) first saw many of his mistresses. They were not mistresses in the sense that prevailed at the Court of the French Bourbon kings. None of them ever aspired to, or attained, political or social power, for the distance between the sacrosanct sovereign and common humanity was too great for that to be possible in Castile. They were just the creatures of Philip's caprice, and the

[1] The rooms in the top floors were called *desvanes*. The attic rooms were often occupied by priests.

momentary playthings of his passions, none of them
retaining hold upon him but for a very short time.

Of his thirty and more illegitimate children,
of whom eight were recognised, the only one that
was given princely rank was that Don Juan of
Austria who was beloved by his father above all
others of his offspring. From the theatre, at the
period which we are now writing, Don Juan of
Austria sprang. It was at the Corral de la Cruz
in 1627 that Philip first set eyes upon the girl
whom one of Olivares' agents had sent from the
country to act upon the Madrid stage. Her name
was Maria Calderon, and at the time she appeared
in the capital she was not more than sixteen years
of age. She was no great beauty, but her grace
and fascination were supreme, and her voice was so
sweet and her speech so captivating that Madrid
fell in love with her at once.[1] The King from
his *aposento* was enamoured of her the first time
he saw her, and for him to desire was to enjoy.
She was immediately summoned to the private
apartment, that the King might listen more closely
to her lovely voice, and when he heard it the
King's love grew fiercer still. From the corral to
the palace was but a step when Philip willed it,
and thenceforward the *Calderona* became the King's
best beloved mistress. She still acted upon the
stage, though gifts and tokens of affection were
piled upon her by the love-lorn King. She, proud
of the ineffable honour vouchsafed to her, became
rigidity itself in her virtue, and turned a hard face
to all other lovers.

[1] Contemporary Italian MS. in British Museum, MSS. Add. 8703.
"Ritratto della nascitá qualitá ed accioni di Don Juan d'Austria."

The tradition in Spain made the position of
King's mistress not by any means one to be coveted
by most women, since it was understood that when
the liaison ended the lady must immune herself
in a convent for the rest of her life, to prevent such
a sacrilege as for the King to have a successor in
any woman's regards. It is told of one young
lady of the Court to whom Philip was making
unmistakable advances, that she shut herself
behind a locked door when she knew the amorous
King was seeking her, and cried out to him from
the inside: " No, no, sire ; I don't want to be a
nun ! " The Calderona had no such scruples,
either from natural devotion or because she really
felt the honour of the King's love to be overwhelming. Her son by the King was born on the
17th April 1629, and as soon as the *Calderona*
could leave her room she sought the King, and,
throwing herself at his feet in tears, prayed for his
permission for the mother of his son to sin no more.
For it was enough, she said, to have borne a child
to the greatest monarch on earth, and nothing
more was left for her but to devote the rest of her
life to cloistered sanctity. Philip was deeply in
love with her still ; all his children by the Queen,
none of whom had been sons, had expired at,
or soon after, their births, and this boy by
the *Calderona* was held to be the most beautiful
and perfect child ever seen. Philip tried hard to
alter the resolve of his mistress, but she absolutely
refused to cohabit with him again ; and at last,
but with sorrow, he gave way, and the actress Maria
Calderon became the abbess of a remote convent,
whilst her child was sent with semi-royal surround-

ings to be educated with exquisite care at Ocaña,
with a view to his future greatness.

This was the background : a vast conspiracy of
make-shift and of make-believe, before which the
Court of Philip IV. alternately prayed and postured
unconvinced. An utterly decadent society, of which
each individual was striving to get as much as possible out of life without giving anything in return ;
a society which combined besotted superstition and
abject servility to priests and ritual with appalling
impiety, a society that lived from day to day for
such pleasures as it could grasp, knowing that all
was crumbling to dissolution beneath its feet, that
squandered and lavished money, mostly ill-gotten,
in empty splendour, whilst the whole nation beyond
the mud walls of the " Court " was sunk in carking
penury. And amidst the festivities and stage
plays, the poetical recitals, the battues that stood
for sport, and the *autos-de-fe* that stood for holi-
ness, " Philip the Great " moved like a demigod,
knowing in his heart of hearts that all was hollow—
his wealth a lie, his dignity a mask, and he himself
but a poor sinning trifler whose coward conscience
denied him even pleasure in his sin.

Philip's love for ostentation had full opportunity for its exercise in October 1629, when, six
months after the birth of his son by the *Calderona*,
an heir was born to the Spanish crowns. The
month had begun with splendour, for on the 3rd
October the Prince of Guastalla had entered the
capital as the envoy of the Emperor to marry by
proxy the Infanta Maria for the King of Hungary,
heir to the imperial crown. The whole of the
grandees of Spain had gone out to receive him,

o

and his train of thirty-six pages and lackeys in liveries of black velvet and gold, and his thirty-six baggage horses with crimson and gold horse-cloths, the Spanish nobles being so numerous and smart, as Soto says, that " Madrid looked like another Indies for richness." Before the splendours of Guastalla's welcome had become dim, the prince of so many prayers was born, and Madrid settled down to another orgy of festivities. The magnificence of the baptism in the Church of St. John near the palace need not be detailed in full ; suffice it to say that a temporary staircase and gallery splendidly adorned with tapestries descended from the great balcony over the palace portico to the church. Down this corridor, in a sedan chair of silver and crystal, preceded by heralds and followed by crowds of nobles, the child was carried very slowly to its baptism on the lap of the Countess of Olivares. On the left hand of the chair marched Olivares himself, strangely dressed, as was remarked at the time, in a long robe of cloth of silver with sleeves reaching to the ground, his breast crossed by a crimson baldric—some ceremonial dress, it was thought, of the house of Austria. Then came the new Queen of Hungary, her nephew's godmother, and the rest of the high personages, to attend the ceremony. It was against the etiquette for the King to be there, but he was too proud and happy to forego the pleasure of seeing the show secretly, which he did from a closely curtained pew reached from the adjoining house. The Countess of Olivares, as supreme in the palace as her husband was in the Government, held the child at the font, seated upon " a chair of rock

crystal, the most costly piece of furniture ever
seen in Europe," whilst cardinals and bishops did
their best to make Prince Baltasar Carlos of
Austria a member of the Christian Church. As
soon as the Queen was able to appear, which was
on her birthday, she was feted in her turn as she
had never been feted before. Masked equestrian
contests, torchlight parades, bull-fights, and balls
succeeded each other day after day, and in all of
them the King and his brother, Don Carlos, made
a gallant appearance.[1]

The fact that both Philip and Olivares were
accomplished horsemen made equestrian pastimes
and field sports specially fashionable in this the
best period of Philip's reign. At least two realistic
representations exist of hunting battues in which
Philip was seen to great advantage, reproducing
from the brush of the great painter the exact aspect
of such diversions. That in the Ashburton Collection
portrays one of the deer hunts in the leafy glades
of Aranjuez, Philip's spring palace on the Tagus,
twenty-eight miles from Madrid. In the wooded
park the afternoon sun glints through the dark
verdured trees against the cloudless sky, and upon
a wide stretch of sward a great white canvas
enclosure is erected. Into its gradually narrowing
limits the frightened deer are being driven by
beaters, and at the narrow end of the funnel, the
only outlet from the enclosure, the "hunters"
are stationed on prancing steeds. Over the
narrowest part of the funnel neck a leafy bridge
or balcony is built, decked with crimson hangings
and furnished with soft cushions, upon which the

---

[1] All are described *ad nauseam* in the Soto y Aguilar MS.

Queen and her ladies sit, dressed in brilliant colours. Just beneath them, on horseback, are the King, his brother Carlos, and the inevitable Olivares; and as the terrified deer rush past them underneath the ladies' bower, the cavaliers, with big sharp hunting-knives, slash at them, killing some, laming others, and leaving those they miss to the mercies of the hounds that await them beyond. The ground beneath is drenched with blood, but the ladies smile approvingly upon the butchery. The exercise demanded a firm seat in the saddle, and great agility and dexterity in the management of the horse, and it was universally admitted that no one in Spain shone so brilliantly at these battues as Philip himself,[1] though Olivares, courtier like, was only just inferior to him.

The other picture by Velazquez, which is in the National Gallery in London, presents a sport somewhat less repugnant to English eyes. The scene in this case is the hunting seat of the Pardo, a few miles out of Madrid, and the King, within the canvas walls of the vast enclosure, is, from the saddle of his caracoling steed, which he sits like a centaur, thrusting his forked javelin into the flank of the boar as it rushes past, Olivares being close by, whilst other mounted courtiers in different

---

[1] Most of the Spanish kings have been fanatical devotees of the chase in various forms. During the reign of Philip's father it used to be said that " Lerma and the woods were King." Philip IV. spent much time in field sports. In a letter from the Venetian ambassador in Madrid, enclosed in one from Dermond O'Sullivan Bear to an Irish correspondent (March 1628), the following passage occurs: " The King is so inclined to horse exercise and hunting, that Olivares manages to keep him at it all day, thus leaving the King no time to do anything but sign the decisions of the Councils, which suits Olivares perfectly." Record Office, S.P. Spain 34, MSS.

parts of the enclosure are participating in the sport. Inside the enclosure there are stationed some of the heavy leather-curtained coaches then in use, filled with ladies. The mules in every case have been unharnessed and put out of the way of a charge from an infuriated boar ; but as the boars were agile when aroused, and had been known to leap into the carriages themselves, the ladies inside are armed with dainty little javelins to repel any such attempt ; not very easy to happen, one would imagine, as the heavy leather aprons or screens that cover the footplate and serve as doors are closed.

To look upon these pictures is to view the very life of Philip's Court ; the posturing gentlemen outside the enclosure, the prancing gentlemen inside. Beyond agile showy horsemanship and well-trained steeds, nothing was called for on the part of those who joined in the sport. There was no danger, and little exertion needed from the " hunters," for the quarry was all driven into the enclosure, and could not get away. One sees that ostentation and " show-off " are the main attraction and object of the sport ; and in the sports, as in the pleasures and devotions, the same inevitable note is struck : that of selfish epicureanism that seeks to enjoy sensuously without risk or labour. Each poor mortal is marked out in his own esteem as the central point of a brilliant show, and gorges the best of life's banquet to the end, careless of who pays the scot.

CHAPTER VI

RENEWED WAR WITH FRANCE LATE IN 1628—
RECONCILIATION WITH ENGLAND—THE PALA-
TINATE AGAIN—COTTINGTON IN MADRID—HIS
RECEPTION AND NEGOTIATIONS WITH OLIVARES
AND PHILIP—FETES IN MADRID FOR BIRTH OF
THE PRINCE OF WALES—DEATH OF SPINOLA—
TREATY OF CASALE—A "LOCAL PEACE" WITH
FRANCE—SPAIN AND THE THIRTY YEARS' WAR
—POVERTY AND MISERY OF THE COUNTRY—
UNPOPULARITY OF OLIVARES — HIS MONOPOLY
OF POWER—HIS GREAT ENTERTAINMENT TO
THE KING — HIS INTERVENTION IN PHILIP'S
DOMESTIC AFFAIRS — "DON FRANCISCO FER-
NANDO OF AUSTRIA"—THE BUEN RETIRO—
HOPTON IN MADRID—HIS DESCRIPTIVE LETTERS
—THE INFANTES—PHILIP'S VISIT TO BARCELONA
—DISCONTENT OF THE CORTES—THE INFANTE
FERNANDO LEFT AS GOVERNOR—DEATH OF THE
INFANTE CARLOS — DEATH OF THE INFANTA
ISABEL IN FLANDERS—THE INFANTE FERNANDO
ON HIS WAY THITHER WINS BATTLE OF NORD-
LINGEN—GREAT WAR NOW INEVITABLE WITH
FRANCE

THE Spaniards for all their poverty had never
ceased to send men and money in plenty to the
Emperor for his eternal war against freedom of
conscience in Germany, and to the Infanta Isabel

against Holland. But Richelieu, hampered with
a war with England about the unfulfilled conditions of Henrietta Maria's marriage contract,
had kept the peace with Spain since January 1626.
An English fleet co-operated with the Huguenots
at Rochelle, but Richelieu was equal to the occasion, and he and Marshal Schomberg together
sent back Buckingham and his fleet disgraced and
defeated, with a loss of two-thirds of his force,
after which—late in 1628—Richelieu, relieved of the
terrible siege of Rochelle, could turn his attention
again to the doings of Olivares and the Spaniards.
The pretext for fighting this time was the old
question of the duchy of Mantua, which, being
vacant, was claimed by a French and an Italian
imperial pretender ; and Olivares, thinking in any
case to grab something for Spain, seized the strong
place of Casale in Montferrat, aided and abetted
on this occasion by the Duke of Savoy, who, greedy
and discontented as usual, had again changed
sides. As soon as Richelieu was partially free
from the struggle with the Huguenots, he sent a
French army to oust the invaders from Mantuan
territory ; and once more Philip saw himself pledged
to a national war with France for a cause which
was of no interest whatever to his Spanish subjects ;
a war in which if he were victor he could gain little
or nothing, whilst if he were vanquished he might
lose enormously.

Olivares began by concentrating his resources,
recalling Spinola from Flanders to meet the French
in Italy ; and once more smiling upon England,
where Buckingham, smarting under his ignominious
defeat at Oléron by Richelieu, in the previous year,

was raising another fleet at Portsmouth to relieve Rochelle. He was assassinated by Felton in August 1628, and the fleet under Lord Lindsay arrived too late to succour the heroic Huguenots, who had been at last obliged to surrender in October 1628. France was then free to launch her whole force against Spain, and peace with England, which had been desirable for Spain before, become an absolute necessity. The need was a bitter one for Olivares, for friendship and alliance with a heretic power was an open confession to the world that Spain's proud claim to the possession of a divine mandate to crush heterodoxy throughout the world could not be enforced.

But past insincerities and present inconsistencies on the part of Spain weighed but little with Charles I. of England against the flattering vision of obtaining for his German brother-in-law the restoration of the Palatinate by the influence of Philip, and he welcomed the informal approaches which for some time past had been made to him by Olivares. The plotting with the Irish Catholics, which had been busily carried on from Madrid, through O'Sullivan (Count of Bearhaven), Burke (Marquis of Mayo), the agents of Tyrone and Tyrconnel and the Irish friars,[1] was suddenly cooled by Olivares, much to the disgust of the exiles; and the Irish Dominican, who had been sent from Spain to sound Charles I., reported that peace might now be easily settled in England. Simultaneously Father Scaglia, an Italian friar, had been sent from Turin by the Earl of Carlisle to Madrid

---

[1] See letters from Madrid to Eugene Field in the Monastery of Timoleague, etc., in Record Office, S.P. Spain 34, 1627.

upon a similar mission, and reported that he had seen Olivares, and that everything was ready for Cottington's arrival in Spain to settle terms.[1] Rubens also took a hand in the game. He was painting industriously in Madrid, and was in high favour with Philip, but held secret credentials from Charles I., and wrote enthusiastically about the approaching friendship of the two countries.[2] The preliminaries were not altogether easy to arrange. The Irish exiles in Madrid were still clamorous for armed Spanish aid to their desired rebellion, and were discontented at Olivares' *volte face*, whilst Charles I. himself, who had been tricked before by the Count-Duke, wanted something definite about the Palatinate before he sent Cottington openly to Spain. Scaglia tried hard and hopefully all through 1628 to get matters in train. Olivares was graciousness itself in his usual non-committal way ;[3] but when the need for peace became pressing, he tired at last of this slow progress, and decided to send Rubens to London in the summer of 1629 with the rank of Secretary of the Council and Ambassador.

At length, thanks largely to Rubens' personality,

[1] Scaglia to Carlisle. Record Office, S.P. Spain 34, MS., 19th January 1628.

[2] Rubens to Carlisle. Record Office, S.P. Spain 34, MS., January 1628, etc.

[3] A good specimen of his style is seen in his reply to a letter from Scaglia early in April 1629 (Record Office, S.P. Spain 34, MS.), asking for an audience at the desire of Lord Carlisle, in order to tell Olivares how much Carlisle esteems him. "I will give this audience to your lordship very willingly to-night (writes Olivares), and it will give me most particular pleasure to talk about the Earl of Carlisle, of whom I am the most affectionate servitor, and have been so all through the worst tribulations; although when he was here I always considered him a friend of France. . . . The differences that have taken place between us are all owing to French intrigue."

all the thorny preliminaries were settled, and Cottington started in November 1629, but with strict orders from Charles that he was not to ask for audience until the Spanish ambassador Coloma, who was being sent from Brussels but had been delayed, should present himself in London. For Charles was still distrustful of Olivares, and feared a trick to make him appear the suppliant for peace. Rubens was prompt in conveying this suspicion to Olivares, who was quite shocked that anyone should doubt his sincerity. His letter to Cottington, received by the latter when he landed at Lisbon, elaborately explains the delay in Coloma's arrival in London by the necessity for the ambassador to remain with the Infanta in Flanders for a time until the Marquis of Aytona arrived there, owing to the loss of Bois le Duc, and ends in a holograph postscript deploring that he should be so distrusted : " You cannot think how this business has distressed me ! " [1]

Nothing was left undone by Olivares to win Cottington, always a pro-Spaniard. He was offered as a present the whole of the customs dues (£5000) on a great English ship's cargo of goods, allowed by special licence to enter Lisbon at the same time as he did, which gift he refused, and all along the road from Lisbon to Madrid evidence of thought for his comfort met him. On the other hand, Charles I. could not do enough to honour Coloma when he came to a state dinner at Whitehall on Twelfth Day, 1630, where there were so many ladies to do him honour, writes Lord Dorchester to Cottington, " that there were many fallings out

[1] Record Office, S.P. Spain 34, MS., December 1629.

amongst them for spoyling one another's ruffs, by being so close ranked." [1]   But amiable as were the appearances, the distrust was deep, especially on the side of the English.   When Cottington arrived within a day's journey from Madrid, he sent his coadjutor, Mr. Arthur Hopton, ahead to discover what preparations were made to receive him.   He learnt, to his surprise, that Philip was absent from the capital, having gone to escort his sister, the Infanta Queen of Hungary, on her way to her new home, and that Olivares had been left behind to do the honours to the English envoy. Cottington was determined that this should not be, so he dodged the host of grandees, who had been sent out with coaches and guards to welcome him, and entered Madrid secretly by night.   No sooner had he arrived at his lodging than Olivares presented himself, but the Englishman flatly refused to receive him there, and, entering a coach, drove off to the palace to offer his respects to the Queen in the absence of the King, and seek audience through Olivares as first minister.

There, in his apartment, Olivares kept Cottington in converse until midnight, using all his blandishments to persuade the Englishman that he meant to deal straightforwardly this time.   " All my art of fence," wrote Cottington, "·could not keep him from entering into the principal business, yet but flashed and intermixed with other points.   He could not doubt, he said, that I had brought orders to renew the peace negotiations at least. I said yes, if I found good resolutions to give satisfaction to my King (Charles) and his friends

[1] Record Office, S.P. Spain 34, 10th January 1630.

and allies. I know your meaning, he said, ye would have restitution of the Palatinate. Yes, said I; but that is not all. You know that my King has made a league with the States, and their interests must also be considered." The protestations and heated disputes continued between them thus for hours; the point of Olivares evidently being to secure the marriage of the Palgrave's son with a daughter of the Emperor or other Spanish nominee without a prior restitution of any part of the Palatinate. At last Olivares rose, and, taking Cottington by the hand, said : " The King of England shall do the greatest work in Christendom, for by his means the Palatinate shall be entirely restored, and by his means also the King of Spain shall find peace in those northern parts." [1]

Whilst the two statesmen were talking, the Countess of Olivares entered with a message from the Queen, to ask after the health of King Charles. Cottington was rigid. King Charles, he said, had sent a letter to the Queen by him, though she had not written to him for a good many years ; and when he delivered the letter he had a good mind to tell her so, as King Charles was very much offended. Both Olivares and his wife were much concerned at this, and asked Cottington what had better be done. You may tell the Queen, he replied, that she might write a letter to King Charles, and send it to the Spanish Ambassador in London before the King of England's letter was delivered to her. This was promised, and when finally Cottington was led to the Queen he found her all smiles and

[1] Cottington to Dorchester, 29th January 1630, Record Office, S.P. Spain 34, MS.

kindness for the ambassador of her brother-in-law, for matters were complicated terribly by the fact that she was the sister of Queen Henrietta Maria.

Philip was not expected to return to Madrid for several days, and in the meantime it was necessary for Olivares somehow to worm out the nature and extent of the Englishman's instructions. On Monday, two days after the interview just described, Olivares made the excuse of taking Cottington out hawking, to get him quietly in the country and alone all day from morn till dark. But they had no sport, says Cottington ruefully, for the Count-Duke was so eager in his talk that he forgot all about the hawks. The disputations, now on horseback, now in a coach, often waxed angry. The States would not have a peace, but wanted a truce, said Olivares. They will not have either, replied the Englishman, unless my King's demands are granted. How can we restore the Palatinate ? blustered Olivares, which is held mostly by Bavaria. Then Cottington in a rage said he should go back to England immediately, as he saw they had been deceived. If you do, retorted Olivares, we will make a league of half Europe against you.[1]

On Friday the King arrived in the capital, and great efforts were made to persuade Cottington to leave Madrid, and make a state entry, but this he refused to do. The next best thing was to send the whole Court in its finest garb to accompany him to the palace for his first audience with Philip. Nothing could exceed the honour paid him, though

[1] Cottington to Dorchester, 29th January 1630. Record Office, S.P. Spain MS.

on that occasion nothing political was discussed. But on the next day, in private conference, Cottington came to close quarters with Philip. The great question, of course, was that of the Palatinate. Philip assured Cottington that he would give every satisfaction on that point if he only had patience until powers came from Germany. As the Englishman left only half convinced, Philip called him back and asked him why the English would not accept a suspension of hostilities. Because, replied Cottington, it would look like a surrender of the point about the Palatinate. There can be no peace, he said, until that question is settled.

The weeks dragged on, every trifling point being utilised by Olivares to keep the negotiations afoot, and relieve Spain of the strain of war with England, without ceding—what it was clear they could not cede—the restoration of the Palatinate, which was mostly held by the Germans. An interminable wrangle took place about the titles to be given to the King of England : whether he should be called Majesty, which the Spaniards always gave grudgingly to any king but their own. Then it appeared that the draft protocols sent by Coloma from London gave Charles the style of " King, etc.," without his full titles, and "Defender of the Faith." Although it was late at night when the courier arrived, Cottington hurried off to complain to Philip of this. The King of England shall be given whatever style he likes, laughed Philip. Then there was a lengthy squabble about the styles to be used by the two sister-Queens in writing to each other. When that was settled, Cottington grumbled incessantly at all this intriguing with the Catholic Irish rebels, and at Tyrone's presence in Madrid. Again and again Cottington, tired of Olivares' shilly-shally, was for returning to England post haste, but the Count-Duke always managed to smooth matters over by assuring him that they would really use all their influence to get the Palatinate restored if he only had patience.

But at length, in March 1630, Cottington's long-suffering gave way. He saw, he says, that he was being played with, and he sent Hopton to England to ask permission for him to come home. Charles was loath to give up hope, but he too was beginning to doubt the good faith of Philip and his minister, and sent instructions that there must be no more delay. Spain wants peace, but before peace can be made by England, Philip must say clearly and promptly what portion of the Palatinate he will guarantee to restore. When this message from England was brought to Madrid by Hopton in the middle of May, Philip and Olivares took fright, for a continuance of the war with England whilst they were at war with France meant certain ruin for Spain, and yet they could not take the Palatinate from Catholic hands and restore it to Protestant Frederick.

So again the blandishments re-commenced. "Pray tell me your real opinion," asked Philip of Cottington. "My real opinion, sire, is that I shall return at once, unless some means be found for making peace with the Hollanders and raising the ban against Palgrave," replied the Englishman. Philip very rarely showed anger or emotion of any sort, but he grew impatient and cross at

Cottington's insistence, which he attributed to his personal desire to return home for domestic reasons. Rojas, the friend of Velazquez, and Olivares' factotum, came and implored Cottington as a friend to deal plainly with him, and tell him whether he was really going home ; and Olivares himself sent for him late at night to ply him with remonstrances and expostulations.[1]

And thus the juggle went on for months, until at last Charles I., himself sorely needing peace, gave way and sent instructions to Cottington to make a treaty with Spain, leaving all questions still unprejudiced, like the agreement of 1604, with which this book began. Thenceforward all was straight sailing, for Olivares had once more worked his way, and attained the peace that was necessary for Spain, and yet pledging Philip to nothing. Whilst yet the final terms were being settled, with which Rubens was to be sent to London, news came to Madrid of the birth of a son and heir to the King of England. On the 15th June, Philip received Cottington in full state to congratulate him upon the news. Never in the brightest time had the old palace of Madrid put on a braver aspect, for now that in the essential matter of peace the King had gained his point, in that of ceremonial rejoicing he was determined there should be no shortcoming. Surrounded by a full gathering of grandees in gold chains, Philip stood under his canopy dressed in his military garb, almost English in fashion, as he stands in the Dulwich Gallery portrait, with a splendidly embroidered scarlet

[1] Cottington to Dorchester, MS. Record Office, S.P. Spain 34, many letters in 1630.

ropilla doublet, a broad lace collar and "paned" hose, his breast covered with rich jewels and with a great feather in his hat.   As Sir Francis Cottington approached him the King expressed his joy at the news.   He was as glad, he said, as if the son had been his own ; and he had prayed upon his knees for the happiness of the young prince.   Then the delighted Englishman visited the two Infantes to receive their good wishes, they being, as Cottington says, " no less brave in attire " than their brother.   In the afternoon another state visit was paid to the Queen, and to the baby Prince Baltasar Carlos, " in cap and feathers and loaded with charms and jewels." Solemn proclamation of the news was made by heralds in the public squares ; the Calle Mayor and the Plaza were illuminated as bright as day with wax torches, and a great firework display was made before the palace.   Every religious house in Madrid held a solemn service of thanks, and all the priors visited the English ambassador with their congratulations.   Four days afterwards, one of the big royal bull-fights, in honour of the birth of a Prince of Wales, was given by Philip in the presence of Cottington in the Plaza Mayor, at which twenty bulls were killed, with many horses and three men.[1]   At length the treaty of peace, the real object of all the plausibility, was settled.   Olivares had won the game again.   England and Spain were at peace, with the Palatinate still unrestored, and Cottington left Spain, that he knew so well, outwitted for the second time by the bland procrastination of Spanish diplomacy.

[1] Cottington to Dorchester, July 1630, Record Office, S.P. Spain MS.

Once more the rivals, Richelieu and Olivares, France and Spain, were face to face in North Italy ; the Pope, Venice, and the new Duke of Mantua (Nevers) being on the side of France. Richelieu was victorious almost everywhere over the Spaniards, Germans, and Savoyards. Carlo Emmanuele sank to the grave broken hearted, leaving his ancient duchy in the occupation of the French conquerors, and Spinola died of grief before Casale at the scant support and ungenerous treatment he received from Spain. His successor, Santa Cruz, patched up an ignominious treaty with the French in the field, to the violent indignation of the Spaniards at home ; for the country which had paid most for the war had gained nothing by the peace. But the treaty of Casale was merely a local pacification between France and Spain. The house of Austria must be crushed, if France were to be raised to the first rank amongst the nations. Olivares unhappily could not shake off the imperial traditions which had been the ruin of Spain ; and for many years to come Spanish men and money wrung from starving Castile were still poured in an endless stream to fill the armies of the Emperor. Year after year the deadly struggle went on in Central Europe. Sweden and the Protestants with France on the one side, the house of Austria and the Catholics of Germany on the other ; with Spain and Spanish Flanders as the milch cow to provide the wherewithal to face all the progressive elements of Europe.

With the vicissitudes of this epochal war between antagonistic civilisations the present book is not directly concerned, but only with such echoes and influences of it as reached the Court of Spain.

Battles and sieges, the death of heroes and the fall of kings, seared their deep brand upon the page of history. Spain, bereft of commerce and almost of industry, might in its agony protest with passionate tears that it could suffer no more, and lower its dark brows when the arrogant minister who ruled the fainéant King was mentioned.[1] But through it all Madrid laughed and rioted with ghastly gaiety and pagan fatalism, eating, drinking, and making merry, lest before to-morrow it should die. Outside its mud walls the fields lay bare and arid, in the provincial cities sloth and apathy ruled supreme over grass-grown market squares and empty streets; but in the Court, " the only Court," the Madrileños boastfully called it, shameless waste ran riot still; flaunting finery elbowed aside the squalid parasites that sought its smiles and struggled for its scraps ; vain shows and vainer posturings filled the hollow days, and the witling who had pompously declaimed a turgid epic upon the nation's glory was held a hundred times a greater hero than he who starved in Flemish dykes, or rotted of putrid fever in overcrowded hosts before a German city, fighting and dying, as scores of thousands of them did, for the vague mirage of Spanish honour, of which the Court of Philip the Great was the centre and the source.

There is no doubt that deep discontent

[1] W. Gardiner, writing to Lord Dorchester when Cottington landed at Lisbon in 1629, says : " This city has now lost all its ancient splendour since I was here seventeen years ago. It is now completely ruined. All the merchants are bankrupt, and all their commodities are gone except their diamonds, Brazil tobacco, and coarse sugar, all of which are dearer here than in Holland. There is great discontent with Castilian rule, and especially some new laws whose object is to bring them more absolutely under the King." Record Office, S.P. Spain 34, MS.

smouldered throughout the country at the results of Olivares' policy. Spaniards were ready enough to acclaim the privilege and duty of their country to set all the world right about religion, and to interfere in the quarrels of Central Europe. The boastful vainglory of Spanish superiority and the hollow pretence of the King's irresistible power and wealth were as popular as ever, though evidence of their falsity was patent in every house in the land. But though by most Spaniards the dire effect was not traced to its true cause, and they never thought of blaming themselves for their sufferings, the minister who was the protagonist of the system was held personally to be the cause of all the trouble. Already the outer realms, Aragon, Catalonia, Valencia, and Portugal, understood clearly that Olivares aimed at destroying their ancient autonomy,[1] and were seething in anger against him and the triflers at Madrid. The greater nobles, even in Castile itself, disgusted at the monopolous arrogance of Olivares, stood ostentatiously aloof from him, only awaiting an opportunity to retaliate. The minister had taken care to place in the councils persons entirely subservient to him, or those whose age or feebleness of character made them innocuous. His principal

---

[1] In a letter sent by Abbé Scaglia to Lord Carlisle in 1628 a long document is enclosed, drawn up by the Marquis of Leganés, who was Olivares' principal instrument and a kinsman, advocating the absorption of Portugal by Spain. The evil and danger of the existing want of unity are pointed out, and the need to arouse a united national spirit is enforced. This document, supplementing those of Olivares himself quoted on an earlier page, show that the propaganda in favour of national unity was pushed persistently, and the outer realms were naturally alarmed and disturbed at the threat implied to them. Record Office, S.P. Spain 34, MS.

subordinate ministers were his own kinsmen,—the Count of Monterey; the Marquis del Carpio; Marquis of Leganés; the Marquis of Aytona; the Marquis of Heliche, who had married his only daughter, but to Olivares' intense grief had been left a widower within the year; and the Duke of Medina de las Torres; Cardinal Zapata, the Inquisitor-General and member of many Councils, who was old, weak, and foolish; and the King's confessor, Sotomayor, was a man of no character, and entirely sold to the minister.

It will be seen, therefore, that Philip was quite inaccessible to anyone not in the interests of Olivares. The Queen resented her husband's isolation, but the minister and his wife kept her also well under subjection, and her love of pleasure made her almost as easy to manage as the King.

If it had been possible, even now, for the whole truth to be told to Philip as to the real causes of the poverty and wretchedness that afflicted the country, a prompt reversal of the policy that caused it might have arrested the ruin. But, in any case, it was unlikely that such change should be made; for Philip himself failed to see, as did the friends as well as the foes of Olivares, that only by a frank acceptance of the fact that Spain must abandon all her old flighty notions and impossible claims, could prosperity be brought back to the country. To prevent the danger of Philip's either discovering for himself or being told by others how deep and growing the discontent of the country was, Olivares plunged the idle young King more completely than ever in the pleasures and distractions that occupied most of his time and thoughts. Hunting,

play-going, religious ceremonies, literary amusements, and other entertainments left no opportunity for investigation and sustained application to
business by the King. It is evident that now,
whatever may have been the case at the beginning
of the reign, the minister deliberately promoted
this waste of time for his own ends ; and his efforts
to distract the King increased as the discontent in
the country and Court grew.

On the 1st June 1631, for instance, the Countess
of Olivares gave a sumptuous entertainment to
the sovereigns, as she was in the habit of doing
on every possible pretext, in the gardens of her
brother, the Count of Monterey ; [1] and this is represented by the contemporary chronicler, who describes both fetes to have aroused the emulation
of her husband to give another entertainment to
the King and Queen on the night of St. John, three
weeks later, that should eclipse all similar occasions.
The document from which I am quoting, written by
a whole-souled admirer of Olivares, is too long
and tedious for reproduction entire here, but a
few extracts from it may be interesting as showing
how desperately the Olivares tried to please.

" Although there were but few days to arrange
everything, the Count-Duke was determined to show
the extreme love and care with which he serves
our Lord the King, and how easily he conquers
the most difficult tasks by means of it. As a
beginning of the preparations for the feast, which

[1] The house and garden of Monterey occupied the centre portion of
the space facing the Salon del Prado, between the Calle de Alcala and the
Carrera de San Geronimo.

was, amongst many other things, to include two
new comedies not yet even thought of, much less
written, his Excellency ordered Lope de Vega
to write one, which he did in three days, and D.
Francisco de Quevedo and D. Antonio de Mendoza
the other, which they wrote in a single day, and
the comedies were handed to the companies of
Avendaño and Vallejo, the two best now on the
boards, to study and rehearse."

Notwithstanding his constant state occupations,
Olivares is said to have worked night and day
in personally making the preparations for the
great fete. Not only the garden of Monterey, but
those on each side of it[1] were appropriated ; and
a great Italian architect, who had designed the
wonderful jasper pantheon of the Kings at the
Escorial, was commissioned to build a beautiful
open-air theatre and a series of improvised edifices
for the accommodation of the principal guests.
Like magic, thanks to lavish expenditure, there
sprang up in the shady gardens a gorgeously up-
holstered chamber or bower with chairs of state for
the King and his two brothers, and the customary
cushions for the Queen, placed in a projecting
balcony from which the stage could be seen, with two
similar apartments, one on each side, for the suite,
and retired nooks or niches between them, we are
told, in which the Count and Countess of Olivares
might watch over the comfort of their guests. A

---

[1] Occupying thus the whole of the space from the Calle de Alcalá to
the Carrera de San Geronimo. That on the north is now covered by the
new Bank of Spain, and that on the south is still the palace of the Duke
of Villahermosa, the descendant of the Duke of Maqueda, to whom it
then belonged.

stage, surrounded and crowned by a multitude of lights in crystal globes, and decked with flowers, faced the royal pavilions, and on each side seats were provided for the ladies of the Court, but no gentleman was allowed to be present. By the wall separating the gardens from the Prado great stands were erected to accommodate the six orchestras and choirs that were ordered to be present, and the gentlemen guests, none of whom were asked to the garden itself. To each of Olivares' great kinsmen already mentioned was assigned a department : one was to superintend the rehearsals, another was to take charge of the marshalling of the coaches and the reception of the royal guests, another had under his care the refreshments, and so on.

On the day before the fête the Countess of Olivares dined in the garden, and witnessed a full dress rehearsal of the whole entertainment ; and Madrid was agog with excitement when, after dark on the night of St. John, all the grand folk from the palace in their heavy coaches lumbered down to the Prado to attend the fête. At nine o'clock the royal party were received by the Countess at the entrance pavilion which had been erected for the purpose, the united choirs chanting a pæan of welcome as the King and Queen advanced to the chamber whence they were to see the comedies. Gentlemen of the Count-Duke's household on their knees offered to the royal guests and their suite of ladies perfumes in crystal and gold flasks, scented lace handkerchiefs, bouquets, scented clay crocks,[1]

---

[1] These very fine pieces of red biscuit clay unglazed and highly scented were much prized ; and it was a vicious fashion, of ladies particularly, to masticate or eat this ware.

fans, etc., on silver salvers. Then, after a flourish of
trumpets and an overture on the guitars, Quevedo's
and Mendoza's new comedy was performed by
Vallejo's company. "*Who Lies Most Thrives Most*"
was the name of the piece, and we are told that it
was crammed " with the smart sayings and courtly
gallantry of Don Francisco de Quevedo, whose
genius is so favourably known in the world." The
principal actress was the famous Maria de Riquelme,[1]
who in verse welcomed the great guests, and praised
the King in a manner that, if he had not been case-
hardened to adulation, would have made an arch-
angel blush, whilst at the same time several strong
hints were introduced that the Count-Duke himself
was only one degree less divine than his master.

For two hours the stage entertainment went
on, with comedies, dances, poetry and music, all
present agreeing that Don Francisco de Quevedo
had in his one day's work put more wit and humour
than other authors would consider sufficient for a
dozen comedies. At one of the intervals, when
the first comedy was finished, the King and Queen
were conducted to the adjoining garden of the
Duke of Maqueda, where they found a series of

---

[1] This beautiful and gifted actress, the idol of the susceptible Madrileños,
was also for a wonder at that period a decent member of society. She
was a member of the charitable fraternity of Nuestra Señora de la Novena,
and was very devout. She died in 1656, and was buried at Barcelona in
the Augustan Monastery of St. Monica, where there was a special actors'
chapel. Fifty years afterwards, her body, and even the veil in which it
was enveloped, were found incorrupt, and she was thenceforward considered almost a saint. Juan de Caramuel wrote of her : " She was a
beautiful girl, gifted with so vehement an imagination that, to the surprise
of everyone, when she was acting her colour changed in accordance with
the emotions she portrayed. If the event represented were a pleasant
one, her face was rosy, whilst pallor cloaked her cheeks when the play
was sad and sorrowful. In this she was unique and inimitable."

beautiful chambers communicating with one another, and constructed entirely of flowers and
leaves. One of these was for the King and his
brothers, another for the Queen, and the third for
the ladies in attendance, and in each of the rooms
were disguises for the guests. For the King had
been provided a long brown cloak, trimmed with
great scrolls of black and silver, and closed by
frogs and olives of wrought silver, a white hat with
white and brown plumes, a shield of scented leather
and silver, and a white falling Walloon collar ;
similar but diverse disguises being provided for
the two princes. Upon a side table in each flower
chamber was a precious casket of morocco leather
and gold filled with choice sweetmeats, a variety
of perfumes, and some of the scented clay vessels of
which Spanish ladies of the day fancied the taste to
nibble and even sometimes to swallow. The Queen's
disguise was like that of the King, but with much
more adornment in the way of spangles and the
like ; and when the whole party had covered their
ordinary garb with these unusual additions, "strange
in shape and fashion," they were led in stately procession with much attitudinising to see the second
comedy, in which, says the awestricken chronicler,
"they lost no jot of the majesty which is not the
least of their inestimable virtues and perfections."

The assumption of these fantastic disguises
by the royal personages is elaborately apologised
for by the chronicler, by whom it was considered
apparently as a somewhat risky and undignified
experiment ; especially as, owing to it, no male
person except Olivares and his household was
admitted to the gardens themselves ; the gentlemen

of the Court being relegated to the stands by the
Prado wall, in order that they might not see the
King unbend sufficiently to don a disguise. When
Lope de Vega's new comedy, "*The Night of St.
John*," was finished, the royal party retired to
a banqueting-room constructed of flowers in the
other garden on the north. Here a sumptuous
supper was served at midnight, the King and Queen
at their high table being served by Olivares and his
wife, everything being done with perfect silence
and order,—"though a multitude of dishes were
carried to the musicians, singers, and gentlemen in
the orchestra stands." By the time the lights
were dimming, and the sky was turning to pearly
grey beyond the trees of St. Geronimo, the whole
stately company turned out in their coaches for
a drive up and down the Prado ; and then back to
the palace, doubtless to sleep.[1] When the dawn
broke fully, it was found that, notwithstanding
the prohibition, a perfect host of people, men and
boys, had surreptitiously found their way in from
the Prado, and, hidden in the copses and under
the stagings, they had witnessed the whole show,
including the questionable proceeding of risking the
majesty of monarchs by a fancy dress ; whereupon the chronicler attributes the quietness and

---

[1] Less than a fortnight after this costly feast, a terrible fire, which
threatened all Madrid with destruction, and demolished in the three
days it lasted half of the Plaza Mayor, took place (7th July 1631). The
loss and terror of the people were great ; but so wedded was the capital
to shows, that almost before the ashes were extinguished a great royal
bull-fight in the presence of the King and Court was held in the still
smoking square. During the corrida a house in the Plaza caught fire
again, and many of the panic-stricken people in their efforts to escape
were trampled upon and seriously injured. It is stated that Philip did
not even rise from his seat, and ordered the bull-fight to proceed.

patience of these intruders to the awe and reverence inspired by a king, no matter how dressed.[1]

As will be seen by this curious account, the hand of Olivares was everywhere. From handing the King his shirt in the morning and drawing his bed curtains at night, to deciding peace and war for the nation, the Count-Duke did everything. The King's amusements and amours were as much his affairs as were the routine duties of Government ; and I unearthed some years ago, and described fully in a former book of mine,[2] a curious series of original manuscript documents which prove that at the period now under review (1630-1635) the most secret domestic concerns of the King were settled by Olivares as a matter of course. The first document of the series [3] is a note written by Olivares to the King in 1630, saying that it was high time that a certain little boy, whose age is given as four years, should be concealed, and taken away from the people he was then with ; so that all trace of him may be broken. He has, he says, been thinking very deeply how this is to be done, and, as was usual with him, had found objections to every solution that has presented itself. But he thinks, upon the whole, that the child should be secretly put in the care of a certain gentleman of his acquaintance living at Salamanca, named Don Juan de Isasi Ydiaquez ; and the Count-Duke proposes that this gentleman should be summoned to Court without telling him why he was wanted ; and " after seeing him, your Majesty may decide."

---

[1] MS. account reproduced in Mesonero Romanos' *Antiguo Madrid.*
[2] *The Year after the Armada, and other Historical Studies.*
[3] Egerton MSS. 329, British Museum.

Across this document Philip has written in his big straggling hand : " It appears very necessary that something should be done in this matter, and I approve of your suggestion."

The rest of the papers unfold the poor sad little mystery. The babe in question was one of Philip's illegitimate children, christened Francisco Fernando, and he was probably his first son ; born, as we are told in these papers, at the house of his grand-parents, who were gentlefolk, between eleven and twelve at night on the 15th May 1626 ; Don Francisco de Eraso, Count of Humanes,[1] leading the midwife thither and being present at the birth, the infant being conveyed immediately afterwards to the house of Don Baltasar de Alamos, Councillor of the Treasury, where a nurse awaited him, in whose care he remained until he was delivered by Olivares to his new keeper, the hidalgo of Salamanca, who belonged to a notable bureaucratic and secretarial family. The subsequent short career of the infant does not enter into our present subject ; but it is fully detailed in the documents : the periodical reports of the child's progress, the grave discussions of Olivares with physicians and keepers as to his diet and health ; the provisions for his proper education, his clothing and diversions, his infantile ailments, the most trivial circumstances of the child's life, are all considered and passed in review by the minister, upon whose bowed shoulders the whole work of the State rested. The little left-handed royalty, for all the care with which his life was surrounded, failed to resist the bleak air

[1] This was a well-known noble poet and friend of Philip's in his dramatic amusements.

of Salamanca, and on the 17th March 1634 the
King's Secretary of State, Geronimo de Villanueva,
of whom we shall hear again, wrote to the hidalgo
Isasi Ydiaquez, saying " that his Majesty had
received with the deepest grief the news of the
death of Don Francisco Fernando, who showed
such bright promise for his tender years, and his
Majesty highly appreciated all the care that had
been taken with him." [1]   And a few days later, the
little corpse, dressed in a red and gold gown, and
enclosed in a black velvet coffin, was carried with
all secrecy to the Escorial, where, in the presence
of the inevitable Don Geronimo de Villanueva, the
secretary and confidential agent of the King, the
" body of Don Francisco Fernando, son of his
Catholic Majesty Don Felipe IV.," was handed to
the bishop of Avila in the porch of the church, and
buried by the friars in the vaults of their monastery.

The frowning old Alcazar on the cliff overlooking the Manzanares, so often mentioned as
the scene of Philip's festivities, was unfit for gaiety,
and offered but few attractions to him.   The
Escorial for similar reasons was never a favourite
residence of his ; and Aranjuez was always in-
salubrious except in the spring.   The Court therefore was usually in residence in Madrid itself, or in
the neighbouring hunting seat of the Pardo.   But
there was in the extensive and beautiful grounds
attached to the monastery of St. Geronimo at the
east gate of the capital a suite of apartments used

---

[1] Philip showed his appreciation of the services of Don Juan Isasi
Ydiaquez in the most flattering way, by at once appointing him governor
and tutor of his legitimate son and heir, the promising little Don Baltasar
Carlos, then five years old.

by the royal family for religious or mourning re-
treats, or for an occasional guest house. It occurred
to Olivares in 1631 that this place might be made
more attractive, and used more frequently as a
relief to Philip from the stern mediæval palace
at the other end of the town. The idea began
with the mere levelling of an inequality here, the
clearing of a lawn there, and the building of an
aviary and a few fountains and summer houses.
But very soon the Count-Duke's ambition grew, and
he and Philip became fascinated and absorbed in the
building of a palace which became to the reign of
Philip what Versailles was to that of Louis XIV.

The palace of the Buen Retiro was intended by
Olivares, and truly was, a fit setting for the elegant,
chivalric, and poetic surroundings of the King, a
light and pretty retreat in the midst of enchanting
gardens, where upon stages under the trees or in
high and gilded halls the witty dissolute comedies
might be played to an audience of the elect. Nothing
that the inspiration of genius, the efforts of flattery,
or the exercise of unrestrained expenditure could
compass was spared by Olivares in making the
Buen Retiro perfect for its purpose of keeping the
King diverted. An immense territory, in addition
to the monastery grounds, was appropriated for
the purpose,[1] and Olivares exhausted all the
horticultural knowledge of the time in laying out

[1] The vast park of Madrid represents part of the grounds which ran
up from the present line of the Prado to the extreme end of the present
park on the east, and included the whole space from the Alcala to the
Atocha. Olivares had kept his plan secret from the King as long as he
could, having gradually acquired the ground without disclosing his intention. The Venetian ambassador Corner mentions in 1635 with surprise
that the whole place had sprung up in two years.

the grounds with lakes, grottoes, and cascades;
whilst in a very short time there arose in all its
beauty the palace that in future was to be the symbol
of Philip's elegant, picturesque, but useless reign.

Even before the building itself was finished,
the place was inaugurated by a ceremony characteristic both of Philip and his minister. On
the 1st October 1632, the King paid his visit
to see the preparations being made for the festival
to be held in celebration of the birth of an heir to
his sister the Queen of Hungary. When he approached the new royal house, he was met by
Olivares, who had conferred upon himself the
post of honorary Constable of the Palace, bearing
upon a silver salver the gold master-keys of the
Buen Retiro.[1] Kneeling, he handed them to the
King, who, touching them with his hand, signified
that the bearer should retain them; and when,
later, the festivities commenced in the recently
built rooms, to continue thereafter for many days,
Philip and his wife fairly fell in love with the place,
whose lightsome grace was a revelation to them
after the dark old Alcazar.

First there was a showy cane tourney, in which
the King on horseback, with Olivares at his side,
led a glittering troop of riders, Philip taking part
in the festivities, as the flattering poet said, " not
as a king but as a most gallant skilful gentleman."
This splendid show the greatest poet of his time,
Lope de Vega, then rapidly sinking into the grave,
celebrated in verse. " The Vega del Parnaso,"

---

[1] The only portions of the palace now remaining are the Artillery
Museum, and the fine concert hall, built by Philip V., and decorated by Luca
Giordano.   The ancient church of the monastery, of course, still exists.

dedicated to the first festival of the new palace, was an appropriate swan's song of the great dramatist, whose inexhaustible wit and invention had done so much to lead the thoughts of his countrymen to the theatrical expression of which this new fairy palace was to be the apotheosis. Afterwards there was one of the usual bull-fights ; then running at the ring, with rich prizes of silver plate, of course won by the King, and afterwards a ball was held in the unfinished halls, at which, as at a modern cotillon, "perfumed purses of ducats and rich dress lengths" were given to the lady dancers.[1]

Only a few months before this, the Church of St. Geronimo had been the scene of another of those stately ceremonials which were the birthright of Spanish princes. There, upon a splendidly decked staging before the high altar, the tiny Prince Baltasar Carlos, who had been carried thither the day before, received the oaths of the Commons of Castile as heir to the throne. There were two violent altercations for precedence between nobles, even in the King's presence, before the ceremony ; but all was silence as the chubby princeling, in crimson plush embroidered with gold, toddled up the nave to the staging, held in leading strings by his two uncles Carlos and Fernando ; the first in a few months to sink into the grave, a silent, amiable young enigma to the last. The little Prince, we are told, carried a miniature sword and dagger covered with enamel and diamonds, and wore a black hat trimmed with bugles and diamonds, and adorned by scarlet plumes. It is

---

[1] At all these festivities it was the fashion for the company to pelt each other with egg-shells filled with scent.

to be remarked that in most of these festivities
Philip himself was faithful to his love of brown
for his dress ; and on this occasion is described
as wearing light brown velvet embroidered with
gold thread, and wearing the collar of the Golden
Fleece, whilst he rested his hand upon the
shoulder of his gentleman-in-waiting, the Count
de Galve, clad smartly in crimson satin and gold.[1]

In the meanwhile, over the tinkling of all this
courtly gaiety, there echoed the distant rumbling
of the storm. Mr. Arthur Hopton, the new English
ambassador, left in Madrid to look after English
commercial interests, and to push the eternal
question of the Palatinate, wrote to Lord Dorchester in February 1631 : " All the Spanish
Barbary garrisons are starving, but the want of
corn here is so great that every grain from Andalusia is sorely wanted for Castile." [2] But the
extravagant expenditure on the Buen Retiro and
on the never-ending war had to be met somehow,
and Olivares had to incur increased odium by in-
venting now exactions. " The Count of Olivares,"
continues Hopton, " being the most industrious
man in his master's service, and more so in the
matter of his revenue than anything else, hath
made him an instrument by directing a new imposition on salt, making the King the owner of all
the salt that is spent, and delivering it out at 40
reals the fanega (i.e. 1½ bushels), whilst remitting
12 per cent. on the wine and oil excise that had
nine years to run. This is a pretty way of imposing

[1] MSS. Add. 1026, British Museum.
[2] Sir Arthur Hopton's Notebook MS., British Museum, Egerton,
1820.

he should be sent to command in Portugal or Catalonia ; but in the summer of next year, 1632, as will be told, he sickened and died unmarried, greatly, no doubt, to the relief of Olivares, who dreaded the possibility of his being made a figure-head by his enemies.[1]

It was not easy to send Fernando to Flanders, even after it was decided to do so, and many months passed before even the money could be raised and preparations made for his going. Hopton wrote in August 1631 : " The Infante Cardinal hastens his going to Flanders, and has arranged to borrow of the Fucars 240,000 ducats at 40,000 per month. The matter is so forward that the brokers have received the first payment, but I do not believe that he will go ; for if he do it will be no easy matter to stay Carlos going to Portugal, and it is not likely that the King will leave the realm so destitute of his brothers, *and expose them to the familiarity with those who may be dangerous to him.*" A month later he reported that, after all, the young Cardinal was not to go that year, " but may slip away secretly, in imitation of our King's coming hither."

In fact, serious news had suddenly reached Olivares from Central Europe. The battle of Breitenfeld, in which the Emperor's best General, Tilly, had been routed by Gustavus Adolphus, had made the latter master of Germany, and if he chose to march on, Vienna itself was at his mercy. Dismay reigned amongst the imperialists at this crushing blow, and as soon as Olivares received

---

[1] There is an extremely curious medical report on the health and habits of Carlos in one of Hopton's letters from Madrid, in July 1632. MS. Notebook.

the news at the end of September he sent for Hopton, late at night. The Englishman found him in great agitation. " There is no time for words," he said, " but for God's sake send to England post haste, telling them to send to Vienna at once every offer that may facilitate an arrangement with the Emperor. I speak out of my goodwill to England, and I am sending to Vienna with the same object." The real end of Olivares' move is evident. In the critical position of the imperialists, with most of the Emperor's feudatories falling away and John Frederick of Saxony in arms against him, joined to Sweden and France, this was the opportunity, if ever, for England to strike an effectual blow for the Palatinate. It is true that the Marquis of Hamilton and some Scottish mercenaries were already with Gustavus Adolphus, but this was not national war ; and if England could be diverted into diplomatic negotiations during this time of the imperialists' adversity, all might be well, but if she joined the allies the house of Austria was ruined ; and for the next few weeks, whilst the danger lasted, nothing could exceed the amiability of Olivares to the English.[1]

---

[1] This was indeed the crucial time in the fate of the Palatinate. In the contest of ambitions in Germany, only a bold course, both towards Spain and the Empire on the part of England, would have been effectual. But poor Frederick at the Court of Gustavus promptly came to understand that whilst his English brother-in-law held aloof from the war he could expect little consideration. At this very period Charles I. was principally interested in adding to his picture gallery. Cottington, writing to Hopton, 10th November (O.S.) 1631, says : " You must tell the Count of Benavente from the King that the copie of the Venus of the Prado is now ready for him, with a picture of his Majesty, if he will give him his St. Philip for them. You must remember to send the King the painted grapes which the poore fellow hath drawn for him," Hopton's MS. Notebook.

Blow after blow continued to fall upon the imperial cause. Gustavus at Mayence was practically the master of Europe, the Spanish fleet had been defeated off Flanders. Tilly was utterly crushed and killed at Ingolstadt, and a revolt had broken out in Spanish Sicily against the new taxes of Olivares. Worst of all, when the minister decreed that the salt tax should be levied in the autonomous Basque provinces, the assembly there flatly refused to pay it. Olivares blustered that he would send 30,000 soldiers to make them. " We will await their coming," replied the assembly, " with 3000 and beat them." [1] And so gradually the policy of Olivares, which kept Spain at war with Europe for a barren idea, was leading the outer realms of the Peninsula itself towards rebellion, a thing unheard of for generations, because of their fear that they too were marked out by the minister to undergo the same fate as unhappy Castile.

In the midst of all his difficulties at home and abroad, the consummate skill with which Olivares played upon the English statesmen is almost amusing at this distance of time. Hopton's spirits rose and fell from week to week, as those of Anstruther did in Vienna. Olivares and the Emperor understood each other perfectly, and had no difficulty between them in keeping England quiet with the old bait of the restoration of the Palatinate. A specimen from Hopton's letters will illustrate the clever way in which Olivares beguiled his interlocutor.

" In the time my memorial was in debate

[1] Hopton's MS. Notebook.

I sometimes took occasion to see the Conde
(*i.e.* Olivares). On one it happened that the *Ave
Maria* bell rang, and when he had ended
his prayer he examined me in all the material
points of our religion, wherein, I perceive, he is not
ignorant. In the sacrament of baptism I said all
the essential parts are the same in both Churches.
But, he said, here they say, ' O ! he was christened
by a minister ; but I (Olivares) tell them that I see
no cause why a man may not as well be saved being
christened by a minister as by a priest.' This was
in the palace, on the occasion of the christening
of our Princess, of whom they have begun to talk
of as theirs.[1] When the Duke of Lennox went to
kiss the Prince's hand, the Countess of Olivares,
who was present, bade the Prince ask for his cousin's
hand, and said, ' You have a mistress there ;
and then, turning to us, she said, ' We are beginning
to *galantear* (*i.e.* to court) already.' He (Olivares)
examined me upon the Lord's supper, and was
much pleased to know the chiefest difference is
in the manner of the presence. He asked me
concerning divorces, and approved of the practice
of confession, though, he said, that it was too
lightly practised amongst them. Did we, he asked,
receive the blessed Virgin ? I said he who did so
was not considered a good Christian. He said,
' The top of the difference is the Pope's supremacy,
and the chiefest scruple was in temporalities,
because you would not have him meddle in matters
of Kings.' I said yes ; whereupon he shook his
head and said no more. I know his meaning, as

[1] Mary Stuart, afterwards Princess of Orange, whom it was proposed
to betroth to the Prince Baltasar Carlos.

things stand between him and the Pope. He said that if that point could be agreed I think it would not be hard to reconcile Protestants to the Church." [1]

All this talk about marriage and reconciliation in religion had done duty only ten years before ; but apparently the English diplomatists were as ready as ever to follow the Will o' the Wisp until the time of danger for Spain had passed and they could safely be shelved. The young Duke of Lennox was flattered and treated with almost royal honours, and Hopton himself was quite confused by the sustained amiability of Olivares. But at length even he began to doubt ; and presented a strongly worded memorial to Philip, calling upon him to have the Palatinate restored. After inordinate delay the reply to this was simply another promise to instruct the Spanish ambassador with the Emperor to urge the matter again upon him. In very truth this eternal shuttlecock between Vienna and Madrid was growing stale again ; and the English Government did now, when it was too late, what it should have done at first, namely, talk of preparations for war. But it was only talk ; and though it frightened Olivares for a week or two, Hopton deplored that the preparations were not being made a good earnest to fight ; " for this is the only way to bring Spain to reason, and they themselves are making preparations for a big war."

In fact it was quite evident now to everyone that unless Spain promptly withdrew her pretensions a great war to the death would have to be fought with France. Her troops in the Emperor's

[1] Hopton's MS. Notebook, January 1632.

armies had never ceased in Central Europe to meet in combat those of Louis XIII., but the impending resumption of rule by Spain over Catholic Flanders was an event that again threatened the integrity of France itself; for with Spanish frontiers, north, south, and east of her, the old position that had led to the great wars between Charles V. and Francis I. in the previous century would be repeated; and the new France which had arisen under Henry IV., and had been strengthened by Richelieu, would never suffer without a struggle a return to the old state of affairs. Money, constant, never-ending money, was the first desideratum of King Philip, if such a war as that foreshadowed, in addition to the struggle in Germany, was to be undertaken. The outer realms, and especially Portugal, were in a condition of sulky apprehension; but Philip was forced to meet the legislatures before he could get money from them. It was a necessity that he and Olivares dreaded and hated, but it had to be faced. All the Cortes therefore were summoned. "All to get money for their great engagements: how great they are they know not themselves," wrote Hopton.

But money had to be got somehow, even before the Cortes could meet or King go to his eastern realms. All the taxes had been anticipated, the loan-mongers had run dry, and the silver from the Indies had not arrived. Writing in February 1632, Hopton says: "They have levied heavy contributions on the tradesmen of Madrid,[1] but they

---

[1] There is in the Biblioteca Nacional, Madrid, a draft of the royal order, petitioning those who could afford it to come to the assistance of the King with money at this juncture (January 1632).

press them not hard yet, trying mild means first, and then passing to violent. However, they spare not those who are known to be moneyed men ; for they have sent to the Duke of Bejar for 100,000 ducats, and to the Duke of Medina Sidonia, and others in proportion. It will be a very great sum in all, but will be needed for the war next summer." Cardinal Borgia contributed 50,000 crowns, and nobles, merchants, and churchmen were squeezed as they had never been squeezed before, even in the time of Lerma.[1] In the Cortes of Castile (February 1632) a spirited protest for once was made, representing the poverty of the country, and saying that it was unjust to impoverish the land in order to send vast sums of money to the Emperor for a war useless to Spain.[2] But, as usual, the deputies, who were bribed heavily, ended in voting despairingly what was asked ; and after taking the oath of allegiance, as has already been described, to Prince Baltasar Carlos in the Church of St. Geronimo, they were promptly dismissed.

The journey of the King to Aragon was an

[1] Hopton, writing at this time, says : " The King told the Cortes that if the war goes on he will have to call upon them again. Though how the country will beare it I know not, for in all the kingdom of Castile their poverty is not to be dissembled. I am informed for a certainty that the procuradores of Andalucia have told the King plainly that if the peace with England be kept they will be able to serve him, but if not they cannot do it." MS. Notebook.

[2] Hopton, writing during the session of this Cortes, 4th March 1632, gives an account of the anger of Olivares and the King at the cities that had not given their representatives full powers to vote supplies, whilst the cities themselves were very angry at the demand for 6,000,000 ducats (i.e. in three years), and a renewal of the excise in addition to the salt tax. " A decree is lately issued for a donation through all the realm, which is put into practice by sending gentlemen of qualitie to every man's doore and taking their almes down as lowe as foure reales." Hopton's MS. Notebook.

anxious matter. Olivares had complicated the situation by aiding Marie de Medici and Gaston Duke of Orleans in their armed revolt against the government of Richelieu, to the openly expressed fury of the people of Madrid, who hated disloyalty to a King, even if he were King of France ; and the rumour prevailed that in revenge for the action of Olivares a French army was preparing to invade Catalonia and carry the war into Spain itself. The risk and danger of the King's journey were urged upon Philip, and discussed at length in his Council ; but Olivares, whilst admitting the risk, concluded that, " considering the penury of your Majesty's treasury, . . . the suffering to be incurred and the risk of annoyance from the Cortes would be lesser evils than the loss of the two millions (of ducats) we hope to get." [1] But though the voyage was decided upon, of one thing Olivares had quite made up his mind, namely, that the King's two brothers should not be left behind to plot at liberty the downfall of the favourite they hated. Don Carlos, left to himself and excluded from all affairs by Olivares, had fallen into a dissipated mode of life ; and both he and his abler brother Fernando were on terms of intimate friendship with the Count-Duke's enemy, the Admiral of Castile and his kinsmen, especially with Don Antonio de Moscoso, who was the inseparable factotum of Don Fernando. A most interesting paper, transcribed at length by Novoa as being written at the time by Olivares to the King on the subject of the two Infantes, shows how bitter and unscrupulous the

[1] Decision of the Council of State, 23rd March 1632. Danvila, *El Poder Civil en España.*

minister was towards these two young Princes.
The vilest suspicion is expressed as to their loyalty,
and the most cynical distrust of all their actions
and words. It had been decided to send Fernando
to Flanders, but for various reasons he had not
yet been allowed to start; and when the voyage of
the King to Barcelona was decided upon, Olivares
made his cowardly secret attack upon him and his
brother Carlos in the document in question.[1] The
nobles who are friendly to the Infantes are all represented as traitors and scoundrels; and the Princes
themselves are credited not only with unworthy
behaviour, but also with evil plots and designs.

" In any case," says Olivares, " they must
both be separated from all their friends, and this
voyage to Barcelona will offer a good opportunity
for doing it without attracting public notice.
" Fernando," he continues, " is already kicking
over the traces, and assuming airs on the strength
of his going to Flanders ; and the money he has
command of is making him dangerous. He and
Carlos are close friends, and their secret communications indicate an evil bent. Under the pretext of
these Cortes in Barcelona your Majesty might get
Fernando and his servants out of Madrid, saying
that you wanted him to look after ecclesiastical
affairs there, and the noble and university members
of the Cortes, leaving him there when you return
to deal with and close the assembly. Moscoso,
who has a wife in Madrid and does not like travelling,
would stay here, . . . and if he was bold enough
to disobey orders and try to join the Infante, we

[1] *Memorias de Matias de Novoa*, vol. i. p. 133.

would soon find means to upset his projects. As
for Don Carlos, when the Admiral is away from him,
and the Prince absent, his household will assume
a very different aspect. Seeing the musters of
enemies on our frontiers and the dangers threatening
us on every hand, it will be a good plan to send
the (Catalan) nobles to their own estates, to see
what troops they can raise, giving out that Fernando
is to be their leader, surrounding him with grey-
heads to keep him more enclosed, and even imprisoned, for it is a grave crime for him to show
annoyance as he does at your Majesty's orders.
. . . So, Sire, if we get the Admiral away from
here there will be a way to prevent him from
returning, and the Infante Fernando may remain
in Barcelona better occupied than he is now, whilst
Carlos, quieter and in better frame of mind, may
stay by your Majesty's side."

Philip as usual accepted his mentor's recommendation. The two Infantes, fully informed by
Olivares' enemies of the reason for taking them
away from Madrid, had to accompany their brother
to the east, the Queen remaining behind as Regent.
Philip and his brothers, with a large following of
the minister's kin and friends, left Madrid on
12th April 1632, the two young Princes being almost
without attendants. Fernando's reduced household were sent ahead to Barcelona, and the Infante
cried out aloud that this meant that he was not
to return to Madrid, and that the whole journey
to Catalonia had been got up solely to get him
away from Court for good. The Princes, indeed,
were almost in open revolt against Olivares ; and

it was noticed that they travelled with loaded pistols at their saddle-bows, a thing never seen before. After a stay of a week in Valencia, where Cortes were convoked and swore allegiance to the little Prince Baltasar Carlos, the whole Court moved on to Barcelona, where the great struggle for money was expected, for the stout Catalans were determined now that they would make a stand against the encroachments of Olivares on their liberties. The Viceroy, the Duke of Cardona, met the King at Murviedro, and warned him that the Catalans were in a dangerous mood. They objected to vote any more money, objected to a royal Prince for a Viceroy,—it was the duty of the King himself, they said, to come to them, and remain whilst the Cortes were in session, and they would not be contented unless the King stayed at least four months with them. All along the road the King and his favourite found the people scowling, and at Tortosa they broke out in subversive cries because he only stayed a few hours in the town.

At Barcelona the King found the Cortes of Catalonia more recalcitrant than ever, opposing endless difficulties to everything proposed, and advancing all sorts of old claims with regard to ceremonial and ancient privilege, each one of which had to be discussed interminably.[1] At last the ordinary supply was voted without increase, and the Infante Fernando was accepted by the Catalans as Governor with a sufficiently ill grace. Fernando himself was furious, and protested to his brother and Olivares hotly that he was being

---

[1] They are all set forth in the documents reproduced in Danvila's *Poder Civil en España.*

R

isolated in the interests of the latter, without the chance of distinction and elevation that he would have gained in Flanders. But he was at last reconciled by mingled flattery, cajolery, and appeals to duty, and remained as Governor to continue the Cortes, closely surrounded by mentors in the interests of Olivares.[1] Lerida had refused to send members to the Barcelona Cortes at all, and as Philip approached the city on his way home it was given out that he intended to punish it for its disobedience. Terrified, the city fathers came to meet the King and pray for pardon, which, only with difficulty and a complete submission, was partially accorded to them. When the Court arrived at Almadrones, two or three days' journey from Madrid, they were met by Antonio Moscoso, with an ostentatious train of followers and servants, on his way to join the Infante Fernando at Barcelona. This could never be allowed, and the King's confessor ordered Moscoso to return to Madrid at once. He appealed and wept in vain at the humiliation of such a return ; but was told that the King's orders must be obeyed without reply. When he went to kiss Philip's hand, the King, immovable as a statue, drily asked, " When are you leaving ? " " I must speak to the Count-Duke first, your Majesty," replied Moscoso. " You will be too late," said Philip, " for he was going to rest at once, and

[1] There were endless squabbles between the Infante Fernando and the Catalan deputies on all manner of subjects. He objected to the deputies being covered before him ; they insisted upon it as their right. He forbade them to repair and strengthen the city walls ; they at once employed three times as many men on it as before. But, said Hopton, writing on the subject : " He is doubtless a most sweete young Prince. All are ready to forgive him and lay all the blame on Count Oñate, who is with him." MS. Notebook.

would not awake till ten at night, in order to set out on the road from twelve to one."[1] So Moscoso was fain to turn back with a heavy heart, explaining by the way to Olivares that the Infante had sent for him, and he meant no harm. But though Olivares tried to lay the whole of the responsibility upon the King, this insult rankled deeply in the breast of the Infante Fernando, and was one more mark for vengeance scored up by the enemies of the minister. An indignant and formal complaint was made to the King by his brother, and in order to ensure its attention it was handed to Philip by his wife, much to the dismay of Olivares, who knew now that Isabel of Bourbon was the head of his foes, and that he could not dispose of her as he had done of the Infante.

As soon as Philip returned to Madrid, at the end of June 1632, the occasion was celebrated by another great *auto-de-fe* in the Plaza Mayor, where the King and Queen with the Infante Carlos sat in their balcony from eight in the morning (3rd July 1632) till late in the afternoon, witnessing the indictment, the preaching of prosy sermons, and the reading of legal documents, reciting the errors and heresies of the poor wretches who stood upon the high scaffold in the midst of the square, dressed in *sambenitos*. The ghastly rejoicing, such as it was, soon turned to mourning. The Infante Carlos had fallen ill on the way home from Barcelona, but had partially recovered on his arrival at Madrid. The summer was the most oppressive that had been experienced for years, and the young Infante—he

---

[1] The heat was very great, and the King consequently travelled by night. Novoa.

was only twenty-five—fell ill of fever in Madrid, and died in a few days ;[1] and Olivares had one less difficulty to contend with, though the amiable, unambitious young man was of himself inoffensive.

Nor was it long before the other Infante was removed from the path of Olivares. The old Infanta Isabel ended at last her strenuous life in 1633, and Fernando was sent by way of Italy to the States of Flanders to govern the fatal dominion for Spain once more, to Spain's ultimate undoing. Fernando was able and ambitious. From Milan he was to lead a large Spanish force to Flanders. But affairs had gone ill with the imperial cause. Gustavus Adolphus, it is true, had fallen ; but in the fight at which he fell he had beaten Wallenstein, with the loss of 12,000 men on the imperialist side. On the appeal of the Emperor, Fernando turned aside, and a critical moment when the imperialists were delivering the attack he arrived before the Protestant city of Nördlingen (September 1634). His presence turned the scale, for a relieving force

[1] On the 29th July, Hopton wrote : " Don Carlos was sick for seventeen days with ordinary ague at first, but at the end of eight days it turned to tabardillo (spotted typhus) with convulsions. My man has come in from the palace whilst I am sealing up this, and says he is not yet dead, but cannot live two hours. All things for his funeral are prepared, and blacks taken up, and servants that are to wait on his body to ye Escorial are commanded to be in readiness, so that your honour (Coke) may take it that this gallant young Prince is a dead man." Hopton's MS. Notebook. In another letter he wrote of the distress of the people at the Infante's death : " The mourning could not be more hearty for the King, and they have good reason, for he was a Prince that never offended any man willingly, but did good offices for all ; being bred upp amonge them to as much perfection as they could expect." Writing an unofficial letter to Cottington on the same day, Hopton gives some extremely curious private details of the causes of the Prince's illness, which cannot be here trans-lated. But he continues : " The poore Conde de Olivares is the scape-goat that must bear all men's faults ; but he is very much afflicted, for he was very sure of this Prince's love, whatsoever the world sayeth."

of Swedes was just approaching, and the ensuing
battle, one of the most decisive in the Thirty Years'
War, was a crushing defeat to the Swedes and the
Protestants. The Cardinal Infante passed on his
way triumphant to his new governship, crowned by
the laurels of victory and the plaudits of his countrymen. But his active intervention in the war with
Spanish Government troops changed the aspect of
the war. The Swedes were no longer the leaders
of a federation of Protestants against a federation
of Catholics. It was clear to Richelieu that unless
with the whole force of France he threw himself
into the fray against the house of Austria, not
only Protestantism in Germany would suffer—for
that indeed he cared nothing, but the vital interests
of France. And so it happened that when the
Cardinal Infante was entering Brussels in pompous
triumph, Richelieu had already heavily subsidised
the Dutch for an active renewal of their war against
him ; and within a few months, early in 1635, Spain
herself was in the grip of a great national struggle
with France, a struggle which extended as time went
on from her Flanders dominions to her Italian possession, and from the Franche Comté to the sacred soil
of Spain itself.

CHAPTER VII

INTRIGUES TO SECURE ENGLISH NEUTRALITY—HOP-
TON AND OLIVARES—SOCIAL LAXITY IN MADRID
—CHARLES I. APPROACHES SPAIN—THE BUEN
RETIRO AND THE ARTS—WAR IN CATALONIA—
DISTRESS IN THE CAPITAL AND FRIVOLITY IN
THE COURT—PREVENTING LAWLESSNESS—THE
RECEPTION OF THE PRINCESS OF CARIGNANO—
SIR WALTER ASTON IN MADRID—THE ENGLISH
INTRIGUE ABANDONED

As Spain drifted nearer and nearer to the inevitable
war with France, Olivares became more friendly
with the English. He hinted that Spain was
getting tired of the burden of the Emperor's wars,
and might soon be pleased to give up the Palatinate.
At another time he told Hopton that the Palatine
business might be settled in a few hours ; and
through all the reverses that were daily befalling
the imperial and Spanish cause the Count-Duke
kept a good face. " I never saw him merrier,
nor with greater appearance of confidence. God
grant he may have reason," reported Hopton in
the summer of 1632. Rojas, too, who was
the mouthpiece of Olivares, harped constantly
on the same string. " They were most desirous
of close friendship with England ; but had such
crosses with Germany." At the same time the
talk of war with France grew throughout the

country ; though Hopton could not understand how it was possible for them to raise armies or money, for all their talk, " having neither men sufficient to man their ships nor to till their ground."

The penury of the country, indeed, was greater than ever. The American trade, a close monopoly nominally, had previously been the ultimate resource of Spanish kings in need ; but that was failing now. In June 1632 the silver fleet came into Seville, and instead of the treasure being delivered to its legitimate owners, most of it was seized by the Government. The merchants utterly lost heart, and when the time came for the return fleet to leave Seville in the autumn, Hopton wrote :

" The Indian fleet is ready to sail, but there is no merchandise nor merchant ships, and it will cost the King more than it will bring. The reason for this is that for many years past the trade of the Indies has decayed, being wholly given up by Spaniards, and kept alive by strangers. The Spanish merchants think it not worth while to continue a fleet, as the King keeps in the *Contratacion* (India House) all the silver and gold, and hath assumed to himself first the customs, then the 47 per cent. average, and will not declare his purpose as to the rest. This has caused such disability and unwillingness to send goods, and hath brought trade so low, that whereas licences for strangers to trade there were hardly gotten for 4000 ducats, they are now offering them for 4000 reales ; and I thinke they will shortly be forced to *hyre* adventurers. As for the trade in Portugal, that country cannot do a sixth part of it, and so they are obliged to grant licences to contract with strangers to trade in Brazil, offering such conditions as they may trade safely."

I have transcribed these lines at length, because they show in vivid terms how the suicidal system of finance was ruining every class of the community. The workers, agricultural and urban, especially the former, had been the first to go under, then the smaller tradesmen, crushed by the alcabala tax on all sales, and the tampering with the currency; and the turn now had come of the great merchants and bankers; whilst even the nobles and churchmen had been bled freely by the last "voluntary donation." [1] In these circumstances it is not surprising that the dissatisfaction became almost clamorous in its intensity. Such pasquins passed from hand to hand on Liars' Walk that people said that the ghost of Villa Mediana must surely be walking his old haunts again, so bitter were they. Olivares, it was whispered, had poisoned the Infante Carlos, and had tried to send Fernando by the same road. The French were ready with great armies to devastate Spain, only because Olivares was coquetting with the rebel Orleans. Even the Pope, said the gossips, was being insulted and flouted by this minister, who was but an ill-born Jew in disguise. [2] "If you heard," wrote Hopton to Cottington, in August 1632, " the

[1] An attempt was made to enforce gifts of this donation from foreigners, and four English youths at Bilbao resisted, but on Hopton's representations they were exempt.

[2] In fact, a notification had been sent to the Pope that the Nuncio in future would be treated as any other ambassador, and the large revenue drawn by the Papacy from Spain would be in future taken by the King. Upon this the Nuncio was withdrawn, and much trouble ensued.

libels and foolish inventions of the people against the Conde, you would never desire to be a favourite." [1]

Thus affairs in the capital went from bad to worse. Fanaticism spent itself upon the loan-mongers, mostly Genoese and Jews with Portuguese names, who served Olivares in extremity, and many of them, and the richest, fell into the hands of the Inquisition. There were frequent hints, uttered beneath bated breath, that if all men had their due Olivares himself would be burnt in a *sambenito* outside the gate of Fuencarral, for he had risen by the devilish arts of sorcery, and kept the King in his power by witchcraft.[2] Enormous difficulty was experienced in levying troops for the war, for the country was half depopulated, and many able-bodied men fled: the old spirit of confidence in a sacred mission was gone, and they had now no stomach for a fight provoked by the King's favourite. The Catalans looked on in sulky suspicion, believing that Olivares needed the soldiers to rob them of their liberties; whilst in Madrid itself, though there were only eight

[1] Corner, the Venetian ambassador in Madrid, writing at the same period, says: " He (Olivares) is greatly hated both by the grandees and by the people of all classes, but nobody believes that he can be turned out of his place. . . . He is very austere and hard in his dealings with people, which causes great anger, and the murmurs against him are open and loud, even the preachers in the pulpits denouncing him; and everybody is saying that it is a wonder he can stand against it all."

[2] As if to silence these terrible hints, Olivares had at this time adopted an ostentatiously saintly mode of life. Corner speaks of him as living very quietly and in great melancholy since the death of his only daughter. " He professes to live in much piety and devotion, confessing and communicating every day. He has so many masses said daily, and to all appearance lives the life of a devotee. He has now begun to lie in a coffin in his chamber like a corpse, with tapers around him, whilst the *de profundis* is sung; whilst in ordinary affairs he talks like a capuchin friar, and speaks of the grandeur of this world with the greatest disdain.

companies of troops, " and more idle men to be spared than in half Spain." [1] The shirkers flocked by thousands into ecclesiastical and noble service, or in that of the Inquisition, with little or no pay, in order to escape enlistment.[2] News came daily, too, of reverses in Flanders, and serious riots in Biscay against the salt tax; and in the meanwhile the French armies were mustering upon the Pyrenean frontier to menace Spanish territory when the dread hour should strike. No spot of brightness indeed appeared anywhere.

Olivares had opened secret negotiations direct with Charles I. for an offensive and defiance alliance against France, in union with the party of Marie de Medici and the Duke of Orleans; and again the English were sure for a time that now the Palatinate would be restored,—too late, however, in any case, for poor Frederick, who had just died. But soon another cause for dispute changed Olivares' tone towards England. Behind the amiable talk about the Palatinate large bodies of men for the Spanish service had been raised in Ireland. This, it was seen, would not do. Charles I. was willing to oblige Spain in return for concessions in the matter of the Palatinate; and Scottish, or even English, mercenaries, he said, might be obtained. But

---

[1] Hopton's MS. Notebook.

[2] Hopton, writing soon after this (January 1634), says the levies are going on very slowly. Yesterday a pragmatic was published limiting the number of lackeys and squires, all beyond that number are to be discharged, and so also are those employed in unnecessary trades, so that many will be at leisure to serve the King. But the pragmatics did not dare to attack the greater scandal of all, namely, the enormous number of ruffians who escaped all responsibility to the ordinary laws by becoming nominally " Familiars " of the Inquisition, or servants, in the broadest sense, to the religious communities.

Catholic Irishmen, " utter rebels " ! Olivares was told plainly that he could not have ; " for if ever Spain meant to do us harm it would be by means of the Irish." So the new Irish troops were stopped by England before they were embarked, and Olivares, in a violent rage, said he had been betrayed and ruined, and would never trust an Englishman again. England, indeed, at last was learning what manner of man Olivares was. Suave and diplomatic when it served his turn, but, whilst gaining everything, giving nothing but vague promises in exchange. English shipmasters were still being disgracefully despoiled ; not a step had really been taken for the restoration of the Palatinate ; and Charles was more than justified in insisting upon practical proofs of Spanish friendship before he stretched a point to help Olivares.

Through all this gathering trouble, with deep discontent at home and menace on all sides, the trivial life in Madrid went on in the usual way. " The King hath been very sensible of the losse of Rheinsberg," wrote Hopton in June 1633 ; " and the Conde hath endeavoured to divert him with playes and maskes at a new house (Buen Retiro) he hath built near the St. Geronimo monasterie : a thing of noe great expense for such a King, yet murmured at by the people, who will allow to governors in times of misfortune nothing but care." [1] As time went on, Philip had grown more idle and dissolute than ever ; and the tone of the Court had followed the fashion of the King. The newsletters of the period from Madrid are simply a collection of atrocious scandals touching

[1] Hopton's MS. Notebook.

the honour of the highest people in the Court. The blame for this also was laid, though not very justly, upon Olivares, who, having lost his only daughter, the Marchioness de Heliche, to his endur- ing grief, had now cast the whole of his affection upon his bastard son Julian, whom he subsequently legitimated, and rechristened Enrique Felipe de Guz· man, to the fury of the nobles who were opposed to him. But this fact, although it contributed osten- sibly to his fall, as the Queen was persuaded that he had induced Philip to legitimate his own favourite bastard Don Juan in order that he, Olivares, might have a good precedent to do likewise with his, was really but a venial fault in a Court so corrupt as this.

In his private letters to Cottington, Hopton occasionally allowed himself to tell some of the current scandal concerning courtiers, who were, of course, well known to Cottington. He appears in one of his letters to have hinted at a terrible misfortune as having happened to some highly placed ladies in Madrid, but without giving details. Charles I. saw the letter, and was much offended apparently that the scandal should be mentioned vaguely. Hopton (26th October 1633) wrote an abject letter of apology to King Charles, beseeching pardon, and saying that he had only mentioned the scandal and avoided particulars in order to save the lady's honour ; but in obedience to his Majesty's orders he would now tell the whole story.

" The tragedy began in Cardinal Zapata's house, where there is a niece of his, daughter of his sister the Countess de Valenzuela, a very fine lady, and exceedingly well beloved by her uncle,

who married her about two years ago to the eldest
son of the Count de Sevilla, with whom she lived
about a year, and, being left a widow, returned
to the protection of the Cardinal, her uncle. In
the house there lived a favourite servant of the
Cardinal, one Joseph Cabra, who had entered the
service at Zaragoza as a page, but now occupied
the post of highest trust in the household. The
Count of Sevilla's son was jealous of this man
before he died; but since his death the Count
his father has proceeded criminally against the
young Countess and Cabra, for living in adultery
together and murdering the husband. It is now
certain that since she became a widow she lived
with Cabra and had a child by him, which made
them resolve on a secret marriage. This was concealed for some months, and divulged at last
through a slip of Cabra's, who failed to pay
sufficiently handsomely the officers of the church
where they were married. The whole business
then came out. Cabra fled to his own country,
where he thought he would be safe; and there he
published something vindicating his quality. There
was no reason, he argued, why his marriage with
the Countess should be considered strange. Others
of greater inequality had been married before;
for instance, the Duchess of Peñaranda and her
steward Avellaneda. He knew this, he said, by
his having had access to the secret books of Toledo
Cathedral. The Duchess of Peñaranda was a
younger daughter of the Cardinal Duke of Lerma;
and she was known in her youth to have been
free, but all passed under her high spirits. The
Duke of Lerma had a page called Avellaneda, who,

being a favourite, was appointed to wait upon his daughter in those liberties she assumed, and to be the instrument of justification to her and him. The Duke of Lerma having died, the page was appointed steward, and although he was already married, she (the Duchess) had a child by him, who is now five years old. Eighteen months ago, Avellaneda's wife died, and the Duchess married him. When the bans were published, her son, the present Duke of Peñaranda, happened to be present ; but the names being common ones he did not suspect, though he mentioned the matter to his mother as a curious coincidence. This marriage being discovered by the disclosures in Cabra's pamphlet, threw all the town in a turmoil. The Duke of Peñaranda assembled in the house of his sister, the Marchioness of Villena, his confidential kindred, to consult them as to what had to be done. There it was decided that he must first kill Avellaneda. When this news reached the palace, the King sent for the Duke of Peñaranda, and ordered him to do nothing as he (the King) would take the matter into his own hands. He sent to Illescas, where Avellaneda was, and had him brought in a cart to the common prison here ; the Duchess being sent to the royal convent of nuns of St. Domingo el Real,[1] where she still remains. Cabra, who had caused all this trouble, was also imprisoned, and his wife as well, though she in her justification said : ' Why punish me, who try to live in the grace of God ?—let them look to those who live like strumpets ' ; and amongst those who did so she

---

[1] This was an ancient Dominican religious house near the palace, at the corner of the present Cuesta de Santo Domingo in Madrid.

mentioned the Dowager Duchess of Pastrana. The affair has caused dreadful scandal, but has been hushed up. The good old Cardinal (Zapata) has taken so much to heart the misfortune of his niece, who, after having been committed to the custody of an Alcalde de Corte, has been sent to a nunnery, that ill-meaning people say that she is really his daughter. He is so troubled about it that he has moved to six different houses in six months, and much mistrust exists. Another thing has arisen out of the affair. The great distaste to the house of Peñaranda has caused the Duke to retire from Court. The King was quite willing for him to go, but did not like his wife to go with him. She is the daughter and heir to the Marquis of Valdonquilla, the uncle of the Admiral (of Castile), who, without taking any notice of the King's displeasure, forced her to follow her husband. But they say the commerce is established."

This budget of scandal sent to the King of England shows how utterly rotten was the moral condition of the Court, when it sufficed for one disgraceful episode to be made public for a whole string of others to follow touching the honour of those who stood highest. This scandalous immorality, arising apparently from the absolute degeneration of religion into a formula, and of its ceasing to be a guide of conduct, extended to all classes of society, and terrified stories were told of horrible irreligious rites being carried on in the conventual houses themselves by a secret society called the "illumined ones" (*alumbrados*). The particulars of one awful scandal of the sort, which was investigated by the Inquisition at this time (1633), caused great excitement in Madrid. It related to the proceedings of the nuns of St. Placido of Madrid, who were pronounced by the Benedictine chaplain, Fray Garcia, to be nearly all possessed of the devil ; and on the pretext of exorcising them he was with them almost day and night. This went on for three years, when the fact that twenty-eight out of the thirty nuns in the convent were said to be possessed appeared so strange and suspicious, that the Inquisition intervened ; and, in the course of a long inquiry and much torture of the chaplain, uncovered an appalling story of sacrilege, black magic, and immorality combined, for which all the persons implicated were severely punished ; though a few years afterwards (1638) an attempt was made to whitewash the condemned.[1]

It is needless to say that in such a society as this, idle, depraved, and to all effects pagan under its morbid devotion, the race after pleasure became ever keener, notwithstanding the disasters abroad and the misery at home. The Saints' days were excessively numerous, and the parishes vied with each other in the attractions of their religious performances ; the *autos-de-fe* alternated with the constant bull-fights, cane tourneys, and the other festivities so often described in earlier pages ; the amorous adventures of the King became more frequent, or at all events were more talked about, than before ; and the new palace and garden of the Buen Retiro formed a more suitable background for such proceedings than the old palace

[1] Particulars of the case will be found in the contemporary MS., D. 150, Biblioteca Nacional, Madrid.

had been. Every birth in the King's family, every reception of ambassadors, every royal anniversary, was made the excuse for one of these long series of festivities. Hopton, writing to Coke in October 1633, says that the King was then boar killing at the Escorial and Balsain, and that already the capital was preparing to welcome him back in the following week with a series of bull-fights and cane tourneys.

" Great preparations are being made to warme a new house built near by the monastery of St. Geronimo, and contrived by Olivares. . . . The business seems to be a matter of Olivares' or the King's affection, or both, as about 1000 men are at work to have the place ready in time. They are working day and night, as well as Sundays and holidays. I doubt what will happen when the place is burdened with such a posse of people as usually resort to such pastimes, the mortar being yet greene, the building will run some hazard. There is much talk in the town about it, generally against the charge thereof being taken from the bellys of the people by an imposition on wine, flesh, etc. They suffer it worse because they say it is a fancy of the Conde's (Olivares)." [1]

[1] On a portion of the site of the Buen Retiro the Countess of Olivares had formerly had an aviary with a collection of domestic poultry, in which she and her husband had taken great interest. The wits of the capital had dubbed the place " the hen-coop " ; and the name was the peg upon which the satirists and poets hung their scurrilous gibes at the new palace. Corner, the Venetian ambassador at this time, writes : " The origin of the edifice has become a subject for great ridicule. The site was occupied by a collection of poultry the Countess had, and although the hens were curious and pretty of their sort, it was a source of much wonder and derision that the Count, who is occupied in such grave business, should have taken such interest in the hens. . . . Everybody calls it (the palace) the ' hen-coop,' and numberless pasquins have been

S

In another letter, Hopton mentions that the house-warming of the Buen Retiro is to last four days; with bull-fights, running at the ring, wild beast fights and other similar sports; in which " I may say without flattery, the King, with his excellent comportment, exceeded all that came in with him. The house is very richly furnished, and almost all by presents; for the Conde hath made the matter his own, by whose means it hath wanted not friends.[1] And then, as if to furnish a fit commentary upon all this wasteful frivolity, the English ambassador proceeds to say that trade with the Indies was dead, and that, " if things go on like this they will not be able to re-establish it, and that Portuguese Indian trade has been almost quite killed by neglect." [2]

Whilst the drums were beating in Madrid and other great cities to enlist recruits to face the French in the coming war, and Olivares, almost in despair, was casting about for fresh ways of getting large sums of money, he ceaselessly endeavoured to win England to his side. It was clear that the old method and the old bait would have to be changed somewhat, for bland verbal assurances from the Spaniards in favour of a restoration of the Palatinate, whilst the Emperor was left un-pledged, could no longer impose upon the least suspicious of diplomatists. The new move was an extraordinary one, and displays vividly the falsity of Charles I. For some time previous to

written about it, even Cardinal Richelieu joking about the hens and the hen-coop to a secretary of the King (Philip) who was in Paris."

[1] Hopton's MS. Notebook. Corner also says that anybody who wished to stand well with Olivares hurried to send some precious thing to adorn the Buen Retiro. [2] *Ibid.*

the beginning of 1634, Olivares had been delighting Hopton by his conciliatoriness, and somewhat mystifying him by arch hints as to the future. Writing on the 24th January 1634, Hopton says that Olivares was very much better disposed in English affairs than he was wont to be. " I have done him several services, and try to leave him contented."

A few weeks after this, an explanation of the Count-Duke's amiability came to Hopton in the form of a private letter from Windebank, the Secretary of the King of England, enclosing the copy of an address made by the resident Spanish agent in London, Nicolalde, to Charles. There had been a talk for weeks of sending some great personage from Spain as a special ambassador ; but in the meantime Nicolalde had cast soundings by suggesting a close alliance between England and the Emperor, in which the Palatine would join. Charles had replied cautiously, saying that he would consider it if the Palatine were confirmed in the possession of the territories he now held, and especially the Lower Palatinate. But the real inwardness of it all was revealed in a private letter of 13th February from Cottington to Hopton, saying that Charles was willing to league himself with the Emperor and Spain on certain conditions, but that Coke, the Secretary of State, was to be kept entirely in the dark about it, the negotiations being carried on with the King (Charles) direct through Windebank. The object of the proposed alliance was, " the expulsion of foreigners from the empire, and the reduction of the rebels to due obedience," which meant the crushing of the Dutch Protestants. King Charles, says Cottington, is quite set upon it. The plan can only miscarry by incredulity on the part of Olivares, or any waywardness of Nicolalde; and Charles, as an earnest of his good faith, offers the escort of an English fleet to the Infante Fernando, if it was intended to send him to Flanders by sea.[1]

Behind this there was another mysterious negotiation going on, relating apparently to a marriage between Charles's eldest daughter Mary Stuart to Prince Baltasar Carlos, both of whom were children of tender years. Many close conversations on the subject took place between Hopton, as the personal mouthpiece of King Charles, and Philip and his minister. The constant claims and complaints of the English merchants and shipmasters of Spanish extortion annoyed Hopton almost as much as Olivares, because they introduced an element of trouble in these loving confabulations. But Hopton, though zealous to serve his King, was clearly ill at ease, as well he might be, for it was a dangerous business for Charles to receive a big money subsidy from Spain, as was proposed, and to turn the arms of England against the Protestants. Hopton goes so far, indeed, as to say in his letters to Windebank that he is not in favour of the subsidy, but that King Charles should fit out a fleet at his own expense against the Dutch. This will, he says, be easier, and will leave Charles more free and able to bring the Dutch to reason. But, he continues, if the matter is undertaken at all, it must be seen through to the end, or Holland will wax too insolent to be borne.

[1] Fernando was in Milan, and was already under orders to march to Flanders overland at this time.

Long discussions with the Council of State and with Olivares kept Hopton busy in Madrid for months ; the while the great betrayal proposed was kept from the Secretary of State and all the responsible ministers in England, a good foretaste of the policy that led Charles Stuart to ruin and the block. To the official Secretary of State, Hopton had much to say about the great preparations being made in Spain for war, but no word about the secret plan for England to join in it on the Catholic side. Great loans and levies are constantly being raised, he reported in April 1634.

" This great ship," he wrote, meaning of course Spain, " contains much water (*i.e.* money), but many leaks, and is always dry. It is certain that they have made loans this year for 13 millions (of ducats), and are still treating of more, yet at the end of the year they will neither have money in their purse, nor army paid, nor nobody contented ; which is to be attributed to the hard terms wherewith they do their business. For being masters of the mines of gold and silver, and withal having but few friends, nobody will serve them but for their interests : and their own subjects are so well conceited of themselves, as they think they cannot be paid enough." [1] " In their present levies," he continues, " though they are sorry men, they give them 3 reales a day, which is 18 pence English, and yet have all they can do to keep them from running away. Subjects are fearfully hardly pressed. The hard usage of business men in the Indian trade has made concealment general, which has greatly reduced the

[1] Hopton's MS. Notebook.

revenue of the crown. Great measures were taken to discover unregistered treasure in the last fleet, and they found 600,000 ducats, and will yet find more. But this again will stop trade."

Everything possible was done by Olivares to please the English at this juncture. The prisoners of the Inquisition at Cadiz were released, Hopton was made much of, King Charles was the most popular potentate amongst the idlers of Madrid; whilst the French ambassador, stoned and insulted in the streets, was fain to take refuge in a monastery twelve miles away to avoid scandal. "They want our friendship now," wrote Hopton, "and we may make our market." The English ambassador had his head quite turned by so much attention, and, to the anger of King Charles, was drawn by the superior diplomacy of Olivares into going beyond his instructions in his promises to the Spaniards. The King of England had been bitten too often by Spanish plausibility not to be distrustful; and Windebank's letter to Hopton, in May 1634, was almost violent in its scolding. Hopton had gone so far as to say that the English had decided to put a powerful army in the field to punish the insolence of the Dutch, whereas King Charles had only broached it as a proposition, and Nicolalde in the meanwhile was pledging the Spaniards to nothing. When Olivares was pressed for guarantees in return for the English aid he craved, the usual story was told; and by the middle of July Hopton wrote to Windebank—

"*The* business, as I expected when I saw them

haggling, has come to naught. They only want to keep us neutral ; and the affair is at an end. I am not sorry, unless the Palatine might be made secure. When I said they would oblige the gratefullest prince living, Olivares replied : ' No hay gratitud entre Reyes ' (There is no gratitude between kings)." [1]

Olivares was beset on all sides. Detested by the nobles, with nearly all of whom he was at feud ; [2] feared and dreaded by the commercial community, whom he had ruined ; overworked, and at his wits' end to face the vast present and prospective drains upon the national resources, striving not only to do all the work of State himself and to direct everything, but also to keep the King in a good humour by providing an endless series of amusements for him, the Count-Duke was " so spent with the burden of business that lies upon him," as Hopton wrote, " as to deserve pity, if he would only pity himself." There was no class of people now that did not feel the crushing weight of the war expenditure, even before the great war with France had begun. In June 1634, Hopton reports that " a new tax had been imposed of one-eighth of the value of all wine sold in Madrid, with no exception allowed, and one twenty-fourth of all that is sold in the Castilian realms. All the shops that sell wine are shut, so that all stock may be registered and an account be rendered of sales. They think thus to charge the retailer under great penalties.

[1] Hopton's MS. Notebook.
[2] At this very period the great Don Fadrique de Toledo, son of the Duke of Alba, was in prison, the victim of Olivares' jealousy, and most of the grandees avoided Court as much as possible.

It is like to be a great trouble, and the greater part of the " benefit will be consumed in officers and false accounts." " I doe much doubte," he continues, " that by degrees those impositions will first be laid upon all things of home fabric and growth, and afterwards upon those things imported from abroad; and your Honour (Coke) may guess to what immoderation the revenues of this crown will grow by this means." [1]

The good, simple ambassador made no allowance for the self-stultifying operation of oppressive taxation, and if he had reviewed the state of affairs a few years later, he would have seen, as we shall in the course of this book, that, so far from benefiting Philip's treasury, these blighting impositions on the exchange of commodities ended in a decrease of the revenue. But whilst the citizens were groaning under impossible burdens, and the curses of a whole nation were following the careworn Count-Duke, the King, as much afflicted with the troubles of his people as anyone, but looking upon them as a visitation of providence, must needs seek in pleasure distraction from his vicarious sorrow which the oppressed citizens themselves could not escape.

"All the Court is at the new house" (i.e. the Buen Retiro) " for a fortnight," wrote Hopton in July 1634, " which time hath been spent in all manner of entertainments, and much to their Majesties' contentment, wherein the Count of Olivares took great pains, all things being ordered by himself; and so well, as it savoured of his excellent

[1] Hopton's MS. Notebook.

judgment in all things, especially in the furniture of the house, which was such as not to be thought there had been so many curiosities in the whole kingdom; and this at very little expense, for it was for the most part done by presents. Howbeit the things that were bought were dearly and punctually paid for, inasmuch as nobody can wisely complain."

Doubtless no one could *wisely* complain, but many had reason to do so, for few great people with art collections escaped spoliation, and the other palaces were to a great extent denuded of their treasures, for the purpose of cramming the Buen Retiro with rarities. Some of the nobles, like the Auditor Tejada, were artful enough to have copies made of their best pictures, and sent the copies as originals to the Buen Retiro. But, as in his case, this was bitterly resented by Olivares if it was found out. The Marquis of Leganés, the nephew of the Count-Duke, had a superb collection of pictures and articles of vertu brought from Flanders and Italy; but when he was called upon to disgorge, his wife stepped in and claimed the whole collection as her dowry, and the Marquis was let off with the present of a piece of tapestry. The chapel was fitted up at the expense of the President of the Council of Castile; the Infante Fernando continued to send beautiful objects, many of them spoils of war from Flanders; Olivares' brother-in-law Monterey had to surrender much of the vast store of pictures he had collected at Naples; and all the painters in Madrid were kept busy copying or designing canvasses for the new palace,[1] under the direction of the King's painter, Don Diego Velazquez, who, having returned from his long visit to Rome, was now, and had been for the last three years, again working indefatigably in his studio in the old Alcazar.

This, indeed, was the period when the great artist produced some of the best of his work, such as the Surrender of Breda (the Lanzas), the portraits of the child Prince Baltasar Carlos, the fine portrait of Olivares reproduced in this book, and the famous equestrian portrait of Philip himself. In the midst of all the growing national trouble, this in many respects was the most brilliant and perhaps the happiest time of Philip's reign, so far as he personally was concerned. His habits were fixed and his pleasures keen. His fits of contrition were frequent, it is true ; but they were always banished by fresh pleasures or amours contrived by Olivares. The

---

[1] Carl Justi. Presents of paintings were also sent from England. Coke, for instance, sent, presumably from Charles I., a picture by Horatio Gentileschi as a present to King Philip. It is extraordinary to note in the correspondence of the English diplomatists at this period the constant mention of the sending of pictures to Spain, and *vice versa*, mostly for King Charles, but very often also for Lady Cottington. In May 1633, Hopton writes to Cottington the following reference to a painter sent to Madrid to copy pictures for Charles I., which I do not think has been noticed before. " The King's painter is sending some pieces. He is a very well governed young man and a good husband (*i.e.* a good manager of money), yet by reason of the dearenesse of this place, and being willing to live in so handsome a manner as a man sent by his Majesty, money goes away apace which I cannot remedy, because I doe not see that he can ; but I conceive his Majesty will have a very good account of him, to whose service I perceive he hath wholly disposed himself." A little later we are told that " the King's painter hath fallen sick of a calenture, and grows worse. I am out of a great deal of money by him. Lady Cottington and others in England were constantly asking for Labrador's flower and fruit pieces to be sent to them, and purchases and exchanges of pictures are often spoken of for King Charles himself.

King intermittently attended to State business himself ; but the interminable discussions and reports by the various Councils upon every subject made the despatch of business peculiarly irksome and tedious. The Spanish system of a consultative and deliberative bureaucracy, indeed, seemed specially devised to disgust anyone but a patient laborious plodder like Philip II. His grandson, impatient of detail and quick of apprehension, loathed the dull pompous discussions of the Councils, and not unnaturally was content to hear a summary of results from Olivares, whose final decision he always confirmed.

Philip's domestic life at this time had every reason to be happy, though the growing tension between his wife and Olivares had to some extent estranged them, and the Queen was, under the influence of the minister, somewhat ostentatiously excluded from public business, not unnaturally to her annoyance. She was, however, a good wife, and shared Philip's frequent pleasures gaily, whilst in devotion of the peculiar Spanish type she was even more emphatic than he. She had a woman's reason for her dislike of Olivares, as well as the political objections to him which were the ultimate cause of his fall. It has already been mentioned that in pursuance of his system of doing everybody's work, the minister had taken under his care the management of the King's affairs of gallantry, and the results thereof. This, of course, was perfectly well known to the Queen, and the satirical poets who wrote so copiously of frailty in high places took care to publish the fact. Even Hopton, when in a gossiping mood, referred to it more than once. Speaking of the skits that were current about Olivares and the new palace, he wrote : " He (Olivares) hath had likewise some harsh words with the Admiral for speaking to the King in disparagement of his new house ; and the Queen hath had her little saying to him also, for some opinion she had of some secret pleasures there brought to the King."

Whatever may have been the sum of Philip's infidelities, and it cannot be denied that they were numerous, they were never more than temporary and vulgar intrigues, which, whilst they would naturally annoy his wife, did not threaten her permanent influence or interfere with her continuous marital life with her husband. With monotonous regularity almost every year the Queen gave birth to a child, usually a girl, whose advent was an excuse for the customary series of costly festivities so often described in earlier pages, festivities that in most cases lasted almost as long as the life of the child whose advent they greeted ; for all the infants up to this time (1634) had died except the sturdy, promising little Baltasar Carlos, who was idolised by his father and mother, and, so far as the oppressive etiquette of the Court would allow, was petted by the whole Court. The little Prince, who was born in 1629, had early developed a love for horsemanship and field sports, and as a baby horseman, hunter, or soldier, he is presented to the life again and again by Velazquez. From Flanders his admiring uncle Fernando sent him many presents, beautiful armour and weapons in miniature, which now adorn the rich Armeria in Madrid, martial toys, and above all in 1633 what

PRINCE BALTASAR CARLOS

From a painting by Velazquez in the Prado Museum

afterwards became the Prince's favourite steed, a
" little devil of a stallion pony," as the Infante
calls him, that had to be lashed liberally before
Baltasar Carlos was allowed to mount him.[1]

The limited number of his near relatives had
become a source of embarrassment to Philip. Of
his two brothers, one, Carlos, had died, and the
other, the Infante Cardinal Fernando, was in Flanders
fighting and working heroically. There were no
other Spanish relatives, but the heir Baltasar Carlos
and the beautiful illegitimate son Juan, now growing into a handsome, clever ·lad in the secluded
castle of Ocaña, whilst the German archdukes had
drifted farther and farther from Spain, as had the
Savoy Princes. It had always been the policy
of the house of Austria to keep the Spanish nobles
powerless in the Peninsula. They might command
Spanish armies abroad and act as viceroys across
the seas, but were never to be trusted with executive
power in the realms of Spain ; and it had become
increasingly difficult, now that the nobles of the
outer realms had grown distrustful of Olivares,
to find men of the respective provinces who were
of sufficient rank and could be trusted to govern
the non-Castilian territories in the name of the
King. The principal difficulty was in Portugal,
where the widest autonomy, and every possible
guarantee against Spanish oppression, had been
granted by Philip II. But, as we have seen, the
tendency for a long time past, and especially under

[1] The charming picture by Velazquez, here reproduced, represents the
little Prince at about the age of nine on his pony galloping near the
Pardo.   There is another charming equestrian portrait of the Prince
in the Duke of Westminster's collection, with Olivares in the background.

Olivares, had been to curtail the rights enjoyed by Portugal since the union of the crowns.

The promise that none but Portuguese should rule in the country had been disregarded almost from the first in the appointment of Viceroys. The Austrian nephew, the Archduke Albert, had reigned under Philip II. ; and Moura, the wise half-Portuguese minister of Philip II., had ruled Portugal for years under his son. But to appoint a Portuguese noble now, with Olivares' known policy, would have been highly dangerous, and the Portuguese would hardly have stood a Spanish noble, even if Philip had dared to appoint one. The policy of conciliation that Philip II. had adopted had left the house of Braganza, which had a better claim to the Portuguese crown than Philip, richer and more powerful than most sovereigns. The reigning Duke of Braganza had married a sister of the Spanish Duke of Medina Sidonia, the head of the Guzmans, of which house Olivares was a cadet ; and in normal circumstances Braganza might have been the ideal man for Viceroy. But the circumstances were not normal. The deepest discontent reigned in the country at the ruin that had befallen its trade in consequence of its union with Spain, and especially at the new taxation for Spanish objects proposed at the bidding of Olivares ; and a subject so powerful and so popular as Braganza was naturally suspect. The difficulty was met at the end of 1634 by going somewhat far afield for a ruler of Portugal. The younger daughter of Philip II., the Infanta Catharine, had married Carlo Emmanuele, Duke of Savoy, in 1585 ; and one of their daughters, Princess Margaret, the widowed and dispossessed Duchess of Mantua, a first cousin of Philip, was brought to Spain to govern Portugal,—the idea being that, as she was a lady and a foreigner, she would be a safe and obedient instrument in the hands of Olivares. In November 1634 she entered Madrid in great state, and at the bull-fights and other festivities held to celebrate her coming she sat by the side of Philip and his Queen, which the Madrileños thought a great and unusual honour, accorded in order to give her higher prestige and authority before she set out for her fateful government, a figurehead for Olivares' attempts against Portuguese autonomy.

Catalonia was more uneasy even than Portugal. There had been a talk all the summer of the King's going thither to ask for more money, and the Catalans were in anger at the very idea. So great was the ill-feeling, that the Viceroy, the Duke of Cardona, a humble servant of Olivares, thought it safer to keep out of the way of his subjects; and the Castilian soldiers were daggers-drawn with the people, in whose houses they were billeted, in defiance of the Catalonian constitution.

The growing danger from these provinces, and the busy intrigues of Richelieu with the Dutch, to the intended detriment of Spain, again drove Olivares to seek a renewal of the suspended negotiations intended to draw Charles I. into the Catholic camp. At the end of July, Olivares sent for Hopton in great excitement, to show him an intercepted letter of the Prince of Orange, which, he said, disclosed a dangerous plan against England and Spain. "Ah!" said the Count-Duke, "we ought to have carried out that league of ours." "It was your fault," replied Hopton, " that it was not concluded. Nicolalde in London was not authorised to give the necessary pledges." " Well," retorted Olivares, " the matter may be arranged now, if you like." The hint was enough for Charles. The first thing, he said, was to get rid of Nicolalde, who was unsympathetic ; and he sent an English agent named Taylor to Madrid to recommend this course to Philip.

Soon negotiations were in full swing again. Some great personage, the Count of Humanes probably, was to be sent to England, whilst the Duke of Medina Celi was to go to France, and endeavour to secure the return of Marie de Medici the Queen-Mother and her son Orleans to France, which of course would have meant the paralysation of Richelieu. When the news came of the decisive battle of Nördlingen (page 260), gained over the Swedes and Weimar by the Infante Fernando, the great rejoicings and festivities with which Philip greeted the victory (October 1634), the bonfires and bull-fights and *Te Deums*, did not disguise the fact that war with France sooner or later must now be inevitably faced, and the efforts to come to an agreement with England proceeded more warmly than ever.

In October, at length, Windebank sent to Madrid the draft of the agreement, and one stands aghast at the unwisdom of Charles and his secret advisers, in thus showing willingness to betray the Protestant cause at the hollow charming of Olivares. England was to provide twenty ships of at least 400 tons each, ostensibly to protect the coast of England and Ireland ; but as soon as the fleet was at sea, notice was to be given to the Dutch in the form of an ultimatum to surrender to Spain, or the English would attack them. Spain was nominally to lend, but really to give, to Charles 200,000 crowns, and 100,000 a month for every month the fleet was at sea.[1] When Hopton saw Philip with this draft, and as usual raised the question of the Palatinate as a pendant to the agreement, only evasive answers were given to him, and again the negotiations flagged, whilst desperate efforts were made in Spain itself to force the nobles to raise and arm soldiers to take the field against France when the expected war should begin in the spring.

But whilst Olivares was thus striving to obtain at least the neutrality of England on the easiest terms for Spain, there was other diplomacy at work at least as profound and more generous than his. The battle of Nördlingen had broken up the effective league between Sweden and the German Protestants, and John Frederick of Saxony, with the other German Lutherans, soon made terms of compromise with the Emperor, by which they gained the toleration they sought, and the Thirty Years' War came to an end, so far as the religious struggle in Germany was concerned. But the far-reaching schemes of Richelieu would have been frustrated if the war had ended here, leaving Spain free from the drain of helping the Emperor ; for then she would have had power to deal with Holland effectually, and re-establish her waning hold over Italy to the injury of France. So, as war with Spain was necessary for Richelieu, he

[1] Hopton's MS. Notebook.

T

took good care to isolate his opponent before it began. He first effected an alliance with the United Provinces, and intrigued in Catholic Flanders with the nobles. Then he drew into his net Savoy, Mantua, and Parma; he occupied the Valtelline again, and Sweden was coupled to the car of France anew by Axenstiern, whilst, as a last stroke, he strove hard to include Charles I. in his league with the Dutch.

At the end of 1634, Olivares sent to Hopton in a great fright at news that he had heard, to the effect that Charles I. had joined France and Holland in their league ; and bitter complaints were made of the treatment of Spanish cruisers in English ports and in the Channel. In one case a Dutch prize had actually been taken away from the Spanish captors by English vessels, and brought into Dover. What was the meaning of it ? asked Olivares in a towering rage. Was the King of England going to throw them over after all ? A mention of the Palatinate only made him more furious still. Thus the bickering and bargaining went on all through the year 1635 ; Hopton urging Olivares to send some news worth the carrying by Taylor to London about the Palatinate, and the Count-Duke wrangling over the details of the agreement about the subsidy to England, which he swore that Charles had altered without consultation with Nicolalde. " He (Olivares) is in a good humour now," wrote Hopton on one occasion ; " but he is of a most dangerous nature, to which we shall always be subject as long as the business of the Palatinate shall last."

At length, when Olivares had exhausted the possibilities of prevarication in Madrid, the secret draught agreement was sent back to London for further discussion and amendment, and the continued neutrality of England at least was secured for another breathing space. One is struck with positive admiration for the masterly way in which, with this stale bait of the Palatinate, England was beguiled by Olivares from year to year, and prevented from joining the enemies of Spain. Richelieu had been bidding for English aid or benevolent neutrality too, and this was a chance which, if Charles had possessed any statesmanship worthy of the name, or any national ambition apart from the advantage of his dynasty, might have enabled England to play the part of the arbiter in Europe. But, as usual, the chance was missed by the instability of Charles, and when the cloud of war burst in the spring of 1635, the negotiations between London and Madrid were still dragging on. There was a talk at one time of a partition of the Spanish Netherlands between France and Holland after they should have been conquered, and this made Charles more eager than ever for the alliance with Spain to prevent such an eventuality, whilst both Olivares and Richelieu were glad to keep him wavering with insincere negotiations. His own condition, moreover, in England was already becoming difficult; for he had levied the ship money, and had taken the first fatal step by deciding to dispense with his Parliament; so that a strong ally with ready money was desirable to him.

Windebank wrote to Hopton on 27th May 1635:

" The French ambassador is pressing King Charles very hard to make a league with them; and it is, not the fault of the Spaniards that it is not already concluded, for they are going the right way to thrust us upon the French, though they cannot send a letter or pass an ambassador without us. This is a strange fascination, and they deserve to smart for it, as they will dearly if Dunkirk be besieged and his Majesty help them not." [1]

A little later Hopton writes : " Their (the Spaniards) only hope for Flanders and at sea is the friendship of our King. And yet they retain their gravity, as if they were the arbiters of the world. I saw the Conde yesterday, and, though he was a little troubled, yet he is very confident that all would end to their honour."

The conclusion of the precious alliance with King Charles had evidently at last to be carried through, or further delayed, by more highly-placed ambassadors than Hopton and Nicolalde ; and it was decided that Sir Walter Aston should go to Madrid and the Count of Humanes to London. Olivares was, or pretended to be, apprehensive of the coming of a new English ambassador, but was assured by Hopton that Sir Walter was all that could be desired from the Spanish point of view. Humanes, on the other hand, was reported to be " an honest gentleman, but with a good enough conceipt of himself. Thinking to get great things, he will be a little hard to deal with in England." But the seas were crowded with Dutch and French cruisers, and the land route through France was of course closed to Spaniards, so it was a difficult thing to get Humanes to England at all, unless he went

[1] Hopton's MS. Notebook.

back in the English ship that brought Aston. And so month after month of 1635 slipped by, the war proceeding actively in Flanders against the Infante Cardinal, and the French troops threatening Catalonia from Perpignan, whilst the English treaty with Spain was still on the balance. Hopton, in June 1635, told Olivares that this coldness and delay in his proceeding was producing a bad effect in England, and that unless they stirred themselves King Charles might look elsewhere. " Upon what ground do you say that," asked Olivares. " Upon Nicolalde's way of proceeding, and the delay that is taking place. It makes us think that the whole thing is a pretence," replied Hopton. " Everything is now practically settled with very few alterations, and there need be no more delay," Olivares assured him.

In July alarming news came to Madrid, that the Infante Cardinal had sustained severe defeat in the Low Countries (at Tirlemont), and was in personal danger. The Infante was intensely beloved in Spain, and the evil tidings " caused great care to their Majesties and the whole Court, for I cannot express what tenderness all sorts of people show to the Infante," wrote Hopton ; and, almost for the first time, Philip flew into a violent rage with Olivares, when he learnt that a letter written by the Infante, asking for further resources, had been concealed from him. Olivares found himself faced now, as he had never been before, by a determination on the part of Philip to act in opposition to his advice. Philip had no lack of personal courage, and under stress was capable of prolonged exertion. He was burning, too, to distinguish himself in arms, as his brother had done ; and, urged thereto by many of Olivares' enemies, he was insistent in his wish to lead his armies in person on the Catalonian frontier, now threatened by the French. Olivares, knowing that if the King were in the field he could not keep him isolated, or hope to retain his exclusive hold upon him, resisted the King's desire to the utmost, and almost daily squabbles took place between them on the subject.

It was clear now to Olivares that the aid of English ships in the Channel was really in the circumstances desirable for the success of Spain in Flanders. The road through Lombardy had been rendered difficult by the adhesion of the several Italian princes to Richelieu's league, and the war that was proceeding on the Rhine ; and the sea route was equally dangerous by reason of the Dutch and French squadrons. So the Count-Duke made another desperate attempt to buy Charles Stuart cheaply, and on trust. Late in July 1635, Olivares sent a very pressing message to Hopton that he wanted to see him, and when the ambassador presented himself in the palace, the Count-Duke asked him if he had a confidential English servant he could lend him, to hurry off to England at once with despatches for Nicolalde in London. "Yes," replied Hopton, "my man David Matthew will serve your turn " ; and before many hours had passed David Matthew was speeding on his way to London, with instructions to the Spanish agent that the maritime treaty was to be settled at all costs. The question of the Palatinate, Olivares told Hopton again, should really be settled now, though, not unnaturally, Hopton had his doubts ; for he knew secretly that the rebel Earl of Tyrone had been brought disguised to Madrid by the Emperor's ambassador, and was plotting even then with Olivares to raise sedition in Ireland if King Charles turned to the side of the French.

Nicolalde in London still went no further than amiable speeches; but at least Olivares' urgency had the effect of deciding Charles to send Sir Walter Aston to Spain, though poor Humanes died in Madrid, whilst still waiting for a ship to carry him, and was replaced as ambassador in London by Count de Oñate, much to Hopton's delight, who looked upon the appointment of so highly placed a personage as a great compliment. " For what he cannot do, nobody can. He is very honest, but somewhat hasty. In any case it is good to be rid of Nicolalde, who hates us." Aston, when he arrived at Corunna in September 1635, was received with ostentatious warmness ; and it was evident that his coming meant more than the mere ratification of a treaty already nearly concluded. Cottington sent by him what he calls " a merry letter " to Olivares, to tell him " how French I have become, for the Queen (Henrietta Maria) dined with me at Hanworth awhile since, and not long after the new French ambassadors, who now are become my friends, after complaining to the King of my ill affection to their master's service, calling me Conde de Olivares." It is plain that Sir Francis Cottington's " merriment " was intended to convey a hint that unless Olivares was really prompt this time in closing the deal, Charles would go over to the French. Hopton was hopeful but doubtful of Aston's better success than his own, for he knew that the Palatinate still stood in the way, and that Catholic Philip could never force the Emperor to restore it to a Protestant. " I believe they wish for a close union," he wrote, when he was leaving to return to England, " and this King might revoke the impediment if he liked, but I shall never be convinced he will do it till he comes to the point." [1]

Money, as usual, was the great desideratum for Philip, if the war was to be carried on with hope of success. Cortes were summoned both in Castile and Barcelona, and the former, as usual, did as they were asked, and voted 3 million ducats for the year; [2] Olivares having at the time laid by,

---

[1] It is curious that during all this period of great international anxiety and important negotiations, the talk about pictures is still constantly to be met with in the diplomatic correspondence. At one time, in June 1635, Suero de Quiñones wished to send two pictures as a present to King Charles. " I (Hopton) and King (Charles's) painter have seen them, and think they are good, particularly a Venus and Adonis of Luqueto. The other piece is by Tintoret. Suero de Quiñones is poor, but of quality. I know not why he should give his pictures away thus." But Quiñones, urged doubtless by poverty rather than his quality, did not give them away after all, and perhaps never intended to do so : for Hopton writes months afterwards : " Quiñones has played the knave, and sold his pictures." On another occasion (July of the same year), Hopton expresses his delight to Cottington that Labrador's paintings had come to hand at last. " The painter who made the landskips," he continues, " is now dead, and his pieces are much sought after and highly prized. I have a few of them, and am using diligence to get some more, at your lordship's service. If the man had lived I think I had carried him with me to England ; for he was grown much out of love with his own country, and was much my friend." MS. Note-book.

[2] After they had voted this usual 9 millions to extend over three years, the Cortes were thunderstruck, in the following January 1636, by a demand of Olivares that they should vote an additional 13 millions. The members were all paid and submissive ; but this was too much even for them. They flatly refused to vote the sum, which they said it was quite impossible for their constituents to pay. The

as we are told, no less than 8 millions, "which he will make 16 before the war begins in earnest." Spain was fortunate that year 1635, too, with the Indies fleet, which arrived in June with 14 millions of ducats, "of which the greater part will reach the King, besides the good profit he will get out of the confiscations." The Cortes of Barcelona was, as always, difficult to deal with; and for a time they were obstinate in their refusal to vote anything at all. But it was their own country now that was threatened, and on the promise of the King to relieve them from the levy of men for his armies, the Cortes of Catalonia agreed to vote him 400,000 ducats, and promised as much more as they could afford.

Philip's great dispute with Olivares was with regard to his wish to visit Barcelona during the session of the Cortes, and to remain there with his army, ready to lead it either to Italy, France, or elsewhere, as the events of the war might demand. The favourite was shocked at the King being exposed to such danger, and especially at the idea that he might leave the country; and he opposed with all his experience and authority the King's plan. "If Olivares can hinder the King from engaging his person he will do so. He pretends to give way, so as not to cross the King, who is set upon it, but he will not fail of ways to compass

royal Council then at once commenced criminal proceedings against them, whereupon the members prayed for time to consult their constituents, and orders were given by the Council to levy the 13 millions if necessary without the vote: to this abject state had representative institutions been reduced in the realms of Castile. See Danvila's *Poder Civil en España, Documents*, and Rodriguez Villa's Newsletters, 1636-37.

that which he wishes." [1]   But though Olivares was determined, Philip was obstinate; and when the minister, as was his wont, told the King that the Council of State was opposed to his going, Philip addressed a rescript to the Council, ordering them to discuss and vote on the question of his going, but that every Councillor should give his reasons individually to him for the advice he tendered. This was not in accordance with the usual procedure, and under Olivares' guidance the Council declined to do it, saying that the Count-Duke's knowledge of their opinions was so complete that he would report them to the King. It appears that Philip had given peremptory orders to Olivares to make every preparation for his immediate departure, and this was the subject submitted by the minister to the Council for discussion. With the arrogant Count-Duke dominating them, the Councillors, who were all his humble servants, of course agreed with him against the King. Money was short, they said, for the journey; and the recent successes in Flanders might perhaps make the voyage unnecessary. In any case, they begged the King not to undertake the matter lightly. Philip made the best of this halting dissent, replying that he accepted the advice as to not going for the moment, but ordered that everything should be made ready for his going at twenty days' notice if it became necessary. [2]

In the meanwhile the never-ending trivial show of Madrid went on. The idlers still paraded up

---

[1] Hopton to Coke, 13th June 1635. MS. Notebook.
[2] Council of State Deliberations of 19th November 1635. Danvila, *El Poder Civil en España.*

and down the Calle Mayor or gossiped on Liars'
Walk for the greater part of the day. Philip issued
ferocious but ineffective pragmatics against extravagance in dress and household appointments ;[1]
both the public playhouses were filled, and the
comedies applauded by eager crowds as usual.
But, on the other hand, famine had laid its grisly
hand everywhere on the arid lands of Castile,
the excise had been increased until even in the
capital itself starvation was not a threat but a
reality ; the ecclesiastical revenues were drained
as they had never been drained before, and salaries,
pensions, and State debts were either not paid at
all or else ruinously curtailed. In Madrid, penury
was now evident even amongst the better classes ;[2]
and Philip, who always lived frugally in his own
person, was obliged to write to his brother Fernando, begging him to save to the utmost : not to
allow his household to wear other than plain cloth,
and not to spend a ducat unnecessarily.

Spanish troops were fighting under the Infante

---

[1] There was one pragmatic which touched Madrid to the quick,
namely, that which forbade the use of carriages except to a very few
privileged people. So great was the outcry against this, that it was
found to be impossible to enforce it, as the driving about in coaches
was the main pleasure and amusement of every one who could afford
it, and of many people who could not. Whilst, therefore, the pragmatic
was rigidly enforced in the provincial capitals, licences were issued to
anyone in Madrid to own a coach on payment of 100 ducats.—Rodriguez Villa's Newsletters, January 1636. Other pragmatics were issued
at the time, regulating the courtesy titles, as it was found that too many
people were calling themselves *Lordship*.

[2] In the Rodriguez Villa's Newsletters at this period, hardly a week
passes without reference to the selling up of some nobleman's belongings
for debt. One of the most ostentatious nobles in Madrid, the Marquis
de las Navas, was soon after this fined for some offence, and as he had
no money an execution was put in on his coaches and horses, which it
was then found were not his own but hired ; and his furniture and even
the tapestries of his palace belonged to other people.

for the preservation of Flanders, in Germany, in Italy, in the Valtelline, wherever the enemies of the faith or the allies of Richelieu defied the Spanish claims; and yet it never entered the head, apparently, either of Olivares or his master, that these terrible sacrifices were useless to Spain, except that it was a point of honour to hold the Catholic States of Flanders that had been the ancient inheritance of its royal house. Holland was really lost beyond all recovery, though the stiff-necked pride of Castile would not acknowledge it; the religious question in Germany had already practically settled itself, and had left Spain hardly an excuse for fighting for orthodoxy there. All that was needed, even now, for Spain was to eat her unavoidable leek, to recognise facts patent to all the world, and to abandon her impossible pretensions; and peace with France and Holland might have been attained with ease. But through all the suffering and stress, that if continued meant national exhaustion, there was no indication anywhere of the conviction that Spain must voluntarily humble herself or bleed to death.

The process of social decadence had gone on apace, as was inevitable in such circumstances. Scandals were of constant occurrence. At the end of 1635, when the grave matters referred to were under discussion, two nobles, the Marquis del Aguila and Don Juan de Herrera, came to blows with each other in the theatre of the Buen Retiro Palace, in the presence of the King himself;[1]

---

[1] Both of them got safe away abroad, and the Marquis del Aguila was condemned to death in his absence. Herrera subsequently issued a public challenge for the Marquis to meet him and fight in Switzerland,

and whilst they fled from justice, a greater noble still, the Count of Sastago, Captain of the King's Guard, was accused of inciting them to the disturbance. As was invariably the case, no sooner was one offence mentioned than a dozen were added to it. The Count, it was said, had sold the sergeancy of the guard for 1100 ducats; the provedor of the guard paid him fifty reals every day, filched from the mess bill; he ill-treated his wife, . . . and much else of the same sort; and as soon as Count de Sastago was under lock and key for these offences, no less than three other noble Counts were competing and quarrelling with each other for his place as Captain of the Guard;[1] whilst, a few days afterwards, Zapata, the Lieutenant of the Guard, was carried to prison for making a disturbance at the entrance of the palace, and breaking down the barriers to get in, against the royal orders, whilst Prince Baltasar Carlos was coming out.

On New Year's Eve 1636, we are told, " their Majesties went to dine at the Buen Retiro, where there was in the afternoon a sort of comedy or festival never seen before in Spain. First there appeared the poet Atillano, who has come from the Indies, and who may justly be called a prodigy of the world, as he proved himself to be on this occasion; for such is his poetic rage, that he utters

and thus explains the affray. The Marquis, he asserts, said in the theatre that he was drunk, and though he made no reply to this, an hour afterwards he came behind him and struck him a great blow on the back of the neck. He (Herrera) then drew his sword, and he and the Marquis were both seized by the Guard.

[1] *La Corte y Monarquia de España en* 1636–1637, a series of newsletters written by an anonymous grandee in Madrid, edited by A. Rodriguez Villa.

a perfect torrent of Castilian verse on any subject proposed to him,[1] and, withal, in very remarkable style, with much taste and adornments from the Scriptures and classical authors, brought in most aptly, with comparisons, emphasis, digressions, and poetic figures, which strike his hearers with astonishment, many believing that it can only be done by devilish arts, for he never drops a foot or forgets a syllable. . . . After Atillano came Cristobal, the blind man, well known at Court ; and he also showed his skill in turning out couplets impromptu, with his usual prettiness and propriety, and quite in courtier-like fashion. But as he lacks erudition, and the other man possesses much, you may well imagine the difference between them. After the poets came Calabaza, the dwarfs, the little negro, and the girls they call the *Count's wrigglers* ;[2] and they represented their figures and played a hundred monkey tricks to raise a laugh. Afterwards the party ended by a ball and masquerade. It was

---

[1] Philip had grown very fond of these tests of literary promptitude, at which he appears to have shone. In Morel Fatio's *Espagne au XVI. et XVII. Siècle* there is reproduced the programme of a great burlesque *Academy* of this sort, which took place at the Buen Retiro during the fetes of 1637. There are fourteen items for competition, of which the following are good specimens: A romance declaring which stomach is most to be envied, that which will digest great sorrows or great suppers. An epigram in two Castilian couplets, declaring which is the most foolish, to be a fool sometimes or to be always discreet. Sixteen roundels, about a procuress who was dying, much comforted that there were no proper men left in the world ; and just as she is about to expire, a young man comes in whom she receives with delight, saying to him, " My friend, you are just in time ; there are two beautiful lasses in there, as good as gold ; one dark and the other fair." And as the youth was hesitating which to choose, the expiring old woman cried, " My son ; for heaven's sake take the dark one. This is no time for me to deceive people." The tale has been drawn out thus, because they say it is true.

[2] Las Sabandijas del Conde.

very good and diverting ; and my lady Countess
of Olivares gave the collation to their Majesties."

The year thus fittingly begun in the Court was
signalised by the Cardinal Infante Fernando in
Flanders and France by military capacity which
recalled the great days of the Emperor a hundred
years before. The French and Dutch allies were
already suspicious of each other, and were not
co-operating cordially ; so that Fernando had been
able to wear out the resistance of the French
without a general engagement, and whilst they,
disorganised and decimated with famine and disease,
retreated into France, the Infante overran Picardy
and Champagne. He pushed his advance beyond
the Somme and to the banks of the Oise, threatening
Paris itself, and elated Olivares planned a simultaneous invasion of France under the Admiral of
Castile, and yet another from the side of Germany
over the frontier of Burgundy. The only one of
these attacks that came to anything was that of
the Cardinal Infante ; but even he, either from
want of resources or lack of boldness, lagged on
the line of the Somme and Oise until the French
had recovered from their panic. Orange was also
marching to aid his ally, and Paris had raised a
great army of citizens to resist further attack ; and
early in 1637 the Spaniards, under the Cardinal
Infante, had retreated into Flanders again, forced
once more to stand on the defensive. But the net
result of the temporary display of Spanish vigour
had been to free the Catalonian frontier from
imminent fears from the French, and Philip had
found no excuse for insisting further upon his

desire to place himself in command of his troops in Barcelona.

A perusal of the gossiping newsletters of the times, though, of course, much that they record is merely trivial, throws a lurid light upon the utterly lawless condition of the capital at this grave juncture, when the nation was supposed to be straining every nerve to prevent humiliation at the hands of its implacable enemy. It would be profitless to give details of all, or of any large number, of the scandals mentioned by the chroniclers from day to day ; but as a specimen a few entries belonging to this year 1636 will give an idea of the state of affairs in Philip's Court at the time. In January, Don Antonio Oquendo, the famous naval commander, was at Mass in the church of Buen Suceso,[1] when a challenge to immediate combat was brought from the rival admiral Nicholas Spinola. Oquendo just gave himself time to confess, and then met his opponent, both being mounted and armed with knives. One of the combatants was wounded before the passers-by could interfere, and the other fled to hiding.[2]

A day or two later, proclamation was made in the streets that the King ordered all the Portuguese murderers in Madrid to leave within a week, or they would be apprehended and sent before the judges, who were considering their cases. " The intention of this," sapiently says the chronicler, " appears to be that they may thus be forced to

---

[1] This church was at the end of the Puerta del Sol, where the Hotel de Paris now stands.

[2] Oquendo, only a few weeks later, took command of the galleys at Cadiz to attack the French fleet, and received 200,000 ducats.

enlist as soldiers, and the pragmatic with regard to the number of lackeys allowed had a similar object." At the same time a scandalous quarrel was going on between the officers of the Inquisition and the alcaldes of the Court, or judges of first instance, on some trivial point of etiquette, but which ended in wholesale excommunication of all the alcaldes in a body, and several inferior officers on both sides being condemned and imprisoned by the rival authorities. In the summer another panic occurred in the Church of St. Philip and on Liars' Walk, because a heretic shouted some sacrilegious words in the church; and soon afterwards an offended soldier murdered by a pistol shot a gentleman named Bilbao on the steps leading to the crowded atrium of the church, the most frequented spot in Madrid.

On the 28th July there was a great bull-fight in the Plaza Mayor, which had attracted a vast concourse of people, as the bulls were said to have been unusually savage. They must have been so, for several men were killed; but worse than this, daggers were drawn and a slashing match commenced under the King's very eyes. Philip, outraged at such disrespect, ordered the offenders to be arrested. They were handed by the alguacils to the Archers of the Guard, from whom they managed to escape. Philip quite lost his temper at this, which he very rarely did, and rose wrathfully to leave the arena. The Queen pulled him by the cloak, and coaxed him into sitting again whilst two more bulls and many horses were done to death. But the King was still unappeased, and as he went out past the Archers of the Guard

U

he told them "that they had managed it very nicely. Why were they Archers, he wondered, and what were they paid for?" the matter ending in mutual recriminations between the Archers and the alguacils, and the punishment of the former.

Matrimonial scandals succeeded each other daily in the Newsletters, and the highest names in the Court are treated with the utmost scurrility in this particular; whilst accusations of corruption on the part of judicial authorities and priests are quite as common. The authorities whose duty it was to keep order appear to have been as lawless as the rest of the citizens. The Corregidor [1] (Governor of Madrid) had occasion in October to call upon the King's upholsterer and valet de chambre, who was also captain of a newly raised company of militia. The soldiers in his courtyard, for some reason not stated, snatched the Corregidor's wand of office from the page who carried it, and, having broken it, belaboured the boy's back with it. The Corregidor, offended in his dignity, told the soldiers angrily that he was a member of the Council of

---

[1] This was the Count of Montalvo, who must have been more quarrelsome and punctilious than most of his compeers, for only a few weeks after the contention here described he had a violent quarrel with the Council of Castile, the supreme judicial authority, which ended in the Corregidor himself being imprisoned and heavily fined. It appears that he had ordered an alguacil to attend him, which the alguacil refused to do, as he was not under his jurisdiction. The Corregidor's answer was to cast the man into prison; whereupon the alguacil appealed to the President of the Council of Castile, who told the Corregidor that he had exceeded his powers. The touchy Corregidor in a rage burst out with: "A rebuke to me. By Christ's body, his Majesty the King has many ministers who do not know what they are doing." The scandalised president without more ado cast the Corregidor into prison, from which only after much trouble he was released.

War, and their master ; whereupon one of the men-at-arms thrust his pike against the august breast of the Corregidor, and threatened to kill him. Upon this a free fight took place between the alguacils in attendance on the Corregidor and the soldiers, and after much uproar one of the soldiers was overpowered and borne off in triumph by the alguacils to the prison of the municipality, " notwithstanding that it was the feast day of our seraphic father St. Francis." The Corregidor lost no time, but sat in judgment at once, and of course found the soldier guilty. But before the trial was done a great rabble of soldiers assembled outside the Guildhall (*Casa de la Villa*) to rescue their comrade from the hands of justice. The town officers read an order from the balcony that every soldier was immediately to withdraw, and the stout-hearted Corregidor himself arrested the ringleader, and, kicking and cuffing, thrust him into a cell. That afternoon the Corregidor accompanied the first offender through the streets of Madrid, whilst 200 strokes of the lash were administered on the poor soldier's bare back, and when the Corregidor returned to the Guildhall he stood by whilst the other offender was tortured on the rack. Out of this arose a quarrel royal between the Council of War, who took the soldiers' part, and the Royal Council, who were for the civil authorities ; and for weeks afterwards recriminations and punishments were abundantly exchanged.

There was, indeed, in all spheres a shocking absence of real dignity and restraint. Crimes of the most horrible description are mentioned as

being prevalent in the better classes ; [1] and after
the first outcry they were allowed to go almost un-
punished and unchecked. As may be supposed, in
such a state of society superstition of the grossest
description was common. The proceedings of the
miracle-working nun of Carrion, to whom, it will
be recollected, the Infanta Maria had recommended
the Prince of Wales, had become so notorious that
the Inquisition had taken her in hand, and condemned her as a witch and an impostor. But this
appears only to have increased her fame for sanctity,
for several books in her praise were burnt by the
Inquisition, and every measure taken to expose her
frauds by the Holy Office ; but with so little effect,
that after her death, early in 1637, an edict was
read in every church in Madrid pronouncing major
excommunication against all those who retained
images, portraits, signatures, crosses, certificates,
beads, or books relating to her.[2] When the Marquis
of Aitona was unwilling to start from Madrid to
take up the governorship of Milan in the spring
of 1636, and delayed his departure from week to
week, a fresh pretext for delay, and one generally
praised, was that it would be most unwise for

[1] Particulars of these may be found in Rodriguez Villa's *La Corte y
Monarquia de España en* 1636–1637, p. 50, and in Barrionuevo's Newsletters of a subsequent date. With regard to the period now under
review (1636), one of the accused persons under torture was hastily
taken down from the rack, " as he showed an intention of accusing
half Madrid." On this occasion two obscure persons were burnt alive,
but scores of aristocrats whose names are freely mentioned in the letters
escaped with short banishment from Court or no punishment at all.

[2] It was afterwards stated that one bishop had surrendered thousands
of the nun's letters to the Inquisition, and the Cura of Santa Cruz had
" a room full of crosses, medals, images, and old rags belonging to her,
whilst the Duke of Arschot had two thousand made specially to be blessed
by her." Rodriguez Villa.

him to leave Madrid on the Ides of March, because it was the anniversary of the murder of Cæsar.

The lawlessness was not confined even to grown people, but extended to children. It appears that late in 1636 a pragmatic had been drafted, but not yet officially promulgated, decreeing that no man in future might wear in Madrid the long wisp of hair before the ears (*guedejas*) that had recently become the fashion ; and women were strictly forbidden to appear in the strange farthingales or very wide hoop skirt, flattened back and front, called *guardainfantes* ; "although," says the chronicler, "it has not yet been proclaimed, the boys are already hunting women who wear guardainfantes as if they were cows, hissing and whistling at them, and insulting them dreadfully. To such a length has this insolence been carried, that mounted alguacils have been posted to prevent violence, two boys having been killed in the street last Thursday by attendants upon the women, who had turned upon the boys." [1]

Whilst Olivares bore upon his bowed shoulders the whole burden of government, resorting to the most empirical means to raise money, such as calling in the copper coin and restamping it to three times its former value,[2] the King had to be distracted and kept amused by never-ending entertainments, such as those that have been described

---

[1] Rodriguez Villa's Newsletter, October 1636.

[2] This, as Aston wrote, made gold and silver a mere merchandise. The pragmatics, it is true, fixed the premium on silver at 25 per cent., but it was at once raised in the open market to 34 per cent. and more, the resulting distress and dislocation of business being appalling. Aston to Coke, 29th May 1636. Record Office, S.P. Spanish MSS. 38.

in former pages.[1] Hardly a week passed without some pretext for a long series of such shows, which now usually took place at the favourite Buen Retiro. Aston, in one of his letters to Coke in May 1636,[2] describes the festivities of Whitsuntide that year.

"Three days of noble feasting," he calls it ; "the first day a masquerade on horseback, in the evening, and bull-fights on the other two days, with cane tourneys. I was invited to all of them, and had the particular honour on the first night to be placed in a balcony in the King's own apartments with the grandees ; this being an unusual honour. On the other days I occupied a special balcony with my own people. When the welcome news of the Cardinal Infante's victories in Picardy came to Madrid late in September 1636, the rejoicings were frantic. His Majesty and all the Court rode to Our Lady of Atocha to give thanks. . . . They returned at night through the streets, illuminated by countless torches ; all the Councils having been ordered to make a celebration in honour of the occasion, they all complied famously, and with great sumptuousness, each feast having cost 2000 ducats, and others are yet to come which will surpass them all." [3]

[1] In April of this year, 1636, for instance, Philip for some reason or other was in depressed spirits on Sunday, 26th, and was for a time secretly closeted in the chapel alone in prayer. At once, we are told, "great and sudden preparations were ordered to be made in the palace for comedies and interludes, and the comedians were warned to play as many buffooneries as they could to make his Majesty laugh." An account in MS. of all that happened in the Court from 1636 to 1642, Biblioteca Nacional, Madrid, H. 38.

[2] Record Office, S.P. Spanish MSS. 38.

[3] Newsletter. Aston also describes the rejoicings on this occasion,

A few weeks later, an excuse was found in the expected arrival in Madrid of the French Bourbon Princess of Carignano, wife of Prince Thomas of Savoy, who was fighting for the Spanish under the Cardinal Infante, and it was determined that in her honour the Buen Retiro should surpass itself. Before the Princess had even embarked for Spain, the great preparations were begun " to finish the new arena at the Buen Retiro. Experts have been despatched to the country around Madrid to obtain the 80,000 planks which will be needed for the barriers that are to surround it. The work is going on so actively, both in levelling the ground and erecting the wood-work, that there is no cessation, even on Sunday or feast days ; and the Corregidor has erected there a scaffolding with a (neck) ring to punish the workmen who do not complete their task pro-perly, as an example to the others. A triumphal car is also being made, of which the cover alone is to cost 4000 ducats ; and it will be enclosed in glass, in order that the inside may look more beautiful." [1]

Another fine feast is described by Aston in June 1636. Writing to Coke, he says :

" The King and Queen retired to Buen Retiro to enjoy the curious gardens and new waterworks con-trived by Olivares, and a great variety of festivals. One on Midsummer night was of the greatest ostenta-tion and curiosity I have ever seen in my life. I had

and mentions that Philip " let fall some expressions of regret that his brother-in-law's affairs had fallen into such bad case." This was a curious expression, as the brother-in-law in question was the King of France, and it was Philip's own army that had put him " in bad case."

[1] Rodriguez Villa.

the honour to be invited to it, and had extraordinary favour and respect shown in the place that was given to me. The entertainment was a play that was made on purpose to be acted by the three several companies of players of this town, the intention whereof was so good ; the place where it was acted being set out with three several scenes of much ostentation, and the disposition of the lights so full of novelty and delight, that I am highly tempted to give your honour a larger description of it, but that it would prove to be business enough for a large letter." [1]

It was not all feasting and play-going for Sir Walter Aston at the historic " house with the seven chimneys." When he arrived to replace Arthur Hopton, early in 1636, the famous agreement between Philip and Charles was still uncompleted, and the complaints of the English shipmasters against Spanish oppression were louder and more insistent than ever. Tyrone and the Desmonds were in Madrid negotiating for the raising of fresh Catholic Irish regiments for the Spanish service, and urging Philip to make no terms about the Palatinate unless Charles would restore the lands of O'Neill. But the aid of an English fleet in the Channel became more and more desirable to Spain as the war went on ; and it was clear that the old vague promises and smiling plausibilities of Olivares had at last lost their efficacy with Charles. An instructive light is thrown upon the methods by which Olivares still strove to cope with the situation, by an original holograph letter in the Record Office [2] from Olivares' confidential secretary Rojas,

[1] Record Office S.P., Spain MSS. 38.   [2] Ibid.

to the imperial ambassador in Madrid, asking him by King Philip's orders to " give some words of hope to the English ambassador about the Palatinate." " It is of the utmost importance that we should make use of all such expedients as present themselves ; as it appears that the King of England is extremely busy preparing a powerful fleet to be used to the detriment of this Crown, . . . probably against Brazil, in co-operation with the Hollanders."

On the 18th June 1636, Olivares wrote a serious letter to Aston, evidently intended to bring affairs to a crisis. He, Olivares, had news, he said, of a design of a French naval attack on the English coast. Aston replied coolly that he had no doubt due measures would be taken in England to repel any attempt; but in the subsequent interview he succeeded " in persuading," as he says, " the Conde to assent to the terms for the co-operation of the English fleet, and Count de Oñate was instructed to start for England at once. They are really trying to prove that they desire the King of England's friendship. Indeed, in the present state of things it is needful for them, and I hope our King will make wise use of the opportunity." [1] But, withal, the Palatinate, which was the question nearest to Charles's heart, was still left open, though Arundel in Vienna was pushing the point there industriously, while the Palatine himself appealed personally to Philip by a letter which received no answer.

When Count de Oñate eventually presented himself before King Charles at Whitehall, the English King left no doubt that the Palatinate

[1] Aston to Coke, 30th June 1636. Record Office, MSS. S.P., Spain, 39.

was uppermost in his mind. Speaking in Latin, he asked Oñate three questions—"Whether, having notice of the final answer of the Emperor to Arundel, he hath any power by way of interpretation or otherwise to qualify the said answer ? Whether he hath power from the King of Spain to deliver to King Charles, or the Prince Elector, that part of the Lower Palatinate in his (Philip's) possession, and also by this mediation that part held by the Emperor ? Whether he hath commission to set down in particular those conveniences that his father told Arundel the King of Spain would insist upon ? Whether, in accordance with the assurance given by the English ambassador in Spain, King Charles may expect by him (Oñate) any more particular and full satisfaction than hath yet been delivered ? " [1] Needless to say that Oñate had no clear answers to any of these questions, nor instructions to forward the matter of the Palatinate definitely ; and once more discouragement fell upon those who had hoped to carry through the treaty.

Hopton, when he arrived in London and heard the news, wrote to Aston by Richard Fanshawe, who was on his way to Spain :

"A greater change has taken place in our purposes in the last month than in years before. Our eyes are now opened to the intention of the house of Austria to keep hold of the Palatinate. They must have a very mean opinion of us to treat our King with so little courtesy. If his Majesty gives way to the opinion

[1] Record Office S.P., Spain MSS.

of his subjects about the Palatinate, it will prove to Spain their error. It is incredible that they should act thus. They will certainly lose us if they be not careful." At the same time, the Spaniards were boasting in Madrid that " the Palatinate has been put to bed, and the King of England will not dare to break with us about it."

The need of Spain for English co-operation was now once again growing less urgent, for the star of Richelieu was temporarily dimmed. The coalition of the Italian princes against Spain had fallen to pieces, the Dukes of Mantua and Savoy died, and Parma was forced to submit to Spain. The Valtelline was retaken and occupied by the Spanish troops, and the Grisons conciliated ; whilst Cardinal la Valette's campaign in 1637 against the Infante Cardinal partially failed. In Germany, too, the French were defeated all along the line, and, worst of all, France lost Alsace. Richelieu, moreover, was faced by the dangerous Court intrigues of Gaston of Orleans and his cousin Soissons, and half France was in smouldering revolt against the taxation imposed by the great Cardinal. The way across Lombardy and Tyrol to Germany and Flanders by land was now open to Spanish troops ; and Olivares, having kept unstable Charles of England on the tenterhooks all these years with the bait of the Palatinate, could now snap his fingers at him, and for a time drop the mask.

CHAPTER VIII

FESTIVITIES IN MADRID—EXTRAVAGANCE AND PEN-
URY—NEW WAYS OF RAISING MONEY—HOPTON
AND WINDEBANK—BATTLE OF THE DOWNS—
VIOLENCE IN THE STREETS OF MADRID—REVOLT
OF PORTUGAL—FRENCH INVASION OF SPAIN—
REVOLT OF CATALONIA—PHILIP'S AMOUR WITH
THE NUN OF ST. PLACIDO—THE WANE OF
OLIVARES — PHILIP'S VOYAGE TO ARAGON —
INTRIGUES AGAINST OLIVARES — FALL OF
OLIVARES

NOTHING even in Spain could exceed the magnificence with which Philip greeted the Bourbon
Princess of Carignano. She was really a person of
little importance, but her significance in Spain for
the moment was that she was a sister of the Count
of Soissons, who in France was in arms against
Richelieu ; and a foe of the Cardinal was a friend
of Spain. The proud dame was equal to the
occasion, and, after endless discussions as to the
exact behaviour of both at a proposed interview
with the English ambassador, Sir Walter Aston
decided that he could not, with due regard for his
dignity, meet the Princess at all. The points of
difference seem trivial enough : when Aston was
to take off his hat, how many steps upon the dais
the lady was to advance to meet him, and so on ;
but the Princess was indignant that the English-

man should thus haggle over the courtesy due to her, and all Madrid took malicious part in the squabble.[1] The usual round of festivities for the Princess, with the addition of a great pig-sticking day with twenty wild boars at the Pardo, were followed in a fortnight by another series more sumptuous still, to celebrate the election of Philip's brother-in-law to the kingship of the Romans and to the succession of the imperial throne. Many detailed accounts of these extraordinary feasts, the greatest ever given in the Buen Retiro, exist ; [2] but so many similar celebrations have been described in this book from Spanish sources, that it will suffice in this case to quote only Sir Walter Aston's short description of what he saw. "On the 7th February 1637 the King came from the Pardo to the Buen Retiro, and he has been busy ever since arranging the festivities for the election of the King of the Romans. The feasts began on the 15th, the King being present. A large place had been specially cleared and levelled before the Buen Retiro, and built about with uniform scaffolds two storeys high, the posts and divisions

[1] She ended by utterly wearing out her welcome, and disgusting everybody in Madrid by her pride and rapacity and the turbulence of her followers, and before she left she was supplanted by another great French lady, the Duchess of Chevreuse, who came to Madrid from London as an emissary of Marie de Medici, and was received with great distinction, much to the Princess of Carignano's anger. Needless to say that nothing came of either of the intrigues, and that Richelieu kept his hand firmly on the helm until he died in 1642.

[2] These two series of festivities, which together lasted about a month, certainly mark the high-water mark of the splendour of the Buen Retiro. Full descriptions of parts of them have been published by Mesonero Romanos in *El Antiguo Madrid*, by Morel Fatio in *L'Espagne au XVI. et XVII. Siècle*, and by at least three contemporary writers—Mendez Silva, Andrés Sanchez del Espejo, and the Newsletters in Rodriguez Villa's *Corte y Monarquia de España*, etc.

all beautified with paintings and gilding. The King and the Conde (Olivares) dressed themselves in the house of Carlo Strada, the *asentista* (loan-monger), by whom they were richly presented, not only with jewels but with the whole furniture of the apartments,[1] which he had provided for each. His house is in the Carrera de San Geronimo, where the King and Conde took horse, and, attended by 200 of the nobility and persons of quality, and two triumphal chariots drawn by 20 oxen apiece, entered the Plaza, where they performed a curious masquerade after their manner full of changes, the one half of the horsemen being led by the King and the other half by the Count-Duke ; the King and Conde and all the rest being richly clad after the same kind. The Plaza was round about set full of torches in several heights, and postures which had so much delight and magnificence in the appearance, that those who have looked curiously into the entertainments of former times say that amongst the Romans they have not read of any greater ostentation.[2] The charge hath

[1] The contents of the King's apartment, given by Strada to Philip, " with a very precious reliquary," was valued at 20,000 ducats. But this splendid gift did not save Strada from a fine of 200 ducats a few weeks afterwards, for having addressed Camporedondo, the senior member of the Council of Finance as " Lordship," whereas by the pragmatic he was only allowed to be addressed as "Worship." The house Strada lived in was one he rented from Spinola, his fellow-Genoese. As an instance of the prevailing corruption, it may be mentioned that Strada paid 300 ducats to the author of the official account of these festivities for the favourable references to him in it.

[2] The Newsletters say that there were 7000 wax lights, which alone cost over 8000 ducats, the cost of this one day's feast being 300,000 ducats—afterwards increased to 500,000 ducats. This enormous expenditure shocked everybody who thought about the matter. " The gossips," says the Newsletter, " assert that this great event, which had no other end than pastime and pleasure, which indeed was pure ostentation,

certainly been very great, but hath cost the King nothing ; for it hath long used this town to defray all extraordinaries either for his honour or his pleasure. Since then there has been a bull-feast and some fresh entertainment every day. On Sunday last there was a masked carnival fit for the Shrove-tide season ; so full of variety of different figures, antique shapes, and several dances, that I have not seen in a ridiculous way any of more pleasure. Late advices have given them little contentment ; but however their business may go abroad, they are resolved to make themselves merry at home." [1]

However " merry " the Court might be, the need for money was more pressing than ever. In the same letter that describes these entertainments, we are told that the Marquis of Castel Rodrigo had been sent to Seville to demand 800,000 ducats for present needs in Madrid. " Though he is to demand it as a donature, this King's requests are

was to show our friend Cardinal Richelieu that there is plenty more money left in the world to punish his King." But many persons who dared in the subsequent carnival to blame this waste found themselves in the dungeons a few days afterwards ; and several priests who preached before Olivares at St. Geronimo in the ensuing Lenten retreat, and ventured to denounce such wicked extravagance, were banished from Court. Rodriguez Villa's Newsletters have much to say about this.

[1] Aston to Coke, 20th and 25th February 1637.—Record Office, S.P. Spain MSS. 38. This part of the entertainments had been arranged and paid for by Philip's state secretary and confidential friend, Geronimo de Villanueva, Marquis of Villalba, of whom we shall hear later. On the following Tuesday the regular public carnival took place, and the licence appears to have been shocking in the extreme. In one of the cars a donkey was represented as dying in bed, with pretended priests and friars mocking the most sacred mysteries around him, whilst the supposed doctors were going through indecent antics. One masker was covered with habits of knighthood, crosses, and noble insignia, with the significant motto, " For Sale." Rodriguez Villa.

understood to be commands, and admit of no reply.[1]
The donature has already begun in this Court, and
is to go through the whole kingdom, everybody
being told by way of request what he has to pay."
The Pope, too, who had been for months striving
to bring about peace or a truce, was persuaded to
consent that the Spanish clergy should be mulcted
in 500,000 ducats ; and when the Indies fleet
arrived, Olivares ordered a similar amount of private
treasure in it to be seized in exchange for assign-
ments, which, says Aston, is commonly a very slow
and lame payment. But the greatest novelty in
the way to raise funds was invented at this juncture
by a Jesuit priest in Madrid named Salazar, and was
at once seized upon by Olivares to become until
our own days a principal source of revenue in all
civilised States ; namely, the device of using
government-stamped paper for all official and
formal documents. This new impost was published
in Madrid early in 1637, there being four denomina-
tions of stamped paper ; respectively of 1, 2, 3, and
4 reals per sheet, to forge which was an offence
punishable by death. The lawyers and people were
up in arms against it, though financiers said it
would bring in two million ducats a year, and the
Nuncio and priests flatly refused to conform to

[1] Amongst other devices at this period, Olivares in the King's name
appropriated one-third of all the household plate and manufactured
silver in private hands, and ordered each member of the Councils of the
Indies and Castile to provide each month 200 ducats in silver to be
exchanged (for depreciated copper) at the exchange of 25 per cent., the
current rate being 38. A young Irish student at the Escorial
came and said that he had discovered how to convert a mark of silver
and a mark of copper into two marks of pure silver. Olivares accepted
the youth's offer to demonstrate his discovery at the palace before experts, but after two attempts he ignominiously failed and was imprisoned.

it for the ecclesiastical courts, etc., without the special order of the Pope.[1]

The prices of commodities in Madrid had risen enormously in the previous few years, thanks to the tampering with the coinage and the oppressive operation of the alcabala tax on all sales ; and the figures given by Hopton at the time to Coke are very significant of the increased cost of living. Aston, sore and humiliated at the final failure of the treaty, begged to be recalled ; and Hopton, who had not long returned to England disappointed, and, as he said, shelved, was again nominated for the embassy at Madrid. But Coke informed him that his allowance for diet would be in future reduced from £6 to £4 per day, " as it was in the time of Queen Elizabeth." Sir Arthur Hopton (he had only just been knighted) wrote feelingly on this matter, pointing out how unjust the reduction was.

" All the diet of table and stables is three times as dear as in Sir Charles Cornwallis's time, when the £2 a day was first added. A loaf of bread

---

[1] As may be imagined, Father Salazar's invention produced a perfect torrent of satires, and the Jesuit himself was sternly reproved by his ecclesiastical superiors for busying himself in financial affairs. So bitter was the feeling against him, that he was forced to leave the Society. Amongst other rumours about him was that he had devised a government monopoly of drinking water. In the ensuing Lent the pulpits of Madrid rang in denunciation of Father Salazar ; and at the carnival a masker dressed as a peasant bore a banner inscribed—

> Sisas alcabalas y papel sellado,
> Me tienen desollado.

> With food excise and tax on all I sell,
> And now with paper stamps, you've flayed me well.

The unfortunate masker had to fly to hiding to escape the wrath of Olivares.

X

was then worth 12 maravedis, and is now worth 34.[1] An azumbre [2] of wine was then worth 12 maravedis, and now sells for 30 ; a pound of mutton, which was then worth 17 maravedis, is now worth 40 ; a fanega [3] of barley then cost 6 reals,[4] and 16 now. I myself have paid as much as 26. If this new rule be enforced, the English ambassador cannot maintain his position, for some of the small Italian ambassadors have as much as £6."

But Hopton need not have exerted himself to obtain the full pay ; for before he could make ready to return to his post a change came over the scene. Aston had long been puzzled as to what was being arranged in London. Rumours had reached him that some agreement was on foot between England and France, but Hopton from London had emphatically assured him, on the 23rd May 1637, that nothing of the sort was in- tended. By the next courier Aston received an enigmatical letter written by Charles's own hand, which only made the mystery deeper, and drew from the ambassador an impatient exclamation that he could not give any useful warning to the English merchants on such a riddle as that. Why was he not told, he asked, if war was really intended, and he then could make some use of his knowledge. The King's letter is a characteristic one,· and as it has not to my knowledge ever been printed, I give it in full.

[1] Thirty-four maravedis at the normal value would be equal to 2½d.

[2] An azumbre is ancient liquid measure of about 2 quarts.

[3] A Castilian fanega of grain is 1½ bushel.

[4] This is the silver real, then worth 6d.

" Watt. The darkeness of ther inventions could not suffer my resolutions to be cleare : so that it was impossible to send you a right light to walke by. What that is (though uncertaine yet) Secretary Windebanke will send you worde. They may be assured of my friendship, but then ther actions not their words must doe it. So referring you to my Secretaries despatch, I rest your friend Charles R. Theobalds, the 15th June 1637." [1]

Aston had not to wait many days for partial enlightenment. Hopton wrote reminding him of Olivares's dictum that there was no gratitude amongst princes; but said the Count-Duke might have been more grateful on this occasion with advantage to himself. Now it was too late ; for a great change had been effected in English policy, and a treaty had been arranged with France. A few days later, Windebank wrote a long official despatch, setting forth all the causes for complaint against the house of Austria, and announcing an alliance with Louis XIII.[2] But still Aston did not know whether

[1] Record Office, S.P. Spain MSS. 39.

[2] Although not immediately touching our subject, a very curious set of letters included in the above in the Record Office may be mentioned. They relate to Secretary Windebank's young son Christopher, or Kit Windebank, as he was called. He had been sent under Aston's care to Spain to see the world ; and had been quite carried away by the *genius loci* of Madrid, and got out of hand altogether. The scapegrace makes the best of his proceedings in his letters to his father and mother, but Aston's reports tell a different tale, and Kit is very angry when his money is stopped. The worst of it was that he fell in love with a Spanish girl, and, running away from embassy, married her. At Aston's instance Olivares threw into prison the priest who married them ; but a thousand legal difficulties existed, he said, to obtaining a divorce, especially as Kit swore that he would not give up the girl, who was *enceinte*. At the end, however, he submits sulkily, the girl is sent to

it meant war with Spain, or simply a neutrality with benevolent tendency towards the French and Dutch. He learnt before long that all that Richelieu had needed was to divert Charles from an agreement with Spain, for the Stuart ship was already steering straight for the breakers, and thenceforward no active attack from England had to be feared by either of the parties to the great struggle on the Continent.

Relations between England and Spain almost came to open hostility when, in October 1639, the powerful fleet of seventy vessels which Philip had by a supreme effort fitted out was almost destroyed by the Dutch in the Downs, and in English waters, where they had taken refuge from Tromp's pursuing fleet. When the Spanish agent in England sought from Charles the protection due to a belligerent in neutral waters, the King at once attempted to bargain for conditions about the Palatinate. But Tromp was in no mood for scrupulousness, and, taking the matter in his own hands, whilst Charles was huckstering, boldly attacked and routed the Spaniards as they lay on the coast of Kent. Olivares was furious, and demanded redress from the King of England, who, he said, had aided the Dutch in their attack. Admiral Pennington, to keep up appearances, was imprisoned for not defending the neutrality of English waters ; but that was all. The Battle of the Downs was a deathblow to Spain's spirited attempt under Olivares to become again a great naval power, and the loss of prestige and material then suffered was never fully recovered.

By the neutrality of England settled in 1637,

a convent, and young Kit returns home ; doubtless to commit bigamy in due time in England, and continue the knightly family of Windebank.

and the cessation of the war in the Valtelline and in Italy, the area of the duel to the death between France and Spain, between Richelieu and Olivares, was gradually narrowing ; but this concentration of the struggle brought nearer the danger to Spanish territory itself. Great as had been the pressure brought to bear upon all classes to obtain funds for the war, the threat of invasion made the cry for money more peremptory than ever. Not only every noble, but now every knight of an order, was summoned to provide a horse and arms for himself and servant, and to hold himself in readiness to join a company ; and coach and cart horses were seized for government use everywhere.[1] A new " donativo " was decreed for Madrid, and rich men were unmercifully drained.[2] Even the beggars who lived in squalid plenty were passed in review, in order to find how many impostors there were who in purse or person could serve the King. It was found by this inquiry that of 3300 people who lived by public mendicancy in the capital, only 1300 were really poor and deserving.[3] On the other hand, as we have seen, at this very time, with the danger hourly growing, ostentatious expenditure on pleasure exhausted in a day sums large enough, in relation to the national revenue, to have provided to a great extent for the more pressing needs.

Peculation and personal lavishness were as remarkable as the public waste. A Portuguese Count of Linhares, who was Philip's Admiral of the Galleys of Sicily, arrived in Madrid in February

---

[1] It is curious to note that when the census of private coaches was made in Madrid for this purpose, it was found that there were 900 in use.
[2] March 1637, Rodriguez Villa's Newsletters.   [3] *Ibid.*

1637, and in his first audience he gave to the
King a string of diamonds, which was said to
be the handsomest ever seen in Europe, its value
being estimated at considerably over 60,000
ducats. The Count then went to salute the Queen,
to whom he offered a casket with a pair of marvellous earrings. The Queen, we are told, fell in
love with them at once, and without waiting for
ladies or tire-women, snatched her own ornaments
from her ears and put in the new pair. Whilst she
was admiring the effect of them in a mirror the
King came in, delighted, to show her his string of
diamonds, which he wore in his hat ; and they
exchanged many jokes at each other's vanity.
What the Count-Duke received as his present from
Linhares is not stated; but that he was so pleased
with Linhares' generosity that he said, "This
is the sort of ministers and viceroys for his
Majesty"; and he thereupon appointed Linhares,
much to the latter's chagrin, Viceroy of Brazil,
which post he would only accept on all manner of
new and favourable conditions.[1]

[1] The Portuguese in question was splendidly repaid for his generosity,
and when he left Madrid at the end of the year he had received the
following grants,—"Marquis of Viseu, Count of Linhares for his eldest
son and successors, the post of Marshal of Portugal for his second son,
that of Governor of Ceuta for his third son, an extension for three years
longer of the revenues of the governorship of Sofala (i.e. Mozambique),
a grant of 24,000 for his own expenses, 5000 ducats per annum for ever,
2500 ducats perpetual pension for his daughter-in-law, General on land
and sea during his stay in Brazil with the title of Viceroy, and the title
of Lieutenant-General in Portugal so long as the Duchess of Mantua rules
there, grants for a second life of all the pensioned knighthoods he holds,
and four pensioned knighthoods to be disposed of as he likes, and a
renewal for three lives of the pension he holds from the crown." It was
said that these grants were worth 700,000 ducats. This is a fair specimen of the lavishness to quite a second-rate personage at a time when the
nation was in the deepest distress. Rodriguez Villa's Newsletters, 1637.

It was in all respects high time that the noble courtiers who surrounded Philip should be made to occupy themselves in real warfare against the enemy of their country, for their quarrels and turbulence had already reached a point that made them a public reproach. It had been for more than a century a fixed policy of Spanish kings to keep the territorial nobles as much as possible excluded from executive activity in the Peninsula, and to attach them to the personal service of the monarch at Court. The peerage had been enormously increased under Philip III. and IV., and the numerous class of newly enriched and ennobled courtiers and officers that thronged Philip's Court, utterly idle and corrupt as they were, with no great feudal or military traditions, had become insolent and pretentious beyond measure.

The broils of the nobles during the month of festivities in the early part of 1637 were so scandalous, that it was seriously considered by Philip and Olivares how they could punish the highly placed law-breakers, and positively forbid duels altogether. First, the quidnuncs on Liars' Walk were regaled at the end of January by the sight of four gentlemen of birth being led past the Calle Mayor to be hanged instead of beheaded. These criminals had plied their impudent trade of cloak-snatchers in every street in Madrid, and had, amongst many other outrages, killed a priest who had objected to part with his raiment. The Duke of Hijar, a great friend of Olivares and a notable boaster, had been relieved not only of his cape, but of his sword and buckler as well; and a considerable band of these ruffians, led by a young noble of nineteen, one of those hanged, had so terrorised the streets of the capital as to make them unsafe in broad daylight. The next day, ten men and women, mostly people of good position, were whipped through the Calle Mayor as thieves and receivers ; and some highly born gentlemen were condemned to death as housebreakers. " This place," wrote an eye-witness, " simply swarms with folks of this sort, and the efforts of the ministers of justice are powerless to stop them." [1]

One morning soon afterwards, Madrid woke up to find the walls placarded with a public challenge from Don Juan de Herrera to the Marquis del Aguila to meet him and fight to the death in Switzerland. These were the two nobles who had fought in the presence of the King (page 300), and had fled from justice to foreign parts ; and the subject of discussion amongst the idlers and satirists in Madrid was whether or not the Marquis was bound to accept the challenge. But in three days this subject had to give way to another excitement. Don Juan Pacheco, eldest son of the Marquis of Cerralbo, had asked the manager of one of the theatrical companies of the capital, Tomás Fernandez, to represent a new comedy, in honour of the recovery of his sweetheart, the daughter of the Marquis of Cadreita, from fever. Fernandez had made other arrangements for his company, and declined to do so ; and Pacheco at once hired a bravo to stab the comedian as he was walking and chatting with other actors in the open space near the Church of St. Sebastian, called the " Liars' Walk of the Comedians." When the

[1] Rodriguez Villa's Newsletter, 1637.

assassin delivered the blow, this noble employer, who was standing close by, shouted: "That is the way to serve varlets."

Hardly had the exclamations on this event ceased, than another affray between gentlemen in broad daylight interested the gossipers. On the 10th February there was dress rehearsal of the mounted masquerade in the new arena at the Buen Retiro, which has been described on page 318. The populace broke into the ring, and the royal guard had much trouble to clear the space for the riders. During the process of clearing, young Spinola, indignant that he, a Genoese noble, should be hustled, called out offensively to Don Francisco Zapata, the lieutenant (whom we have seen in trouble before): "Hi, Don Francisco! don't you know who I am?" to which Zapata replied: "I don't care who you are"; and in spite of his threats of vengeance Spinola was "moved on." As Zapata left the gates of the palace afterwards, he met Spinola waiting for him in the Prado. "I have a word to say to you," cried the Genoese. "I have no sword," replied Zapata. "Then I will wait whilst you go and fetch one," said Spinola; and with that Zapata leapt in a rage from his mule, and, snatching a sword from a bystander, he fell upon his opponent, though the pair were separated before blood was shed.

Another foolish fray over punctilious trifles took place on the following day between the Count of Salazar and one of the gentlemen in attendance on the Princess of Carignano, a Milanese Spanish subject who bore an Italian title of Count de Pozo. The Spanish nobles always sneered at Italian titles;

and Salazar shied at calling Pozo " Lordship."
The latter had retaliated by calling Salazar himself " Worship " instead of `` Lordship,'' and when he
met him in the Calle Mayor had neglected to bow
to him. Worse still, when they met again in the
passage of the Buen Retiro palace leading to the
Count-Duke's apartment, Salazar doffed his hat,
and Pozo neglected to return the salute. In a
moment Salazar turned back, and, snatching off
Pozo's wide-brimmed felt hat, gave the owner a
tremendous buffet on the face with it. In a moment
swords flew from scabbards, and the two angry
nobles grappled ; but they, too, were separated,
Salazar taking refuge in the German embassy,
whilst Pozo fled into hiding. The " discoursers "
in this case decided that Salazar was in the wrong ;
but he had many friends, and held a perfect levée
in the German embassy, closely isolated from
suspicious visitors, to prevent a hostile message
reaching him that would need his going out to
fight. But by a trick one of the pages of the
Princess of Carignano obtained admission, and
handed him a challenge from Pozo. When the
antagonists met next morning at the place appointed, on the outskirts of the town, they were
both arrested ; and even then the two alcaldes who
arrested them had a violent quarrel as to which of
them should take Salazar.

These, and several other scandals of the sort,
all happened within the space of a fortnight ; and
it is little wonder that the Royal Council, at the
instance of Olivares, discussed the matter and reported to the King that something must be done.
The step decided upon was very Spanish. All the

old fire-eaters and officers of experience were fighting under the Cardinal Infante in Flanders, and to
them the whole subject was referred for consideration and report ; "after which a very strict pragmatic will be drawn up and published forbidding
duels under heavy penalties, and even making
them cases for the Inquisition, or at least that
the principals and their descendants should be
degraded. Either of these two courses would
touch Spaniards deeply." Needless to say that,
long before the report from Flanders came to
Madrid, if it ever came, these good resolves were
forgotten, and the affrays of noble ruffians disgraced Madrid uninterruptedly as before.

Philip and his minister, indeed, had plenty of
other things of greater moment to occupy them than
this. From the first we have seen that Olivares
recognised the absolute need for fiscal unity and
equality of sacrifice from all Spain if the old dream
of supremacy was to be enforced and France humiliated. Portugal, Aragon, Catalonia, and Valencia,
naturally jealous of ancient rights which each
successive ruler had sworn to respect, were determined to resist any attack by the favourite upon
their autonomy. I have on many occasions pointed
out that the main explanation of the past, and
problem of the future, of Spanish history is the
intensely local and regional character of the patriotism of the people. In our times the rapid means
of intercommunication between the parts, and the
existence of a unified administrative system for
two centuries, have in some directions rendered
this feeling less conspicuous than it was ; though
in others, and particularly in Catalonia and the

Basque Provinces, it is still strong and clamant. But in the time of Olivares the sentiment was absolutely unimpaired. Philip II., even after the rising against him in Aragon, had done little really to injure the ancient *fueros*, whilst in Portugal he had gone to the very extreme of prudence in recognising the separate national rights of his new subjects. Any attack, or even threat, therefore, on the part of a new and much hated minister like Olivares upon this, the strongest racial and traditional sentiment of the most active and enterprising communities in the Peninsula, was certain to lead to conflict.

The need for money, nevertheless, was pressing, and however statesmanlike the aim of the minister may have been if its execution had been gentle and cautious extending over many years, it became the height of rashness when forced to an immediate issue. Olivares was very far from being foolish or naturally rash, and when his policy was first explained to Philip, soon after his accession, he did not disguise that his object was difficult to attain, and must be a work of time.[1] But when once he had embraced the policy which forced upon Spain

---

[1] The following words occur in the famous Memorial on the subject referred to on page 142, etc.: "Let your Majesty hold as the most important affair of your State to make yourself *King of Spain*. I mean, Sire, that you should not content yourself with being King of Portugal, of Aragon, of Valencia, Count of Barcelona, but that you should strive and consider with mature and secret counsel to reduce these realms of which Spain consists to the laws and form of Castile, without any distinction. If your Majesty succeeds in this, you will be the most powerful Prince in the world. Nevertheless this is not a business which can be carried through in a limited time, nor do I suggest that it should be disclosed to anybody, however confidential he may be; because the desirability of the object is indisputable, and what is to be done in preparation and anticipation can be done by your Majesty yourself.

costly wars abroad, defeat and ruin for himself was the only alternative to the dangerous plan of making the autonomous realms pay their share of the cost of wars undertaken by the King, and of the rampant waste amongst the decadent crowd in Madrid that had already bled Castile to exhaustion.

For some years the Portuguese had been justly irritated by the giving to Spaniards of administrative offices in Portugal, and by the contemptuous way in which Olivares habitually received representations or remonstrances as to the injuries suffered by Portuguese subjects in consequence of the union with Castile. The principal instruments of the Count-Duke in his attempts to rule Portugal on Castilian lines were two creatures of his—Miguel Vasconcellos and Diego Suarez, both Portuguese of obscure origin, who had practically superseded the Duchess of Mantua, Philip's nominal figurehead, who was personally not unpopular. In 1637, at an attempt to impose a tax on all property in Portugal for Spanish purposes, risings took place in the Algarves and Evora, and protests loud and deep came from other Portuguese cities. Madrid at once announced that the King himself would go with a large force and conquer his realm of Portugal ; but though this was untrue, the Duke of Medina Sidonia marched into the Algarves with a Spanish force, whilst another threatened the north of Portugal, and the Portuguese, unready as yet for the conflict, were cowed by the threat. But the injury rankled deeply, and when, in the following year 1638, Olivares summoned to Madrid the Portuguese archbishops, seven nobles and three

Jesuit priests, to discuss the closer unity of the two countries — an assembly which coincided with the imposition of a new illegal tax upon the Portuguese as a punishment for the risings —Portuguese nobles and people alike knew that unless they were to be enslaved by Castile they must needs fight for their national existence.

Thenceforward the great conspiracy that was to bring independence to Portugal never ceased until victory crowned the attempt. The Duke of Braganza, the Portuguese pretender with the best right to the throne, was prodigiously rich and over cautious, but his virile Spanish Guzman wife was eager and ambitious; whilst her wealthy brother, the Duke of Medina Sidonia, head of the Guzmans, silently helped forward the scheme which would make his sister a Queen, and afford him, the most powerful vassal of the Castilian crown, a precedent for the creation of an independent principality for himself in Andalucia, free from the weak and corrupt bureaucracy led by his cousin Olivares in Madrid.

In the meanwhile the war with France had taken a new aspect. The much vaunted Spanish invasion of France through Bayonne under the Duke of Nocera had turned out a ridiculous fiasco, and it was soon evident that Richelieu meant to make an effort to revenge the attempt by an invasion of Spain, as well as to retrieve the reverses he had sustained elsewhere in the previous year. Anna of Austria, the Queen Mother of France, did her best privately to persuade her brother and Olivares to terms of peace acceptable to her son; and she sent to Madrid for the purpose, in the summer of 1637,

a Minorite friar, who had many interviews with
Olivares on the subject. But the war had now
entered into a phase which involved the personal
rivalry of two all-powerful statesmen, as well as
the prestige of two great nations, so that it had to
be fought to a finish. The blinded courtiers in
Madrid, moreover, openly scoffed at the idea of
making peace with France until Spain had asserted
its incontestable superiority ; [1] and all that the
Minorite friar took back with him to France was
the little finger of Saint Isidore the Husbandman,
the patron of Madrid, which was secretly cut from
the body of the saint in his church in the Calle de
Toledo at midnight, to be sent as a venerated relic
to Philip's sister Anna in Paris. [2]

In the summer of 1638, Richelieu was ready to
strike his blow on Spanish soil. Crossing the
river Bidasoa at St. Jean de Luz, a French army
rapidly captured Irun and the fine harbour of
Pasages, and laid siege to Fuenterrabia both by sea
and by land. The Prince of Condé (Henri de Bourbon)
and the Duke de la Valette were in command on
land, and the Bishop of Bordeaux at sea. An attempt
was made by the French to storm the hill upon
which the fortress stands, but the Admiral of Castile
and the Marquis of los Velez, with 6000 men from
Navarre and Guipuzcoa, eager to fight for their
own provinces, came opportunely upon the scene.
A dashing charge threw panic into the French
camp, and the besiegers fled headlong to their boats.
Spaniards were always ready enough to fight
when well led, and they were fighting for their own

[1] Rodriguez Villa's Newsletters.
[2] Aston's letters, MSS., Record Office S.P., Spain,

provincial frontiers ; and though La Valette was accused by Richelieu of treachery, and condemned to death in his absence in England, whither he had fled to join Marie de Medici, his men on this occasion were fairly beaten by Spanish soldiers, who were irresistible when they were defending their own provinces.

The same thing was seen in Catalonia in the following spring, where, counting upon the notorious disaffection of the Catalans with Olivares' policy, Condé in the spring of 1639 invaded Roussillon, which then belonged to Catalonia, and captured Salcés. Peremptory demands for help came to Madrid, but Olivares was in no hurry to help the Catalans, and preferred that their own impotence to defend their country without the aid of Castile should be first demonstrated. The provincial authorities were stout and determined, and rapidly raised an army of 10,000 men. But the Catalans had no leader yet worthy of the name ; and, though they fought bravely, they fought for a time in vain. They were badly and timidly led ; and 8000 of them died of the plague before Salcés, in which fortress the French were shut up. Condé, late in the autumn, came back from Provence with a new French army of 20,000 foot and 4000 horse to reinforce the French ; and though the case seemed hopeless, the Catalans, ever a dour race, determined to stand and fight them. Full of confidence, the French army stormed the trenches of the besieging Catalans on the 1st November. But the ditches and moats were swollen by autumn rains, and regiment after regiment rushed to the attack, only to be repelled with terrible loss by the

stout Catalans, behind their earthworks and gabions.
Discouragement at last seized the French, and
they fled, leaving the Catalans masters of the field,
and Salcés unrelieved. The fortress surrendered
to famine at the beginning of the year 1640, and
the second attempt of Richelieu to invade Spain
failed. Nor were the attempts upon the Catalan
coasts by the French fleet under the Bishop of
Bordeaux more successful ; for, after some depredations and the temporary occupation of Spanish
ports, the French fleet was scattered by a storm
and returned disabled to France. Once more it
was proved that Spaniards were indomitable when
they were fighting for a deep-seated sentiment. The
deepest of all was local loyalty. Whilst the sentiment of religious selection had been dominant it
had given Spaniards a strength not their own ; but
that burning faith was ashes now,[1] and the only
thing worth fighting for, beyond the inborn love
of contest, was the independence of the province
that gave them birth, and for this, rather than for a
Spain that for most of them was but a geographical
expression, Spaniards were still ready to sacrifice
their lives without stint.

It was a wretched story that King Philip had to
tell the Cortes of Castile that were assembled in

---

[1] How completely the old crusading spirit had decayed is seen in
the derision with which the courtiers in Madrid greeted the saying of
Antonio Mascarenhas, the dignified old-fashioned hidalgo governor of
Tangier. When he visited Madrid he went to present his respects to
the little Prince Baltasar Carlos. " Who are you ? " asked the boy. " I am
the gentleman," replied the Portuguese, " who by and by will help your
Highness to conquer the Holy Sepulchre." It was the answer of a knight-
errant, sneered the courtiers, and so it was, but it was this fervent knight-
errantry which had given to Spain the strength it had possessed, and
which under the scoffers and mockers it never could possess again.

Y

Madrid in the summer of 1638. His treasury, he said, was more empty than ever; "for he had been obliged by his duty to oppose all the heretics in Europe in defence of the Catholic religion, as well as the enemies of his house in Italy, Germany, Flanders, and Brazil, and a greater war was now on his hands than had afflicted Spain since the time of Charles V. And although peace had been discussed through various channels, as yet unsuccessfully, the surest way to attain tranquillity was to arm more powerfully than ever, and strike their enemies with dismay." Seventy two millions and a half of ducats had been raised by loans at 8 per cent. interest, and spent in the previous six years on war, in addition to two millions and a quarter for the army in Spain itself. This was an expenditure unheard of previously in Spain, and it meant that a sum greater than ever was demanded now of Castile in the form of an enormous addition to the food excise, and an increase of the alcabala. The country was depopulated and starving, said the deputies; [1] but withal the duty of his Majesty as a Christian prince was clear, and, no matter at what sacrifice, the means for fighting the battle of the Church and Spain must be found by his faithful vassals.

And so, through 1638 and 1639, as has already been told, the war went on, not on the whole unfavourably for Spanish arms, for the French invasion, at least, was repelled; but more disastrously than ever, for the overtaxed and ruined people upon whom the crushing burden lay of providing

---

[1] The speeches are given *in extenso* in the documents printed in Danvila's *Poder Civil en España*.

funds. Talk of peace went on in Madrid all the while. A secret agent of Richelieu named Pujol was in close though cautious negotiation with Olivares for three years, both ministers professing ardent desires for an agreement. But it was clear that neither was disposed to give way an inch in his claims, and again and again the Spanish agents declared that on no account would they recognise the Dutch otherwise than as recalcitrant rebels against their King. In the circumstances, therefore, peace was impossible ; for Holland had not held her own for seventy years to bow the head now, and in the summer of 1640 the internal storm which had long been gathering burst upon Spain, not, we may be sure, to Richelieu's surprise, and all hope for peace fled.

The fatal burden of Philip's inherited task, and the traditions imposed at his baptism, had led him to embark in impossible wars for an idea ; the need for money to support a policy of Quixotic adventure had drained Castile ; and the unhappy insistence of Olivares in exacting from the autonomous realms a similar sacrifice, had at last sapped their loyalty to the sacred personality of the sovereign. Philip, in the prime of his manhood, after nineteen years of rule, found himself face to face with rebellion of his own people, as well as with a great war abroad ; whilst the centre of his realm, whither all wealth flowed and whence all power emanated, was sunk in pagan epicureanism, pride, pretence, and sloth.

In earlier chapters we have seen that on both the occasions that Philip had personally attended the Cortes of the eastern realms, he, and especially

Olivares, had quarrelled bitterly with the deputies and had returned to Madrid in anger, leaving a rankling discontent behind. Olivares since then had lost no opportunity of dealing hardly with Catalans particularly, — their causes in Madrid being treated with ostentatious neglect, and their interests passed over, in order, as Olivares said, to teach them the lesson of obedience ; whilst the Catalans, whose qualities certainly do not include submissiveness, repaid this treatment by passively resisting the orders that came to them from the Court. When Roussillon was invaded by the French in the autumn of 1639, Olivares had been slow to send succour from Castile. As we have seen, the drain for the foreign war was tremendous, and both money and men were scarce, even if Olivares had desired to send prompt aid. But such was not the case ; and the main efforts by which the French were expelled and Salcés captured were those of the Catalans themselves. The Viceroy was Queralt, Marquis of Santa Coloma, who, although a Catalan, was devoted heart and soul to Olivares, and had been chosen as a more pliant instrument for the minister than his digni-fied predecessor, the Duke of Cardona.

To Santa Coloma, whilst the Catalans were straining every nerve to defend their principality from the French, Olivares and the King con-tinued to send messages calculated to arouse the deepest resentment of the people.

" Do not," wrote Olivares, " suffer a single man who can work to absent himself from the field, nor a woman who can bear on her back food or forage. . . .

If the enterprise can be effected without violating the privileges of the province, well and good, but if in order to respect these the service of the King is retarded by one single hour, he who dares to uphold them at such a cost will be an enemy to God, his King, his race, and his country. . . . Make the Catalans understand that the general welfare of the people and of the troops must be preferred to all rights and privileges. . . . You must take great care that the troops are well lodged and have good beds ; and if there are none to be had, you must not hesitate to take them from the highest people in the province ; for it is better that they should lie on the ground than that the troops should suffer.''

The reinforcements from Castile and elsewhere that eventually reached Catalonia under Spinola, Marquis of Balbeses, arrived after most of the fighting was over, and the French had retired ; but orders were given that these troops should remain quartered in the province. This was a violation of one of the most cherished rights of the Catalans ; and Spinola made matters worse by his marked insolence to people of the country, and his public instructions that in every case the troops lodged in a place were to be stronger than the inhabitants, so that they should always be the masters. Protests and indignant remonstrances met with the same contemptuous treatment from Olivares, Santa Coloma, and Spinola ; and as the months wore on the mood of the Catalans became ever more dangerous. It was announced in the spring of 1640 that the King would go and hold

a Cortes in Barcelona ; but to hold Cortes, it was
remarked that he did not need the strong armed
force he summoned to attend him.   The knights of
the orders were again placed under contribution,
and protested in vain that it was an abuse to press
them thus for subordinate military service ; the
grandees of Castile were each commanded to provide and pay for four months 100 soldiers each ;
and this, on the top of other swollen demands,
aroused higher than ever their hatred of Olivares.
The Duke of Arcos said that he had already paid
900,000 ducats ; the Dukes of Priego and Bejar,
800,000 each, and others in like proportion, and
that they were at the end of their resources.[1]   The
Portuguese nobles saw in the summons only a
pretext for withdrawing them from their own
country, and many went into hiding to avoid
compliance with it, whilst others with feigned
acquiescence procrastinated until they could safely
throw aside the mask.

Whilst Philip was still trifling in Madrid with
the usual merrymakings at the Retiro to celebrate
the feast of Corpus Christi in June 1640, there
came flying news from Barcelona that the threatened tempest had burst.   The Catalans, driven to
desperation by the exactions and insolence of the
polyglot rabble of troops quartered upon them,
had risen and massacred every Castilian soldier
and officer they could hound down.   Santa Coloma
himself in flight had sunk by the wayside, and
had been hacked to death by his maddened countrymen ; and from Barcelona through all Catalonia
the fiery cross had been borne with cries, it is true,

[1] Novoa, *Memorias*.

of " Long Live the King " ; but still louder shouts
of " Vengeance," " Liberty," and " Down with the
Government." In a vain attempt to stem the
flood the old Duke of Cardona was reappointed
Viceroy ; and, after his death shortly afterwards,
was succeeded by the aged Archbishop of Barcelona.
But it was too late, and anarchy soon ruled unchecked. Cardinal Borja, himself a Valencian and
an active minister of Philip's thenceforward, openly
declared in the Royal Council at Madrid that "the
revolt could only be drowned in rivers of blood."

Again the screw had to be turned, and Olivares
was almost in despair. But he worked like a giant,
cajoling and humouring Braganza and the Portuguese nobles into what he hoped was a better
frame of mind, whilst he depleted the Portuguese
frontier of the forces with which he had up to that
time terrorised the sister kingdom. The details
of the Secession War in Catalonia cannot be told
here.[1] Suffice to say that again Philip, supported
by the enemies of Olivares, clamoured to be allowed
to lead his troops against the rebel subjects ; but it
suited the minister to keep him amused with poetical academies, comedies, amours, and devotions,
rather than to bring him in touch with realities, and
enable him to learn the whole of the dire truth.

The Marquis of los Velez was sent to Catalonia
with such an army as could be got together, and
in the summer he swept through the province,
almost without resistance, until he came to Tarragona and Barcelona, which places had been
occupied, by the invitation of the Catalans, by

[1] The best contemporary is that by General de Melo, *Guerra de
Cataluña.*

French troops. Epernon, who commanded them, again showed the white feather, and retired ; but the stout Catalans, though deserted by their allies, formally renouncing the rule of the King of Castile and acknowledging Louis XIII. as their prince, manfully stood behind their trenches to defend the capital. The attempt to storm the outworks was made on the 26th January 1641, the Earl of Tyrone leading the Irish regiment, and falling dead at the first onset. The battle was a desperate and sanguinary one, but just as victory seemed assured for the Castilians, a panic seized them ; a Catalan attack in their rear completed the demoralisation, and Barcelona, untaken and victorious, proclaimed itself a French city, whilst the routed Spanish army retreated to Tarragona, a mere rabble. Thenceforward French government troops poured into the principality ; and Philip, amidst his alternate wanton pleasures and agonised remorse in Madrid, realised that the realms of his fathers were crumbling apart, and that the King of France ruled with the consent of Spaniards over some of the richest provinces of Spain. The knowledge struck like death to the heart of Philip, for up to that hour, kept in the dark by Olivares, he had never understood the tenacity of the autonomous States, or the danger of tampering with a deeply rooted national tradition.

But the news of the secession of Catalonia, terrible as it was, came only a few weeks after another blow which had affected Philip even more. The King, in the earlier days of December 1640, was presiding over one of the ostentatious bullfights that he loved, given in honour of the Danish ambassador, when a courier from the Portuguese frontier galloped post haste to the quarters of Olivares in the palace. Soon Liars' Walk and Calle Mayor were full of grave faces and important whispers that dreadful news had come from the sister kingdom. In the palace, even in the Plaza where the bull-fight was being held, everybody knew or guessed the story that had come ; yet none dared whisper a hint to the King, for the sallow, frowning face of the Count-Duke was rigid, and until he spoke the word none might break the silence. Hours passed ; the bull-fight came to its usual end, and, on returning to the palace, the King sat at play with his friends. To him entered the Count-Duke, gay and smiling. " I bring great news for your Majesty," he said. " What is it ? " asked the King, with little concern. " In one moment, Sire, you have won a great dukedom and vast wealth," replied the minister. " How so, Conde ? " inquired Philip. " Sire, the Duke of Braganza has gone mad, and has proclaimed himself King of Portugal ; so it will be necessary for you to confiscate all his possessions." The King's long face fell longer still, and his brow clouded, for all his minister's jauntiness. He was no fool, and he knew this was tidings of evil moment. " Let a remedy be found for it," was all he said, turning anew to his game ; and the Count-Duke, as he left the room, looked sad, as if he saw the beginning of his own eclipse.

In three hours the long prepared conspiracy had come to a head. Braganza himself had done little, though he had artfully kept himself out of the trap which Olivares had cleverly baited for him.

On the 1st December 1640 the cry had rung

through Lisbon, " Long live King John IV." The hated Vasconcellos had been murdered first, literally torn to pieces by the crowd ; the Duchess of Mantua, Philip's Vice-Reine, had been respectfully conducted to safety in a convent, and the Castilians in the city had been interned in the fortress. Resistance there was none, and no adequate Spanish force to make any ; and although for the rest of Philip's sad life the pretence was kept up of treating the Portuguese as rebels, and intermittently war was pushed on the frontier to regain Castilian hold over the country, the separation was permanent, and Portugal never lost her independence again.[1]

The volume of discontent against the minister grew apace, and all Olivares could do was to keep Philip amused, whilst he isolated him more and more from those who could open his eyes to the true state of affairs. Several attempts had been made in the past years by rash individuals to open the King's eyes. Once a young courtier named Lujanes had thrown himself at the feet of Philip in the royal chapel, and had shouted to him to beware of Olivares, who was bent upon his ruin. He was hurried away, and the servile friends of the Count-Duke shrugged their shoulders and said the poor fellow was a lunatic ; but the next day he died mysteriously in confinement, and the gossips made no hesitation in saying that he had been poisoned. Other cries to the same effect had from time to time greeted Philip in the streets and public diversions ; but now they became more frequent and out-

[1] The details will be found in *Historia de la Conjuracion de Portugal; Revolutions de Portugal*, Vertot ; *Historia del levantamiento de Portugal*, Seyner ; and Canovas de Castello's *Estudios del Reinado de Felipe IV.*, vol. i.

spoken. As he was going on a wolf-hunt, cries arose : " Hunt the French, sire ! They are our worst wolves." The disaster of a great part of the Buen Retiro being burnt down with its sumptuous contents, during a splendid carnival in February 1641, a few weeks only after the reception of the ill news from Barcelona and Lisbon, gave fresh cause for complaint against Olivares. Twice previously the King had been in danger there by the bursting of reservoirs, and now he ran a worse risk by the place catching fire.[1] The place was accursed, said the grumblers ; and when the irreparable loss of precious works of art by the fire had to be made good by " voluntary " offerings of similar things from private collections, and 60,000 ducats for rebuilding were extorted from the deputies of the Cortes, with 20,000 from the municipality of Madrid, 30,000 from the Council of Castile, and 10,000 from the Council of War, whilst the soldiers in the field were unpaid and starving, all those who were not absolutely slaves to the Count-Duke openly cried shame.[2]

Another trouble occurred at this time which embittered Philip's heart and conscience for years to come ; and this, again, whether true in all its particulars or not, was added to the heavy account that the people at large had against the Count-Duke. It will be recollected that a horrible scandal had taken place in the convent of San Placido in Madrid in 1632. The matter was hushed up and condoned in 1638, and the nuns went into residence

[1] The King was actually dressing at the time, and with the royal family escaped to one of the hermitages in the park, though at one time in danger. Many ladies who were yet in bed fled in their night garb, and were rescued with difficulty. Novoa.

[2] Ibid.

again. Now, the patron of San Placido was the King's confidant, and Olivares' henchman, the protonotary Geronimo de Villanueva, whose mansion in the Calle de Madera adjoined the convent. Villanueva had always been one of the useful ministers of Philip's amours, and when his convent was rehabilitated in 1638 he brought stories of a very beautiful young nun that he had seen there. Philip and Olivares insisted upon seeing this paragon of loveliness, and Villanueva, exerting his authority as patron, obtained entrance into the locutory for the King in disguise ; and for many nights in succession the interviews took place.

The affair, though very carefully concealed, began to be whispered, before the King and his friends had penetrated beyond the grille which separated them from the beautiful nun ; and though Philip's conscience after an offence was tender enough, it usually did not operate until after the offence was committed. So determined was he to approach more nearly to the object of his passion, that Olivares and Villanueva together managed by bribes and prayers to persuade the nun to consent to a violation of her vows, and to admit the King. A passage was made from Villanueva's house to the cellars of the convent to facilitate the entrance of the King ; but before the secret work was finished, the nun, either conscience-stricken or afraid of consequences, told the abbess what was going on. The punishments meted out by the Inquisition a few years before had probably been enough for this good lady ; for she besought Villanueva to desist from so terrible and dangerous a crime. But Villanueva, anxious to please the King,

and being, like most of the courtiers of his generation, a religious cynic, turned a deaf ear to her
entreaties. When later he led the enamoured
King through the secret passage into the sacred
cloister, and to the room where it was arranged
that the meeting should take place, the pair were
horrified to see that the abbess had laid out the
nun upon a bier, her eyes closed, her hands crossed
upon her breast clasping a crucifix, whilst tapers
were burning at the head and foot of the bier. This
was too much for Philip, and he fled; but subsequently affairs were arranged more comfortably,
and the amours, we are assured, continued for
some time.[1]

By and by the Inquisition heard something of
what was going on from its spies. What could
be done ? The King was too high even for the
Holy Office to touch ; yet so awful a sacrilege
as this could not be allowed to go on. The Inquisitor-General was Friar Archbishop Sotomayor,
Philip's own confessor, a creature of Olivares, and
a man of indifferent character ; but even he took
the King to task severely and repeatedly for his
crime. Subsequently, when Philip probably was
tired of the intrigue, he desisted, and then, after
interminable secret inquiries by the Holy Office, it
was decided that Villanueva was guilty of sacrilege
of the worst description, and must be arrested.
The King, remorseful or panic-stricken, was for
letting the matter take its course ; but Olivares,
trembling now for himself (in 1642), went to the

---

[1] The only part of the story which appears open to question is the
continuance of the intrigue after Philip's remorseful flight. There
seems to be some doubt about this.

Inquisitor-General, Sotomayor, with two decrees signed by the King, one dismissing him and banishing him from Spain, the other giving him a pension of 12,000 ducats a year for life, on condition that he resigned the Inquisitor-Generalship and retired to Cordova. Sotomayor naturally accepted the latter alternative. At the same time strong measures were taken in Rome by Philip's agents to induce the Pope to demand the reference of the case to him. The Inquisition obeyed the Pope's command, and sent the whole of the papers in a casket to Rome by one of its own confidential officers. Olivares managed to delay his departure whilst one of the King's painters, perhaps Velazquez, made several sketches of the messenger's face, which sketches were sent off post haste to the King's officers in various parts of Italy, with orders to capture the original secretly wherever he appeared, and send him closely isolated to Naples, whilst his precious casket of papers was to be forwarded intact to Olivares.

The unfortunate messenger, Paredes, landed at Genoa, where he was at once kidnapped and spirited off to the strong castle of Ovo at Naples, fated to be kept in close confinement for the rest of his life, fifteen years. The casket was conveyed with great secrecy to Olivares,· who, with the King, reduced it and its unread contents to ashes in Philip's private room. The new Inquisitor-General was a Benedictine frair in the confidence of Queen Isabel, one Diego de Arce ; and as no news came from Rome of the case, letters were written by him and the Council of the Inquisition to the Pope. The latter, primed by Philip's ambassador, still kept silence ; and as the minutes of the trial of course could not be found, and the wretched messenger had apparently vanished from the face of the earth, there were no proofs forthcoming against Villanueva, who remained under interdiction and in partial seclusion.

This, however, could not continue for ever ; and when, in 1644, Olivares had disappeared from the scene, and nothing more was to be feared from him, Villanueva was formally arrested by the Inquisition, and carried off to Toledo, where he was taken before the judges *in penitenciæ* ; and, without any particulars being recited, was admonished that he had sinned enormously by sacrilege and irreligion, whereby he had incurred the heaviest penalties ; but that the Holy Office in its clemency would absolve him, only imposing upon him the obligation of fasting on Fridays for the rest of his life, of never entering a convent again, or speaking to a nun, and of giving 2000 ducats for charity to the Prior of the Atocha. The King then restored Villanueva to his post, and imposed perpetual silence with regard to the case against him.[1] What penalty Philip himself paid for his terrible offence is not known ; though it is said that the clock of the convent, which played the dirge for the dead each hour, and which existed well within the memory of the present writer, and perhaps exists still, was one of the King's peace offerings to the outraged cloister.

[1] The story is told with many embellishments, but the above version is the most trustworthy. It comes from a contemporary MS., written after the fall of Olivares, transcribed by Mesonero Romanos in *El Antiguo, Madrid.*

The clouds gathered ever blacker over Olivares. The demands he was forced to make now for resources to face the French in Catalonia, and to present some show of attempting the recovery of Portugal, drove the Castilian nobles and people of means into almost open revolt. The copper currency was again tampered with, being reduced to one-sixth of its previous value ; [1] and large demands were assessed in silver upon persons who were assumed to be able to pay. In Madrid alone on this occasion, 150 people were sent to the dungeons for their inability or unwillingness to pay all that was asked of them. In addition to the public causes for the hatred of the people against the minister, there were also personal reasons of rapidly increasing strength for his unpopularity with his own class. His arrogance had always offended the nobles of high lineage, and he now added to it, as if in mere wantonness, an offence for which even his own kin never forgave him. His only daughter had died soon after her early marriage ; and whatever may have been Olivares' faults, he was an extremely fond father. He had, as he grew older, practically adopted his nephew Don Luis de Haro, son of the Marquis del Carpio, as his heir ; but suddenly there appeared at Court a young man of twenty-eight, up to that time known by another name, and passing as the son

[1] August 1642. Novoa, an eye-witness, referring to this time, says : " Trade and commerce were confused, and the prices rose enormously, so that people could not find money for boots and clothes ; and even provisions could not be had, as no one would sell. The copper money was valueless, and people threw it about or forced it upon those to whom they owed money, as the law gave it currency. The agony and desperation of the people were intense, and utter despair consumed the hearts and lives of the people." Novoa, *Memorias*.

of a small government official in Madrid. The
name now given to this person was Enrique Felipe
de Guzman, and Olivares brought him to the
palace and to the King's apartments, introducing him as his son. The young man was a person
of no breeding or attraction, and his mode of life
was far from exemplary, but Olivares appears to
have been perfectly infatuated with him. Following his own bent, the son had married a lady of good
house in Seville ; but Olivares had higher views
for him, and, by dint of great and costly efforts,
caused the marriage to be declared invalid. No
people in the world were more tenacious of purity
of blood than the Spanish nobility, whose open immorality of life, indeed, added to their strictness
with regard to their legitimate succession ; and,
much as Olivares favoured his new son, and lavishly
as, at his instance, Philip endowed him with rank,
resources, and offices, it was difficult to get him
acknowledged as an equal by the proud Guzmans,
and much less by the nobles, who were already
bitterly opposed to the minister. But Olivares
was powerful and determined. At his instance,
the handsome, gallant young son of the King, and
of the actress the *Calderona*, who was now twelve
years old, was brought to Madrid, and by decree
was given the same semi-royal honours as had
been bestowed on the other Don Juan of Austria,
the son of the great Emperor. Queen Isabel had
but two living children, young Baltasar Carlos, the
heir, and a younger girl, Maria Teresa. Baltasar
Carlos, who was the same age as his half-brother,
was a promising, sturdy little Prince, immensely
popular with the people of Madrid as he pranced

z

about on his pony, or raised in his name fresh regiments for the war. But naturally the Queen his mother was jealous that another son of the King, even better looking than Baltasar Carlos, should be brought into such close competition with her own legitimate offspring.[1]

The significance of the legitimation of Don Juan was seen in a family council summoned by the Count-Duke, in which Olivares' three sisters, all great ladies, and their children, were required to greet Enrique Felipe de Guzman as " Excellency," and a relative.[2] All the Castilian nobility was up in arms at such an insult ; but the disgust was infinitely deepened when Olivares demanded of the Constable of Castile, the Duke of Frias, the hand of his daughter for Enrique Felipe de Guzman, and when the Constable, a weak man, consented to the indignity—

> Soy de la Casa de Velasco,
> Y de nada hago asco,
>
> Here great Velasco's chief you see ;
> Nothing is too vile for me,

---

[1] Don Juan was acknowledged in 1642, and the occasion was taken for a great series of festivities to celebrate the event, though the state of public affairs at the time was more deplorable than ever. The Nuncio Panzuolo took a prominent part in the affair, and gave the Pope's blessing to the young Prince ; but it was noted that the Queen, usually so hearty and debonnaire, was cold and haughty when Don Juan was led up to kiss her hand and that of Prince Baltasar Carlos. It was noticed that the latter, prompted apparently by his mother, addressed his half-brother as *Vos*, You, which was the manner usually adopted towards nobles, but not to royal personages. An interesting unpublished paper in Italian in the British Museum gives many curious particulars of Don Juan's youth, and the details of his legitimation. Add MSS. 8703, "Ritratto della nascitá qualitá costumi ed accioni de Don Juan d'Austria."

[2] A most amusing account of this family council is given by Novoa, who hits off the respective characters of the three sisters—the Marchioness of Carpio, Marchioness of Monterey, and Countess of Alcañizes—very heatly.

was written by one of the poets of the Calle Mayor, and another scorpion was added to the lash preparing for the back of Olivares.

The minister was no weakling, and his hand fell heavily upon those who dared to oppose him. Quevedo's trenchant pen had scarified the vices and weaknesses of Madrid in a dozen satires : he had scourged the slothful, vain, pretentious crew that filled the gutters of the slums and the galleries of the Buen Retiro ; but so long as he was friendly to Olivares none dared to touch him. The moment he turned his glib verse and bitter prose, addressed to the poet-king himself,[1] to an exposure of the

---

[1] The terrible Memorial, written by Quevedo, exposing in burning words the state of the country, and calling upon the King to arouse himself, should be read by anyone who desires confirmation of the pictures I have tried to trace in this book. The paper was slipped under the King's napkin at dinner, and was accompanied by a parody paternoster, beginning as follows—

> Filipo, que el mundo aclama
> Rey del infiel tan temido,
> Despierta, que por dormido
> Nadie te teme, ni te ama ;
> Despierta, rey, que la fama
> Por todo el orbe pregona
> Que es de leon tu corona
> Y tu dormir de liròn,
> Mira que la adulacion
> Te llama con fin siniestro
>   " Padre Nuestro."

Hail, Philip, King whom all acclaim,
In fear the infidel to keep,
Awake ! for in thy slumber deep
No one doth love or fear thy name.
Awake ! oh King, the worlds proclaim
Thy crown on lion's brow to sit,
Thy slumber's but for dormouse fit.
Listen ! 'tis flattery's artful wile
That sunk in sloth thy days beguile,
And calls thee, its base ends to foster,
  " Pater Noster."

evils arising from the policy of the favourite, then isolation in a dark and filthy dungeon was Quevedo's reward. There, until the favourite's fall, the poet, loaded with chains, was kept, whilst the vices he had scourged grew greater with impunity.

The streets of Madrid became more scandalous even than before. Bravos and assassins almost openly stood for hire; murder and robbery were so common in broad daylight as to attract only passing notice, and in one fortnight at this period (1641) there were 110 murders in Madrid alone, many of them of persons of position.[1] Devout in form as were the people, even sanctuary was now no protection, and the most hideous sacrilege went hand in hand with grovelling sanctimoniousness. Fresh pragmatics, with penalties ferocious in their severity, denounced evil living, but little notice was taken of them after the first few days. Women still clattered up and down the Prado and the Calle Mayor on high jingling pattens, and with great swelling farthingales, their faces covered and their breasts exposed; cape snatchers still plied their trade at the street corners, and ruffling bullies picked quarrels for gain with peaceful citizens.

[1] At this time three of the principal grandees of Spain were banished from Court by Philip, for scaling the walls of the Retiro at night and clandestinely making love to the maids of honour. Two years previously affairs had reached such a scandalous length with the nobles, that Philip ordered a special commission to inquire into the matter. As a result a large batch of nobles, two marquises and one of Philip's chamberlains amongst them, were expelled as persons of known evil life. But suspicion is aroused by the terms of the decree that their dissoluteness was not the sole cause of this disgrace, as they are said to have " frequented gambling houses and there murmured without any reason at all against the present Government and the higher officers of the State, although some of them are deeply obliged to the same." Rodriguez Villa's Newsletter.

In Catalonia the Spanish armies and fleet were being beleaguered and beaten hopelessly (1641). The French King had received the oath of allegiance from Barcelona, whilst powerful French armies under Schomberg, De la Motte, and Meilleraie, with Richelieu behind them, held the principality firmly, cordially seconded by the Catalans themselves. All Spain, even Madrid, now almost at the end of its resources, saw that the country was upon the rapid slope that led to utter ruin. Portugal gone, with hardly as yet a pretence of winning it back. Catalonia gone, apparently as hopelessly, Andalucia almost in revolt,[1] and Naples simmering in discontent : a great empire of formerly loyal people falling into impotent disintegration, and all fingers pointed at the heavy, frowning, yellow-visaged man, who worked night and day doing everybody's work, and desperately keeping the King immersed in trifling pleasures, as the author of all this ruin and disgrace.

It was inevitable that it should be so ; but it

---

[1] An extremely dangerous conspiracy hatched at this time in Andalucia was discovered, and contributed much to the increased unpopularity of the Guzmans. The principal plotters were two of Olivares' greatest kinsmen, the Duke of Medina Sidonia, brother of the new Queen of Portugal, and the Marquis of Ayamonte, the object of the conspiracy being to make Medina Sidonia King of Andalucia by the aid of the new King of Portugal. Ayamonte had already betrayed to the Portuguese a conspiracy hatched by Olivares in Lisbon ; and then suggested to Medina Sidonia that the discontent in Andalucia and the disorganisation in Madrid offered a good opportunity for him to proclaim himself an independent sovereign. The proud magnate consented, but the plot was discovered. Olivares did his best to minimise the matter, and the Duke was let off with a heavy fine, much humiliation, and a challenge to fight John IV. in single combat ; but Ayamonte lost his head, although his life had been promised if he divulged the whole plot, which he did. A curious account of how the plot was discovered is in MSS. Egerton, 2081, British Museum.

was, of course, unjust. At the beginning of the reign, and for long afterwards, the policy that caused the trouble, that of persisting in the inflated claims of a century before, had been heartily endorsed by the whole people. They wanted glory, pride, supremacy. They wanted still to act the part of God's militia, to dragoon the world into one belief —their own—to boast of the riches of their King and the greatness of their country. But when at last they understood that a policy abroad of bombastic meddling and of domestic waste at home was costly, they turned to rend the man who had carried their vain aspirations into acts. Olivares was no wiser than other Spanish statesmen of his time. He could only see with the eyes of his own generation.; and his share of the blame for the ruin that had ensued upon his rule was only greater because more conspicuous than that of the whole people, who were blinded and besotted by the foolish hope of enjoying advantages, national and personal, which were beyond their means.

In April 1642, Madrid was panic-stricken by the news that the last reinforcements sent to the seat of war, and raised with such terrible suffering from the exhausted people, had been overwhelmed by Marshal de la Motte ; and Castile was now powerless to send adequate forces to make any head against the absolute domination of Catalonia by the French. The satires and epigrams fell as thick as autumn leaves in Madrid, urging Philip to wake up and act the man. Louis XIII. was to be present with his army on Spanish soil at Perpignan, and was already playing a worthy part in a great national crisis ; whilst Philip, his Spanish brother-in-law, still dangled about the Buen Retiro, busy in arranging comedies, even writing them, some said; planning ostentatious shows and affected literary competitions, or, as a change, speared driven boars at the Pardo. The Queen, a Frenchwoman though she was, added her tears and entreaties that her husband himself should go whither his duty called him, no matter at what sacrifice of his ease and pleasures.

To do Philip justice, he personally was eager to fulfil his duty; but long custom had made him almost incapable now of shaking off the yoke of Olivares and having his own way. For a time the minister and his obedient Councils opposed every obstacle to the project of the King's joining the army in the field. The personal danger was made most of; the incommodity of the voyage, the inconvenience to the troops to be weighted with the additional responsibility of the safety of the monarch; the risk of assassination by rebel subjects; even the positive lack of money for the journey, was urged, again and again, upon Philip by Olivares. It was useless, moreover, he said, for the King to go without large reinforcements. On the other hand, the Queen and the higher nobles, even many of the Councillors, urged that the case was desperate, and that without the King's personal example Catalonia was lost for ever to Spain. They even began to whisper that cowardice was the reason of Olivares' obstinate resistance to the journey; and at length Philip, aroused for once in his life, put his foot down, peremptorily silenced the remonstrances of the Council, and tore up its Memorial opposing his going.

Again the drums were beaten. The cities of Andalucia were appealed to in the name of loyalty ; the nobles and their sons were once more squeezed. The son of Olivares, with his father's money, raised a chosen corps with which he made a brilliant show before the King, and gave an excuse (says Novoa) to put pressure upon other young nobles to do the like. At last, with infinite effort, a new force was got together to accompany the King to Aragon ; the Queen, working strenuously, selling her jewels, putting pressure upon pious ladies and ecclesiastics to subscribe, making much of the popularity of her son Baltasar Carlos ; and for the time putting aside the frivolous pleasures that had delighted her, to play a part worthy of the daughter of the gallant Béarnais, Henry of Navarre.

When news came to Madrid that Louis XIII. was on Spanish soil in Roussillon, Philip finally determined to go to the front in spite of Olivares. He would go by Aranjuez, he said, and if the Count-Duke did not like to join him there he should go without him. This was open rebellion, but Olivares was too old a hand to gainsay the King, who, like all weak men, was obstinacy itself when once his mind had been made up. On the 26th April, Philip, on a splendid charger, with pistols at his saddle-bow and sword by his side, rode to the Atocha church to pray to the famous image of the Virgin, and thence by Barajas and Alcalá de Henares, on his way to the war. Like a lighted powder-train the enthusiasm flew through the country as the King passed onward. Not in the memory of living men had a monarch of Spain thus rode forth to war to fight for his inheritance, and the foul miasma of sloth and ignoble enjoyment was swept from the hearts of thousands of young Spaniards, whose spirits were aflame and whose chivalry was touched anew with the spirit that in times past had made their sires invincible.

The Queen was left in Madrid as Regent, with the President of the Council of Castile and the Marquis de Santa Cruz to aid her; and Olivares, who knew well the danger of the course he was obliged to acquiesce in, lagged behind in the capital as long as he dared,—afraid of the war, sneered some; afraid of leaving the Queen alone, whispered others; whilst, as time went on, the opinion became general that the King's going was all a feint to get more money and men. There seemed good reason for the suspicion; for when Olivares at length joined his master, it was with plans formed to beguile Philip in the usual way. Two days were passed in devotion at the shrine of St. James at Alcala; then a pompous visit with long festivities to Olivares' own house at Loeches; and thence to Aranjuez, where and in the neighbourhood nearly a month was passed in hunting parties, tourneys, and the like, with frequent visits from the Queen. Again the war spirit in the country flagged, and the people despaired at so much trifling, when, as the saying went, there were three Kings on Spanish soil instead of one.[1]

At length Philip shook himself free again, thanks to the exhortation of his wife; and on the 20th May rode forth from Aranjuez, now with a numerous unwieldy train of servants, carriages, and baggage, and followed by Olivares in terror

[1] That is to say, Philip, the King of Portugal, and the King of France.

of assassination, surrounded by guards whom he beseeched to allow no one to approach him.[1] Olivares was in mortal fear, too, of an interview between Philip and his cousin the Duchess of Mantua, the expelled Vicereine of Portugal ; whom, much to her indignation, the minister had forbidden to come to Madrid, and had secluded under formal restraint at Ocaña, which lay in the road by which the King must pass. The Duchess, if once she got ear of the King alone, would tell him how, and why, Portugal had been lost ; and in the long drive during which the Duchess shared the King's coach on his way to Ocaña, she laid such a story before him, of oppression, cruelty, and unwise government, as to leave Philip shocked and angered that so much had been hidden from him.

Visiting noble houses and shrines on the road, and seizing every opportunity for delay, Olivares managed to spin out the journey to Saragossa until the 27th July, when Aragon itself was half overrun by French raiders. Philip's entry into the city was more fitting for a monarch's triumphal return from victory than for the opening of a campaign by a soldier. Soon after his arrival he heard with dismay that Monzon, the ancient legislative capital, had been occupied by the French ; whilst everywhere his troops were either retiring before the enemy or being beaten hopelessly. The greater nobles, both Castilian and Aragonese, systematically avoided contact with Olivares ; but the

---

[1] It must not be forgotten that Novoa, who says this, was an enemy of Olivares; though there is no doubt that the minister did believe at the time that his death was planned.

presence of Philip in the Aragonese capital offered a good opportunity for a visit of the grandees to him, in order to take counsel as to what could be done in so calamitous a state of affairs. Olivares received them almost rudely, and refused them collective access to the King, whereupon the nobles in high dudgeon shook the dust of Saragossa from their feet, and to a man swore to be avenged on the insolent upstart who, they said, was keeping the King prisoner. In fact, Philip was practically isolated in two rooms whilst at Saragossa, on the plea of the risk to his life if he went out. Olivares rode forth every day in a coach closely surrounded by guards, and no one was allowed to approach him.

For all the months that Philip passed in the Aragonese city he never saw his army or approached the enemy, his main amusement being to watch tennis matches from his window.[1] Roussillon was lost in September, never to be recovered, when Perpignan fell ; and thenceforward every week brought some story of disgrace and defeat for the Spanish arms ; whilst Philip, in inglorious despair, moped in his seclusion, bereft even of his cherished amusements. Olivares was growing desperate. Every courier brought from the stout-hearted Queen Regent in Madrid messages of encouragement and good cheer. She was working bravely, and with wonderful success ; collecting funds from hoards hitherto unsuspected, gathering troops and putting heart into them. With her

---

[1] These particulars are taken from an interesting Italian MS. in the British Museum, Add. 8701, from the pen of the Venetian ambassador in Madrid at the time, and also to some extent from Novoa.

son by her side she reviewed soldiers, and made herself the idol of the populace, who for a time had plucked up some hope and pride in the future of their country. But with the Queen's cheery news to her husband there always went open or covert blame of Olivares. To the minister she sent all the plate, jewels, and treasure she could collect ; but he saw from the comparative ease with which she could raise it, whilst he could not, that she held the winning hand and had the people behind her. In despair of beating the French in the field, he stooped to conspire with Cinq Mars against the life of Richelieu himself. The conspiracy was discovered, and made the feeling against him personally more bitter than ever.

Philip could not be kept quite ignorant of the misery and ruin around him, or of his own undignified position, and he grew moody and irritable with the minister who had led him to such a pass. Without even consulting him, he appointed the Marquis of Leganes, a cousin of Olivares and an experienced soldier, to the chief command of what was left of his army ; and Olivares, foreseeing his disgrace, craved leave to retire. But this Philip would not allow. He had no other minister to replace him ; he was in the midst of a disastrous war, and he had neither the energy nor the knowledge necessary to take matters in his own hand at this juncture.

The Queen in Madrid had no lack of friends and advisers, all of them enemies of the Guzmans, especially the Counts of Castrillo and Paredes ; but the ostentatious legitimation of Olivares' son Enrique had also alienated his own most influential kinsman, the Haros, represented by the Marquis of Carpio, whose son he had disinherited so far as he was able ; and these with other former adherents now joined the Queen's friends. All Madrid knew that the Queen was against Olivares ; and, safe now from his presence, she made no concealment of it. " My efforts and my boy's innocence must serve the King for eyes," she said ; " for if he use those of the Count-Duke much longer my son will be reduced to a poor King of Castile instead of King of Spain."

When la Motte defeated Philip's army under Leganes before Lerida late in the autumn (1642), the last hope seemed gone. Torrecusa, the Neapolitan general who had fought so well in the previous campaigns, went to Saragossa, and, forcing his way to the King, told him that all was lost unless a change was made in the direction of affairs. Torrecusa was mollified with a grandeeship on the spot ; but Philip, overweighed and almost at his wits' end, was fain to return to his capital, in the desperate hope of raising another army in the spring, though the citizens of Saragossa prayed him to stay and defend them against the all-victorious French and Catalans.[1] Alas ! he had neither troops nor money with which to defend them,—no spirit, no counsel, no hope.

On the 1st December 1642, Philip turned his face towards Madrid, after signing decrees, drafted by Olivares, imposing upon Castile new and crushing impositions with which to raise a fresh army. Another " voluntary " levy of money was ordered, a new loan authorised, the seizure of all the church

[1] Novoa ascribes their desire for his presence to the money spent by the Court.

and domestic plate decreed, and a tax of 7 per cent.
upon all real property demanded. Well might the
subjects stand aghast at this. Where, they asked,
was the actual money to come from ? The copper
was so debased as to be worthless ; the only standard
was silver at a high premium (38 per cent.), and of
this there was not enough available for currency,
much less to represent the new demand. When,
therefore, Philip entered Madrid by the side of his
wife, all spirits were prepared and eager for the
change they saw must come. As the royal pair
passed in their coach from the Retiro to the palace,
blessings loud and long greeted the Queen, such as
Philip had never heard before.

Olivares understood the signs of the times too.
Summoning his brother-in-law Carpio, he tried to
reconcile him, but in vain, and complained bitterly
that all the gentlemen of the King's chamber had
turned his enemies. He talked, indeed, about
retiring ; but Philip never moved a muscle of his
face, and the minister knew that the course which
had served him so often was powerless to help him
now. The Countess was strong and resourceful, and
undertook to bring Philip round. When she met
him in the palace that evening, she spoke much of
her husband's services and efforts, and of the
excellent arrangements he was making for carrying on a successful war in the following spring.
Philip bowed gravely, but made no reply. The day
afterwards (14th January 1643) a courier came from
the Emperor, bringing more bad news to Philip and
bitterly attacking Olivares, and this also sank into
the King's mind.

Moodily the King walked to his wife's apartment that afternoon. There, to his surprise, he found with her the heir Baltasar Carlos, now aged fourteen. Casting herself at the King's feet with her son by her side, the Queen solemnly exhorted him, for the sake of what remained of their child's inheritance, to cast aside the evil councillor who was dragging them all to ruin. The King was troubled, for everything with him was a case of conscience, and he felt that he could trust no one. On his way from his wife's apartment he traversed a passage where he was intercepted by an old woman, his foster-mother, Ana de Guevara, who had been banished by Olivares and had returned without leave. Kneeling, she in her turn implored Philip to listen to those who loved him best ; and then with a torrent of impassioned eloquence she impeached the favourite and all his acts : spoke of the national ruin, of the people's misery, of fields untilled, of looms idle, of the foreigner reigning over Spanish land, and of people who once were the soul of loyalty now in revolt against their King, all, all through Olivares. Philip was overwhelmed, and could only raise her, saying, "You have spoken truly."

But still one more blow was to be struck that night at the falling favourite. The Duchess of Mantua, secretly summoned by the Queen, had fled from Ocaña, and as fast as post-horses could draw her carriage through the winter storm she had come to Madrid. Suddenly appearing in the office of Olivares, she said she had come to see the King, and required lodging and food. The minister treated her with great rudeness, and made her wait for four hours before he provided a bad lodging for her in the house of the Treasury. But she was the

King's cousin ; and the next day the Queen introduced her into Philip's presence, where, this time with documentary proofs, she brought home to him the responsibility of Olivares and his creatures for the loss of Portugal.

That night Philip wrote to his minister, saying that the leave to retire he had so often craved was now accorded him, and that he might go where and when he pleased. Olivares, we are told by one who saw him, stood as if turned to stone as he read the letter ; but at length, recovering his serenity, he turned to his wife and told her that he needed rest and change, and would shortly leave for a stay at Loeches, his seat some twelve miles from Madrid, if she would start at once and prepare the place for his coming. Guessing the truth, she resisted as much as possible, but was at last forced to obey. On the following morning, according to his invariable custom for so many years, the minister entered the King's room early, and knelt before him for a time in silence. Then he launched forth an eloquent denunciation of those who had slandered him in the eyes of his master, and in justification of his efforts. He had failed, he acknowledged ; circumstances and the venom of his enemies had wrecked his best laid schemes for the exaltation of Spain and the glory of his Sovereign ; but at least he prayed that his loyalty should be recognised, and that, in the retirement to which he willingly went at the King's behest, he might carry with him the regard of the master he had so strenuously tried to serve.

No word of reply came from the King, whose long sallow face remained as expressionless as if

moulded in putty, and Olivares left the presence
for the moment defeated ; but still revolving in his
mind other expedients to regain Philip's favour, or
at least to delay his own fall.   First he wrote to his
energetic and spirited wife at Loeches, telling her
the whole truth ; for where he had failed he thought
she might succeed.   When her husband's letter
reached the Countess, she was just taking her seat
at table for dinner, " and on reading it not only
did her natural colour fly from her face, but the
rouge with which she covered it, as is the fashion
in the palace, paled and left her like a corpse." [1]
Leaving her dinner untouched, the afflicted woman
hurried back to Madrid ; and after an interview
with her husband tried her blandishments upon
the King as he was on his way through the
corridors to visit his children as usual.   She found
him unmoved and silent, and then, rushing to the
Queen's apartment, she threw herself at her feet.
But Isabel had suffered under her hard rule too
long, and answered coldly : " What God, the
people, and evil happenings have done, Countess,
neither the King nor I can undo."

Then Olivares summoned to the Retiro his
nephew, Don Luis de Haro, Carpio's son, who he
knew was in high favour with the King.   He had,
he told him, been a bad uncle to him ; but he had
brought his father and him from their remote
grange at Carpio, and had made them rich and
powerful ; and he begged him, notwithstanding
later jealousy, to be a good nephew to him and
plead his cause.   Haro saw the King, and gave
him account of several secret points of politics

[1] So one of her servants who was present told Novoa.

2 A

on behalf of the fallen minister, and asked in his name many and expensive favours for his servants, all of which Philip granted,[1] but kept silent with regard to Olivares himself.

Soon the news was whispered in Madrid ; and Liars' Walk was like a swarming hive. At first men were incredulous. It was all a sham, they declared ; just another trick to squeeze more money out of them on the pretext that the hated Olivares had gone. But by and by the happy truth gradually forced itself upon them. The nightmare that had sat for all these years upon the heart of Spain had been shaken off at last ! And then there burst out such a frantic flood of rejoicing as Madrid had rarely seen before. We have a King again ! cried the crowds that stood in the great square before the palace ; and squibs and pasquins were handed from hand to hand by the score.[2] But still day followed day and yet Olivares tarried in the vain hope of averting his fate. A hundred excuses were found by him for delay : the difficulty of transport, the condition of his health, his desire to see all those who had served him well provided for, and much else. Hints reached him in plenty that his

---

[1] " I got a pension of 400 ducats," says Novoa ; and he relates the whole of these grants and favours to those who had served Olivares.

[2] Amongst the skits was a placard that was stuck upon the palace gates, saying—

El dia de San Antonio
Se hicieron milagros dos ;
Pues empezó á reinar Dios,
Y del rey se echó el demonio.

Saint Antonio's day did bring
Of miracles this twain,
'Twas then the Lord began to reign,
And devil cast from the King.

absence was desirable, though he admitted no one to see him. His keys were demanded, and he sent them ; once he saw the King in public audience, and talked to him of affairs for a quarter of an hour, but those who stood by remarked that Philip's eyes never once rested upon him ; and again he retired discomfited, with tears coursing down his cheeks. As the King and Queen, with the Duchess of Mantua in their coach, went on St. Anthony's day (17th January 1643) to the Convent of Discalced Carmelites, the people, who now knew everything, impulsively surged around them with joyous cries : " Our King is King at last !—God save the King ! "

At length Philip grew impatient at the delay, for he would appoint no new officers until he was clean quit of Olivares and his crew, and he decided to hunt for two days at the Escorial in order that measures might be taken in his absence. No sooner had he left than the Countess of Olivares made another tearful appeal to the Queen, who dismissed her promptly ; and on the second day (20th January 1643), when Philip was approaching Madrid on his way back, a great gathering of nobles came out to meet him. Through Melchior Borja they said that they wished to place themselves and their possessions at the disposal of their King once more. Hitherto they had stood aloof, for reasons now known to him ; but so soon as that evil cause was removed they were willing to stand by him to the death. Then they urged him to change all his councils and administrative officers, and begin a new régime.

When Philip entered the palace, he turned to Don Luis de Haro and asked, " Has he gone ? "

" No, Sire," was the reply.   " Is he waiting for us
to use force ? " grumbled the King ; and soon the
hint was conveyed to Olivares, and, convinced
now of the hopelessness of his case, the man who
had ruled Spain over the King for two-and-twenty
disastrous years slunk out of the capital by un-
frequented ways, accompanied by only four attendants in a coach with closely drawn curtains, in
mortal fear of assassination ; for, as his spiteful
biographer says, the very children in the streets
would have stoned him to death if they had known
of his flitting.[1]

Not until the fallen favourite had left Madrid
well behind him did Philip feel himself safe.
Summoning to his workroom in one of the corner
towers of the old palace, Cardinals Borja and
Spinola, and a number of the nobles who had
opposed Olivares, he addressed a long speech to
them. He was, he said, ardently determined to
take the details of Government into his own hands
in future. The Count-Duke had served him long,
well, and zealously ; but his health had broken
down and he needed repose. Thenceforward he
(the King) would have no confidential minister,
but would work himself as minister, with the aid
and counsel of his hearers, from whom he asked
now reports and suggestions for future remedial
action. Oñate, an old man and vain, hoped for
some days that he was to replace Olivares as sole
minister, but the King promptly undeceived him,
and declared publicly that in future he would have
no other minister but his wife, whose energy,

---

[1] Novoa and, also for other details, Newsletters in Valladares' *Semanario Erudito*, vol. xxxiii.

wisdom, patriotism he now understood for the
first time.

As for the once powerful minister who had gone
into obscurity broken-hearted, none was so poor
as to do him reverence, few magnanimous enough
to give him a good word. Those who had be-
slavered him with adulation were the first now
to load him with ignominy; even the Constable of
Castile, who had so willingly married his daughter to
Olivares' base son, now stripped of all his honour,
claimed that young Guzman's earlier marriage
had been valid after all. When it was pointed
out to the Constable that this would leave his
daughter dishonoured, he replied : " I would rather
see my daughter a bawd and free, than an honest
woman and Guzman's wife." [1]

The many scathing attacks published upon
Olivares and his administration, provoked by his
fall, found but one able, though imprudently frank,
answer, which was called *Nicandra*,[2] and is
ascribed to Ahumada, the Prince's tutor, and to
that staunch friend of Velazquez and of the Count-
Duke, Francisco de Rioja ; but now that the dust
of the convulsion has cleared away, we see that
it was Olivares' methods rather than his principles
that were the cause of the disasters of his rule.
The foreign policy which he represented was not
his alone, but was the policy of the immense
majority of his countrymen at the time; and if it
had not brought him into antagonism with the

---

[1] Many of these particulars are taken from the Venetian narrative,
British Museum MSS., Add. 8701.

[2] The work was confiscated by the Inquisition, and the supposed
authors and the printer prosecuted ; as were the attacks that gave rise
to it.

provincial and autonomous traditions of the outer realms of the Peninsula, the principal factor of his fall would not have existed. The vast wealth which it was said he had heaped upon himself, amounting, so his enemies asserted, to the enormous total of 400,000 ducats a year, was not accumulated for personal gratification or greed, as had been the case with Lerma, nor were the sums he obtained larger than were appropriated by his great rival Richelieu. He lived very quietly, almost humbly, giving the whole of his time to work, and spent his revenues largely in the entertainment and convenience of the King.

From Loeches he soon, with the King's permission, retired to Toro, far away from Court. Even there, divested of his dignities and power, the envy and hate of his enemies pursued him. More than once in the two years that followed his retreat the King seemed inclined to recall his old minister. But watchful eyes and jealous heart always frustrated such an idea, if it was entertained. Many a time, in fear of such a calamity to them, the nobles, especially those of Aragon, urged the King to punish with death a man who had thus betrayed his confidence; but Philip was neither cruel nor unjust, and naturally drew back from such a course as this. Once it seemed as if the enemies of Olivares had almost succeeded; for in reply to an address from the ex-minister upon public affairs, in which the latter offered his services again, the King wrote from Saragossa: " In short, Count, I must reign, and my son must be crowned King of Aragon. This is difficult unless I deliver your head to my subjects, who demand it unanimously, and I cannot oppose them any further."

Alas! the head of Olivares was useless to them or to anyone else thenceforward, for the letter sent him raving mad, and he died on the 22nd July 1645, only two years and a half after his disgrace. Thenceforward Philip, for good of for evil, stands alone. What is done he does, and no powerful minister is interposed as a shield between him and the responsibility for his acts. "Philip the Great" meant well, but he had yet to learn the lesson that broke his heart : that good intentions alone are not sufficient to ensure success ; and that the despairing struggles of one conscience-haunted man are powerless to save a nation that has lost its faith in itself, and its dependence upon labour as a means to salvation.

CHAPTER IX

DEATH OF RICHELIEU AND OF THE CARDINAL IN-
FANTE — PHILIP'S GOOD RESOLUTIONS — HIS
CORRESPONDENCE WITH THE NUN OF AGREDA
—PHILIP WITH HIS ARMIES—DEATH OF QUEEN
ISABEL OF BOURBON—THE WAR CONTINUES
IN CATALONIA—DEATH OF BALTASAR CARLOS—
PHILIP'S GRIEF—HE LOSES HEART—INFLUENCE
OF THE NUN — HIS SECOND MARRIAGE WITH
HIS NIECE MARIANA—HIS LIFE WITH HER—
DON LUIS DE HARO — NEGOTIATIONS WITH
ENGLAND — CROMWELL'S ENVOY, ANTHONY
ASCHAM — HIS MURDER IN MADRID — FRIEND-
SHIP BETWEEN PHILIP AND THE ENGLISH COM-
MONWEALTH — CROMWELL SEIZES JAMAICA —
WAR WITH ENGLAND

THE disappearance from the scene of Olivares
seemed to the people of Madrid to change the
national winter into summer. All the evils under
which Spain had groaned so long would vanish,
they thought, like snow before the sunshine ; and
once more Spain, powerful and rich, would dictate
the law to Europe. Philip swore in solemn fashion
to forsake dissipation and devote himself thenceforward to the welfare of his people. It was a
golden dream whilst it lasted, and for a time it
really did lift Spaniards into some semblance of
the old-time faith and confidence. All the gang

of Guzmans were thrust into the background, and those who had stood aloof were now summoned to the Councils of the King. Quevedo came from his dungeon, cynically triumphant ; the distribution of business amongst a multitude of unimportant juntas subservient to Olivares was abolished, and the great Councils again took executive and administrative charge of the affairs entrusted to them. The active and intelligent influence of the Queen was exerted everywhere ; and new life was breathed for a time in the languishing body of the State.

There were also other great changes nearly coinciding with the fall of Olivares that increased the hopefulness of Spaniards for the future. Richelieu died some months before, and the personal rivalry between the two ministers, which had done so much to embitter the war, disappeared. Then, in May 1643, the King of France, Louis XIII., died, and Philip's sister, Anna of Austria, became Queen-regent of France for her five-year-old son, Louis XIV. Anna had always been a true daughter of Spain, and deplored the war between the land of her birth and that of her adoption ; and it was hoped that she would find a means to end the differences. Another event had occurred at the end of 1641, which, whilst adding to Philip's gloom, made the continuance of the war in the Netherlands more hopeless than ever. The Cardinal Infante Fernando, his frail physique worn out by constant campaigning and enfeebled by fever, died at Brussels ; [1] and Philip had no relative now to

---

[1] A pathetic account of his deathbed is given by Novoa. After eighty-eight days of continual fever, the miraculous image of Our Lady of Bois le Duc was brought to his sick chamber. As the image entered

stand for Spain in the ancient patrimony of Burgundy.

With all these changes in the space of two years,
the spring of 1643 seemed to blossom with hopes of
peace once more, humiliating as the terms might be.
But again Spanish pride stood in the way, and after
long discussion Philip's new councillors determined
that honour demanded the expulsion of the French
from Spanish soil before any negotiations for peace
with them were undertaken. With infinite difficulty
money and men were got together somehow [1] for
Philip to take the field again in Aragon, where
the French had arrived within a few miles of Saragossa. Before he could start on his way thither,
there came from Flanders news of a crushing defeat
sustained by General Melo, who had replaced the
Cardinal Infante in the command. Melo at first
had done well ; for he was skilled and bold, and had
more than held his own against the allies. But
on the 18th May 1643 the terrible battle of Rocroy
was fought, in which Melo himself was captured,
Count de Fuentes was killed, and the Spanish
army of 20,000 men, the tried veterans who were
the last remnant of the once invincible *tercios*,
whose fame was world-wide, were put to utter rout
by the genius of the youthful Enghien (Prince of
Condé). The Spanish infantry never regained the
prestige they lost at Rocroy, which was to the army
of Spain what the defeat of the Armada was to her

the door the Prince chanted the hymn, " Mater, Mater Gratia," and
when he reached the words " Mater Misericordia " he faltered and
died.

    [1] The Cortes of Castile voted 4,000,000 ducats a year for six years
in June 1643, and the silver fleet arrived in Seville intact with a large
treasure, which was seized by the Government as a forced loan.

navy ;[1] and with the knowledge that disaster
was pursuing him on all sides, for the Portuguese
were raiding far into Castile and the French were
threatening the capital of Aragon, Philip left
Madrid, his heart well-nigh breaking, early in June
1643.

In the five months that had passed since he
had dismissed Olivares the King had tried hard ;
but already his indolence was casting its paralys-
ing blight over him ; and most of the work of the
Government was handed to Don Luis de Haro,
the nephew of Olivares, who went with the King to
Aragon. This time Philip was accompanied by
a modest train, and by little of the ceremonial
state that Olivares had deemed needful for his previous voyage. He travelled slowly, nevertheless, and
on the 10th July, as he approached the Aragonese
frontier city of Tarazona, he halted at the humble
Convent of the Immaculate Conception at Agreda,
which in the previous few years had been founded
by a lady whose fame for sanctity and wisdom had
already become wide, though she was but forty
years of age yet. Maria Coronel had written
several mystically religious books, and the convent
under her rule was known for its rigidity in an age
when most cloisters had grown lax. Philip probably visited the house and its abbess as a usual
compliment and duty ; but the visit, whatever its
motive, set its mark upon him for the rest of his
life.

The abbess, Sor Maria, as she was called, must
have been a woman of worldly wisdom as deep as

---

[1] The story of the battle of Rocroy is told in minutest detail by
Canovas del Castillo in *Estudios de Reinado de Felipe IV.*, vol. ii.

was her piety. She must have impressed the King, moreover, powerfully as being absolutely disinterested and free from mundane temptation. He was, as we have seen, almost in despair at the magnitude of the tasks before him ; the strong spirit upon which he had leant since he was a boy had passed out of his life, and he knew not whither to turn for unselfish counsel. Sor Maria, saintly, but keen, with her sad yet half humorous face, and her shrewd, kindly eyes, seemed to him a very rock of refuge, and in the long talk he had with her she spoke so wisely, yet so fearlessly, of the oppressive governance and ungodly methods of Olivares, she urged the King so powerfully to trust to God and himself alone, to work and pray and make his people cleanly, that he went forth from Agreda refreshed in faith and hope, leaving with Sor Maria his command that she was to write to him her private counsel when she listed, and to pray for him and his unceasingly with all her saintly soul.

Thenceforward until death snapped the spiritual link that joined them, the heart of Philip was bared in all its sorrow, its weakness, and its sin to Sor Maria alone. The haughty face with the pathetic eyes and great projecting jaw remained unmoved before the world, only the deepening furrows in it showing the storm that raged within. Men thought that he was callous and cold ; for he suffered silently behind his mask. But Sor Maria knew, and none but she under heaven, the true secret of the King's gilded misery. His cry of agony, of remorse, of pity thenceforward came to the cloistered nun as a surer way to reach the throne of grace than to all the cardinals, confessors,

Sor Maria
de Jesus

and bishops who waited upon his smile, and gently hinted disapproval of kingly vice.

At the end of July 1643, Philip entered his city of Saragossa, this time, to the delight of the jealous Aragonese, unattended by the crowd of dissolute nobles and courtiers who made love to their wives and threatened their political liberty.[1] No time was lost now in moving against the French, who were threatening the centre of Aragon, and the new commander, Felipe de Silva, whom Olivares' jealousy had consigned to a prison, showed great energy, and soon changed the appearance of affairs. It will be useful for our purpose to reproduce the principal paragraphs of Philip's first letter to the nun on the 4th October 1643, five weeks after his arrival at Saragossa, the precursor of so long and important a correspondence.[2]

" SOR MARIA,—I write to you leaving a half margin, so that your reply may come on the same paper, and I enjoin and command you not to allow the contents of this to be communicated to anybody. Since the day that I was with you I have felt much encouraged by your promise to pray to God for me, and for success to my realm ; for the earnest attachment towards my well being that I then recognised in you gave me great confidence and encouragement. As I told you, I left Madrid lacking all human resources, and trusting only to divine help, which is the sole way to obtain what

[1] Newsletter, Valladares' *Semanario Erudito*, vol. xxxiii.
[2] Many isolated letters have been known, and some of them published, at various times ; but in 1885 the whole correspondence, so far as it is known, was published by my lamented friend, Don Francisco Silvela.

we desire. Our Lord has already begun to work
in my favour, bringing in the silver fleet, and relieving Oran [1] when we least expected it ; whereby
I have been able, though with infinite trouble and
tardiness for want of money, to dispose my forces
here so that we shall, I hope, start work with them
this week. Although I beseech God and His most
holy Mother to succour and aid us, I trust very
little in myself ; for I have offended, and still
offend very much, and I justly deserve the punishments and afflictions which I suffer. And so I
appeal to you to fulfil your promise to me, to
clamour to God to guide my actions and my arms,
to the end that the quietude of these realms may
be secured, and peace reign throughout Christendom. The Portuguese rebels still raid the frontiers
of Portugal, acting against God and their natural
sovereign. Affairs in Flanders are in great extremity,
and there is risk of a rising unless God will inter-
vene in my favour ; and though affairs in Aragon
have somewhat improved with my presence, I
fear that unless we can gain some successes to
encourage people here they are liable to lose
heart and to take a course very injurious to the
monarchy. The necessities, of course, are numerous

---

[1] Oran, a Spanish fortress on the African coast, was closely beleaguered
by land and sea by the Moors, at the instance, so it was said, of the
new King of Portugal. The Duke of Arcos, Governor of Valencia,
managed to run the blockade with two English ships full of provisions,
and the place was thus relieved. The superstitious Madrileños of the
time atrributed the relief to a miraculous painting of the Virgin that
had just been discovered in Madrid. A servant girl had begun to sing
a hymn of praise and dance before the figure, when she saw the fingers
of the painting move. Her cries brought the crowd to see the miracle,
and all Madrid was stirred. The painting was taken to the convent of
Discalced Carmelites. The next day it was exposed in the church, and
the news came of the relief of Oran. Newsletters, Valladares.

and great ; but I must confess that it is not that
which distresses me most, but the certain conviction
that they all arise from my having offended our
Lord. As He knows, I earnestly wish to please
Him and to fulfil my duty in all things ; and I
desire that, if by any means you arrive at a knowledge of what it is His holy will that I should do
to placate Him, write to me here, for I am very
anxious to do right, and I do not know in what I
err. Some religious people give me to understand that they have revelations ; and that God
commands that I should punish certain persons,
and that I should dismiss others from my service.
But you know full well that in this matter of
revelations one must be very careful, and particularly when these religious persons speak against
those who are not really bad, and against whom I
have never discovered anything injurious to me ;
whilst others are approved whose proceedings
are not usually thought well of. The general
opinion about these persons is that they love
turning things over, and that their truth cannot
be depended upon. I do hope that you will keep
your word to me, and will speak with all frankness
as to a confessor, for we kings have much of the
confessor in us. Do not let yourself be influenced
by what the world says, for that is little to be
depended upon, seeing the aims of those who
move such discourse ; but be guided solely by
the inspiration of God, before whom I protest (and
I have just partaken of Him, in the Sacrament)
that I desire in all things, and for all things, to
fulfil His sacred law and the obligation which He
has laid upon me as a King. And I hope in His

mercy that He will take pity on our pains and help us out of those afflictions. The greatest favour that I can receive from His holy hands is that the punishment He lays upon these realms may be laid upon me ; for it is I, and not they, who really deserve the punishment, for they have always been true and firm Catholics. I do hope you will console me with your reply, and that I may have in you a true intercessor with our Lord, that He may guide and enlighten me, and extricate me from the troubles in which I am now immersed.— I, THE KING. Saragossa, 4th October 1644."

In addition to the invaluable and unquestionable glimpse which this letter affords of public affairs, it gives us the key, more entirely perhaps than any of the six hundred letters that followed it, to the real character of the King. He was weak ; he confesses to have no confidence in himself, although in his heart of hearts he is striving to live well and do his duty. He is unable to struggle successfully against the worldly pleasures that have captured him, and which he pursues still, whilst hating himself for doing so. Conscience-haunted, he is the only sinner, and the terrible conviction forces itself upon him that his personal sins of omission and commission are to be visited in awful punishment upon whole nations of innocent people. His natural justice and his knowledge of men cause him to rebel against the suggestions that come to him, even under the cloak of religion, to punish those who in his eyes have done no ill ; and behind the regal purple and the stately port of his great office we see the poor soul, so remorseful

in the knowledge of its sin and insignificance as
to feel unworthy even to pray without a poor
nun's intercession to the appalling deity he thinks
he has incensed. And yet, with all this humility,
how the true Spaniard peeps out in the conviction
that God has His eyes specially on *him* ; how
God's designs for the universe revolve around *his*
fortunes, *his* acts, and *his* transgressions. Only
by the light of these self-revelatory letters can we
see how penetrating was the genius of Velazquez.
The tragic, haunted face of Philip, when age had
palled his pleasures, only told its tale to the painter ;
and its pride, its weakness, its mercy and despair,
an enigma until now, are explained to us when, after
looking upon his portrait, we read the King's own
words, meant for the eyes of the cloistered nun alone.

Whilst Philip was, for the first time for twenty
years, manfully struggling against his indolence,
and facing his enemies in Aragon, the Queen, as
regent of Castile, was straining every nerve to
provide money for the campaigns ; and during the
autumn (1643) an army of 16,000 men was mustered
in the various provinces, and sent to the King.
Queen Isabel too put her hand to the Augean stable
of Madrid. Murders in the streets and armed
affrays upon trifling pretexts were as numerous as
ever, one Newsletter (25th August) enumerating four
or five of such fatal scandals during the previous
few days ;[1] one of which—although that was in
Valencia and is given as an instance—is curious :
one Iñigo Velasco, an actor, we are told, having been
beheaded "because, forgetting the humility of his
calling, he courted ladies as impudently as any

· Valladares' Newsletter.

2 B

gentleman could have done." But it was noticed in Madrid that the punishment now followed the crime more surely and more promptly:[1] that immorality was attacked more earnestly than before, and that the large public houses of ill-fame were being rapidly cleared out by the new President of the Council of Castile.

The financial officers and others were also having rather a ruthless time, for secret commissions descended upon them and their papers without notice one after the other, and scores of thousands of ducats of ill-gotten plunder had to be disgorged; whilst the friends of Olivares who had survived his fall, and kept their places, were gradually made to understand that things had altered for them.[2] The Countess of Olivares thus far had held firmly to her footing as Mistress of the Robes, notwithstanding the frowns of the Queen ; but the Duchess of Mantua brought matters to a head with her. As the Countess aspired to sit upon a seat in the royal carriage instead of in the doorway, the Duchess rose and said that that was not her place, and she would leave the carriage. The Queen placated her, but a few days afterwards

---

[1] The punishments were terrible. In a Newsletter written during this winter it is mentioned that two young gentlemen of birth had been hanged that week as known thieves. " A young girl who was their accomplice did not accompany them, as she was not old enough to be hanged. But they gave her two hundred lashes, and cut off her ears under the scaffold, after which they kept her all day hanging by the hair in sight of the public ; so that she died of the punishment within two days. Valladares.

[2] The famous Villanueva, we are told, had to dance attendance upon Secretary Andres de Rozas instead of keeping everybody waiting in his antechamber ; and the King's former confessor had to pay his respects in the cell of Friar Santo Tomas, who was now the King's spiritual guide.

the Queen's coach was surrounded in Madrid by a crowd that cried, "Long live the Queen, and down with the Duchess of Olivares"; and soon orders came from the King in Aragon that the lady was to follow her husband into retirement.

The legitimated son, too, Enrique Felipe de Guzman, who had kept close to the King as a gentleman-in-waiting, found that the atmosphere at Court, and especially amongst Aragonese, was antagonistic to him; and he also was dismissed to join his father.[1]

The only subject of difference between Philip and his wife now was the rivalry between his two sons. Young Baltasar Carlos had been granted a separate household, and was already assuming the state befitting the heir of Spain. Philip was devotedly attached to him, as was his mother; for, after allowing for all the adulation of courtiers, the Prince must have been a manly and gracious youth. But Don Juan was infinitely more handsome, and it was said of extraordinary talent, although it is fair to say that the actions of his later life hardly justified the fame of his youth. In any case, Philip was very proud of him, and now gave him a separate household, with many noble attendants and officers about him, and, as a separate residence, the suburban pleasure house called Zarzuela. Don Juan was to be called Serene Highness, and was to address gentlemen as Vos, You, as if he had been a royal Prince. To

---

[1] A Newsletter of the time gives rather a quaint instance of the feeling against him at Saragossa. Don Antonio de Mendoza, the poet, entered a room where Guzman was playing cards. Guzman impatiently said: "How tiresome that man is to me." Mendoza stood behind his chair to watch the game. "Get away from there," said Guzman, addressing

add to his importance, he was now made Grand Master of St. John, and delighted the courtiers with his boyish assumption of sovereign dignity.[1] Isabel looked askance at all this, and Baltasar Carlos saw little of his half-brother ; but Philip, having before him the example of his great-grand-father and the other Don Juan, evidently destined his left-handed son for great things. He had, moreover, no near male relatives now, and it is clear that there were ample opportunities for use-fulness open to a semi-royal Prince in Philip's wide dominions.

Philip and his little army in Catalonia and Aragon did well. Monzon was captured by Silva from the French on the 3rd December, to the immense solace of the King, who had been be-seeching the nun's prayers for the victory ; and with the laurels still on him he returned in triumph to Madrid to pass the Christmas with his wife. The Queen had ordered dinner to be prepared for his reception at the Buen Retiro (14th December), and had gone to meet him at the Atocha, where the holy image had to be thanked for his safe return. But Philip was a changed man since the nun's weekly letters of exhortation and encourage-ment had reached him ; and the palace of past frivolities was not in accordance with his mood. He would not even enter it, but went, gaily dressed, through the cheering crowds to the old palace, which if gloomy was yet kingly. Philip

the noble as " Vos," You, instead of " Your Worship." This was repeated, when Mendoza in a rage said : " I am not ' Vos ' to you, and don't intend to be," and flung off to complain to the King.

[1] Valladares' Newsletter, 28th July 1643.

went the next day to the Discalced Carmelites to
pray ; but the Queen did not accompany him,
for the proud, exacting Savoy Princess, Duchess of
Mantua, who lived in the convent, occupied the
royal apartments, and all manner of questions of
etiquette would have arisen if the Queen had
gone with her husband.

During the few days of staid rejoicings for
Christmas, for the splendid old entertainments
were now discontinued,[1] the King wrote to Sor
Maria to ask her to help with her prayers the expected arrival of the silver fleet from Mexico ; and
as a mixture of mystic devotion and worldly aims
the King's letter is quaint.

" The promise you gave me when I was with
you, that your prayers should not fail me, delighted
me much, and I remind you of it in the greatest
necessities. We are expecting hourly, by God's
help, the arrival of the galleons, and you may
imagine what depends upon it for us ; and although
I hope that, in His mercy, He will bring them safely,
I want to urge you to help me by supplicating His
Divine Majesty to do me this favour. It is true, I
do not deserve it, but rather great punishment ; but
I have full confidence that He will not permit the
total loss of this monarchy, and that He will continue the successes that He has begun to give us.
I should very much like to succeed in carrying out
the advice you give me in your letter of the 6th

---

[1] The King's good example had as yet done but little to wean the
Madrid people from their bad habits.   On the 26th December a gentleman
was shot dead before the Church of St. Sebastian, and the next day a
murderous affray in a playhouse about a seat ended in two deaths.

instant.[1] I can assure you I will try to do so ; and for my part, I will use every effort to comply with the will of God, both personally and in official matters. May He give me grace to do it. I cannot help telling you of the joy it gave me to come hither and see the Queen and my children, for my absence had seemed to me very long. They are, thank God, very well ; and although I shall feel keenly leaving such company, I am preparing to return ; for the welfare of my realms must be placed before all things, even before the pleasure of being with such treasures as these. God send me the time when I may enjoy them with more tranquillity."

The King's and the nun's prayers were satisfied. A few days after the letter was written, Madrid was rejoiced to know that the galleons had arrived safely, " which on this occasion were sorely needed ; for the loans for the frontier fortresses, and for Italy and Flanders, were held back, and the lenders would not do business without this guarantee. . . . They bring five millions (of ducats) for the King, and almost as much for private owners, with much

---

[1] The advice to which this refers is significant, and was evidently intended to be so by the nun, although the words she uses are very cautious and involved. " I supplicate your Majesty, as your servant, to make yourself thoroughly versed in everything touching you. This admonition is very important, and in order to adopt it with full knowledge of facts, your Majesty should choose, guided by your own sound judgment, someone whom you can depend upon, and listen to him with the fitting dissimulation. God will not deny this boon to your Majesty ; and when you have learnt the truth, the execution should be rapid ; for the evil is great and the remedy needs resolution. God assist your Majesty and rule your heart." This probably refers to the reform of the social and moral evils in Madrid, as that subject had been broached by the nun in her first interview with Philip.

indigo, etc. . . . It is believed that the King will not take any from private people or from the treasury pensions, so that we all breathe again." [1] In these somewhat alleviated circumstances, Philip, full of hope, started for Aragon on 6th February 1644, having signalised his short stay in Madrid by giving the gold key of chamberlain to Diego Velazquez, " who, they say, is at the present time the greatest painter in Spain. I understand there are to be no more honours given this Twelfth Day, as in other years." [2]

Philip, with a very small suite, hurried to Aragon ; for already in his absence his officers were quarrelling amongst themselves about ridiculous questions of style and precedence, and on the very frontier a deputation of Aragonese notables met him to ask for the dismissal of his Commander-in-chief, Felipe Silva, the most successful General he had ; and, although not immediately, Silva, disgusted by the jealousy that surrounded him— a Portuguese—ultimately went into retirement, to the lasting loss of Spanish arms. Whilst Philip was busy in Aragon ordering the coming campaign, the welcome news came to him in March 1644 of the pregnancy of his wife ; but soon his joy was dashed with the intelligence of her miscarriage and illness. The gossips said that, attended only by the Marquis of Aytona, he rushed to Madrid secretly for a few days to see her ; but whether the cloaked cavalier who came post from Saragossa was indeed the King is uncertain. In any case, Philip was with his army during the summer, gradually making way before the French, and

[1] Valladares' Newsletter.   [2] *Ibid.*

keeping up his resolution to live an exemplary life ; although the nobles and others were beginning to grumble that Don Luis de Haro was almost as powerful a minister as his uncle Olivares had been.

Philip was still rejoicing over the capture of the important city of Lerida at the middle of August 1644, and the relief of Tarragona in September, when ill news came to him of his wife's health. She had, it seems, on the 28th September suffered some sort of choleraic attack with erysipelas. Messengers were sent to the King, whilst the doctors, as was their wont, bled the patient copiously until they had left her bloodless, though with symptoms which now would be recognised at once as those of diphtheria. Then, in their desperation, the dead body of St. Isidore the Husbandman and the sainted image of the Atocha were brought to the palace ; though the dying woman protested that she was unworthy to have them brought to her bedside. But the inflammation of the throat increased, notwithstanding all the charms of the Church and the prayers of young Baltasar Carlos, who was devotedly attached to his mother. There was no church nor convent in Madrid that did not bring out in procession its crucifixes and most sacred images in prayer for the Queen's restoration to health, and the fervent prayers of a whole people went up in rogation that her life might be spared.

On the 5th October the Queen tried to make a new will, but she was too weak to sign it, and only left verbal testamentary instructions before witnesses for the King to be informed of her wishes. At noon that day she sent for a *fleur de lys* which

formed one of the ornaments of the crown, and
in which there was a fragment of the true Cross.
This she worshipped fervently, and her two children,
Baltasar Carlos and Maria Teresa, were brought
to her ; but she would not suffer them to approach
her for fear of infection, though she blessed them
fervently from a distance. " There are plenty
of Queens for Spain," she sighed ; " but Princes and
Princesses are rare." The next day, at a quarter
past four in the afternoon, stout-hearted loyal
Isabel of Bourbon breathed her last, aged 41.
Garbed as a Franciscan nun, the body of the Queen
was borne to the Convent of Discalced Carmelites,
where she had so often prayed and diverted herself ;[1] and thence soon afterwards it was carried
back again to the palace in grand coffins of lead
and brocade, to lie in state with flaring torches and
all the pomp and circumstances of royal mourning.
" Isabels always bring happiness to Spain," shouted
the crowd that adored her, after the fall of Olivares. She, poor soul, had brought happiness neither
to Spain nor to France, though she did her best
and was truly mourned. She had always been
devoutly Catholic ; and since the commencement of
the war she had grown stronger in her devotion,
and in her determination to reform the scandalous licence of the Court.[2] Frenchwoman though

[1] Only a few weeks before her death, she had gone to the Discalced
Convent to visit the Duchess of Mantua with Baltasar Carlos. When
she entered the apartment she noticed that the cushions placed under
the canopy for her to sit upon were of black velvet. She thought black
unlucky, as the King was in danger ; and she made an excuse not to
sit down. When she had sent her son off to play about the convent,
she sat upon the carpet rather than risk the ill-luck of sitting on black
cushions. Valladares' Newsletter.

[2] One of her last acts had been to issue a stringent decree—probably

she was, no breath of suspicion of her loyalty to her husband's people had ever been heard during all the years of war with her brother's realm.

Philip hastened home as fast as relays of mules would carry him. At Maranchon, about fifty miles from Madrid, where the King had alighted to dine at a wretched *venta*, the courier bringing the news of the Queen's death met him. The ministers and courtiers around the King, knowing how he loved his wife, avoided telling him the evil tidings at first ; for the anxiety and fatigue of the voyage had told upon him, " and he had only just dined." But a few miles farther on, at Almadrones, the news was broken to him in his carriage by the Marquis of Carpio and his son, the favourite Haro, and the bereaved King begged to be left alone with his grief. Turning aside from Madrid, now a city of mourning for him, Philip retired to the Pardo, where, with his son Baltasar—all that was left to him now, for Maria Teresa was but a child—for a few days he indulged his sorrow in private. Thence he went for the official mourning in the old apartment at San Geronimo ; whilst, with the gloomy pomp traditional in Spain, the body of the Queen was carried at dead of night across

suggested to Philip by the nun of Agreda, with regard to the comedies, of which in her happier days she had been so inordinately fond. In future it was ordered that no fictitious plots should be represented, but only scenes from the Scriptures or from history. No actors, male or female, were to dress in gold cloth ; and no unmarried woman nor widow was to be allowed to appear on a stage, only married women, whilst gentlemen were not permitted to visit an actress more than twice. New plays were not allowed to be produced more than once a week ; and plays in private houses were forbidden ; whilst the managers were not to receive in their companies any actors but those known to be decent and well behaved. Valladares' Newsletter, March 1644.

the bleak Castilian plain, with hundreds of monks
and nobles following, to the gorgeous new jasper
pantheon at the Escorial reserved for Kings and
mothers of Kings, which, from very dread, Isabel
had never dared to enter in her lifetime.[1]

Three days after the Queen died her wraith
appeared, it is said, before the nun of Agreda,
asking for the prayers of the godly to liberate
her from purgatory for the vain splendour of her
attire during her life.[2] Philip himself was overwhelmed at his loss, and the nun wrote to him
exhortations to resignation and patience ; but it
was a month before he could gather sufficient
courage to reply : his grief, as he says, and the many
calls upon him having prevented him from doing it
before. " I find myself in the most oppressed state
of sorrow possible," he wrote, " for I have lost in
one person everything that can be lost in this world ;
and if I did not know, according to the faith that
I profess, that the Lord disposes for us what is best,
I do not know what would become of me."

The following spring again saw Philip in the
field in Aragon. Things were going badly with
him now, and he was again losing heart. To the
nun he wrote on the 25th March 1645—

" Your letter indeed arrived at a good time ; for
the cares that surround me had much afflicted me,
and your words have encouraged me. I now trust
that God in His mercy, looking to all Christendom,
and to these realms, which are so pure in their

---

[1] Novoa; Valladares' Newsletters; Florez, *Reinas Catolicas*, and
Martin Hume's *Queens of Old Spain*.
[2] *Life of Sor Maria*, quoted by Florez.

Catholic faith, will not allow us to be ruined utterly, but will shield and defend them, and grant us a good peace. Short are the human resources with which I have returned hither; and what appals me most is to see that my faults alone are sufficient to provoke the ire of our Lord, and to bring upon me greater punishments than before. But the greater the punishment, the greater will be my appeal to faith and hope, as you say; and I will continually supplicate our Lord to supply with His almighty hand what we need. I for my part will do all I can, trying not to displease Him, and to comply with the obligations He has placed upon me, even though in doing so I risk my own life. I have not hesitated to give up the comforts of my home, in order to attend personally to the defence of these realms : for, whilst I thus fulfil this duty, I trust our Lord will not fail me; but in any extremity I submit to His holy will. I have wished for the Prince to begin to learn what will fall upon him after my days are done; and so, though alone, I have brought him with me, and have confided his health to the hands of God, trusting in His mercy to guard him, and to guide all his actions to His greater service." [1]

The campaign brought reverse after reverse to Philip. Jealousy had lost him the services of Silva, his best General; and the new French Viceroy of Catalonia, Count de Harcourt, scattered the Spaniards at Balaguer, and all Catalonia and most of Aragon lay at his mercy, if he had been sure of the loyalty of the Catalans, who, truth

[1] *Cartas de Sor Maria.*

to say, were getting somewhat disappointed and tired of their French masters.

The Aragonese mostly remained faithful to Philip, but held firmly to their privileges ; and when in the autumn of 1645 he summoned the Cortes of Saragossa and Valencia to swear allegiance to Baltasar Carlos, they drove a hard bargain, and Philip was forced to concede many legislative demands of the members, in return for sparing votes of supply. The tale he told to the Castilian Cortes summoned early in 1646 in Madrid was disconsolate in the extreme. All was spent : the wars still went on in Flanders, Germany, Italy, and Catalonia, as well as on the Portuguese frontier, and the regular revenue was utterly insufficient. The deputies were as much afflicted by the penury of their constituents as the King was by the emptiness of his treasury, but with many groans they voted an immediate grant of a million and a half of ducats in money, and in the following year an extension of the special war taxation upon food, and leave to sell pensions was granted.

Almost every week beseeching letters went from Philip to the nun, praying for her intercession with the Almighty to aid him in his troubles ; and the replies of the good woman were always wise, as she inculcated hope and labour without remission. Sometimes Philip's faith weakened, and he almost despaired, for he was convinced that all the national trouble arose from his personal sins, and yet, as he says, he could not help sinning. In the meanwhile disasters fell upon his arms thick and fast, and the national distress became more intense. He could suffer his own troubles, wrote Philip, for he knew that he had deserved them ; " but to see the sufferings of so many poor innocent people in these wars and conflicts pierces me to the very heart, and if with my life's blood I could remedy it I would expend it most willingly."

When Philip returned to Madrid for the winter of 1645–46, Sor Maria's constant exhortations had prevailed upon him to make a determined attempt to cleanse Madrid of some of its blatant vice in order to win God's favour. She was particularly strong in her condemnation of the dress and demeanour of the women of the capital, and a severe pragmatic on the subject was issued : the playhouses, to the dismay of the comedy-loving people, were rigorously closed,[1] the press-gangs that scoured the country for recruits were enjoined to be merciful to the poor in their operations, and other measures urged by the nun became the law of the land, whilst the lethal crimes so common in Madrid were prosecuted now with merciless severity.

Leaving his capital at least outwardly more decent, Philip travelled north again in April 1646, accompanied by his promising young son, now approaching manhood ; Pamplona, the capital of Navarre, being taken on the way, in order that the Navarrese Cortes might swear allegiance to the heir. No sooner had they entered Pamplona, late in April, than Baltasar Carlos fell seriously ill of tertian fevers ; and the nun's prayers were frantically supplicated for the boy by his afflicted father, who would not leave his son's side, although the Aragonese were getting clamorous for his coming to

---

[1] Avisos de Pellicer.

direct the campaign, which had already been opened by the enemy, who were actively besieging Lerida. After two months' delay, Philip at length entered Saragossa in June, when he received the news of the death of his sister, the Empress Maria, who had been betrothed to Charles, Prince of Wales. This, coming on the top of all his other troubles, almost broke the poor King down. " If I did not recognise that my troubles are sent by God, as warnings for me to prepare my own salvation, I could hardly tolerate them. . . . Help me, Sor Maria, to pray to Him ; for my strength is small, and I fear my weakness."

A greater blow than all fell upon him soon afterwards. An insincere embassy had been sent to England some little while before, in order to frustrate the betrothal of Mary Stuart, daughter of Charles I., with the Prince of Orange ; and the means employed had been the old suggestion of the marriage of an English Princess with Baltasar Carlos. It came to nothing, and, so far as the Spaniards were concerned, was a mere feint from the first, for the real wish of Philip's heart, as it had been that of his father, was still further to cement the two branches of the house of Austria, by marrying his heir to the Emperor's daughter. Imperial ambassadors were at Saragossa when Philip arrived, and the King wrote cheerfully to the nun soon after, saying that the marriage of Baltasar Carlos had now been settled, and that his niece Mariana of Austria was betrothed to his heir. " My son is very much pleased with his new state, and I am so too, to have chosen such a good daughter-in-law, as I hold this marriage certain to produce very beneficial effects to the Catholic religion, which is my sole aspiration." [1]

Not many weeks afterwards, on the 7th October, the King in great trouble writes to the nun—

" I have received your letter, but I confess that I am not in a condition to reply to it, for our Lord has placed upon me a trial through which I can hardly live. Since yesterday my son is oppressed with very extreme fever. It began by severe pains in his body, which lasted all day ; and now he is delirious, and we are in such fear that we hope it will turn to smallpox, . . . of which the doctors say they see signs. I know, Sor Maria, that I deserve heavy punishments, and that all that may come to me in this life will be insufficient to repay my sins ; but I do cry now to the divine mercy of our Lord, and the intercession of His holy Mother ; and I beseech you to help with all your strength."

Three days afterwards, the heart-broken father writes in dull despair that his son had died. " I have lost," he wrote, " my only son, and such a son, as you know he was." And for this pain the consolations of the good woman, though salutary,

[1] The Prince, who had seen the nun on his way to Saragossa, wrote the following artless letter to her about his betrothal. " Mother, two or three days ago my father gave me a letter from you congratulating me on the marriage that my father has made for me with the Arch-duchess Mariana. I am the most pleased in the world to have taken this state, especially with my cousin, who was the one I wished for ever since I had use of my reason ; and it seems impossible to me that I could have come across any other woman so much to my taste. So I hope His Divine Majesty will let us be very happily married, which is all I can hope for. I ask you to pray for this. Our Lord guard you. —I, THE PRINCE. Saragossa, 20th July 1646."

were weak. Philip bowed his head, and to all outward seeming was resigned to his loss. He did not rail against the decrees of Providence that had left him alone in the world, but his resignation now was a fatalistic hopelessness ; for this blow had finally convinced him that the Most High had doomed him to affliction, and his people to suffering untold, solely for his sins. There was no way out of it, even by prayer ; and Philip for a time gave up trying to be good.

Don Luis de Haro already did most of the work of the State, and Philip grew still more idle after the death of his son, one of the results of his indolence being a weakening of the struggle he had fought for four years against the temptations of the flesh. Sor Maria from her convent took him to task somewhat seriously for his remissness, and for the first time Philip defended himself with some spirit [1] with regard to his dependence upon others. He was anxious to do right, he assured her ; but his great predecessors and all other monarchs had been obliged to employ ministers, and he did not think he could be doing wrong in following their example. One man cannot, he says, look into the execution of all his commands, and must trust to others ; " for it does not accord with the dignity of a monarch to go from one office to the other to see personally that his decrees are being properly

[1] Her reproaches were curiously framed. Just as after the Queen's death she had tried to reform the extravagance of women's dress by pretending to have seen Isabel's ghost in trouble for her fine garments on earth, so she now appealed to Philip to keep hard at work, by saying that the soul of Baltasar Carlos had told her that he was troubled to see his father surrounded by people who looked after their own interests rather than after those of the nation. *Cartas de Sor Maria*, 30th January 1647.

2 C

carried out." When he first came to the throne, he reminds the nun, he was only sixteen, and, quite naturally in his inexperience, depended upon a man of more knowledge than himself. Where he had erred was in keeping that minister supreme too long. Since he dismissed Olivares he had tried to avoid having a favourite; and the minister who people now say does everything was brought up with him as a boy, and has always been irreproachable; but even so, he (Philip) had always refused to give him the post of sole minister, and he only does what the King cannot do, namely, look after the raising of funds, and hear the opinions of people with whom the King cannot discourse. " I, Sor Maria," he wrote, " do not shirk any labour, for, as anyone can tell you, I am here seated in this chair continually with my papers before me and my pen in my hand, dealing with all the reports that are sent to me here, and with the despatches from abroad; resolving points in question immediately, and trying to adopt the most proper decision in each case."

The nun even took upon herself, as the winter wore on, to tell the King that it was high time to arrange the new campaign, and follow up the brilliant defence of Lerida which had ended in the defeat of the French under Condé himself. The Aragonese thought so too, for the troops there refused to move for a time unless Philip would come to Saragossa, as in previous years, to direct the campaign personally.

The nun could hardly speak very clearly in reprehension of the King's moral backsliding, although her hints even in this respect are pretty

broad.   But his confessor and the other friars
around him did not hesitate to do so ; and people
other than friars were saying that with no heir to
the crown the King must marry again.   So long as
Baltasar Carlos lived, Philip had gently put aside
these suggestions by saying that his hopes were
centred in his son ; but when after his heir's death
his excesses in the intervals of his poignant contrition shocked the devotees of his Court, and they
added their censure to the pressure of the lay-
men for another Queen-Consort, Philip consented,
though without enthusiasm, to marry again.   He
was only forty-two, but anxiety and dissipation
had aged him, and he was approaching the years
when most of his ancestors had developed the
peculiar strain of mystic devotion that borders upon
madness, but his people clamoured for a male
heir, for the Infanta Maria Teresa was only eight,
and Don Juan of Austria, popular as he was, was
impossible as King.   In the letter which Philip
wrote to the nun, on the 9th January 1647, he says :
" I have received a letter from the Emperor condoling with me for the loss of my son, and at the
same time offering my niece to be my wife.   As this
agrees with my own feelings, I think I may decide
to accept this marriage, which is doubtless the most
fitting one for me ; so I hope that our Lord will
help this with His powerful hand, so that the business may tend to His service, and to that of my
own country " ; and a few weeks afterwards he
conveyed to her the intelligence that the match has
been arranged.

Mariana was as yet a child, and the daughter
of Philip's sister Maria.   That such a companion

can have been really congenial to him it is difficult
to believe, but his subjects needed an heir. The
unhappy tradition that imposed upon Spain the
belief in its duty to dictate orthodoxy to the world
was not yet dead, and the solidarity of the house
of Austria was a first condition for its success.
Spain had already paid dearly for such Austrian
help as she had obtained, and the price now given
for the further union was a high one indeed ; for
by this dire incestuous union of Philip and his
niece the consummation of his country's ruin and
the extinction of his dynasty was wrought. What
for the time being was worst of all was, that the
support of Austria in the wars that were finally
to exhaust Spain was withdrawn even before the
marriage took place.

For three years the representatives of the Powers
of Europe, invited by the Emperor, had been laboriously discussing terms for a general pacification
at Osnabrück and Münster. Philip wrote to the
nun that the French demands were so insolent
that it was clear that they did not want peace ;[1]
but the Hollanders were more inclined to an accommodation, for they had grown suspicious of the
ultimate designs of Mazarin. After interminable
intrigues and self-seeking, however, an arrangement
was arrived at which practically ended the Thirty
Years War ; and Spain, beaten to her knees, still
burdened with war in Catalonia, on the Portuguese
border, and in Flanders, with her kingdom of
Naples in full revolt, was obliged to accept, at last,
what the world had seen to be inevitable for many

[1] One of their proposals was to evacuate Catalonia in exchange for
Spanish Flanders.

years past, the recognition of Protestant Holland
as an independent Power. For nearly a hundred
years the war with her Protestant former depend-
ency had dragged Spain down, and made her an
easy prey to the French, and at last from the sheer
impotence of Spain to struggle longer the Treaty
of Münster (October 1648) was signed by her, which
made Holland free and gave Alsace to France.
The central European Powers were satisfied, the
religious compromise was ratified, there was nothing
more for the Emperor to fight for, and he retired
from the war with France, leaving Philip to fight
her enemy alone. The long dream of Spain's
supremacy over an orthodox Catholic Europe was
indeed dissipated at last ; she had now to fight
for the integrity of her own soil and her continued
existence as a great nation, and in this hard strait
the empire deserted her.

All through the year 1647, Philip remained in
Madrid, whilst the wars in Flanders and Catalonia,
as well as on the Portuguese frontier, dragged on
with various fortunes, but on the whole not disastrously for Spain. The great revolt of Massaniello
in Naples for a time threatened Philip with the
loss of the kingdom ; when the happy thought
came to him of sending his brilliant young son,
Don Juan, thither as his Commander-in-chief. He
arrived at a time when Guise, the French pretender
to the Neapolitan crown, had disgusted the fickle
populace which had formerly acclaimed him, and
by a fortunate *coup de main* Don Juan recaptured
the city for his father in February 1648, to the joy
of most of the inhabitants, who were tired of the
anarchy which had lasted for a year. The exploit

raised the popularity of the young Prince almost as
high as that of his famous namesake after Lepanto,
and the rejoicings in Madrid to celebrate the victory
made the capital for a time seem its old self again.

But though the lieges might still enjoy their
brilliant shows as of yore, Philip himself had
become introspective and gloomy ; and he attended
the bull-fights and parades with sad, weary face.
He wrote weekly to the nun deploring his frailty,
and beseeching her intercession ; but it is clear
that he had thrown over most of his good resolutions, for Don Luis de Haro was as necessary to
him as Olivares had been ; and the fragile beauties
of the capital found in him again as ardent an
admirer as ever.[1] The departure of the bride
who was to rescue him from his evil life was long
delayed for want of money, both on the part of
her father the Emperor, and of Philip ; [2] and, notwithstanding the King's saintly contrition after
his faults, the talk of his loose and idle life began
to make him personally unpopular with many,
who thought that his place was with his army
in Catalonia rather than in the Retiro sunk in
slothful pleasures.[3]

---

[1] Writing to the nun on 15th July 1648 from Madrid, in reply to her
expressions of sorrow at the vice prevalent, he says : " It pierces my
heart, too, to see the vicious state at which the world has arrived. I
recognise it as clearly as you do, and as I cannot remedy it so quickly
as I should like I am greatly troubled ; although I do what I can. God
grant that I may succeed in remedying it, and that I may begin by
my own amendment ; for there is no doubt that I need it more than
anyone. Pray for me, Sor Maria, . . . for I have need of your help
against my own frailty." *Cartas de Sor Maria.*

[2] *Ibid.*

[3] How deep this feeling was is seen by the courtier Novoa's words
at the time (*Memorias*). " The only place where the war was carried on
with activity was here in Castile, and that in a most unheard-of way,

In September, a great Aragonese noble of turbulent antecedents, the Duke of Hijar, with three other nobles of rank, were suddenly seized and committed to prison in Madrid. The accusation against them was that they had plotted against the crown : some said in favour of the King of Portugal, others in favour of France ; but the King specially assured the nun that there had not been discovered any design against his life. The Duke, as soon as he was arrested, endeavoured to implicate Sor Maria in the plot, and produced a letter from her to him. In a note in her own hand on the King's account written to her of the execution of the prisoners in December, she explains the matter. Hijar, it appears, had written to her hinting at some plan against the Government being in contemplation, and asking her advice. She had replied deploring such wickedness, and had referred him to the King. The nun says that many had been the attempts to bring her into trouble about it ; but that in all his letters to her referring

---

by disarming subjects and divesting them of their property on the pretext of the war. Even the treasury warrants which had been specially exempt from deduction were again seized and forced to yield a half. When those who had to pay were advised not to do so, because whilst the war lasted so long would the Government cut their purses and would soon take everything, a certain person asked: 'Why do they give habits?' (of knighthood).—'Because they are cloth,' was the reply. 'Why do they give keys?' (*i.e.* the office of chamberlain).—'Because they are iron.' 'Why do they give titles?'—'Because they are air.' 'Why do they not give money?'—'Because that is the essence and substance of everything, and they do not wish anyone to have it.' And he added: 'God save us from him who is liberal to vice and stingy to virtue, for the only people now who are comfortable and placed aloft are concubines and the women who look after them, low and common women, and those men who have been base enough to marry them.'" This was pretty plain speaking for a courtier ; but, of course, the Memoirs were not made public for many years after.

to the plot the King had never even mentioned her connection with the matter, which showed that he, at least, did not believe that she was culpably concerned. The King, indeed, in his letters rather makes light of the affair, as being "the most foolish conspiracy ever conceived," and he evidently did not think that the Duke of Hijar was the prime mover in the affair ; as repeated torture having failed to wring any incriminatory admissions from the Duke, the judges sentenced him to perpetual imprisonment only, though we are told that the torture had made him a cripple for life, both hand and foot. One of the other conspirators died of a fit in the prison soon after the death sentence was passed, his fate, as Philip wrote to the nun, being worst of all, since he had died unabsolved.

The public execution in the Plaza Mayor of the two principal conspirators, both nobles, Don Pedro de Silva, Marquis de la Vega de Sagra, and Don Carlos de Padilla, moved excitement-loving Madrid profoundly, and several eye-witnesses of the scene have left their impressions of it. From one unpublished account in the British Museum [1] the following description is condensed as an example of a Spanish execution, of the first importance at the time.

Shortly before noon, on Saturday, the 5th December 1648, the massive doors of the Carcel de la Corte, opposite the Plaza de Santa Cruz, near the Atocha entrance of the Plaza Mayor,[2] opened for

---

[1] Egerton MSS., 367, 181.

[2] The " prison of the Court " still stands nearly opposite the Plaza de Santa Cruz, at the end of the Calle de Atocha, and near the entrance

a sombre procession to issue therefrom. First came seventy alguacils of the Court ; then followed, amidst tapers and swinging censers, two famous figures of Christ from the parish church of Santa Cruz opposite, with the attendant clergy. Then came a saddle mule covered to the ground with housings of black baize, and led by an executioner. Upon the mule sat Don Carlos de Padilla, who only on the previous day had been divested of his honourable habit of a Knight of Santiago. Now, as he rode disconsolate, a crucifix in his hand and closely surrounded by many Jesuit fathers, he wore a long gown of black baize, with a cap of the same, and a steel chain dangled from his right foot. It was noticed, too, that instead of the almost universal golilla he wore a white starched Walloon collar unblued.

After him came on another draped mule the Marquis, Don Pedro, similarly garbed ; but, instead of the collar, wearing the tippet of a Fellow of the College of Cuenca at Salamanca. Following the condemned men came crowds of alguacils, notaries, and officers of justice ; and as the procession swept along dismally, heralded by tolling bells and the dreary call of the criers for the people to pray for the souls of the departing, vast crowds stood at every coign of vantage, and were held back at the end of each side street by guards and alguacils. The procession did not enter the Plaza by the nearest gate, that of the Atocha, but debouched into the

to the Plaza Mayor. It was built in 1634 by the same Italian architect who had designed the Buen Retiro, and is a very handsome building. It is now used as the Spanish Foreign Office, which was formerly housed in the basement floor of the royal palace.

Calle Mayor, in order to enter the Plaza by a
principal, Guadalajara, portal. It was noticed
that as Don Carlos Padilla reached the entrance
by the Guadalajara gate his face lit up radiantly,
and the word passed along the awestruck crowd
that a heavenly vision had brought comfort to
him, now that all earthly comfort had fled.

The Plaza Mayor itself had been cleared of all
its fruit stalls, as if for a bull-fight ; and in the
centre (where now stands the statue of Philip
III.) was erected a scaffold, upon which were two
uncovered chairs side by side. Don Carlos de Padilla
ascended first the fatal stair, and, taking his seat
upon the left-hand chair with much serenity,
slowly arranged his long gown decorously, whilst
the swarm of priests and friars around him continued their sacred ministrations. The doomed
noble's hands and feet were firmly bound to the
chair, and a strip of black baize blinded his eyes.
Then the executioner, stepping forward, with a
large butcher's knife slashed the throat across
again and again. It was remarked that Don
Carlos, being a robust man, shed an immense
quantity of blood. Then going behind him, the
executioner with several heavy blows on the nape
of the neck severed the head entirely, and the
deed was finished.

Then came the turn of the Marquis, Don Pedro
de Silva, to mount ; and as he reached the top his
eyes perforce rested upon the dead body of his
comrade, still bound to the chair. " Blessed be
the name of the Lord," he exclaimed in horror at
the ghastly sight, as he took his seat on the adjoining chair. The strip of baize that had bound the

eyes of Don Carlos was too much soaked with blood to be used for the second time, and another had to be brought ; Don Pedro devoutly repeating the Creed in the meanwhile. It was noticed that Don Pedro, being a dry, shrunken little man, shed but little blood ; and when his head at last was severed from the back, as that of Don Carlos had been, the King's justice was satisfied. The bodies remained in the chairs all that day ; but at one o'clock in the morning the executioner and the widows shrouded the bodies by the light of two candle-ends, and enclosed them in rough coffins, in which they were carried in procession, with the parish cross and eight wax tapers before them, across the Calle Mayor to the churchyard of St. Ginés for burial. The two Christs of Santa Cruz went with them too, though the clergy were not allowed to accompany them ; for they had claimed the right of burying the bodies in their own church, which is the parish in which the prison is situated, and the King had ordered the sepulchre at St. Ginés.

The King had taken no part in the trial of the prisoners, and had strictly enjoined the five judges specially appointed to investigate the case to be absolutely impartial, though the nun herself had almost violently urged that no mercy should be shown against men who aimed at overturning the Government. The real object of the conspiracy appears to have been the overthrow of Don Luis de Haro, and the adoption of a conciliatory policy which would end the warfare in Catalonia and Portugal, even at the cost of a sacrifice of pride and territory to Spain.

Already, when the impressive sight just described

was passing in Madrid, the new girl Queen-Consort was slowly, very slowly, making her way from city to city of her father's dominions, Tyrol, Hungary, and Italy, on her way to the expectant arms of her elderly avuncular bridegroom. Festivities and celebrations greeted her in every town she entered, and everywhere the inexperienced girl enjoyed her new importance without restraint. At Trent, Philip's representatives met her, and thenceforward she travelled as Queen of Spain, staying on her way for many weeks at each place.[1] The reasons for so long a delay were several. First, money was scarce for the conveyance of the tremendous company of 160 Spanish nobles with their households who accompanied the Queen ; secondly, the plague was raging throughout eastern Spain, where she had to land ; and thirdly, she herself was as yet quite immature, being barely fifteen.

During all this long delay, which lasted until the late autumn of 1649, Philip continued to write to the nun, deploring his inability to overcome the frailty of the flesh, and fervently invoking her aid in prayer to make him as perfect as he wished to be. Though the world knew it not at the time, it is quite certain from these letters that the ecstatic religious mysticism that had taken possession of his father, grandfather, and great-grandfather at a similar age, had at this time firmly captured Philip IV. But he, unlike them, still retained his pleasure-seeking instincts, and with him it was a

---

[1] A tedious account from day to day of her doings was written by Mascarenhas, Bishop of Leiria, who accompanied her. *Viage de la Serenisima Reina*, etc., Madrid, 1650.

never-ending battle between the spirit and the flesh
which prevented him subsequently from sinking
into the monkish seclusion of his ancestors.

At length, whilst Philip was in Madrid in September, a messenger, bringing for him a beautiful
jewel from his bride, came to announce her landing
on Spanish soil at Denia ; [1] and the King at once
wrote in delight to the nun, to tell her the news
and ask her blessing, to which the good woman
replied by urging him to begin a new life on his
marriage. Mariana had been received at Denia
by all the nobles of Valencia, where the Sandoval
interest was strong, and jealousy surrounded her
from the first hour ; the Duke of Najera and Maqueda, who had conducted her from Italy, being
dismissed in disgrace as soon as he landed for some
lack of respect reported of him.

Mariana troubled her head little about such
things. She was a red-cheeked, full-blooded lass,
with bright black eyes, and an insatiable ambition
to enjoy and make the most of life. Selfish and
hard-hearted she proved herself to be later, but
now in her florid spring she seemed a gay, happy
girl, whose high spirits nothing could damp, even
the prospect of matrimonial life with a worn-out,
disillusioned voluptuary in chronic anxiety about
his soul. As she slowly moved onward through
Valencia and Castile, she was entertained everywhere with feastings and shows which delighted
her. At one place, after dinner, some of the King's

[1] Some days before arriving at Denia the Queen's flotilla had anchored
at Tarragona to water, and amongst other ceremonies the Queen was
amused during the necessary delay by the representation of a comedy
by Roque de Figueroa on the quarter-deck of her vessel. Pinelo,
Anales.

dwarfs and buffoons were introduced to amuse her, at whose antics she screamed with laughter. The stately Countess of Medillin, a Sandoval, her Mistress of the Robes, shocked at such a breach of etiquette, reminded her that sovereigns of Spain never laughed in public. But Mariana snapped her fingers at such stiffness, and avowed that she should laugh as often as she saw anything to laugh at ; and when the same great lady informed her that it was a violation of all the Court traditions for her to walk, she obtained a similar answer.

As she approached Madrid, Philip, with his young daughter, Maria Teresa, moved to the Escorial, to be within easy riding distance of the village of Navalcarnero, where the royal wedding was to be celebrated.[1] Every few days, letters, gifts, and loving messages had passed between Philip and his bride since her arrival on Spanish soil, and he evidently desired to act his part of the anxious lover irreproachably. When, therefore, he learnt that the Queen was to arrive at Navalcarnero, on the 6th October, he complied with the traditional usage of the Spanish Court, and set forth on horseback, and in perfectly transparent disguise, to look upon his new wife incognito and without formality for the first time. That he did so to his satisfaction is on record in his subsequent letters to the nun, for Mariana was a buxom lass, and as she sat gaily smiling at the comedy with which she was being entertained before her evening meal, she doubtless looked an attractive bride. The King

---

[1] I have remarked in my *Queens of Old Spain* that the reason why these wretched villages were often chosen for royal weddings was the custom to free them thenceforward from seigniorial tributes.

retired that night to a little neighbouring hamlet called Brunete; and betimes in the morning, with a brave array of courtiers, he rode up to the humble house in which Mariana was temporarily lodged, whilst she stood smiling and blushing beneath her plentiful rouge until he approached, when she made as if to kneel; but he raised her without a word, and led her to the adjoining chapel, where mass was celebrated before them, and the marriage was performed by the Primate of Spain, Cardinal Moscoso Sandoval, with all the state which Navalcarnero could contain.

After their dining in public at noon, there was a long series of bull-fights and comedies to go through before the royal pair and their Court in the great swaying coaches moved on the Escorial, where the early days of the honeymoon were to be passed. A league from the palace they were met by the Infanta Maria Teresa, who at once became the friend and play-fellow of her stepmother, only five years older than herself, and thenceforward her inseparable companion. The stern old monastery palace of Philip II. tried its hardest to look gay for the occasion, with its 11,000 wax lights and its array of fine courtiers; but gaiety sits badly upon it. Here in diversions, especially in hunting, the time passed happily for three weeks before the pair proceeded to the Pardo, nearer Madrid, whilst the capital was busy putting on the festal garb it loved so much, and had missed for so long.

At length all was ready. From the Retiro to the old palace, the entire length of Madrid, a series of beautiful triumphal arches were erected, spanning the road. All the fountains, which were ordinarily unpretending enough, had been turned to account and made to appear classic temples, whence the Olympian gods and goddesses dispensed refreshing nectar to the world. The shabby house-fronts were masked by erections of imitation marble, or hung with splendid tapestries and armorial shields ; in fact, Madrid once more, almost ruined though she was, managed somehow to raise money enough to make herself handsome again for a space. Mariana, with her white teeth, rosy painted cheeks, so full and round, and her frank, unabashed gaiety, captured the hearts of the Madrileños at once, as she rode on her splendidly caparisoned milk-white palfrey, from the Buen Retiro by the Carrera de San Geronimo, across the Puerta del Sol, and up the Calle Mayor to the palace. They did not know yet, as they learned later, that she was greedy and hard, caring nothing for Spain except for what it could give her.[1]

Philip was too much immersed in the delights of his honeymoon to write to the nun for several

[1] Soto y Aguilar gives interminable accounts of the festivities to celebrate the entrance of the Queen into Madrid. The entertainments lasted nearly a month. Novoa says that on the 27th November the King himself took part in a " masquerade " on horseback, as in old times, running in a pair with his first minister and favourite, Don Luis de Haro; "all the nobles and gentles in the realm taking part in this show, which in liveries and splendid appointments surpassed all others. It was indeed a day of marvellous brilliancy. A proclamation was issued by sound of drum, by which the King gave leave to men of business and capitalists trading abroad for them to fit out eighty ships and trade with them in his ports and those of his allies, but not with the French Catalans or Portuguese. Politicians talked much of this, thinking it would be of the greatest advantage to the country." The chronicler, however, says that no advantage was taken of the permission, as merchants thought that the ships would be seized for the King. This shows how completely confidence had been lost in the honesty of Philip's Government, even by his friends.

MARIANA DE AUSTRIA ; SECOND WIFE OF PHILIP IV.

From a portrait by Velazquez at the Prado Museum

weeks after his marriage ; but when he did write, on the 17th November, he testified to his full satisfaction with his new wife. " I confess to you that I do not know how I can thank our Lord for the favour he has shown me in giving me such a companion ; for all the qualities I have seen up to the present in my niece are great, and I am extremely content, and desirous not to be ungrateful to Him who has granted me so singular a boon : showing my gratitude by changing my life and executing His will in all things."   The nun in her reply places much stress upon the need of the country for an heir to the crown, and urges the King to be faithful to his wife, if only for that end ; " trying to fix your whole attention and goodwill upon the Queen, without turning your eyes to other objects strange and curious." Philip had no great difficulty at the time in following his friend's advice ; for he really was smitten with the fresh charms of his fifteen-year-old niece-wife. He was full of good resolves and saintly protestations ; he would never go astray again, for he was as anxious for a son as his people were, though he confided to the nun that he was in doubt whether his wife was as yet mature enough to bear children, " although others of her age, which is fifteen years, are so. But it is easy for our Lord to remedy this, and I hope in His mercy that He will do so." [1]

In the meanwhile, Mariana, the depository of all these hopes, was diverting herself as best she could, in girlish romps with Maria Teresa, and in the constant shows, comedies, and masques which were offered for her pleasure. Once more the

[1] *Cartas de Sor Maria.*

2 D

Buen Retiro rang with mirth and blazed with lights. The playhouses of the capital again were allowed to open their doors ; and the Madrileños did their best to evade, bit by bit, the sumptuary enactments that had kept them in sober garb and outward gravity of demeanour for seven years of war and trouble. Neither the war nor the trouble was yet over, for the plague came almost to the doors of Madrid, and scourged whole provinces ; whilst the war with the French still went on in Catalonia and Flanders, and Portugal continued to defy successfully the arms of Philip. But, withal, the drain upon Castile, bad as it still was, became somewhat less pressing ; for Mazarin had his hands full in France with the revolt of the Fronde, which, of course, Spain helped to the extent of her possibilities ; and the Catalans were far less enamoured with their French masters than they were at first. Don Juan, the King's son, moreover, who was now in command in Catalonia, was doing well, and winning popularity on all sides, whilst the recognition of Dutch independence by Philip had freed his Indies fleets from their greatest danger.

The novelty of the King's honeymoon soon wore off, and in his letters to the nun he refers to his wife thenceforward kindly and with solicitude, but as it seems somewhat wearily, and usually in connection with her many more or less disappointed hopes of maternity, or to her love for shows and festivities ; which it is quite evident from his tone now palled upon him. Pleasure and the joy of living absorbed most of Mariana's attention, and, immersed as the King was in business

and devotion, he could have little in common with
his young wife. His own habits were absolutely
fixed, and an observer at his Court at the time
says that it was possible to foretell a year beforehand exactly what the King would do on a given
day and hour.[1] His demeanour in public was like
that of a statue, and when he received ambassadors
or ministers it was noticed that no muscle of his face
moved but his lips, and he rarely showing any
emotion, even by a smile. Already the haughty disillusionment, represented by Velazquez so finely in
the later portraits, had been fixed indelibly upon his
features, and his eyes had grown blear with remorseful tears.

In 1651 a daughter was born to Philip and
Mariana, and christened with the usual extravagant
pomp Margaret Maria,[2] but, though oft expected,
the longed-for son came not. Mariana felt her
husband growing colder, and guessed his infidelity.
Then she fell homesick and disappointed, and
Philip became anxious. A splendid series of
festivities were arranged at the Buen Retiro to
solace and enliven her, an ingenious Florentine
being requisitioned to invent novelties to attract
her attention. But it was all dust and ashes to
Philip now. He speaks in his secret letters always
gently of his young wife, sometimes even almost
with enthusiasm of her goodness; but it is plain to

[1] Aersens van Sommerdyk.
[2] Florez relates that at this sumptuous christening the little Infanta
Maria Teresa was god-mother, and in drawing off her glove she dropped
a very precious bracelet of brilliants. A lady in the crowd picked it
up and offered it to the Infanta, who even thus early had learnt the
haughty traditions of her house, to take nothing from the hand of anyone
but certain officials, made a sign that the lady was to keep the bracelet,
Reinas Catolicas.

see that there was little sympathy between them,[1] for his terrible remorse at his moral fragility and evil life, and his grief at the troubles he firmly believed he was bringing upon his people by his own backsliding, show that the struggle between the spirit and the flesh had begun again as severely as ever, and that Mariana was powerless to keep him entirely faithful to her. She, on her side, had soon learnt the lesson of the Court. Her face grew cold and haughty, and her ostentatious German sympathies and repellent Austrian manner cooled the warm-blooded spontaneous Spaniards towards her. Thus, with all stately dignity, decorum, and solemnity in outward seeming, the ill-matched pair lived : passing from Madrid to Aranjuez and the Escorial at stated seasons, wearily going through the dull, depressing tale of pre-arranged devotions and duties ; the Queen seeking such distraction as was possible in comedies and the like, the King spending much time at his desk, reading the never-ending reports of his Councils brought to him by Don Luis de Haro, and scribbling in his big straggling hand on the margins " *Como parece*," or some similar sentence signifying his acquiescence in the conclusions arrived at by his advisers.

And behind this dreary changeless round there was, unknown to all but one lonely cloistered woman, a human soul in mortal pain for transgressions real and imaginary, which it was unable to avoid, and yet was convinced were dragging the

---

[1] He usually speaks of her in the earlier years as " my niece," not as " my wife," or " the Queen," and very frequently mentions her and his daughter together as " the girls."

man it animated and millions of the people that
he loved and pitied to suffering and sorrow.
Philip's constant correspondence with the nun had
changed him much ; for it is evident, whatever
may have been his shortcomings, that her exhortations to him to be brave, dutiful, and faithful,
and her wise insistence upon unceasing work and
prayer, had made the King watchful of his own
weakness, and kept him from sinking into in-
difference. It is highly probable, indeed, that in
his constant self-reproach his failings at this time
were exaggerated by him, as those of his father
had been on his deathbed. Certainly, from this
time forward he tried his best, according to his
lights and strength, to live worthily, and to rescue
his country from the trouble into which the policy
of his ancestors and himself had dragged it ; though
still there was no glimmering of true statesmanship such as was needed in circumstances so
difficult. Philip's spirit was a poor one ; and his
faith, notwithstanding his devotion, was far from
robust. He continued to look upon himself and
his country as doomed irrevocably by the Almighty
to suffer for his personal sins and those of his
generation, and the only remedy presented to his
mind was to plead fervently for mercy through
a saintly soul untouched by the sins of the time.
Of the efficiency even of this resource he needed
constant reassurance, and for ever foresaw disaster
whilst he was frantically praying for triumph.

Lacking in statesmanship as were Philip and
all his advisers, it would nevertheless be unjust to
attribute to their ineptitude alone the troubles
that overwhelmed Spain. It has been pointed out

that Philip inherited both his policy and his methods; and so fixed were they upon the tradition of Charles V. and Philip II., that nothing short of a real genius or a sudden great catastrophe could have altered them. But Philip was specially unfortunate in the international circumstances of his time. The deadly rivalry between the house of Austria and the house of France had existed since the earliest years of the sixteenth century; and wars between them had been frequent since that period. But England had always provided a check to prevent such wars being fought to the bitter end. It had been a fixed canon of English foreign policy that the Flemish dominions of the house of Burgundy, that had descended to the Spanish Kings, must never be allowed to fall into the hands of France, and when such a danger threatened, England invariably interfered in favour of Spain; whilst any aggressive action of France against England, either in Scotland or elsewhere, usually brought Spain to the side of the English sovereigns. But the revolutionary war which had overthrown the monarchy of the Stuarts had for years doomed England to impotence in the struggles of Europe; and Richelieu and his successor Mazarin had been able to disregard an influence which had always previously stepped in to prevent the final humiliation of Spain. Without this immunity from England's interference, France would never have been free to foment rebellion in Catalonia and Portugal; and it may be said that Philip to a great extent owed the extremity of his tribulation to the internal disturbance in England.

It will be recollected that after the diplomacy

of Olivares had secured the neutrality of England
in the war with France, Sir Arthur Hopton remained
in Madrid as English ambassador, having little to
do but to press the constant complaints of English
shipmasters against the authorities of Spanish
ports, and other maritime questions. But in the
late summer of 1641, Olivares had sent to Hopton,
and in a long interview with him had complained
that Charles I. had received an ambassador from
the Duke of Braganza, the usurping King of
Portugal. Hopton says [1] that the Count-Duke
spoke modestly and without much bitterness in
the matter, and the English envoy at once pointed
out that Charles did not presume to judge of the
Duke of Braganza's right to the crown, but that
as English interests in Portugal were very large,
it was needful that he should negotiate with the
power wielding effective control in the country.
Sir Arthur, moreover, slyly pointed out that words
only had passed between his King and the Portuguese envoy, whereas it was with much more than
words that the King of Spain had aided Bavaria
to keep the Palatinate. Indeed, with the exception
of constantly harping on the Palatinate in his discussions with Philip and his ministers, and complaining of the action of the Spanish ambassador in
London, Don Alonso de Cardenas, against Charles
I., Sir Arthur Hopton confined himself practically
to the negotiation of shipping claims,[2] until affairs
in England and his lack of money necessitated his
return home in 1644.

---

[1] Record Office MSS., S.P. Spain 42.
[2] See Hopton's summary of his proceedings in Spain. Record Office
MSS., S.P. Spain 42.

When at last the axe fell in Whitehall, on the 30th January 1649, upon the neck of the Stuart King, Don Alonso de Cardenas, who was accredited to Charles and not yet to the Parliament, was without definite instructions how to proceed, and for that or some other reason he did not identify himself with the Dutch ambassadors in their protest against the death sentence pronounced upon the King. This may have been an accident ; but it is certain that there was little love lost between Charles I. and Philip since the visit of the former to Madrid, and his French marriage. It is true that large numbers of Irish and English troops had been raised for the Spanish service with his consent even during the course of the civil war, but his sympathy with Braganza, and the ostentatiously French leanings of Henrietta Maria, had, as Charles's troubles increased, estranged Philip from him personally. It was, moreover, of the highest importance to Philip that, whoever had command of the English fleet and the Channel, should be friendly with him.

It was a serious thing, nevertheless, for Philip, the soul of legitimacy, to have dealings with rebels and regicides ; and when Cardenas conveyed to Secretary Geronimo de la Torre in Madrid the news of the tragedy of Whitehall, Philip and his Councils discussed as usual interminably the best course to be pursued.

" Truly," wrote Cardenas, three days after Charles's execution, " I am as grieved as so dreadful a tragedy as that which has befallen this unhappy Prince demands. The events both in this country and abroad have contributed to it, and especially the turmoils in France. . . . You will now see that what I wrote to you on the 20th August was a true forecast, and indeed I wrote it from certain knowledge I possessed of the designs of these people; namely, that they would try to do without a King, and if they could not succeed in that they would choose the Duke of Gloucester. . . . We are here in utter chaos, living without religion, King, or law, subject entirely to the power of the sword, and this faction is bearing itself as the conqueror of the realm, wherefrom many novelties will spring." [1]

The next letter from Cardenas, on the 19th March (N.S.), warned the Spanish Government that the English were in negotiation with the French, and that unless prompt steps were taken the danger to Spain would be great. This intelligence set Philip's Councils considering again; for unpleasant as it would be to make friends with these " heretic " regicides, their threatened alliance with France in the war would have meant certain ruin for Spain. As usual, the Councils deliberated frequently and at length, and, equally as usual, followed their tradition of avoiding as long as possible decisive action of any sort. An agent of the Parliament came to Cardenas in April 1649 to say that the English Government was desirous of continuing in friendly relations with Spain, and desired to know if King Philip would receive an ambassador from them. This was disconcerting; but the embarrassment was increased by

[1] MSS. Simancas, *Estado*, 2526; Canovas del Castillo, *Estudios del Reinado de Felipe IV.*

a letter which Sir Francis Cottington wrote to Cardenas from the Hague, saying that the Prince of Wales (Charles II.) had instructed him to go to Madrid as his ambassador, and to ask assistance in his attempts to regain the crown of England. The Council was determined, if possible, to prevent Cottington from coming until the attitude of the French towards Charles was known, but they were very doubtful, on the other hand, about receiving a republican envoy, and accrediting the Spanish ambassador to the Parliament, and thus putting Philip in the unenviable position of offending Charles II. and the legitimist elements in Europe.

The result of many weeks of deliberation in Madrid was that which might have been confidently foretold from the first, namely, to cast upon some-one else the responsibility of deciding. Philip accordingly wrote to the Archduke Leopold, his Governor of Flanders, asking him, in the first place, to stop Cottington by any pretext until he discovered what his instructions and object were, or to prevent his going to Madrid at all if possible without offending him. Cottington was to be assured secretly of Philip's sympathy with Charles, but to be told that the best way for Charles to regain his father's crown was to bring about peace between Spain and France. The Archduke was instructed to rap Cardenas sharply over the knuckles for saying so much to the agent of the Parliament, and to instruct him to hold the English revolutionary Government at arm's length for the present, " until at least it was solidly established." [1]

In the meanwhile no formal declaration was

[1] Simancas MSS., *Estado*, 2526 ; Canovas del Castillo.

to be made on behalf of Spain, either to Charles II.
or to the Parliament ; although, with characteristic duplicity, the former was given the title of
Majesty in a letter antedated, so that the Parliament,
if they learnt of it, might think that it was written
before the Stuarts had been excluded from the
succession." [1]   And, as if to counterbalance this,
Cardenas was unofficially to convey to the Parliament Philip's satisfaction at their friendliness.
This non-committal attitude, of which Spanish
statesmen were always so fond, soon tired the
downright English politicians of the Parliament,
and they began to show their teeth. In July
Cardenas was informed that he would not be
treated as an envoy unless he produced new credentials addressed to the Parliamentary Government, and he begged Philip either to recall him
or to send new credentials. Philip and his Councils
were very loth to do either, intent, as usual, upon
running with the hare and hunting with the hounds.
At first it was agreed by Philip's Council that
the King should not recognise the English Parliament until it was quite clear whether it or Charles II.
was likely to prevail in the end ; whilst the Stuart
Prince in Holland was to be treated with full
ceremony, but nothing else. Other Councillors
consulted later thought that, as the Parliament
was strong and threatening, the Archduke Leopold
in Flanders should be empowered to give Cardenas
temporary leave to go to Belgium on the pretext
of ill-health ; but that if any grave occasion should
arise another envoy might be sent temporarily,
duly accredited to the Parliament of England ; and

[1] Simancas MSS., *Estado*, 2526 ; Canovas del Castillo.

a small number of Councillors, whilst deploring the necessity, were in favour of new credentials being sent to Cardenas at once. The matter was finally submitted to Philip himself, who decided that the Archduke should act as he thought best.[1] Being in closer touch with the realities and dangers of the situation in Flanders than were Philip and his Councillors, the Archduke promptly sent credentials to Cardenas addressed to the Parliamentary Government of England ; and thus it happened that the ultra-Catholic King of Spain was the first sovereign in Europe formally to recognise the Puritan revolution in England, and the Stuarts had to pay thus for the reception of an envoy of the Braganza King of Portugal by Charles I. years before.

The chain of grievances between the Stuarts and Philip was unbroken. The rebuff in Madrid in 1623, the insincere juggling of the Spaniards about the Palatinate, the marriage of Charles I. to a French Princess, and the recognition of the Portuguese pretender led now, in 1649, to the strange and paradoxical position in which Philip, whose Dominican baptism was described in the first pages of this book, and who ever since had been the champion of Catholic orthodoxy, made friends with the stern Ironsides and Puritans of the Long Parliament.[2] It was important also for Cromwell so to deal with the continental Powers as to prevent them from extending to Charles the aid he was so industriously

---

[1] Canovas del Castillo.

[2] I have remarked elsewhere (*Spanish Influences in English Literature*) the strange approximation of the Spanish mystics (such as Sor Maria) with the English Puritans.

soliciting for the re-establishment of his family on the throne of England; and if France and Spain, from which Cromwell had most to fear, could be conciliated, the main danger from without which threatened the English republic would be avoided.

It was therefore natural that the Parliamentary Government should be desirous of establishing as early as possible full diplomatic relations with Spain. The question was on several occasions pressed upon Cardenas in London; but it went against the grain for so proud a sovereign as Philip to receive an ambassador from a Government whose very existence was a negation of the principle of Spanish sovereignty. He dared not, however, drive England into the arms of France against him, and after the usual protracted deliberation the Spanish Council of State reported upon the letter from Cardenas in these words: " It was a matter of the gravest importance to pass over so serious an excess as that which the English had committed in publicly beheading their King and born ruler; and it would be very worthy of great monarchs to contribute to the punishment of those who were guilty of such an atrocious crime." [1] But, nevertheless, whilst they recognised this, they saw the difficulties in the way of Philip's doing so. Again they took shelter behind the former reception of the Portuguese envoy by Charles I., and decided that as yet no other Power had recognised Charles II. there was no reason why they should take the lead in doing so, especially as Prince Rupert's fleet was still finding welcome in Portuguese ports with his prizes. After much preamble of this

[1] MSS. Simancas, *Estado*, 2526; Canovas del Castillo.

sort, Philip's Council made a clean breast of it to each other : the Parliament of England, with its fleet, was too strong for Spain to offend, and, distasteful as it might be, the ambassador from the English Parliament must be allowed to reside in Madrid. Cardenas had recommended that a bargain should be made, and that Cromwell, in return for the reception of his envoy in Spain, should refuse to receive a Portuguese envoy in England ; but Philip was afraid of drawing the cord too tight, and gave orders that the Puritan ambassador should be placed upon the same footing as the other ministers from foreign Powers resident in his Court.

The man chosen for the post was one Anthony Ascham. He must have been in an advanced stage of consumption ; for, when he was first appointed in October 1649, he was doubtful if he could go, and wrote to Lord President Bradshaw, saying that the hæmorrhage of the lungs from which he suffered was so bad that he must go to his father's house at Boston to recover before he could set out.[1] However, although still in wretched health, he safely arrived at Cadiz, though not without an attack on the voyage from a French man-of-war, on the 17/27 March 1650. The great Andalucian magnate, Duke of Medina Celi, received him with all honour, and took him across to Port St. Mary to lodge at his palace. Ascham wished to go to St. Lucar, as being a quieter place, and better fitted for an invalid ; but, to his surprise and indignation, he learnt from the Duke that he was not to be allowed to leave Port St. Mary until instructions came from Madrid. The Duke, indeed,

[1] MSS. Record Office, S.P. Spain 42.

expressed haughty astonishment that the Parliament should have presumed to send an envoy at all until they learnt King Philip's pleasure in the matter. Philip knew all about his coming months before, Ascham replied; and whatever orders came from Madrid to the Duke, he, Ascham, would only acknowledge a direct reply to the letter of the Parliament to King Philip.

It was clear that, although fear forced the Government in Madrid to receive the envoy, they were determined to snub him as much as possible, and during the time Ascham was detained at Port St. Mary, not unwillingly, for he was still very ill, it was decided that although he might be sent to Madrid with an escort to ensure his safety, when he arrived there he was to be kept waiting on various pretexts as long as possible before even being received by Don Luis de Haro, who was to avoid all negotiations or agreements when he did see him, until he knew the tenour of his instructions and his object in coming to Spain;[1] the intention of Philip and his Councillors evidently being to compromise themselves as little as possible until it was proved which party in England would ultimately triumph. Ascham was kept in Port St. Mary's until almost the middle of May, though treated with ostentatious respect; and at last, with an escort of six Spanish officers, headed by a colonel, slowly moved on through the burning Andalucian summer to Madrid.

He had naturally expected to be taken, as was usual, to some good private house retained by the King for his accommodation; but, much to his

[1] *Consultas del Consejo de Estado*, Simancas.

surprise, the colonel who was the chief of his escort led him on the day of his arrival, Sunday, 5th June, to a poor inn kept by a widow named Pandes in the Calle del Caballero de Gracia. Ascham, who was accompanied by a secretary named Fischer, an Italian interpreter, and an English servant, remonstrated against being thus exposed to the discomfort and danger of lodging in an open posada without locks or bolts upon the doors. The colonel was very haughty and off-handed about it, doubtless prompted by his superiors, and told the envoy that his duty was ended in bringing him safely to Madrid ; but that he would return in the morning. Ascham, in high dudgeon, remained at the inn that night, and early in the morning sent for an Englishman named Marston resident in Madrid, who came at once, accompanied by another Englishman who was with him at the time, one Laurence Chambers.[1] To them Ascham, in alarm, stated the case. Here he was, he said, without even a lock on his door, in a Catholic country swarming with enemies of his Government and his religion ; with Sir Francis Cottington posing at the Spanish Court as the representative of Charles Stuart ; and yet the colonel, who had just visited him, had told him that he must look after his own safety, for he had done with him.

Ascham had that morning sent his interpreter to see Secretary Geronimo de la Torre, who had

[1] The present narrative is compiled from (1) the details of Ascham's murder, given to the English Council by Laurence Chambers on his return to England (Record Office MSS., S.P. Spain 43); (2) the letters of Fischer, the secretary, in the same packet; and (3) an unpublished manuscript deposition of the prisoners in Bib. Nat., Madrid, i. 325, transcribed by me.

expressed surprise at the colonel's action; and had
promised to place some of the King's own guard
at Ascham's disposal. " But in the meanwhile,"
said Ascham, " here I am in hourly danger of my
life, for I cannot trust these people." His own
ignorance of Spanish had prevented his understanding his escort's instructions, and whether
the safe-conduct sent to Medina Celi covered his
stay in Madrid and his return to the coast. " If
not," said poor Ascham, " I am a dead man."
Marston and Chambers agreed as to his danger,
and at once set out to find him a fitting lodging in
a safe house.

Whilst the Englishmen were house-hunting for
the unfortunate ambassador in the forenoon of
the 6/16 June, another party of their countrymen
were drinking in a tavern within a few doors of the
posada where Ascham was lodged. For years
Catholic Irish and North and West countrymen
from England had been incorporated in the Spanish
armies; and at the final break up of the royalist
forces in England many of Charles's late soldiers
enlisted under the same banner. They were a
turbulent, swaggering lot, though good soldiers,
and were wont to hang about the Catholic Flemish
cities and Madrid until new companies were formed
in which they could serve. Five or six men of this
sort it was who were drinking in the tavern in the
Calle del Caballero de Gracia. There was Major
Halsey, a man from Lancashire; Captain Prodgers,
a Welshman; Captain Williams, his compatriot;
Valentine Roche, an Irishman; and one Sparkes,
a merchant's book-keeper from Oxford, as well as
a Scottish trumpeter named Arnet. The talk

turned upon the arrival in Madrid on the previous
evening of the Roundhead ambassador, sent by
the men who had murdered his Sacred Majesty
King Charles. It were a good deed to kill such a
crop-eared knave, said one of the swashbucklers ;
for he had even written a scurvy book defending
the regicides. The wine was heady and cheap ;
and as they talked thus and drank, the project grew
in favour, for were they not in Catholic Spain,
where to kill a heretic and a rebel, envoy or no
envoy, was a godly deed that all men praised ?

In the meanwhile Marston and Chambers
came back to the posada, which was still without
a guard, and informed Ascham that they had found
an excellent and secure lodging for him. Mr.
Fischer was asked to go with them to see the house
and settle the bargain ; but dinner being on the
table in the room on the first floor occupied by
Ascham, the latter asked his countrymen to partake
of the meal before going. Marston declined, and
earnestly recommended the envoy to forego his
dinner and move to the new lodgings instantly,
since the guard had not come, and he had reason
to feel apprehensive for the envoy's safety. The
Italian interpreter, John Baptist Arribas, made
light of the danger, and persuaded Ascham to dine
first and then to transfer his lodging, whether the
King's guard came or not. With this Marston and
Chambers, accompanied by the secretary Fischer,
went out, leaving Ascham and his interpreter at
dinner, attended by the English serving-man.

Presently a tramping upon the stairs was heard,
and the Lancashire soldier, Major Edward Halsey,
entered the room, followed by Williams, Sparkes,

and Arnet ; whilst the others remained at the door
and the head of the stairs. Halsey advanced as if
to salute the envoy, and the latter rose, but seeing
the three others following Halsey he drew back
towards a side table upon which some loaded pistols
were lying. Before he could reach it Halsey seized
him by the hair and cried out, " Traitor ! " whilst
Williams thrust him through the arm with a dagger,
and another stabbed him in the temples. The
unhappy envoy fell at once, and the murderers
hacked him about the head and body as he lay ;
whilst the Italian, in mortal fear, made as if to fly,
crying out in Spanish, " I am not the man ! "
But as he ran towards the door he was slashed
across the stomach by Halsey and another of the
ruffians, and was just able to stagger into the bedroom beyond, where he fell dead.

Then the six assassins fled, as they had arranged
to do, to the Church of St. Andres, a door or two
away in the same street, where before the high
altar they claimed sanctuary. In a few minutes
all the quarter was in an uproar, from the Red de
San Luis at the top of the street to the Convent of
St. Hermenegildo at the bottom. Grave alcaldes
carrying white wands, and followed by alguacils,
surrounded the posada, and on entering the upper
room they found Ascham and the Italian interpreter lying dead, and the English serving-man
uninjured, but almost beside himself with terror.
The case was so scandalous that the alcalde ordered
the murderers to be taken from sanctuary, a
most unusual thing, which was looked upon askance
by those who saw it. But Philip had been determined, since he had enjoyed the support of the nun,

to allow no immunity to open assassination in the capital; and with shouts of indignant protest five of the prisoners were led off to gaol.

Much interrogation there was of Mr. Fischer. Why had they come to Spain? What was their religion? and finally, the poor secretary had his money and papers seized, and was borne off to remain in strict seclusion in the alcalde's house pending the orders of His Majesty. Philip was intensely annoyed at the news of the crime, which rendered his position with Cromwell's Government more difficult than ever. He found himself, to begin with, at issue with the ecclesiastical authorities, who peremptorily demanded the restoration of the prisoners to sanctuary; the murderers, moreover, openly boasted of their deed, and competed with each other in claiming the leading part in it. The feeling in Madrid was, of course, strongly in favour of them; for was it not a virtue to kill an unrepentant heretic and rebel regicide? Every Madrileño who had enjoyed himself at an *auto-de-fé* knew that it was a saintly act and not murder which these men had done; and they in their prison were the heroes of the hour.

Philip personally could hardly be expected to look upon it otherwise; for in his eyes a King, however bad, was sacrosanct. Yet how could he let the murderers of a political envoy under his safe-conduct go free, and thus arouse the ire of Cromwell, who with his Council now wielded the power of England, and could ruin Spanish commerce as well as ensure the victory of the French in the lingering war. Again political expediency won the day; for Philip refused to surrender the prisoners to the Church or to the Inquisition, and they remained in prison until the affair blew over and circumstances changed ; when all but one of them, who had died, were quietly let out and disappeared.

In the meanwhile Fischer assumed the part of agent in Madrid for the Parliament, and was treated by Haro with marked politeness and respect. " Had Fischer any authority to negotiate an alliance ? " asked Don Luis.   " No," replied Fischer. " The Parliament is not so much perplexed at the murder of their agent as at the tardance thereby of a firm league between the two countries." Haro said that the King was still just as anxious to be friendly as the English were.   " Are not the French and the Portuguese the enemies both of the Parliament and of King Philip ? " "Yes," replied Fischer ; " but the Parliament will be very scrupulous about sending another envoy until they know how Ascham's murderers are to be punished." [1] " Cottington," writes Fischer, " is still here, and lives in good fashion, by his Catholic Majesty's charity ; although I am confident he can work little with him,—but he passeth better here than he can elsewhere, so he thinks not of departure.   Had the Parliament once capitulated with his Majesty (*i.e.* Philip) I suppose he would be quickly cashiered." [2]

Fischer was not a man of sufficient standing to bring about an international agreement ; and by Cromwell's orders he returned to England in

[1] Fischer's letters and full account of his negotiations are in Record Office MSS., S.P. Spain 43.

[2] Fischer to the Council, 26th November 1650.   MSS. Record Office.

1651, without having negotiated an alliance. But
thenceforward Cromwell and Philip were polite
and friendly to each other to an extent that filled
English royalists and Catholics with indignant
surprise. A high noble, the Marquis de Lede,
was sent from Spanish Flanders to congratulate
the Lord Protector upon the assumption of his
new dignity ; and Cardenas had nothing but kind
messages to give from his master to the English
Puritans. Cromwell, however, wanted something
more solid than amiable messages. He knew full
well, as indeed Fischer wrote, that fear, not love,
made the Spanish King so courteous. Cromwell
had, it is true, secured something when he prevented
Spain from helping the Stuarts, but he wanted
also as conditions of the proposed alliance with
Spain that freedom should be given to English
ships to trade in the West Indies, that the power
of the Inquisition over Englishmen in Spain should
be limited, that reciprocal advantages in the
matter of duties should be given to English and
Spanish trade, and that English merchants should
be allowed to buy wool in Spain.

The two first demands were flatly and haughtily
refused by Cardenas in Philip's name, and Cromwell
looked around for a means of coercion, for he was
in no humour to take the traditional view of
Spain's awesome superiority. He found it in
Mazarin's difficulties in France, and his urgent need
to end the war quickly at any cost. The aid of
England on the sea would make all the difference,
and if he obtained it Spain must bow the head
and accept the terms he offered them. So he bade
higher than Philip for Cromwell's friendship,—Dun-

kirk, a Spanish Flemish port to be jointly captured,
being the bribe ; and Blake, who had long been
co-operating with Philip to suppress Moorish piracy
in the Mediterranean, suddenly sailed with the
Parliament fleet, and without a declaration of war
fell upon the Spanish silver fleet in the Atlantic,
whilst Penn and Venables attacked Mexico and
St. Domingo unsuccessfully, and without warning
captured from the Spaniards the rich island of
Jamaica.

This was in May 1655 ; and the news fell upon
Philip like an avalanche. Panic spread through
Seville and Cadiz, and curses loud and deep of
the falsity of heretics rang through Liars' Walk
and the Calle Mayor. For all these years poor
overburdened Spain had kept at bay half the world
in arms, but hitherto the diplomacy which had
successfully kept England neutral had saved her
from being utterly overwhelmed. Now, as hope
was dawning that her great antagonist was fainting
from the domestic strife which crippled Mazarin,
and that terms honourable to Philip's pride and
respectful to the integrity of his territory could
be attained, the new and strong republican England had cast her glaive into the scale on the side
of France ; and Spain, already exhausted, plague-
ridden, and bankrupt, was face to face with two
great enemies instead of one. Well might Philip
write to the nun when he heard of the intentions
of the English fleets, and the probable outbreak of
hostilities : " If this should happen it would be
the final ruin of this realm ; and no human power
would be able to stop it : the Almighty hand of
God alone could do it ; and so I beseech you most

earnestly to supplicate Him to take pity upon us, and not to allow the infidels to destroy realms so pure in the faith and so religious as these are. Blessed be His holy name ! " [1]

[1] *Cartas de Sor Maria*, 30th June 1655.

CHAPTER X

MORAL AND SOCIAL DECADENCE IN MADRID — PHILIP'S HABITS—POVERTY IN THE PALACE— VELAZQUEZ—THE MENINAS—BIRTH OF AN HEIR — THE CHRISTENING — THE PEACE OF THE PYRENEES—PHILIP'S JOURNEY TO THE FRONTIER—MARRIAGE OF MARIA TERESA—CAMPAIGNS IN PORTUGAL—DON JUAN—DEATH OF HARO— PHILIP BEWITCHED—DEATH OF PHILIP PROSPER —BIRTH OF CHARLES—FANSHAWE'S EMBASSY— LADY FANSHAWE AND SPAIN—ROUT OF CARACENA IN PORTUGAL — PHILIP'S ILLNESS — THE INQUISITION AND WITCHCRAFT — DEATH OF PHILIP

By great good fortune there have survived descriptions and accounts of life in Philip's Court at the time of which we now write (1654–1660), so minute and so photographic in their fidelity, as to provide absolutely trustworthy material for a true comparison of the condition of affairs after five-and-twenty years of a disastrous reign, with that which had existed on the King's accession. A writer of keen observation, insatiable curiosity, ample opportunity, and much literary skill, the noble churchman and poet Jeronimo de Barrionuevo, from 1654 for several years wrote almost every week a chatty letter from Madrid to his friend the Dean of Saragossa and others, setting forth with perfect frankness everything worth recording that passed in Madrid. At the same time, an observant Hollander named Aersens van Sommerdyk visited Spain, and stayed in the capital long enough to write an account of the social and political condition of the Court as it appeared to an intelligent foreigner ; whilst shortly afterwards the sparkling narrative of life in Madrid, written by the Frenchman Bonnecasse, came to confirm the impressions of the Spaniard and the Dutchman.[1] If we add to these Philip's own weekly letters to the nun, and the reports of the Venetian ambassadors, which are also in print, we have a mass of contemporary evidence which cannot be contradicted, especially in matters upon which all agree.

It is well that this should be so ; for the picture to be presented of life in the capital of the Spains at the end of Philip's reign is so gloomy, that the historian who ventured to produce it without full contemporary warrant would be accused of bias

---

[1] *Avisos de Barrionuevo* (Coleccion de Autores Castellanos), Madrid, 1892 ; *Voyage en Espagne* (1655), Aersens Van Sommerdyk, Amsterdam, 1666; *Rélation de l'État et Gouvernement d'Espagne*, Bonnecasse, Cologne, 1667. Barrionuevo, who was brother of the Marquis of Cusano, was a " character." He was a jovial priest, not ashamed to boast of his love affairs, of his good looks, of his bravery ; and he belonged to a turbulent family who were always getting into affrays of some sort. He himself records without any word of reprobation a murder committed in the open streets of Madrid by his kinsman, Francisco Barrionuevo, upon a man who had boasted of making love to his wife ; and the chronicler quite unconcernedly predicts that the murderer, who had fled to sanctuary, will get off. Barrionuevo confesses that he is insatiably curious, and gathers news from everyone, going every morning to the palace to learn what was passing there. His brother, who was Spanish ambassador in London, also kept him well posted as to what happened in England. See Barrionuevo's biography by Señor Paz y Melia in the first volume of the *Avisos*.

and exaggeration. At the beginning of the reign we saw a fairly numerous class of nobles, church-men, and officials, still rich with royal grants and government plunder ; whilst the mass of the people were sunk in poverty. At the time of which we are now writing the nobles themselves had been bled to a state of bankruptcy. They and the Church were supposed to be exempt from taxation ; but the demands made upon them, and especially upon the nobles, for funds for the war had ended by reducing most of them to the same poverty-stricken condition as their inferiors in rank. The financial and mercantile classes had lost all con-fidence ; for the arbitrary seizure of their property again and again by the Government, and the crushing taxation on exports, even to Spanish colonies, had driven them to universal evasion and contraband, to the further depletion of Philip's resources.[1] Haro, who had a revenue of 130,000 ducats a year, and a few of his kinsmen, were still very rich, and continued to plunder all they could, though there was, indeed, little left to plunder ; and in addition to these, the only people who had much ready money to spend were the colonial officials who had returned home with the booty of their offices.

The idleness and pretension of all classes in the capital had increased now to such an extent, that practically the whole of the necessary work had to be done by foreigners ; there being as many as 40,000 French subjects in Madrid dressing as Spaniards, and calling themselves Burgundians or Walloons, to escape the special tax on foreigners.[2]

[1] Van Sommerdyk.
[2] *Ibid.* The population at this time was between 250,000 and 300,000.

By these people most crafts and callings were conducted, the Spanish working classes being occupied mainly in casual service, petty traffic, and mendicancy ; whilst highway robbery and murder, even in Madrid, was so frequent as to cause no remark. The streets were more filthy and dilapidated than ever, and still the crowd of idlers on foot and in vast number of coaches, drawn by mules now, for the horses had been seized, thronged the promenades, —the Calle Mayor in the winter, the Prado and river bank in the summer ; the humbler classes elbowing their social superiors with perfect effrontery, wearing swords and daggers, claiming equal respect, and, indeed, swaggering more than the nobles.

The two playhouses, which had been reopened on the King's second marriage, were crammed every day with artizans dressed in imitation or cast-off finery, and calling themselves *caballeros*, who had to pay from 10 to 15 sous in all for a seat ; [1] and, whilst the fields were mostly tilled, if at all, and the urban labour was performed, by foreigners, the very cloth upon Spanish backs being made in Holland and England from Spanish wool, the native working classes still vociferously kept up the silly tradition of their own gentility, and of national potency and the overwhelming wealth of the King. The alternate appreciation and debasement of the coinage had enormously raised the price of commodities, and especially of house rent

---

[1] Aersens and Bonnecasse. The charge for entrance was 1½ sous, which went to the actors ; 2 sous were charged for admission to the seated part, which went to the Town Council ; and 7 sous was the cost of a seat in the cheapest part, 1½ sous of which went to charity, and the rest for the lessee.

in Madrid; the houses being still low, shabby, and incommodious, for the most part, owing to the claim of the King to the first floor of every house or its equivalent in money.

But what struck foreigners, and indeed observant Spaniards, at this period, was the appalling profligacy still prevalent in Madrid. Public women almost monopolised the promenades; their shameless impudence in broad daylight having the effect of lowering the standard of behaviour, even of decent women, who thought it no insult, but rather the contrary, to be addressed in amorous terms by strange men in the street.[1] The women, for the most part, still went about, notwithstanding the prohibition, with shawls covering their faces except one eye, and this facilitated intrigue in all classes to a shocking extent. The Government were in despair about the utter disregard by women of the dress regulations; for the wide farthingales, stiff, extravagant wigs, and fine stuffs were worn in spite of all pragmatics, since the Queen and her ladies set the fashion; and the only persons punished were the unfortunate shopkeepers who supplied the offending things.

The whole moral situation in Spain was indeed a social problem which can only be explained by the lack of feminine influence in society at the time and previously. There had always remained a taint of Oriental tradition in the treatment of women in Spain. They had been kept in strict seclusion;

---

[1] Bonnecasse says that at this time there were 30,000 women of evil life in Madrid. Even now strangers in Madrid are surprised to see the impunity with which well-dressed, respectable young men dare to make audible remarks of an amorous or complimentary nature intended to reach the ears of ladies unknown to them in the streets.

they were for the most part entirely ignorant, and had never taken an equal social position with men, usually dining apart from their husbands, visiting each other in closed chairs or coaches, and spent their time squatting on the ground in circles talking trivialities or devotion, whilst the men were rarely accompanied by their woman-kind in public. It was therefore no wonder that in such a state of society as this, ladies and modest women for the most part abandoned the streets and public places to utter profligacy; and that men, free from the salutary influence exercised by the presence of good women, sank deeper and deeper into vice. Philip, under the influence of the nun, had striven hard to make his capital more decent; but the whole tide of feeling was contrary and too strong for him; whilst his own example in this respect was a very bad one, which seriously weakened his efforts. Barrionuevo, in one of his letters at this time, mentions the King as being " a fine hand at bastards, but with very poor luck as regards legitimate children "; and shortly afterwards, during one of Philip's spasmodic attempts to cleanse his capital, the same writer says : " They are arresting all the women they find wandering unoccupied about the streets, and hailing them off by tens and twenties to prison with their hands tied. The gaol is crammed full, so that they have hardly room to stand, and the house will have to be largely extended if this rigour is to go on, or vast supplies of wood will have to be laid in to burn some of them otherwise."

In the matter of men's dress Philip's example had agreed with his precept; and here he had succeeded in imposing the fashion of sombre modesty. No man was allowed to enter his presence, or even to tender a petition to him as he went to Mass through his lines of red and yellow halberdiers, unless apparelled entirely in black, and wearing a *golilla*. The style of dress had changed somewhat since the King's accession. The hats were much smaller, and often of silk instead of felt, and profusely trimmed with black lace. The doublet, trunks, and cape of the men were usually of black baize, as was the *ropilla*, a close - fitting unbuttoned tunic reaching to the thighs, with open sleeves hanging from the shoulder ; though gentlemen often wore black silk doublets and trunks in the summer. The trunks or breeches were now cut quite narrow, with buttons at the knee, like modern knickerbockers ; and the fashion was to wear thin black silk stockings over thick white ones, and the shoes were tied with very broad black ribbons.[1]

The King was now rarely seen in public, except that on two days in the week he sat almost motionless for an hour in public audience to receive petitions, which with a slight inclination of his head he referred to Don Luis de Haro. The various Councils, as before, discussed at great length every point touching their respective departments, and, unseen, the King might listen to their deliberations ; but practically his intervention in their business was confined now to his

[1] A curious craze was universal amongst men in Madrid at this time, and for some years previously, namely, that of wearing large round horn framed spectacles such as are seen in the portrait of Quevedo. The modern name for goggles in Spanish is " Quevedos." The habit of snuff-taking was also a fashionable affectation of the time.

sitting upon his throne every Friday morning, whilst the respective secretaries recited what had been done during the previous week. The King's assent to their recommendations was usually given simply by the words " *Está bien,*" It is well ; but if the matter appeared to demand further attention he turned to Don Luis de Haro, who stood by his side, and told him to speak to him later about it. Don Luis de Haro was in all but name a Vice-King. Everyone, even the Secretary of State, knelt whilst he addressed him, and Philip appended his signature " Yo el Rey," with little or no inquiry, to everything that the favourite placed before him.

His finances were more hopelessly involved than ever, especially after Cromwell joined the French against him : and he told the Cortes of Castile in the previous year, 1654, that out of the 10 million ducats voted to him by them he only received 3 millions. From the Indies in all he received in good years from $1\frac{1}{2}$ to 2 millions of ducats ; [1] whilst about 2 millions came from Aragon, etc. Out of a total nominal revenue, therefore, of about 18 million ducats he only received about 8 or 9 millions, the rest being either anticipated or intercepted by peculation ; and in the year 1654 he confessed to an uncovered debt of 120 million ducats. But, withal, though Philip himself made no secret of his poverty, the country at large, and particularly the people of Madrid, insisted upon boasting still of the boundless wealth at his disposal. There are in Barrionuevo's letters scores of references to the squalid penury that existed

[1] Worth 2s. 8d. each.

everywhere at this period,[1] even in the interior of Philip's palace; but the following short extract from one of them, belonging to the year 1657, will suffice.

" For the last two months and a half the usual rations have not been distributed in the palace; for the King has not a *real*. On the day of St. Francis they served a capon to the Infanta (Maria Teresa), who ordered them to take it away, as it stank like a dead dog. They then brought her a chicken, of which she is fond, on sippets of toast, but it was so covered with flies that she nearly overturned the lot. This is how things go on in the palace. . . . It appears also that the Queen likes to finish her dinner with sweetmeats; but as none had been brought to her table for some days, she asked the lady whose business it is to attend to these things, why they were not served as usual. She replied that the confectioner refused to supply them because he could not get paid, and a large amount was owing to him. The lady then drew a ring from her finger, and said to a servant: ' Run out at once and get some sweetmeats, anywhere, with this jewel.' But the buffoon Manuelito de Gante was present, and cried: ' Put your finger in your ring again, mistress '; and with that he took a copper real from his pocket and said : ' Go and get some sweet-

---

[1] He also cites, however, very numerous cases of professedly poor people having large secret hoards of money. The universal want of confidence had undoubtedly led to the hoarding of coin—especially silver—to a very great extent by all classes, and this will to some extent explain the strange facility with which money was found on emergency even in the midst of poverty.

meats quickly, so that this good lady may finish her dinner.'"

With poverty touching even the Queen's own table, with Philip and his ministers in despair of finding fresh means to extort more money from the empty pockets of subjects, and from the hidden hoards of the Church, lavish waste still jostled carking poverty. Barrionuevo gives an account of an entertainment provided by the Marquis of Heliche, the eldest son of Haro, a few months only before the scene just described (January 1657), to celebrate the visit paid to him by Philip and his wife at the Zarzuela outside Madrid, where, in addition to comedies and the like, a great banquet was prepared.

"It cost 16,000 ducats. . . . There was a dinner served of 1000 dishes ; and there was one monstrous stew in a huge jar sunk in the ground with a fire beneath it. . . . It contained a three-year-old calf, 4 sheep, 100 pairs of pigeons, 100 partridges, 100 rabbits, 1000 pigs' trotters, and 1000 tongues, 200 fowls, 30 hams, 500 sausages, and 100,000 other trifles. They say it cost 8000 reals, though mostly presents. Everything I am telling you is true, and I minimise rather than exaggerate. There were three or four thousand persons present, and there was plenty for everybody, and to spare. So much was left, indeed, that it was brought back to Madrid in baskets, and I got some relieves and scraps. And all this was in addition to tarts and puffs and pasties, sweet cakes, preserves, fruits, and enormous quantities of wine and sweet drinks.

The Venice ambassador presented 500 ducats' worth of glass, and Tutavilla gave a similar amount of crockery. . . . All the scenery and apparatus have been brought to the Retiro, to the new theatre which they have made in the St. Paul's Hermitage there, and the whole affair is to be repeated there this carnival."

It is hardly necessary to say that, in reward for this Gargantuan feast, Heliche was made a grandee a few days afterwards.

Philip took no pleasure personally now in these coarse frivolities ; though Mariana hungered for them, to distract her from the fits of homesick depression into which she periodically sank in the dull monotony of her life and her frequently disappointed hopes of renewed motherhood. The King himself was well-nigh despondent : going through his life like a leaden automaton, signing papers placed before him by Haro, usually without discussion or remark.[1] His condition, indeed, now was closely akin to melancholy religious madness, such was the morbid misery that preyed upon him : in anticipation of an early death, weeping for his own sins, for the utter ruin that seemed impending,

[1] Barrionuevo mentions a malicious caricature which was current in the palace (1655, satirising Philip's helpless despondency in the face of universal corruption. A group represents Haro, the chief minister, saying: "I can do everything"; the Secretary of State, Contreras, saying : "I want everything " ; the King saying : "I see everything"; his Confessor saying: "I absolve everything"; and the devil saying: "I shall fly away with the lot." Aersens, as an instance of the ineptitude and corruption everywhere at the same period, mentions that he saw on the beach at St. Sebastian a great warship in course of construction, but which had not been touched for a long time ; " but upon which more millions had already been spent than would have built a dozen such ; but those who have spent it have alone profited by it."

and for the continued absence of a male heir to his broken realms. One of his strange whims at this time was to pass hours alone in the new jasper mausoleum at the Escorial, to which he had transferred the bodies of his ancestors shortly before. After one of these visits in 1654, he wrote to Sor Maria : " I saw the corpse of the Emperor, whose body, although he has been dead ninety-six years, is still perfect ; and by this it may be seen how richly the Lord has repaid him for his efforts in favour of the faith whilst he lived. It helped me much, especially as I contemplated the place where I am to lie when God shall take me. I prayed Him not to let me forget what I saw there." Soon afterwards, Barrionuevo records that the King had passed two solitary hours upon his knees in prayer on the bare stones of the mausoleum before the niche which was to be his own final resting-place ; and that when he came out his eyes were red and swollen with weeping.

The years went on, and still Mariana's repeated hopes of progeny were disappointed. Her own health was not good, for she fretted much, whilst Philip's troubles had crushed and aged him sadly. The Indian silver, which had previously been so precious a contribution to his revenue, was now regularly captured by Cromwell's cruisers, which closely beleaguered Cadiz. The French on the Flemish frontier and in Catalonia were still holding his territory, though Don Juan was doing his best and not unsuccessfully in Flanders (1656–57). Peace, as Philip well knew, was now a vital necessity for him ; but pride still kept him from surrendering to the foreigner the land of his fathers, and Mazarin's terms were as yet too humiliating for acceptance by a Power which had for so long claimed predominance in Europe.

Girl children had been born to Mariana, but each one had died at, or soon after, birth, though the wildest caprice of the mother was complied with in order to produce favourable conditions ; but after the simultaneous birth and death of the girl child which came in August 1656, all hope seemed gone, and a profound melancholy fell upon both husband and wife, unrelieved by one ray of light. Philip's principal pleasure now, with the exception of his prayers and the immoralities he deplored so much, were the visits he paid every few days to the studio of Velazquez in the old palace. There, beneath the magic brush of the painter, he saw grow in resemblance the portraits of those amongst whom his life was passed,—the dwarfs and buffoons, who tried now so fruitlessly to make him smile, the quaint characters about the palace, the generals and admirals, the councillors and secretaries, whose faces he knew so well ; and, above all, his two little girls and his young wife, with her rouged cheeks, her stiff square wig and her hard eyes. The favourite child—for Mariana was jealous of the elder, Maria Teresa— was the little Infanta Margaret, born in 1651, a fragile, fair little flower of a girl, degenerate from her descent, but in childhood not showing excessively the unlovely features she inherited. The etiquette that surrounded the child and her sister was freezing in its formality. Those who served them knelt, and everything had to pass through several hands before reaching them. Their dress, with the wide-hooped farthingales and stiff long bodices, were utterly unchildlike and cumbrous, but, withal, the charm of youth could not be utterly crushed out of Margaret ; and Velazquez has left us portraits of her as a child which will always remain the ideal of infancy.

The finest painting that ever left the master's easel is that which presents not only a portrait of the little Princess, but also an interior which tells more of Court life at the time (1656) than pages of written description could do. The tiny Infanta stands in her white satin hooped dress, her fair hair parted at the side, in the studio of Velazquez, who, with the coveted cross of Santiago upon his breast,[1] is painting a portrait of the King and Queen, whose faces are seen reflected in a mirror at the back of the room, but who do not appear in the picture itself. The child had probably been brought to relieve the tedium of her parents in sitting for their portraits, and she seems herself to have grown fretful and needed amusing. The young maid of honour, Doña Maria de Sarmiento, kneels before her, handing her, on a gold salver, a cup of water in the fine red scented clay which it was a vicious fashion of ladies of the day to eat. In the foreground lies a mastiff dozing, and close by it are two of the ugly dwarfs who were such important personages in the Spanish Court, Mari Barbola and Nicolasico Pertusato ; whilst behind

---

[1] The tradition is that Philip himself painted the cross of Santiago on the representation of Velazquez as a token of his delight at the master-piece. This, however, is hardly likely to be the case, as the rank was not granted to the painter until two years later. It was no doubt eventually added by Philip's orders, but Velazquez was not a Knight of Santiago when the painting was executed.

THE MAIDS OF HONOUR

Portrait of the Infanta Margaret ; from a picture by Velazquez at the Prado Museum

them, slightly curtseying, is another maid of honour, Doña Isabel de Velasco ; and still farther back in the gloom a lady and gentleman in attendance, the former in a conventual dress ; whilst in the extreme rear of the picture stands the Queen's quarter-master, Don José Nieto, at the open door drawing back a curtain, perhaps that more light may be thrown upon the King and Queen, whom the painter is portraying. The interior of the room, with its special lighting and its unrivalled perspective, fixes for us, as if in a flashlight photograph, one unstudied moment of life in Philip's Court as it was actually passed, and for this reason the picture is invaluable. The existence it crystallises is a dull one, unrelieved from tedium for Philip except by the presence of his little child, and the trembling consolations of his religion.

Soon, however, hope for a time was to blossom again. After months of anxiety, in which his doubts and fears were laid before the nun again and again by the anxious father, he was assured that another child was yet to be born to him, and the astrologers and soothsayers predicted that this time it would be a son, and would live. Philip was in dire straits for money at the time (November 1657), and on the first day of the Vigil of the Presentation of the Virgin he had nothing to eat but eggs without fish ; as his steward had not a *real* of ready money to pay for anything else, and the tradesmen would give no more credit.[1] But yet the most whimsical fancy of his wife now had to be gratified at any sacrifice, and the Buen Retiro soon again rang with jovial music and water parties

* Barrionuevo.

on the lake, merry comedies, novel bull-fights, and diversions of all sorts, which were produced to make Mariana happy. Don Juan sent from Flanders a splendid silver bedstead, with brocade hangings ; and all that care and solicitude could discover to ensure the happy arrival of the looked-for heir was forthcoming.

At last, to the weary, worn-out King of fifty-two, a man-child was born at the end of November 1657. The mother was thought to be dying, but no one had thoughts for her, the birth of an heir to Philip being greeted by rejoicings so tumultuous in the capital as of themselves to prove the lawless condition into which the people had sunk.

" On the day of the birth," writes Barrionuevo (5th December 1657), " not a bench nor a table was left unbroken in the palace, nor a single pastry-cook's nor tavern that was not sacked. In the Admiral's house, too, one of his equerries, and riding-master to some of the greatest gentlemen in Madrid, named Chicho Cristalino, killed his groom in the stable, stabbing him for some trivial cause. . . . He has escaped. He was a Knight of Calatrava. The same night three or four other similar misfortunes happened, and in the rejoicings nobody's cape was safe. . . . To-morrow they say that his Majesty will go on horseback to the Atocha to give thanks to the Mother of God. . . . They say the Prince is a pretty little chap, and that the King wishes him to be baptized at once, before the extreme cold comes on. . . . There are to be masquerades, bull-fights, and cane-tourneys as soon as the Queen gets up to see them, as well as plays with machinery invented by an engineer, a servant of the Nuncio, to be represented at the theatre at the Retiro, and in the saloon of the palace. . . . The municipality, following the lead of the Councils, have gone to congratulate the King, . . . and no gentleman, great or small, has failed to do the like. There have been some funny incidents. Here are two. The little Count de Haro, the Admiral's child, six years old, went, and the King was much pleased with the little man, as he was so serious, and especially when he said to his Majesty, ' But, Sir ! those buttons of yours are against the pragmatic ; they are gold ! ' They were really diamond buttons that the King had put on for the celebration. The favourite (*i.e.* Haro) accompanied him, and one of the courtiers present came up to him and said : ' God bless your Excellency for the boon you have bestowed upon Spain in sending us a Prince,' as if Haro had been the artificer of the work. There was much laughter at this."

Astrologers were busy predicting all manner of glory and good fortune for the new-born Prince, and Philip was full of gratitude and hope that all would now be well. " Help me, Sor Maria," he wrote, " to give thanks to God ; for I by myself am unable to do so adequately. Pray to Him to make me fully thankful for the signal favour conferred upon me, and to give me strength henceforward to do His holy will. The new-born babe is well, and I implore you to take him under your protection, and pray to our Lord and His holy Mother to keep him for their service, for the exaltation of the faith and the good of these realms. If this is not to be, then pray let him be taken from me before he reaches manhood." [1]

For weeks the usual festivities in Madrid went on, though the general penury made them less brilliant than the occasion warranted. But Philip, for his part, seemed almost young again with joy. On the 6th December he rode through the decorated streets of his capital on a spirited Neapolitan charger. Dances, masques, and music greeted him on his way, and the public fountains ran wine instead of water, whilst the night was made as light as day by thousands of wax torches.[2] A week afterwards the baptism of the Prince was celebrated in the royal chapel by the Cardinal Archbishop of Toledo (Borja), whose magnificent preparations of liveries, vestments, and equipages were to cost 50,000

---

[1] *Cartas de Sor Maria.* Philip evidently recollected the bitterness of his losing Baltasar Carlos in the flower of his youth.

[2] In a long doggerel ballad on the occasion, quoted by Barrionuevo, many lines are devoted to the King's delight. These are specimens—

Salió el Rey á verlo todo,
y tambien á que le viesen;
porque todos conociesen
en el regocijo el modo
de salir. . . .

The King came out to see the show,
And also that he might be seen;
For by his gay and happy mien
Thus all the world his joy might know.

En toda mi vida ví
hacer locuras mayores
á plebeyos y señores;
y sin reparar, entrando
al Rey le iban hablando
desde el Grande hasta el rapaz.

Sure never in my life before
Did such mad pranking meet my eye,
By rich and poor and low and high.
For no one cared, but in did walk,
And to the King himself did talk,
From great grandee to urchin poor.

Fué el Rey el dia noveno
á dar las gracias á Atocha,
mas tierno que una melcocha,
y, por Dios, que iba muy bueno
de diamantes todo lleno,
á ese cielo parecia.

And when nine days had taken flight,
Atocha's saint with thanks to greet,
Our King did ride, as honey sweet,
By God! he was a gallant sight,
From top to toe with diamonds fine,
Like starlit heaven did he shine.

ducats ; though, says Barrionuevo, he had not a
real.

"On Thursday the 13th, the corridors and
courtyards of the palace were decorated with great
splendour, and three canopies were erected, one
in each corridor and one in the chapel. There was
a very sumptuous bed adjoining the King's curtained closet, and a step away a staging, with two
steps and a triangle of silver. Upon this was
placed the font of St. Dominic's baptism, and six
great silver braziers very full of fuel, which were
replenished every now and then from the fireplaces, so that the air might be warmed, which it
was until it was like an oven. There were also
sconces which perfumed the air divinely. Shortly
after two the ceremony commenced ; the Inquisitor-
General and the Bishop of Sigüenza, apparelled in
pontificals, assisting the Cardinal, who awaited
the arrival of the Infante near the altar, whilst the
whole chapel was hung with the most beautiful
hangings the King possesses. Don Luis Ponce,
without a cape, led the way with the Spanish
Guard, followed by peers, nobles, and grandees ;
after whom came the Nuncio and ambassadors.
Then came the minister (Don Luis de Haro), dressed
in a gown of cloth of gold and a red sash.[1] Following
him the Prince, richly adorned, was borne in the
arms of the Countess of Salvatierra, seated in a
crystal chair ; and the Infanta (Maria Teresa)

---

[1] It will be recollected that this was the same costume as that which
Olivares wore at the baptism of Baltasar Carlos, and which then puzzled
people.   The dress, whatever it was, seems only to have been worn at
christenings.

walked behind, her train carried by the Mistress of the Robes, after whom marched the heralds and archers of the Guard, who entirely surrounded the space. The Marquis of Priego carried the sacred taper, Alba bore the custode and napkins, the Admiral carried the ewer, which was of a single emerald, very large, and set with diamonds. The marchpane [1] fell to the Count of Oñate, the towels to Medina de las Torres, the salt-cellar to the Prince of Astillano, his son. The ladies of the Court followed the Infanta, their trains borne by pages. The presidents of the Councils, with their two senior officers on each side, were ranged around the chapel, with the grandees before them ; and when the ladies entered they stood in front of the grandees. The lady-in-waiting handed the Prince to the Infanta naked, except for a very short little jacket of plush much adorned, and with false sleeves. The Infanta cried out in a very clear voice : ' Why have you not put his clothes on ? Why do you give him to me so undressed ? ' The lady replied : ' That is done on purpose, Madam, that it may be seen that he is a male.' The water they baptized him with was from the Jordan, . . . brought lately by some friars who came from the Holy House. The Prince screamed lustily when he was baptized, and, attracted by the loud resonant voice, the King, who was looking through his jalousies, ex-

---

[1] What was called " marchpane " at royal baptisms was not really marchpane, which is of course a sweetmeat compounded of almond paste and honey, but a piece of crumb of bread upon which the bishop wiped his fingers of the holy oil after anointing the royal infant during the ceremony. The crumb of bread was often enclosed in an envelope of marchpane and was carried in the procession wrapped in a beautifully embroidered cloth upon a gold salver.

claimed, " Ah ! that does sound well ; the house smells of a man now." [1]

Then, after retailing the baby's names, Philip Prosper, " and the whole litany of saints to follow," and the magnificent presents given to the child's nurse, the narrator gives a curious instance of the overweening pride of the higher Spanish nobles of the time. A staircase had broken down with the crush of people, and the Duke of Bejar, whose duty it was to carry the marchpane, could not get through the crowd. The acting Lord Chamberlain, the Count of Puñonrostro, seeing that the ceremony was being delayed in consequence, asked the King what he should do. " Tell the Constable (*i.e.* the Grand Constable of Castile, the Duke of Frias) to carry the marchpane," said Philip. The proud noble replied that his arm was bad, and he could not do it. This answer only produced a repetition of the command from the King that the Constable was to carry the marchpane. " Tell his Majesty that the Constables of Castile are too big to serve as stopgaps for anybody," said the Constable. Two days later the Duke was being hurried off to Berlanga under arrest. If Dukes and Constables could be impracticably proud, so could scullions ; for only a fortnight after this there was a regular pitched battle in the King's kitchen on some point of honour between the scullions and the guards, in which six of the combatants were killed outright, and twenty were wounded, many more being carried off to the prison of the Court to answer for their turbulence.

[1] Barrionuevo.

Admiration spent itself in praises of the beauty of the infant that had been born to Philip's decline. Never, sure, was such a babe vouchsafed to man as this. Verse and prose galore declaimed its present perfection and coming greatness. But alas ! Philip Prosper, as might have been expected from the offspring of several generations of incest, was a poor epileptic monstrosity, who quietly made his exit from the world four years after he entered it with such a blare of trumpets. The good nun of Agreda, far away from the turmoil of rejoicing at the Prince's birth, had misgivings at the ungodliness and extravagance of the festivities, and remonstrated with Philip upon them. " It is good and politic for your Majesty to receive the congratulations of your subjects, . . . but I do beseech you earnestly not to allow excessive sums to be spent on such festivities as these, when there is a lack of money needful even for the defence of your crown. Let there be no offence to God in what is done. . . . It is good to rejoice for the birth of the Prince ; but pray let us do it with a clear conscience." [1]

Through all these years the wars in which Spain was engaged had gone on. Mazarin's many enemies in France had been encouraged and bribed largely by Spain, and the greatest of French commanders, Turenne and Condé, for a time entered Philip's service against their own country. This changed the aspect of affairs, especially on the Flemish frontier, whilst in the south of France the leaders of the Fronde with Spanish aid kept Mazarin's troops busy there. When Turenne

[1] *Cartas de Sor Maria.*

again returned to the French side the tables were turned somewhat (1655), and after a series of defeats the Archduke Leopold, Philip's Governor of Flanders, had retired, leaving Condé in command of the troops, whilst Don Juan, King Philip's son, succeeded the Archduke as Governor (1656). This brilliant pair of young men did much to restore Spanish prestige in Flanders; but when the alliance between Cromwell and Mazarin was signed Spain was outmatched, and all observers could see that France in the end must be victorious.

One after the other the Flemish frontier places surrendered to the allies; but the great blow to Philip's arms fell in the summer of 1658. Dunkirk, a Spanish port in Flanders, promised to Cromwell by Mazarin, was closely blockaded by an English fleet, and besieged on the land side by Turenne, who was accompanied by young Louis XIV. himself; whilst a Spanish army under Don Juan and Condé, with whom was James Duke of York, now nominal Admiral of the Spanish fleet, was endeavouring to break through Turenne's lines and relieve the place. By a *coup de main* Turenne outflanked the Spanish force, whilst Cromwell's fleet bombarded them from the sea. Panic overtook the Spaniards, who fled precipitately with great loss, and Dunkirk soon after capitulated. This Battle of the Dunes seemed the last drop in Philip's cup of sorrow, for by it all Flanders lay at the mercy of the French royalists, and city after city fell into their hands.

Shortly before this, and soon after the christening of Philip Prosper described above, an equally fatal catastrophe had fallen upon Philip on the Portuguese frontier. There for years a state of hostility had continued, with frequent raids on both sides ; but, growing bolder with Philip's increased exhaustion, the masculine Spanish Queen Mother of Portugal [1] had laid regular siege to the great Spanish frontier fortress of Badajoz. At any cost this daring insolence had to be met, and Philip, with no able commanders now available, Don Juan being in Flanders, entrusted the leadership of his forces of 8000 men, raised with infinite sacrifice and difficulty, to his favourite, Don Luis de Haro. On the news of his approach the Portuguese raised the siege of Badajoz and recrossed the frontier ; but Haro, utterly inexperienced in warfare, was drawn into pursuing them, led into an ambush and put to ignominious flight, with the loss of guns, baggage, and most of his men.

This defeat, followed by the Battle of the Dunes a few months afterwards, proved to all the world that Spain had come to the end of her tether and could struggle no more. Material resources, faith in herself, belief in her mission, even confidence in her God, had all fled, and nothing was left to her but besotted pride and a sanctimonious ritual devotion which lightly covered a scoffing mockery of the noble ideals that had made her temporarily great. Peace had now, indeed, become for Philip absolutely necessary. There had been many efforts made through the influence of Anna of Austria, Queen of France, to come to an understanding with her brother, ever since the treaty of Münster ; but the demands of Mazarin, that the

[1] Braganza himself, John IV., had died in 1656, leaving his son, Alfonso VI., a minor.

French should continue to hold all they had taken, including Catalonia, had in every case frustrated the attempts. But the aspect of affairs was changing. Catalonia was heartily tired of the French, who left the province less liberty than it had enjoyed under the Castilian Kings, whilst the grave discontent and division in France against Mazarin's Government had rendered peace necessary even for him. But that which, above all, contributed to a peaceful agreement was the fact that Philip's health was evidently failing, and that only one life, that of the scrofulous epileptic infant, Philip Prosper, stood between the house of France and the Spanish throne. It is true that when Queen Anna had married Louis XIII. she had solemnly renounced for herself and her family the right of succession to Spain ; but some of the dowry which was to have been paid to her had not been paid, and it might be contended that as one condition of the contract had not been fulfilled the others could not be enforced as against the house of France. Mariana, Philip's second wife, was at Madrid quite as much in the capacity of Austrian ambassador as of Philip's consort, and she had always tried to prevent any closer union between France and Spain ; her object, aided by the German agents who prompted her, being to maintain the fatal alliance between the two branches of the house of Austria, which had dragged Spain to ruin.

In the summer of 1656 a sincere attempt had been made by France to come to an understanding with Philip. A skilled diplomatist, M. de Lionne, in the confidence of Mazarin, had arrived with great secrecy at Madrid, and was lodged at the Retiro,

2 G

where he and Haro held many conferences, with a result that an agreement on many points was arrived at, especially upon the retrocession of Catalonia (though not of Roussillon) to Spain. In one of their conferences Lionne noticed that Haro was wearing in his hat, doubtless for a purpose, a medal impressed with the portrait of the Infanta Maria Teresa. " If your King would give to my master for his wife the original of the portrait you wear," said Lionne, "peace might soon be made." [1] Haro passed over the matter lightly, for in the absence of a male heir to Philip it would have been impossible to marry Maria Teresa to the King of France ; but the idea was not a new one, and the possibility of bringing about such a match as a pledge of peace between France and Spain had often been mooted by the quidnuncs of Madrid. [2]

Lionne's negotiations came to nothing at the time, mainly because the knotty point of the Prince of Condé's position could not be settled ; but when the birth of Philip Prosper provided Philip with an heir, the marriage idea again came to the front, and made both sides in the subsequent peace negotiations much more conciliatory than they otherwise would have been, especially when there was a talk of marrying Louis XIV. elsewhere. He was, indeed,

[1] Lionne's own account of his negotiations in *Recueil des Instructions données aux Ambassadeurs Français*. Ed. Morel Fatio, Paris, 1894.

[2] On Good Friday, 1657, for instance, the procession, as usual, passed before the palace of Madrid, and as the carved group representing the Flight into Egypt passed the royal balconies a large flight of white doves was let loose. One of the doves, Barrionuevo says, flew direct to the window where the Infanta was standing, and settled upon her head, whilst another alighted upon the King's hat. Both birds were caught and liberated by the King's command, and all Madrid was soon talking of the good omen the event presented.

on a courting expedition to the south of France to
meet the Princess of Savoy, when Haro, in May 1659,
sent Antonio Pimentel in a hurry to Mazarin,
reminding him of what Lionne had said three
years before about a Spanish marriage. Anna of
Austria and Mazarin were quite willing ; and in a
very few weeks the diplomatists on both sides had
drawn up a protocol suspending hostilities, and
providing for a meeting of plenipotentiaries of
both Powers in the little Isle of Pheasants in the
Bidosoa River that separates France and Spain.
This was to take place in August, and in the meanwhile ministers were busy drawing up marriage
settlements and agreeing upon the main points in
dispute between the two Powers. Mariana struggled
hard to prevent the agreement by proposing a
marriage between the Infanta and the Archduke
Leopold, the Emperor's heir. She even prevailed
upon her brother to send the Archduke Sigismund
to replace Don Juan in Flanders, and to bring a
strong imperial army with him to defend Spanish
territory there. Before they could meet the
French, however, the truce between Philip and
Louis was signed (June 1659), and the Austrian
interest for the present had to accept defeat.

Peace or war, the stereotyped merrymaking
never ceased for very long in the Court of Madrid.
Like Olivares before them, Philip's ministers were
constantly on the look-out for new musicians,
buffoons, or beauties to distract him, and discovering fresh pretexts for shows.[1] To celebrate

---

[1] On the day of St. Blas, writes Barrionuevo, the King and Queen
go to the Retiro, and on the 8th February (1658) there will be the great
comedy there which will cost 50,000 ducats, with unheard of machines.

the birth of the sickly Philip Prosper, the festivities continued for months ; and in answer to the nun's remonstrances about it, the King invites her to tell him how he can fulfil his desire to withdraw his mind from worldly things, " since it is obligatory for me to live amongst men, and to be present at festivities and other public occasions, which I cannot avoid attending. In the midst of all this turmoil I should like to execute your directions, if my frailty does not prevent me from doing so. Help me, Sor Maria, and pray to God and His holy Mother to aid me in attaining such a boon." [1] In one of Philip Prosper's frequent illnesses a saintly friar from Jerusalem, one Father Antonio, went to see Philip, and brusquely told him, in reply to his request for prayers for the Prince's health, " that he, the King, ought to pray also, and leave off all these comedies and other rejoicings." [2] The Madrileños of Philip's time would no more abandon their idle pleasures than they would their daily bread. Fresh taxes of 2 per cent. more were put upon food, and upon every payment made of any sort ; even fireplaces and windows were taxed more heavily, the idea being to make people redeem these taxes by paying a sum down, and so, as Barrionuevo says, to get money quickly. " All this makes men of business desperate, for it is said that even upon loans and payments of every sort the

There will be 132 performers, 42 of them musical women brought from all parts of Spain. . . . One of them, the *Bezona*, is a very fine lady from Seville, and another one, the *Grifona*, has escaped from her prison, so that the feast will be brilliant, and will last from Shrove Sunday to Ash Wednesday.

[1] *Cartas de Sor Maria.*
[2] Barrionuevo.

tax is to be charged ; so that we shall soon have nothing to pay with but water and sunshine." [1]

Only a few days after this was written, the municipality of Madrid gave a luncheon to the eleven Royal Councils, handsome presents being given to all the guests, the cost of the entertainment being over 550,000 ducats ; and hardly a week passes without the record of two or three costly shows, bull-fights, masquerades, and tourneys, in which smart new clothes are always a notable feature, and the King and Queen are usually present, the young Marquis of Heliche being generally the busiest promoter. Madrid, although suffering from a winter more severe than had been known in the memory of man (February 1658), was full of foreigners and strangers, attracted by these continual shows, and doubtless much of the money squandered came ultimately from them ; but the people themselves must have been in dire straits, for robbery seems to have been openly resorted to, even by priests ; and so highly placed an ecclesiastic as Barrionuevo says of it : " I do not wonder, for the pinch of poverty is such that everybody is forced to do it."

Madrid, at the time, indeed, presented a strange picture of anarchy. The only rich people were the comparatively few who were concerned in the administration, either in Spain or the Colonies ; and they spent their money with the utmost prodigality, whilst the great bulk of the population lived from hand to mouth on the proceeds of this expenditure, gained either by service, work, or robbery. There was practically no industry,

[1] Barrionuevo,

except that carried on in a small way by foreigners ; and the vast majority of the inhabitants of Madrid lived, directly or indirectly, by government expenditure. Philip looked on helplessly, convinced apparently that his calamities were unavoidable, because sent for a special purpose by the Almighty as a scourge for his and his people's transgressions. Preachers unrebuked thundered out of pulpits to him that most of the evils might be avoided by energy. "Your Majesty is poor, and your ministers are rich," cried one to him. "You give grants, favours, pensions, and double pay to people such as these, who beguile you with vain shows. The noblest eagle may be left bare if plucked feather by feather ; and your Majesty is obliged to appeal to these very ministers, whom you enable to settle vast estates, for money necessary for your very food and garments."

In good truth, it was too late to preach to Philip now ; for he did little but register the decisions of others, and go through his dull round of duties with despairing, earthy face ; his great consolation, as he says again and again, being the letters of the nun, which assured him of the divine mercy and of the efficacy of constant prayer. To his great delight another son was born to him in December 1658, though the babe lived only for a few months ; but Philip Prosper lingered on still, through a sickly infancy. In the meanwhile Don Luis de Haro and Cardinal Mazarin were in close confabulation on the Isle of Pheasants, settling the terms of the much-needed peace ; and the death of Cromwell, and the probable restoration of the Stuarts to the English throne, gave a further

hope that, after a long lifetime of constant war,
Philip's days might end at peace with all the world.

In October 1659 the peace negotiations were
sufficiently advanced for a formal demand to be
made to Philip for his daughter's hand on behalf of
her cousin Louis XIV. The ambassador was one
of the greatest seigneurs of the Court of France,
Marshal de Grammont ; and though Madrid, with
good reason this time, assumed its most pompous
garb, and Spaniards held their heads high, yet de
Grammont, as he entered with his brilliant suite
into Philip's capital, consciously represented a new
dispensation that was in process of supplanting
that of Spain. For a century and a half Spain
had claimed precedence over all earthly Powers :
her language was that of culture and fashion ; her
literature, especially of the theatre and the novel,
had given the tone to the writers of Europe ; her
dress had set the fashion ; her soldiers had taught
the art of war ; and her explorers had borne to the
four quarters of the earth her traditions, her tongue,
and her religion. But the stately entrance of de
Grammont with his new airs and graces into the
palace of Madrid, after a devastating war extending
over thirty years, marked the opening of a new
epoch in the civilisation of the world. Spain was
the waning force, France was the youthful giant
with a long life before him ; the Planet King Philip,
spent and weary, was sinking to his yearned-for
rest after a reign of tragic failure ; the Roi Soleil
was climbing in the sky. All the courtly conventions of diplomatists, all the gracious politeness of de Grammont, all the consideration shown
by French statesmen to Spain in the treaty of

peace, could not hide these facts ; nor could it be concealed that this new friendship meant the end of the fatal union of Austria and Spain, whose aim had been to force orthodoxy upon the world.

Mariana frowned and pouted as Grammont and his company of princes and nobles bowed before her ; and the gloomy grandeur of the old palace of Madrid, with the richly sombre dresses of Philip and his courtiers, seemed to the triumphant and gaily dressed Frenchman, fresh from the sprightly youthful Court of Louis, to be in harmony with the old obscurantist régime which was passing. The visitors were liberal in recording their impressions of a society which they regarded as romantic and antique.[1] The description of a theatrical representation in the old palace of Madrid in honour of Grammont, written by one of his chaplains, will give a good idea of a characteric feature of Philip's Court at the time.

" The great saloon was lit only by six enormous wax candles in gigantic silver stands. On each side of the saloon, facing each other, were two boxes or tribunes with iron grilles before them. One of these was occupied by the Infanta, whilst the other was destined for the Marshal (Grammont). Two benches covered with Persian rugs ran along the sides beneath the boxes, also facing each other, upon which sat about twelve ladies of the Court, whilst we Frenchmen stood behind them. . . . The

---

[1] There are three French MS. narratives of it in the Bibliotheque Nationale, written by various hands, as well as a *Journal du Voyage d'Espagne*, by Bertaut, in print, Paris, 1669, and *La Veritable Rélation du Voyage*, etc., Toulouse, 1659. Several Spanish narratives of the embassy also exist in print and MS. in the Biblioteca Nacional.

Queen and the little Infanta entered, preceded by a lady holding a candle. When the King appeared he saluted the ladies and took his seat in the box on the right hand of the Queen, whilst the little Infanta sat on her left. The King remained motionless during the whole of the play, and only once said a word to the Queen ; although he occasionally cast his eyes round on every side. A dwarf was standing close by him. When the play was ended, all the ladies rose and gathered in the middle, as canons do after a service. Then joining hands in a row they made their courtesies, one by one, a ceremony that lasted some seven or eight minutes. In the meanwhile the King was standing, and he then bowed to the Queen, who bowed to the Infanta, after which they all joined hands and retired." [1]

It was far into the winter (1659) before the terms of the pregnant peace of the Pyrenees could be finally settled by the plenipotentiaries on the Isle of Pheasants. More than once the negotiations came to a deadlock, for, comparatively easy as the French conditions were, they were very bitter for the pride of Spain to swallow.[2] She had to surrender the province of Roussillon and most of Artois, as well as many of the principal cities of French Flanders, whilst the English kept her port of Dunkirk. But in return Catalonia willingly

[1] *Journal du Voyage d'Espagne*, par l'Abbe Bertaut, Paris, 1669.

[2] So jealous were the nations of one another still, that Mazarin strictly forbade any of his French followers from crossing the Spanish line during the conference : " *Dans la crainte qu'il avait que les Français, accoutumés à mépriser les étrangers et à se moquer de tous ceux qui ne sont pas vêtus à leur mode, ne fissent quelques déplaisirs aux espagnols, dont le procédé est plus serieux et plus modeste.*" "L'isle de la Conference et le Mariage du Roi," 1660.

became Spanish again under its old constitution, whilst the new King of England and his friends the Portuguese were excluded from the treaty. The rejoicings in Madrid, and the adulation of the favourite Haro, who was made Prince of the Peace, knew no bounds. At last, no matter, thought the lieges, at what cost, Spain was free from the war that had weighed her down for a whole generation ; and now the rebel Portuguese might be punished for their contumacy, and Philip be King of the Peninsula again. Don Juan, the King's son, was to have the honour of reconquering Portugal for Castile ; but for the present all minds were occupied by the ceremonious journey of King Philip and all his Court to the French frontier to conduct his daughter, the Infanta, to her waiting bridegroom.

For many months, notwithstanding Philip's expressed desire that things should be done as economically as possible, the preparations for the voyage had been carried out on a scale of magnificence surpassing that of all previous bridal progresses between Spain and France. The Spanish nobles and courtiers, taking their tone from Haro himself, were determined, even at the cost of their last ducat, that the Frenchmen should see that the country was neither exhausted materially nor humiliated morally. So again the old prodigal pride asserted itself, and Madrid pushed its poverty in the background, as it spent its money on gewgaws, or flocked to see the preliminary turnout of the royal equipages prepared for the King's journey to France.

" There were four litters, and fourteen coaches with six mules each ;—a fine sight ! The table services, newly made with the arms of Spain and France, which her Highness is to take with her, are a marvel of richness and beauty. The jewels for presents and for adornment exceed all price and praise. Each of the gentlemen who is to accompany the royal party is making preparations more in accordance with his spirit than with his means. They say that the Duke of Medina de las Torres will distinguish himself specially. He gives five suits of livery to each of his servants, one set alone of which made in Naples will cost 65,000 ducats ; whilst, as to his Excellency's own dresses, wonderful stories are told of them, and also of the jewels he is taking with him, worthy as they are of the greatness of his heart. The preparations of Don Luis de Haro can only be conceived by those who recollect that he is the luminary of the world upon which reflects and radiates most fully the majesty and brilliancy of our Sun-Monarch. The value of the horses and hackneys, with their harness and housings, alone are said to be worth a vast treasure ; but when we consider the rank of the persons with whom the horses of the Sun will enter Irun, these latter, richly caparisoned as they may be, will be unworthy of an occasion so supreme. It is likely enough that when our In-fanta took leave of the altars of Madrid her eyes were wet with tears ; but our muffled women, who spare nobody, said so in such a way as to hint that the tears were really hearty smiles. The Queen looks very sad at the King's going away." [1]

[1] *Avisos anonimos.*   Appendix to Barrionuevo.

On the 15th April 1660, Philip set forth on his famous journey to the French frontier to give his daughter Maria Teresa to his young nephew Louis XIV. for his wife, and meet in peace once more his sister Anna, whom he had not seen since their early youth, over forty years before. The train that accompanied him surpassed anything of the sort ever seen before in Spain. Don Luis de Haro himself was served by a household of 200 persons, and scores of other nobles vied with him in magnificence.[1] All the sumptuary pragmatics were suspended, and as a reaction after the long insistence upon plain, sombre attire for men, Philip's courtiers were gorgeous in the costly richness of their garb, determined as they were to impress the Frenchmen.

The land through which the long procession slowly made its way, at the rate of about six miles a day, was stark and ruined ; and provisions, as well as beds and all other necessaries, had to be carried for the whole multitude, the cavalcade covering over twenty miles of road. Such of the wretched peasants as were left in Castile [2] saluted their King with frantic joy as he passed ; for he looked so sad and sorry for them, and with so much wealth as he now displayed before their famished eyes, surely he would not grind them down to utter famine as he had done for these unhappy years of strife. All would be well now.

---

[1] A full account of the progress from day to day, written by an eye-witness, is *Viage del Rey Nuestro Señor à la Frontera de Francia.* Madrid, 1667.

[2] So few were they at this time, that it was projected to repopulate the rural districts by large immigration of Irish and Dalmatian families (Barrionuevo).

The Infanta was to be Queen of France, and she would not allow her father's realm to be laid desolate again by those over whom her young husband reigned. Everywhere hope blossomed again. The towns on the way regaled the vast concourse of courtiers with shows, banquets, and bull-fights; long-hidden hoards of money were brought out and spent in rejoicing now, even by the humbler farmer folk, for the great fear that all would be taken from them by the tax farmers had passed away.

At length, after six weeks of tedious travel over miserable roads, where overturns and other mishaps were frequent, the King and his Court entered St. Sebastian, where the first marriage ceremony was to be performed, on the 2nd June 1660. In the crowds of splendidly apparelled Spanish courtiers, whose names were as resounding as their pedigrees were long, there was one olive-skinned man, with a touzled mop of wavy black hair streaked with grey, whose fame was to outlive them all. His office, that of the King's quarter-master, and one of his chamberlains, kept him close to the person of Philip, who loved his company. Upon the breast of his dark, closely fitting tunic was embroidered in scarlet the long sword-shaped cross of Santiago, whilst an enamelled and diamond pendant hung from a rich gold chain around his neck; and Diego Velazquez, the painter, now growing old with his master, looked as distinguished as any in the throng, doing his courtier's service in the famous journey as if he had been merely a grandee of long lineage instead of a poor gentleman who happened to be a genius.[1]

[1] Palamino, *Life of Velazquez.*

All the magnificence that could be crammed into the humble town of St. Sebastian was there on the morning of the 2nd June 1660.[1] In the principal house, under canopies of damask stiff with bullion armorial embroideries, sat upon thrones side by side Philip and his daughter, the Patriarch of the Indies and the Bishop of Pamplona standing in their robes near to them, with Haro upon the steps of the daïs. Every inch of standing room was filled with the proudest nobles of Spain, intermingled with many masked and cloaked figures whom all knew or guessed were French princes, princesses, and nobles, who had crossed the frontier disguised to witness the ceremonies which some still hoped, notwithstanding the failures of past similar attempts, would " level the Pyrenees." One who was there writes : " The ladies-in-waiting were dazzlingly handsome, and all the multitude of people, grandees, peers, noble gentlemen, and others, stood with uncovered heads, their Majesties alone being seated ; whilst Don Fernando de Contreras, the Secretary of State, read aloud the solemn document in which the Queen of France, by oath on a Christ crucified, renounced for herself and hers for ever all claim to the succession of the Spanish throne." For a long hour and more the Secretary of State, on his knees, read the pompous sentences of the act which was in after years to convulse all Europe in war, and change the dynasty of Spain ; but those who listened to it

[1] An eye-witness, from whose unpublished MS. description of these ceremonies I have condensed some passages, says they were " de los mayores y de mayor lucimiento que ha visto Europa en muchos siglos." MS. Biblioteca Nacional, P. v. c. 27.

were more concerned with their own fatigue at standing in a crowd so long than at the vast import of the renunciation, whose effects were hidden in the womb of time.[1] When, at last, Contreras had finished reading, the Bishop stepped forth, and upon the Gospels and the crucifix Maria Teresa swore to keep inviolate the pledge contained in the act.

The next morning the humble parish church of St. Sebastian was transformed, by the " richest hangings and adornments necessary for the greatest wedding that ever was seen in the world, whilst their Majesties and the Court were a blaze of magnificence." Advancing with his daughter, Philip took his seat upon the curtained throne by the side of the high altar, whilst Maria Teresa stood beneath the canopy, and Don Luis Haro, who was honoured by holding the proxy of King Louis to marry her, stood a step below her. The church was crowded with French princes, princesses, and nobles in disguise intermingled with the Spaniards, and, as the pontifical mass was sung with its beautiful ceremonial, appealing to all the senses before that gorgeous assembly, St. Sebastian reached the apogee of its glory, never to be surpassed. When the sacrament was ended the Bishop descended to the canopy, where the Infanta and Haro were standing before the King. In answer to the ritual question whether she would take his Majesty the most Christian King for a

[1] In one of the narratives of the ceremonies from day to day, written by Roque de la Luna, one of Philip's household (MS. Biblioteca Nacional, P. v. c. 31, transcribed by me), he says " Don Francisco took an hour and a half to read it, and as we were all standing it seemed a very long time to us."

husband, the Infanta with streaming eyes turned and sank upon her knees before her father. Philip, himself overcome with emotion, bowed his head and gave his blessing to the daughter who was to be the pledge of future peace between Spain and France ; and the Bishop had to repeat his question three times before the weeping Princess could summon composure enough to reply in the affirmative. Then she and Haro together placed their hands in a great gold dish that stood upon a side table, whilst Haro in the name of King Louis XIV. accepted Maria Teresa of Austria as his legitimate wife. Taking a gold ring from the centre of the salver upon which their hands rested, the Spanish minister placed it upon the rim near the fingers of the Infanta, but without touching them ; and then with a sweeping flood of melody the *Te Deum* burst out, whilst the great guns of the fortress upon the crag overhanging the church thundered their message to the two realms that another Spanish Princess was Queen of France.[1] In the midst of the uproar King Philip led his daughter from the church, followed by all the glittering crowd.

That afternoon the royal party rode to the neighbouring land-locked Port of Pasages three miles away, and so to Renteria for dinner, and by Oyarzun to the ancient fortress village of Fuentarrabia on its jutting peninsula, from which you may cast a stone to France on the other side of the river mouth. The roads were so narrow and bad that the maids of honour were upset on the way ; and Don Luis de Haro, anxious as he was to do

[1] " The noise was so great that it seemed as if the world was crumbling," says the narrator from whose manuscript I am quoting.

honour to the Sovereign who had made him little
less than a King, he was unable to meet him on the
narrow rocky causeway, but perforce had to stand,
surrounded by the King's Guards in their new
yellow uniforms, at the gate of the ancient palace
fortress upon its cliff, that twenty-two years before
had so stoutly withstood the siege of the French by
land and sea.

The following day, whilst preparations for the
public interviews upon the Isle of Pheasants were
being made, Philip embarked with his daughter,
Haro, and a very few attendants, amongst whom
was Diego Velazquez, and landed privately upon
the little island in mid stream. The buildings,
which had been specially erected for the peace conference of the previous autumn, were constructed
with the jealous punctiliousness which always
characterised the intercourse between France and
Spain. The eyot was divided into a Spanish and a
French half, and the houses, each in its respective
territory, were connected by a corridor, the conference hall, which stood upon the dividing line, being
half upon Spanish and half on French soil. Even in
Philip's private meeting with the sister from
whom he had been separated and at war so long,
the utmost precision of etiquette was preserved.
Landing on the Spanish part of the island, and
entering the Spanish house, he bade all his attendants stay behind, except Haro, Velazquez, and one
or two more, who alone accompanied him to the
hall, where, on the French side of the dividing line
across the hall, stood Anna of Austria.

The meeting was a painful one, for when they
had last met Philip and his sister had been in the

flower of youth, full of hope and bright ambition ; and now both were old and broken, with lives of bitterness behind them. Both brother and sister had been slaves of their passions, and had surrendered their regal power to other hands. They had been but figureheads of State ; and though, as was the case with all their house, their family affection had been strong, national aspirations had been too powerful for them, and victor and vanquished, brother and sister, must have felt themselves, for all their grandeur, the helpless victims of forces beyond their control or understanding. Anna of Austria broke down into piteous tears when she saw the unhappy face of her brother ; and, after a few low-spoken words of comfort had passed between them, there came tiptoeing silently behind the Cardinal and Don Luis, who stood behind Queen Anna, a handsome young man with aquiline features and a nascent black down upon his upper lip. He wore, in the French fashion of the time, high red heels to his shoes ; and a flowing black curled periwig fell upon the wide Walloon collar of fine lawn that covered the shoulders of his satin skirted-coat. Peeping over the shoulders of those before him,[1] himself supposed to be unseen, thus Louis XIV. first looked upon his bride, and upon the King the ruin of whose realm and dynasty was to make way for the supremacy of France and the Roi Soleil.

At length, on Sunday, 6th June, all was ready for the ceremonial meeting and delivery of the bride to her new country. At a signal both

---

[1] Narrative of Roque de Luna, MS., Biblioteca Nacional, Madrid, P. v. c. 31.

monarchs stepped into their boats at the same time, Philip in Fuenterrabia and Louis in St. Jean de Luz, followed soon by crowds of other boats filled with courtiers as fine as silks and satins and bullion tissues could make them, for sumptuary decrees were all thrown to the winds now ; whilst strong armed forces, 12,000 troops in all, with loaded arms and new uniforms, stood upon each side of the tiny stream, as many as 4000 cavalry being arrayed on the French bank, with numbers of pikemen and guards ; " all smart looking troops, but both men and horses small," said a Spanish expert, who thought Philip's fine array of red and yellow guards " better troops, smarter and with better horses." [1] As far as the eye reached on either side, crowds of people stood upon the banks, and far away upon the hills overlooking the scene, which for most of them promised peace and renewed prosperity ; whilst the ante-rooms of the conference hall which was to be the scene of the interview were packed to suffocation by a privileged crowd of nobles and courtiers of both nations.

At the same moment the two Kings landed upon their respective ends of the island, and at the same moment they and their suites entered the conference hall by opposite doors, Philip leading his daughter, followed by Haro and a great house-hold, and Louis his mother with Mazarin, and forty ladies-in-waiting behind. Advancing to the line that divided the room, Louis made as if to kneel to Philip, who prevented him from doing so by clasp-ing him in his arms. " My son," said Philip, " I

[1] Narrative of Roque de Luna, MS., Biblioteca Nacional, Madrid, P. c. v. 31.

welcome you. For me this has been the happiest
day I have ever known or shall know; for I see
your Majesty is as well as I can wish"; and then,
pointing to the Infanta, he continued : " the only
person after your Majesty who could have brought
me on this journey is this piece of my own heart,
that I have brought to give you for your wife ; and
I trust that your Majesty will hold her in the
esteem she deserves, not only as Queen of France
and my daughter, but also in consideration of the
goodwill with which I give her to you." [1] Anna
of Austria was weeping copiously the while ; but
Louis himself, not to be outdone in courtesy, was
fully equal to the occasion. " My father," he said,
" only the favours I am receiving from the generous
and potent hands of your Majesty could force me to
confess myself not only unworthy to be the son of
so powerful a monarch, but also your humble
vassal," and with that he warmly returned his
uncle's embrace.

Much more flattering talk there was about
Philip's potency and strength, and the obligation of
France to him. It pleased the Spaniards vastly ;
for words with them ever took the place of deeds
when their pride was touched, and every courteous
word of the Frenchmen was as balm in Gilead to
men who, in their heart of hearts, knew that poverty,
humiliation and defeat had befallen them and
their country. Many tears there were, too, when
Philip formally handed his daughter to her new
husband, and the four sovereigns took their seats
side by side on thrones arranged for them across the

---

[1] MS. narrative of an anonymous eye-witness. Biblioteca Nacional,
Madrid, P. v. c. 27.

line. Then Mazarin came forward with a missal in his hand, upon which Philip on his knees swore to keep the terms of the peace, and the Patriarch of the Indies administered a similar oath to Louis. The public act being thus ended, the hall was cleared of the crowds of nobles that encumbered it, and for four hours the royal party gave themselves up to familiar intercourse ; after which Louis with his Court, " the most enchanting sight ever seen in the world," says the Spanish chronicler, rode off to St. Jean de Luz, and Philip returned by Irun to Fuenterrabia.

Of the costly presents on both sides, of the overwhelming magnificence of the subsequent ceremonies in St. Jean de Luz, where the personal marriage took place,[1] and of the delight of the gallant Spanish courtiers at the nice French fashion of kissing all the ladies, it boots not here to tell ; but as Philip and his cumbrous Court slowly wended their way home again to Madrid, the younger courtiers of both sexes, at all events, took back with them something like a contempt for the old Spanish fashions which had persisted so long.[2] The *golilla* was voted stiff and

[1] Contemporary descriptions of these ceremonies in French are numerous. One, published in Paris in June 1660, is specially interesting. It is called " Le mariage du Roy, célébré á St. Jean de Luz." The occasion remains one of the great glories of St. Jean de Luz, where the house in which Maria Teresa lodged still stands, and is called "La maison de l'Infante." A series of interesting tapestry pictures of the ceremonies may be seen in the exhibition palace in the Champs Elysées, Paris.

[2] Some of the Spanish narrators mention with surprise and chagrin that neither the Spanish troops nor courtiers were so fine as the French. The anonymous Newsletter writer (sequel to Barrionuevo) says : " Many of our courtiers write (*i.e.* to Madrid) that the French gentlemen and ladies who came to the ceremonies were so numerous, and the adornments they wore were so rich and abundant, that we were evidently inferior to them, although much care had been taken on our side to excel, and no expense had been spared. So we cannot say this time, as we have said before, that the French finery was nothing but frills, furbelows, and feathers."

ungraceful when compared with the fine lace cravats of the French ; black-framed goggles looked frumpish ; the *ropilla* and close doublet were not half so modish as the full skirted long tunics, open in the front and showing a smart vest, that Louis and his gentlemen had worn ; and who would care to wear thin lank hair, even when a topknot on the brow and *guedejas* before the ears adorned it, when he could buy a splendid flowing curly periwig such as made the French look so stately ? It is true that the change of fashion that began on the banks of the Bidasoa did not go very deep or far away from Court; for the common people clung to the old modes still, and the wars that divided Spain forty years afterwards caused French fashions, or anything but Spanish, to be loathed by all ranks as unpatriotic. But, nevertheless, this great transmigration of Spanish courtiers to the French frontier in 1660 was the first opening of the door by which some glimpses of light from a new Europe entered Spain, the first inkling to Spaniards that anything outside their own frontiers could be estimable and worth imitating.

Philip was welcomed back to Madrid by his wife and his people, with great rejoicing for his safety, on the 26th June, and even poor suffering little Philip Prosper, tricked out in a military uniform with a sword by his side, was carried in his nurse's arms to greet his father as he ascended the stairs of his palace, though the child fell into a series of exhausting fevers immediately afterwards. The King's base-born son, Don Juan, of whom Queen Mariana was bitterly jealous, was impatiently waiting outside Madrid[1]

---

[1] It was against the etiquette of the Court for a left-handed son of the sovereign to stay in Madrid, or even to visit it without special permission.

for troops and means to be provided for him to conquer Portugal ; Don Luis de Haro, who had ignominiously failed in the task himself, not being at all active in forwarding Don Juan's ambition. It was six months more before an army was at last got together, and, early in 1661, Don Juan crossed the frontier with 20,000 men, whilst Osuna's force of 15,000 co-operated with him in the north. But the marriage of Charles II. of England with a Portuguese wife had given to Portugal the aid of England ; and though Don Juan fought well, he had now Marshal Schomberg with an English force to cope with, in addition to the Portuguese, and he made but little way. Bitter complaints came from him to his father that Haro would not provide him with the resources necessary for the task he had to do. But Haro died at the end of the year 1661,[1] and after that Mariana's influence against him crippled Don Juan more than ever, though at one period the civil dissensions in Portugal enabled him to overrun for a time some of the central provinces of the country.

The loss of Don Luis de Haro affected Philip greatly. The minister was not a strong man, but his conciliatory manner and quiet industry had prevented the existence of such violent antagonism to him as had ruined his predecessors. The nun of Agreda had never ceased to urge upon Philip the need for hard work on his part, and the King had wearily defended himself, again and again, by saying

The rumour, though untrue, that Don Juan was to be allowed to come to Madrid and welcome Philip at this time caused much heart-burning.

[1] The Newsletter writer (*Avisos anonimos*) says that when Don Juan was told of Haro's death, he replied: " My father has lost a great minister ; let us go hunting," which he did immediately, to show his satisfaction.

that it was impossible for him to do everything. Indeed, the whole system was so cumbrous that under it the monarch's whole time was taken up in reviewing the interminable reports of the various Councils, and signing papers placed before him, leaving him no opportunity for initiating policies. When Count Castrillo, Haro's uncle, entered the King's chamber one morning late in 1661, and announced Haro's sudden death, he told the King that all the official papers had been locked up, and requested the King's instructions as to who should take charge of the key. Philip meditated for a while, and then replied: "Put it on that table," much to Castrillo's disappointment, as he expected to be appointed chief minister. Philip, however, thought this time really to do without an all-powerful vice-king, such as he had had all his life; and as soon as Haro was buried he issued decrees dividing the administration between Castrillo, the Duke of Medina de las Torres, the Inquisitor-General, and himself, and ordering that every question from all quarters should be submitted to him before decision. Entering the Queen's apartments a few days afterwards, he found all the ladies chattering upon the floor, as usual, about what a bold preacher had said in the pulpit that morning: that the King was going to show the Councils now that he was really King. Hearing this talk, Philip said: "I am quite old enough now to see things for myself, and I shall be glad if those who know of anything that needs remedying will advise me of it, and I will see to it. Things are not going on as they had been doing."

There appears, indeed, to have been a dead set against Haro's family as soon as he died. The

Marquis of Heliche, his son and heir, claimed, amongst other lucrative offices held by his father, the Keepership of the Retiro. This offended Philip, who refused him the office, and gave it to the Duke of Medina de las Torres. Heliche was soon afterwards accused of a plot to blow up the Retiro, which brought him and his family into the deepest disgrace. One morning in March 1662, three packets of gunpowder, connected by a train with a slow match, was found under the stage of the Retiro Theatre among a lot of heavy stage machinery, which had been used in a comedy recently represented, and designed and paid for by Heliche, but which was now to be used for a play to be produced before the King and Queen under other auspices. As soon as the discovery was made (in time to avert disaster), five underlings connected with the theatre, two of them being Moorish slaves, were arrested ; and when Heliche heard of it he went to the gaoler, saying that as one of the Moors had been punished by him, and had his ears cut off, he would probably say that he, Heliche, had prompted the crime. He therefore offered the gaoler a bribe to kill the Moor, by giving him a slight wound and anointing it with a poisonous unguent which Heliche would send. The gaoler divulged the plot, and the page of the Marquis was captured with the unguent in his possession. The Marquis was then arrested, and though great efforts were made by his kinsmen to obtain his release, four Duchesses kneeling before Philip at one time to beg for mercy, the King refused to interfere, though he said he was sorry the lad had not escaped. In the end the Marquis was let off with a term of banish-ment, apparently on the ground that he was bewitched. His own excuse for the crime was that he did not wish his scenery and stage effects to be used by the Duke of Maqueda. The whole case is an interesting illustration of the morals of the time.

Soon Madrid had something more piquant to talk about even than this ; though for days no one dared to whisper it above his breath. But by and by Liars' Walk became bolder, and, with the accompaniment of many a sign of the cross, the story ran through the city, growing ever larger with additions as it ran, that devilish arts were being practised upon the King. It appears that a certain alcalde suspected that the house in Madrid of a lady, the sister of a judge at Granada, was being used as a factory of base money ; and on going thither to search the premises and arrest the inmates, he discovered amongst the instruments for counterfeit coining, two engraved metal plates, each of which bore the device of a heart pierced with an arrow, one being inscribed with the name of " Philip IV., son of Philip III. and Margaret," and the other with the name and parentage of Don Luis de Haro, with other words taken from the Scriptures ; the hearts themselves bearing the words, " I am thine, and thou art mine." [1] The alcalde thought that this looked serious, and carried the incised plates to the Inquisition, which promptly decided that it was a case of witchcraft, and at once sent its hosts of familiars to worm out the rest of the dreadful story, whilst sweeping into their silent dungeons all who might be suspected of complicity or knowledge, and giving occasion thus for all Madrid to invent its own details. The case dragged on in secret, as

[1] *Avisos.* Sequel to Barrionuevo.

was the wont of Inquisition investigations, but thenceforward until his death the awe - stricken whisper was never long silent that the King lay under a maleficent charm ; and grave heads were shaken knowingly, and crossed fingers kissed devoutly, when any fresh misfortune befell him.

Evil fate, indeed, gave Philip little truce from sorrow. The frail life of his only son Philip Prosper flickered out on the 1st November 1661, and a week later the bereaved father wrote to the nun—

"The long illness of my son and my constant attendance at his bedside have prevented me from answering your letter, nor has my grief allowed me to do so, until to-day. I confess to you, Sor Maria, that my grief is great, as is natural after losing such a jewel as this. But in the midst of my sorrow I have tried to offer it to God, and to submit to His divine will ; believing most earnestly that He will order all things for the best, which is the most important thing. I can assure you that what grieves me even more than my loss is that I see clearly that I have angered God, and that these punishments are sent in retribution for my sins. I only yearn to know how to amend myself, and to fulfil the divine will by avoiding transgression, with which end I will try my hardest, surrendering my life, if necessary, in order to succeed. Help me, as a true friend, with your prayers to placate the ire of God, and supplicate Him, since He has taken away my son, to send a safe delivery to the Queen, whose confinement we expect every hour ; to protect her, and grant that her offspring should be for His service, for otherwise I desire it not. The Queen has borne

the blow as a true Christian, though sorrowfully.
I am not surprised at this, for she is an angel. O
Sor Maria! if I had been able to carry out your
doctrines, perhaps I should not find myself in this
state. Pray to God that my eyes may be opened,
so that I may comply with His will in all things."

And then in a postscript, written a day later, the
King, full of gratitude, conveys the happy news to
his friend that another son had been born to him.

" Our Lord has deigned to send me back my son,
by bringing me another ; for which I am as grateful
as so signal a boon and mercy demands. Help me,
Sor Maria, to prostrate myself at His feet and
beseech Him to preserve this pledge, if it be for His
service, otherwise I desire it not, but to bow my
head to His will. The Queen and the child are well,
and I am content."

The child that was born to Philip's old age was
greeted, as his many predecessors had been, by violent
rejoicings in the capital, though the King took
little or no part in them beyond the religious ceremonies ; for he really was trying hard now to do
without a minister, working early and late at the
drudgery of administration, drafting new stern
pragmatics to reform the corruption of his capital,
which had become more scandalous than ever, and
bringing to book many of those who had grown
rich under Don Luis de Haro. Money was needed
for the Portuguese war, and the coinage was again
debased ; clothes were ordered to be plainer than
ever, no silk was to be worn by officials, and no one
was to have more than two mules to his coach ;

the owners of carriages were to pay for the paving
of the streets of Madrid, which had become simply
quagmires, whilst, to the joy of the populace, the
taxes on food entering Madrid were reduced by one
half. The speculators who farmed these dues cried
out that they were being defrauded, and they were
recompensed by a cession to them of half the 10
per cent. property tax on Madrid.

Thus, with reforms in judicial procedure, the
cancelling of grants and pensions which could not
be justified, and desperate efforts to suppress the
open vice that paraded the capital, Philip, for the
third time in his life (in 1661–1662), tried to carry
into effect the saintly precepts in which he believed.
Much of this new zeal for reform was evidently
owing to the insistence of Sor Maria, who was never
tired of pointing her lesson. Soon after Haro's
sudden death she wrote—

" Let your Majesty order your ministers strictly
to punish the rich and powerful people who cheat
the poor by usurping their property, make your
inferior ministers do justice with equity and im-
partiality, let them punish foul vices and all sorts
of sin, and let the superior government of your
Court assume a better form. And, for God's
sake, moderate some of the taxes the poor people
pay, for I know that villages have been depopulated
in consequence of them ; and that the poor people
only keep body and soul together on barley-
bread and the herbs of the fields. . . . So many
changes in the coinage, too, are most injurious." [1]

Philip did his best, but he was sick and weary,

[1] *Cartas de Sor Maria*, 25th November 1661.

and soon slackened in his personal efforts. Nothing that he did, indeed, seemed to prosper, and in his constant letters to Sor Maria his despairing references to his own sins being the cause of all his troubles became increasingly poignant. With infinite trouble and scraping together of resources, he managed to raise another army and full campaign material, with which his son Don Juan was to reconquer Portugal for the crown.[1] At first in the spring of 1663 all went well with Don Juan, who invaded Portugal and captured the important city of Evora, but he was met near that place by the English and Portuguese and defeated on the 8th June. Attempting to retreat into Spain, he was overtaken, and again the Spanish army suffered a disastrous rout, with a loss of 8000 men, with baggage, standards, and arms. Don Juan himself fought bravely, pike in hand, but was borne away in the flight, and with difficulty escaped to Badajoz. He was then re-called to Madrid, and in long conferences with his father's ministers [2] arranged a new campaign for the

[1] It was necessary for Philip to seize all the securities lodged in the hands of the contractors and money-lenders for the raising and provision of this army, the excuse being that the contractors were swindling him. It appears that they bought barley in Estremadura at 8 reals the fanega (1½ bushels), and sold it to the army for 56 reals. The contractors (Genoese and Portuguese) offered 3½ million ducats for the securities back again, but it was refused. Another seizure of securities left with loan-mongers and contractors was made in the following year, which completed the ruin of several of them. *Avisos*, 1660–1664.

[2] Don Juan was kept in Madrid for many months, much to his own disgust, as he saw that it was in consequence of the intrigues of Queen Mariana to separate him from the army altogether. One of her plans was to induce the King to order Don Juan to conduct to Germany the young Infanta Margaret, who had just been betrothed to her uncle, the Emperor. Don Juan stood out firmly against this. He hated the Austrian connection, and Mariana and her German advisers were his enemies. Affairs came to a head in October 1663, when Don Juan forced the pace by boldly urging his father to make him an Infante of Spain

following year, though it was evident now to
everyone that the reconquest of her lost dominion
was beyond the material and moral strength of
Spain.

Ever since the Restoration in England, Charles
II. had been making tentative efforts to bring about
peace with Spain. Philip it was certain would not
officially recognise the independence of Portugal ;
but perhaps a *modus vivendi* might be arranged, by
means of a long truce or otherwise, so that direct
trade between England and Spain might be restored, and the mutual injuries inflicted at sea be
stopped. The advantage to Spain would, of course,
be great, because the silver fleets were constantly
preyed upon by English privateers ; but the English
shipmasters and merchants also had felt severely
the deprivation of Spanish trade ; and after the
crushing defeat of Don Juan at Amegial, just
referred to, in June 1663, it seemed a good
opportunity for Charles II. to suggest directly to
Philip the advisability of an agreement.

The envoy chosen was that Dick Fanshawe
who had been in Spain in the time of Bristol and
Aston, and had lately negotiated the marriage
with Catharine of Braganza. He, stout loyalist as
he had been during all the Commonwealth, was Sir
Richard Fanshawe, Baronet, now, and in high
favour with Charles, who, it was thought, would
have made him Secretary of State. He was instructed to set forth to Philip the benefit that

---

and first minister. This frightened Mariana and her *alter ego*, Father
Nithard, her Jesuit confessor ; and it had the effect desired by Don Juan,
of obtaining his despatch from Madrid to the army at Badajoz. During
his stay in the capital he had offended nearly all the nobles by his haughty
arrogance. *Avisos.*

would accrue to both States from a reopening of maritime trade, and to say how anxious the King of England was to be friendly with the Catholic King, whom he esteemed so highly, notwithstanding the refusal of Spain to deal with him during the Commonwealth and the expulsion of his agents from Madrid at that time, as well as the closing of the Spanish ports to Prince Rupert's fleet. The matter of Portugal was to be very tenderly handled. Fanshawe was instructed to say that the King of Spain " cannot imagine that we will ever persuade him to deprive himself of his reputed right to the kingdom of Portugal, but whether the determination of that difference may not be advantageously suspended till a more favourable conjuncture, and until the crown of Spain be less liable to accidents, will be his part to judge." [1]

Fanshawe arrived in Cadiz on the 24th February (O.S.) 1664, and nothing could exceed the honour shown to the English ambassador and his wife by the magnates of Andalucia. The keys of the city were tendered to him in a " great silver basin," and he was asked to give the password for the night, which, courtier like, he did in the form of " *Viva el Rey Catolico.*" Very different was the welcome that had awaited poor Ascham in the same port fourteen years before ; though Fanshawe, overcome by all this ceremonious posturing, hoped that it was " not instead of substance, for then it would be very tedious and irksome to me, indeed, but an earnest prognostick of it, which

---

[1] Instructions to Sir Richard Fanshawe. *Original Letters of Sir Richard Fanshawe,* London, 1702.

time will try when I come to treat." [1]   Everywhere,
as Fanshawe travelled towards the capital, he was
treated with almost royal honours ; bull-fights, cane-
tourneys, and, of course, the usual comedies being
offered by nobles on the way : and it was the 7th
May before he reached Vallecas in the outskirts
of Madrid, where he remained for a time, as Philip
was staying at Aranjuez, and no house had been
provided in the capital for Fanshawe's accommodation ; the famous " house with the seven
chimneys" being then occupied by the Venetian
ambassador.

For the next five weeks the exchange of visits
of compliment and ceremonial generalities with
the Duke of Medina de las Torres, now Philip's
principal minister, and many other nobles and
officials, occupied the time of Fanshawe and his
clever wife ; who wrote, " Though the men visited
my husband, I could not suffer the ladies to visit
me, though they much desired it, because I was
so straitened in lodgings that in no sort were they
convenient to receive persons of that quality, in
not being capacious enough for my own family."
The gossips of the Calle Mayor were full of the
visit of the English peace-envoy, and saw all
manner of grave political import in the difficulty of
finding him a house ; though Fanshawe himself attributes it to its true cause, namely, the insufficient
house room in the capital ; though he offered *carte
blanche* as to terms, and to pay a year's rent in
advance in silver. After much delay and resist-

[1] Fanshawe's *Original Letters*. A most naïve and amusing account
of his embassy in Spain, where he died, is in Lady Fanshawe's *Memoirs*,
of which a new and fully annotated edition has recently been published.

ance on the part of the Venetian ambassador, who wished to retain the house after his departure for the accommodation of his successor, the English ambassador was once more housed in the "house with the seven chimneys," after he had stayed for a time at a house standing in its own grounds outside the Fuencarral gate at Santa Barbara.

At length, Philip having returned from Aranjuez, Fanshawe made his state entry into the capital, and had his first audience of Philip.

"On Wednesday the 8/18th June," says Lady Fanshawe, "my husband had his audience of his Catholic Majesty, who sent the Marquis de Malpica to conduct him, bringing him a horse of his Majesty for my husband to ride on, and thirty more for his gentlemen, and his Majesty's coach with his guard, that he (*i.e.* Malpica) was captain of. No ambassador's coach accompanied my husband but the French, who did it contrary to the King's command, who had before, upon my husband's demanding the custom of ambassadors accompanying all other ambassadors that came to this Court at their audience, replied that, although it had been so it should never be again ; saying that it was a custom brought into this Court within less than twenty-five years.[1] My husband, about eleven of the clock, set forth out of his lodgings thus. First went all those gentlemen of the town and palace that came to

[1] The controversy on this point is fully set forth in Fanshawe's own letter to Lord Holles. The French ambassador's exceptional courtesy to the Englishman somewhat disconcerted the Spaniards, who thought there was some political significance behind it.

accompany my husband, then went twenty footmen, all in new liveries of the same colour we used to give, which is dark green cloth with a frost upon green lace. Then went all my husband's gentlemen, and next before himself his *camarados*, two and two (here follow the eight names). Then my husband, in a very rich suit of clothes, of a dark fille (feuille) morte brocade laced with silver and gold lace, nine laces, every one as broad as my hand, and a little silver and gold lace laid between them, both of very curious workmanship. His suit was trimmed with scarlet taffeta ribbon, his stockings of white silk upon long scarlet silk ones, his shoes black with scarlet shoe-strings and garters, his linen very finely laced with very rich Flanders lace, a black beaver buttoned on the left side with a jewel of twelve hundred pounds, a curious wrought old gold chain made at the Indies, at which hung the King his master's picture richly set with diamonds, cost three hundred pounds, which his Majesty in great grace and favour had been pleased to give him at his coming home from Portugal. On his fingers he wore two very rich rings, his gloves trimmed with the same ribbon as his clothes. All his whole family (*i.e.* suite) was very richly clothed according to their several qualities." [1]

In this great magnificence Sir Richard Fanshawe rode through Madrid with the Marquis of Malpica by his side, followed by the Teuton guard, groups of pages and lackeys, and then the royal coach. After that came a coach drawn by four black horses, the finest state coach, says Lady Fanshawe, that ever

[1] Lady Fanshawe's *Memoirs*.

came out of England, and to describe its grandeur nothing but the lady's own words will do justice.

" It was of rich crimson velvet, laced with broad silver and gold lace, fringed round with a massy gold and silver fringe, and the falls of the boots so rich that they hung almost down to the ground. The very fringe cost almost four hundred pounds. The coach was very richly gilt on the outside, and very richly adorned with brass work, with rich tassels of gold and silver hanging round the top of the curtains round about the coach. The curtains were of rich damask fringed with silver and gold. The harness for six horses was richly embossed with brass work, with reins and tassels for the horses of crimson silk, silver and gold. That coach is said to be the finest that ever entered Madrid."

After it followed a host of other coaches, which, fine as they were, must have appeared dull by the side of such a chariot as this. Fanshawe passed through an admiring crowd both outside and inside the palace, for the Madrileños ever loved finery ; and at length reached the presence of Philip, who received him courteously, and many complimentary speeches, meaning nothing, were exchanged ; after which ceremonious visits had to be paid to Queen Mariana and her children, the Infanta Margaret, now called the Empress, by virtue of her betrothal to her uncle, and the scrofulous rickety infant, Don Carlos, now Philip's only son.

A week afterwards, Sir Richard had his first private interview with the King at the Buen Retiro. Philip was ill, and unequal now to much exertion, so that after Fanshawe's long address on the need for peace, and the conditions upon which it might be attained, he could only request that the whole of the points might be put in writing for his careful consideration. Soon after this, on the 27th June, Lady Fanshawe first went to salute Queen Mariana, and thus gives her impressions of what she saw—

" I waited on the Queen and the Empress (*i.e.* the little Infanta Margaret) with my three daughters and all my train. I was received at the Buen Retiro by the guard, and afterwards when I came upstairs by the Marquesa de Hinojosa, the Queen's *Camarera Mayor*. Through an infinite number of people I passed to the Queen's presence, where her Majesty was seated at the upper end under a cloth of state upon three cushions, and on her left hand the Empress upon three more. The ladies were all standing. After making my last reverence to the Queen, her Majesty and the Empress, rising up and making me a little curtsey, sat down again. Then I, by my interpreter, Sir Benjamin Wright, said those compliments that were due from me to her Majesty, to which her Majesty made a gracious and kind reply. Then I presented my children, whom her Majesty received with great grace and favour. Then her Majesty, speaking to me to sit, I sat down upon a cushion laid for me above all the ladies, but below the Camarera Mayor (no woman taking place of her but Princesses). The children sat on the other side, mingled with the Court ladies that are maids-of-honour. Thus, after passing half an hour in discourse, I took my leave of her Majesty and the

Empress, making reverences to all the ladies in passing."

Of the various times the Fanshawes saw the King or Queen no detailed account need be given here, as the descriptions add nothing to our knowledge ; nor is it necessary to dwell upon the accounts given of the Court diversions, which have already been described fully in the earlier pages of this book. Lady Fanshawe's opinions, however, of Spain and Spaniards generally are quaint. She thinks that the usually accepted English idea that Spain is a land of famine is unjust, especially for those who could afford to pay.

" There is not in the Christian world," she says, "better wines than their midland (*i.e.* southern) wines, especially sherry and canary. Their water tastes like milk, and their wheat makes the sweetest and best bread in the world. Bacon is beyond belief good ; the Segovia veal much whiter, larger, and fatter than ours. They have a small bird that lives and fattens on grapes and corn—so fat that it exceeds the quantity of flesh. They have the best partridges I ever ate, and the best sausages, and salmon, pike, and seabream, which they send up in pickle called *escabeche* in Madrid ; and dolphins, which are excellent meat,[1] besides carps and many other sorts of fish. The cream called *nata* is much sweeter and thicker than ever I saw in England. Their eggs much exceed ours ; and so all sorts of salads, roots, and fruits. . . . Besides that, I have ate many sorts of biscuits, cakes, cheese, and excellent sweetmeats. . . . Their olives, which are

[1] The fish she calls dolphins were probably tunny.

nowhere so good. Their perfumes of amber excel
all the world in their kind, both for clothes, household stuff, and fumes ; and there is no such waters
made as at Seville."

The good lady, too, was much enamoured of the
courtesy of Spaniards.

" They are civil to all, as their qualities require, with highest respect ; so I have seen
a grandee and a duke stop his horse, when an
ordinary woman passeth over a kennel, because
he would not spoil her clothes, and put off his
hat to the meanest woman that makes reverence,
though it be to their footmen's wives. . . . They
are punctual in visits, men to men and women to
women. They visit not together, except their
greatest ministers of State to wives of public
ministers from Princes. . . . They are generally
pleasant and facetious company, but in this their
women exceed, who seldom laugh and never aloud,
but are the most witty in repartees and stories and
notions in the world. . . . They work little, but
that rarely well, especially in monasteries (*i.e.*
convents). They all paint white and red, from the
Queen to the cobbler's wife, old and young, widows
excepted, which never go out of close mourning,
nor wear gloves nor show their hair after their
husband's death, and seldom marry. They delight
much in the feasts of bulls and in stage plays, and
take great pleasure to see their little children act
before them in their own houses, which they will do
to perfection. . . . Until their daughters marry
they never stir so much as down stairs, nor marry
for no consideration under their quality, which to

prevent, if their fortunes will not procure them husbands, they make them nuns. They are very magnificent in their houses, furniture, pictures of the best, jewels, plate, and clothes ; most noble in presents, entertainments, and in their equipage." [1]

Fanshawe's mission made but slow progress, for the pride of Spain with regard to Portugal still stood in the way, and Philip was hoping against hope that the campaign of the following year, 1665, would restore to him the crown he had lost. He was still straining every nerve to get money ; and as a last fatal resource in order to relieve as he hoped the distress of the treasury, he now reduced the value of the silver money to half, so that, as Lady Fanshawe says, " the pistole that was this morning at 82 *reals* was now proclaimed to go but for 48, which was above £800 loss to my husband." [2] At length, in the spring, by such devices as this— seizing all the securities lodged for loans, etc. —another army was got together. Don Juan, by the intrigues of the Austrian faction, was recalled and sent into semi-disgrace to Consuegra ; the Count of Caracena, distinguished in the war with the Turks on the frontier of Hungary, being en- trusted with the task of reconquering Portugal.

Philip, indeed, at this time, as his health and strength decayed, was surrounded by intrigue, intended, as it did, to drag unhappy Spain once more into the fatal alliance with the Emperor, in

[1] Lady Fanshawe's *Memoirs*.
[2] Whilst the penury of the country led Philip to adopt such measures as this, the influence of Mariana and her German *entourage* induced him at this very time — November 1664 — to send a contribution of 500,000 ducats to the Emperor's needs.

which Spain was made the catspaw of Austrian ambition, and the milch-cow of Austrian greed. It was no longer to suppress freedom of conscience in the German States. That had been conceded long ago ; and against that alone had it been Spain's traditional policy to fight. The German Queen and her confessor Nithard, with Pöetting, the Austrian ambassador, were all intent now upon obtaining Spanish aid to the wars with the Turk on the Hungarian frontiers.[1] Philip still treated it as a question of conscience, and his letters to the nun breathed continual sorrow at having to deplete his own poverty-stricken subjects to help the Emperor. But it never seems to occur to him that he was really under no obligation whatever to do so, and that Spain would not have been seriously affected even if the Turk had been victorious in Hungary.

His personal health was now very bad, gall-stones and other painful maladies keeping him in almost constant agony. To a letter from the nun, imploring him to care for his health, in March 1665, he answered that he would do so ; " but I can assure you that I only want what may be best for God's service, and neither health, nor anything else, but that the divine will should be executed upon me. This is what I wish you to supplicate His Divine Majesty to grant me, and my salvation, which is my main concern." A few weeks after this was written, in March 1665, the nun sent to her royal friend another letter full of goodly counsel

[1] An interesting volume founded upon Pöetting's correspondence, and dealing with the connection between Spain and the Empire at this time, has recently been published by his Excellency Don W. de Villa Urrutia, Spanish ambassador in England. It is called *Relaciones entre Espaua y Austria*, Madrid, 1905.

and encouragement ; and then the pen fell from her hands for ever, and Philip was left utterly alone. His wife, working hard for her future influence, and in favour of the Austrian policy, had no sympathy to spare for the sufferings of the declining old uncle-husband, to whom political ambitions had given her as his wife. The only son who lived to succeed him was a scrofulous degenerate, who presented, even in his infancy, an exaggeration of his inherited type, which made him a monstrosity, a poor creature who never emerged from puerility, and finally died of senile decay at forty.

There was literally no ray of light on earth for Philip, now that Sor Maria was dead. Around him, as he knew and saw, plans and intrigues were anticipating the time when he should be no more. There were those in the Court, looking mostly to Don Juan, who dreaded to see Spain dragged once more at the tail of the Empire ; for Louis XIV. was already threatening, and most Spaniards hankered for the closer alliance, meaning peace with France, that seemed so firm on the Isle of Pheasants only five years before ; whilst Mariana and the Austrians had gained to their side a large party of nobles, pledged for their own greedy ends to support the Queen when she should succeed to the Regency and hold in her hands the resources of Spain.

On the 20th June 1665 the terrible news had to be broken to the King, that his forlorn hope had been defeated. Count Caracena, from whom so much had been hoped, had been utterly crushed by the Portuguese and their English auxiliaries. Eight hours of carnage had reduced the Spanish army from 15,000 men to 7000, and all the guns had been lost. Philip could, in very truth, do no more. To raise this army every means, legal and illegal, had been resorted to ; private property had been violated, pledges had been broken, injustice had been perpetrated, and suffering had been inflicted upon poor people already sorely oppressed. To this had the great dream come at last : that the King who was held to be the proudest and wealthiest in Christendom was unable to hold even his own territory. For the first time Philip broke down in the sight of men ; for Sor Maria was dead, and to none could he turn now for comfort. Heart-broken, he cast himself upon the ground in a paroxysm of grief, and sobbed out the formula that was his only refuge, " Oh God ! Thy will be done," almost the same words as those which his grandfather uttered when he received the news of the catastrophe that had overtaken his great Armada. But Philip IV.'s case was worse, by far, than that of Philip II. Behind the latter there was still a nation full of faith in its divine selection to dominate the world for the glory of God and His chosen King : behind Philip IV., himself aged and worn with sickness of body and disillusion of spirit, there was a people who had lost all confidence in themselves and their mission, ready to scoff and spit upon the idols that had failed them ; a people whom sloth, vanity, and epicureanism had robbed for a time of their nobleness, and who yet had to pass through the consummation of their woe before, cleansed in the fires of suffering, they should arise again.

Philip knew it ; and, looking back over his long

reign, he must have cursed the fate that condemned him from his birth to the performance of an almost impossible task with utterly inadequate means. He had been dedicated at his baptism to the Dominican ideal of a Christian church purged of dissent at any cost ; and yet, from the time when the Protestant ambassadors of England were the honoured guests at his christening, until now in his despairing age Fanshawe was reminding him daily of his impotence both on land and sea, he had been obliged to woo heretics, and to fight a great Catholic Power which was bent upon the final humiliation of his house. Thus, with bitter irony, some mightier power, with ends incomprehensible to men, mocked at the great designs of those who thought that they and theirs were but junior partners with providence, the chosen agents of the Almighty ; and Philip, in whose days the scales had fallen from the nation's eyes, ascribed the agonised awakening, and the ruin it disclosed, to the vengeance of an offended deity for his own puny sins.

Philip was tired of the struggle, weary of the sordid intrigues around him, and he fell into gloomy despondency that banished from him all interest in life. His bodily sufferings were intense, for the malady that afflicted him was a cruel one. Again the rumour ran that the King was bewitched, and that the late Inquisitor-General had been arranging means to remove the spell when he died. The great ecclesiastics in attendance were convinced that Satan was at the bottom of the King's troubles ; and asked Philip's permission to proceed in their incantations to defeat the evil one who was thus persecuting him. There were those at Court who sneered at the absurdity of attempting to cure a physical malady by such means ; [1] but the Inquisition insisted, and took over the management of the case. The acting Inquisitor-General, Gonzalez, accompanied by Philip's confessor, Juan Martinez, went to the patient and asked him for a little bag of relics which he always wore around his neck, for they feared some evil charm might be amongst them. Then to the Dominican monastery of the Atocha they solemnly carried " an old book of sorcery, some prints of his Majesty transfixed with pins," and other rubbish, all of which they solemnly burnt with much sacred mummery.

This did the King no good, and then the doctors tried their hand with a sweet conserve of mallow leaves, not, one would think, a sovereign remedy for gall-stones. On Monday, 14th September, the physicians confessed themselves hopeless. The hæmorrhage was very great, and the patient utterly exhausted with frequent paroxysms of fever, in one of which he was thought to be dead, and the news spread through the capital that he was so. When he was restored to consciousness, he summoned the new Secretary of State, Loyola, and entrusted him with official papers and his will for Queen Mariana, and then demanded the last sacrament. When the friars brought the viaticum and told the dying man that all hope was gone, he was resigned ; though the Holy Virgin of the Atocha was taken in procession past his windows, and the body of St.

---

[1] There is a very minute account of Philip's illness and death written by one of his attendants, from which I take some of the particulars. Biblioteca Nacional, Madrid, P. v. c. 24. Manuscript, 15 pages transcribed by me.

Diego, with scores of other grisly remains, were kept in the sick-room itself, in the hope that good would come of them. Mariana and her two children came to say good-bye to the dying man on Monday afternoon, and, with tears in his eyes, Philip sighed to the five-year-old weakling who was to succeed him : " God make you happier than He has made me." [1] He took an affecting leave, too, of the Duke of Medina de las Torres, and the other nobles who were attached to him ; pardoned the Marquis of Heliche for the attempt to blow up the Retiro, and granted many titles and knighthoods to his gentlemen-in-waiting. Count Castrillo, always self-seeking, had the bad taste to pester the King, both personally and through the friars, that he should be made Grandee, but Philip angrily referred him to the Queen.

For three days the King lingered on in suffering, confessing again and again and receiving absolution ; never for long abandoning his hold upon the rough crucifix that had comforted the last moments of his saintly predecessors on the throne. The jealous friars and confessors about him quarrelled so violently in the death chamber on one occasion, about administering the last sacrament again, that the Marquis of Aytona turned the King's confessor out of the room and forbade his return. On Wednesday, Castrillo came in full of the great news that Don Juan had presented himself at the palace, and Philip, disturbed and unhappy at the trouble that this portended, sternly sent orders for the Prince to return instantly; for this, he said, was only

[1] *Muerte del Rey Felipe IV.*, a contemporary account by an eye-witness. British Museum MSS., Add. 8703.

the time for him to die, not to enter into mundane disputes.

All that night the King was delirious, until he suddenly recovered consciousness just before dawn on Thursday, 17th September 1665, and then quietly passed away. He had been beloved by those around him, and had been prodigal all his life of favour to the men who served him ; but Mariana and her son were the source of bounty now, and human nature showed its baseness at such a crisis, as it is wont to do in palaces ; for, as my eye-witness authority avers,[1] " Of all his Majesty's household, the Marquis of Aytona and two other servants alone wept for the death of their King and master ; and in all the rest of the capital there was not one person who shed a tear." The Marquis of Malpica, captain of the Guard, came from the death chamber first to the anteroom filled with guards on duty, and announced the King's passing by shouting : " Now, comrades, your duty is to go upstairs [2] and guard his Majesty King Charles." Courtiers were too busy thence-forward looking towards the future to care much for the unhappy Planet King who had laid down his heavy burden. The reading of the will which made Mariana Regent, the constant meetings, and the coming and going of the ministers, kept the palace astir from morning till night ; but a few faithful souls dressed the poor remains of the King in a musk-coloured velvet suit, embroidered with silver, placed a silver sword by his side, a

[1] MSS. Bib. Nac., Madrid, P. v. c. 24.
[2] Philip had died in the entresol-room in the palace, which he always occupied in summer, as it was shady and cool.

diamond cross in his hands folded upon his breast, which was embroidered with the great red dagger of Santiago, and covered the head with a beaver hat. And so, garbed and enclosed in gorgeous silver and red velvet coffins, he was placed high upon a daïs under a canopy illumined by great wax torches, surrounded with the insignia of imperial majesty, and guarded by the faithful halberdiers of Espinosa ; whilst friars chanted and prayed around the bier hour after hour. The hall in which the body of Philip lay thus in deathly state was that which had seen so many gay hours of his hopeful youth ; for it was the room devoted to the stage-plays that he had loved not wisely but too well.

Lady Fanshawe, like the rest of the great people in Madrid, went to see the sight, and thus records her impressions—

"The body of Philip IV. lay exposed from the 18th September, Friday morning, till the night of Saturday the 19th, in a great room in his palace, in which they used to act plays. The room was hung with fourteen pieces of the King's best hangings, and over them rich pictures round about, all of one size placed close together. At the upper end of the room was raised a throne of three steps, upon which there was placed a bedstead raised at the head. The throne was covered with a rich Persian carpet, and the bottom of the bedstead with a counterpoint of cloth of gold. The bedstead was of silver, the valance and headcloth of gold wrought in flowers with crimson silk. Over the bedstead was placed a cloth of state of the same as the valance and headcloth of the bedstead, upon which stood a silver gilt coffin raised a foot or more at the head than at the feet, and in the coffin lay Philip IV. with his head on a pillow, upon it a white beaver hat, his hair combed, his beard trimmed, his face and hands painted. He was clothed in a musk-coloured silk suit embroidered with gold, a *golilla* about his neck, cuffs on his hands, which were clasped on his breast, holding a globe and a cross therein. His cloak was of the same, with his sword on his side; stockings, shoe-strings, and garters of the same, and a pair of white shoes upon his feet."

Seven altars and scores of lighted tapers were erected in the chamber, and offices for the dead King's soul went ceaselessly on, as the courtiers came and went before the painted clay that had been once so potent; but when, late on Saturday, the time came to carry the body through the night across the plains to the snow-tipped Guadarramas glimmering afar off, where in the stately jasper chamber he had wrought for his royal house Philip IV. was to lie amongst the greater dead, few of the high nobles and officers cared to absent themselves from Madrid in these early days; and one after the other they refused to do the last sad offices to him who had so often commanded them with a glance. At last the Duke of Medina de las Torres peremptorily ordered a kinsman of his own to take charge of the body to the Escorial. Even the bearing of the body to the mule litter that awaited it gave rise to a hot dispute, in which threats of

2 K

violence between two sets of officials were flung across the coffin.[1]

With fourscore friars and the great officers of the palace who were obliged to accompany the corpse, the litter, surrounded by torches, travelled throughout the night, and on Sunday, 20th September 1655, the prior of the Escorial relieved the courtiers of the burden of which they were so glad to be free; whereafter they all scurried back, as fast as horses could carry them, to make the preparations and ensure their own important participation in the glorious series of bull-fights, cane-tourneys, masques, and sumptuous parades which within a fortnight were to greet the accession of his Catholic Majesty King Charles II.

There were still thirty-five years more of national humiliation and grief for Spain before the great convulsion that awoke her to a new life; but these years were but a prolongation of the agony preceding the dissolution that had been made inevitable during the reign of Philip IV. The Court over which he was the presiding spirit had exhibited in the forty-five years he ruled it the strange phenomenon of corruscating intellectual activity, accompanied by unexampled moral and social corruption. Literature and art had blazed up with sudden refulgence before they too sank into twilight; and when Philip passed in, the generation of geniuses that illumined his Court were dead or hastening to the grave, whilst all else was sinking deeper and deeper into darkness.

It needed the formation of new ideals, the evolution of a new patriotism, to make Spain

[1] MSS. Biblioteca Nacional, Madrid, p. v. c. 24.

worthy of her history again ; and the outworn, incestuous blood of the Philips was powerless to lead the nation back to health and sanity after its splendid epoch of heroics. Philip did his best, but he himself was but a product of his time and country : a kindly gentleman of noble aspirations and ignoble practice, weak of will and tender of conscience, a poet and a dilettante, doomed to an overwhelming task for which he was unfit. In his long reign he saw moral decadence that he could not arrest, national ruin that even his frantic prayers were powerless to avert ; and he lived through half a lifetime of martyrdom, because he ascribed his failure to the vengeance of a ruthless deity whom he had offended by his sins, and believed that he, gentle-hearted as he was, had brought upon the people that he loved the wide-spread woe he saw around him.

INDEX

517

INDEX

A

Abbot, Archbishop, 109.
Academies (literary contests), 200, 301.
Admiral of Castile (Duke of Medina de Rio Seco), 163, 167.
Aguila, Marquis del, 300.
Ahumada, Father, 373.
Alamos, Don Baltasar de, 237.
Albert, Cardinal, Archduke, 21, 286.
Aliaga, confessor of Philip III., 45.
Alumbrados, the blasphemous sect so called, 271.
Amegial, battle of, 494, 495.
Anna of Austria, Queen of France, 155, 334, 335, 377, 464, 465, 482.
Aragonese Cortes, 141, 159, 162–170, 228, 254–259, 287, 296, 397.
Archy Armstrong in Spain, 100, 120.
Arcos, Duke of, 342.
Arnet, murderer of Ascham, 433.
Arundel, Philip, Earl of, 196.
Ascham, Anthony, Cromwell's envoy to Spain, 429 ; his mission, 431 ; his murder in Madrid, 431–437.
Astillano, Prince of, 460.
Aston, Sir Walter, 77, 81, 106, 124, 292, 293, 295, 311, 312, 313, 317, 322.

Atillano, " the poet," 301.
Auto-de-fé, an, 150, 259.
Avendaño, an actor, 231.
Aytona, Marquis of, 218, 229, 391, 510.

B

Balbeses, Marquis of (Spinola), 341.
Ballard, an English priest in Madrid, 102.
Baltasar, Carlos, Prince, 210, 225, 241, 244, 246, 250, 253, 257, 276, 282, 284, 285, 353, 367, 387, 397 ; his betrothal, 399.
Barbastro, Cortes at, 164.
Barcelona, 167 et seq., 255–259, 297, 337–342.
Bejar, Duke of, 253, 342, 461.
Borgia, Cardinal, 253, 343, 458.
Borja, Melchior, 371.
Braganza, Duke of, 286, 334 ; proclaimed King of Portugal, 345, 423.
Breitenfeld, battle of, 247.
Bristol, Earl of, Sir John Digby, 67, 68, 72, 73, 76, 77, 81, 97, 98, 100, 106, 123, 124.
Buckingham, Duke of, in Madrid, 67 et seq. ; meets Philip, 81–85 ; the state entry, 86–92, 95, 96, 105 ; quarrels with Olivares, 106, 113–120 ; leaves Spain, 121–123, 125 ; his assassination, 216.